TRAGIC AMERICA

THEODORE DREISER

〜〜〜

FICTION

SISTER CARRIE
JENNIE GERHARDT
THE FINANCIER
THE TITAN
THE "GENIUS"
AN AMERICAN TRAGEDY
FREE *and Other Stories*
CHAINS, *Lesser Novels and Short Stories*
TWELVE MEN
A GALLERY OF WOMEN

AUTOBIOGRAPHICAL

A HISTORY OF MYSELF
   DAWN
   NEWSPAPER DAYS
   A LITERARY APPRENTICESHIP (*in preparation*)
   LITERARY EXPERIENCES (*in preparation*)

PLAYS

PLAYS OF THE NATURAL AND SUPERNATURAL
THE HAND OF THE POTTER

TRAVEL

A TRAVELER AT FORTY
A HOOSIER HOLIDAY
THE COLOR OF A GREAT CITY
DREISER LOOKS AT RUSSIA

POETRY

MOODS *Cadenced and Declaimed*
EPITAPH
MY CITY

PHILOSOPHY

HEY RUB-A-DUB-DUB

TRAGIC AMERICA

BY

THEODORE DREISER

HORACE LIVERIGHT, INC.

NEW YORK

CONTENTS

TRAGIC AMERICA

CHAPTER I

THE tempo of this great land is one of speed and contention. Faster cars, more efficient machinery, more and more towering skyscrapers erected in record time, subway trains screeching the extreme necessity of speed, more and larger cities, more businesses, more cares and duties—as though we, of all people, were ordered not only to mechanize but populate the world! But just why? For any known event or spiritual reason? Rather, it seems to me that in this atmosphere, the mental and physical condition of millions of people have either already "blown up" or are about to. They live and die without tasting anything really worth while. The average individual to-day is really tortured; he is so numerous, so meaningless, so wholly confused and defeated.

In short, the general condition of the industrial life of our great cities and towns is enough to destroy the nerves as well as the comfort of many sensitive persons, in some instances driving them to suicide. How persistent and increasing is the number of those who decide to die and get away from it all!

And more, apparent disaster overhangs America as well as countries financially allied to her. In the world crises, England has had to give up the gold standard, temporarily closing the London Stock Exchange and German banks. Repercussion of world finances followed. Norway, Sweden, Denmark and Egypt were forced, likewise, to give up the gold standard. World crisis goes deeper, because to avert it, private banks here recently loaned vast sums to Germany. Although reparation debts to the U. S. Government are supposed to come first, the bankers now want reparation debts canceled a year in order to secure their

1

own loans made on securities they know to be only a second
lien, rather than a first.

More, this disaster is upon America in the shape of millions
unemployed, barely existing and even starving. Those still
working have the crisis of the wage-cut. Soon after the wage-
cut of the U. S. Steel, this big headline appeared on the front
page of *The New York Times:* "Stocks Rise One to Fourteen
Points as Wage Cuts Continue." Here are the broad indications
of disaster. In this book, I propose to ask what is the cause of
the economic conditions in the large to-day? How did they
evolve to the present status?

On the American scene to-day, no one can fail to observe
the approaching clashes as well as the current discontent.

In parts of Kentucky, due to the labor-capital fight, civil
war is feared by *The New York Times.* In Harlan County, Kentucky, the big Morgan, Insull, Ford, Mellon, etc., interests are
grinding the coal miners to uncivilized living conditions. Corporation police have perpetrated lawless terror upon strikers,
and denied them privileges guaranteed by Constitution and
State laws. Scores of miners have been arrested merely to
intimidate them. The judge's family are mine operators. Elections have been tampered with. Yet all this, including dynamiting a strikers' soup kitchen, and workers' relief car, illegally
raiding the homes of striking miners and illegally slugging them
as well as firing on unarmed miners with machine guns, is
caused by a fight between capital and labor—and for the very
sustenance of the worker.

More, this wildly individualistic, and hence wildly capitalistic, tension renders life at once so dull and insecure. Under
"In God We Trust" on our dollar, might be written: "The
Devil Take the Hindmost!"—that is, the laborer. Nor does the
Government, unchastened as it stands by popular scrutiny, any
longer seek to look after all, but only the strongest (who, in their
turn, may look after the rest, if they wish). Millions of people in
America to-day have reason to worry as to where food and
bed are to come from. And yet they are called upon to strive

for these until death ends the struggle. Hence, how can the laborer and the average small businessman, really the prey of the great trusts and banks, make himself safe? The battle is that of man against man, group against group, trust against trust, but all fighting the individual, so that all of life bears out the scientific theory that small particles of energy in continuous motion bump other tiny particles only to increase or lose some or all of their own strength. But why the immense contention, the savage indifference to reason, under which men and women work so hard and get so little? What phases of American life tend to produce the present struggles between capital and labor, the individual and the trust, the Government and its people?

The late War, as we all know, gave rise to enormous business. Contracts for ammunition, clothing and supplies in greater quantities than had ever been imagined, were furnished. But what good did it do? Merely enriched the stockholders of du Pont, Standard Oil, Botany Worsted Mills or their ilk, while American boys gave their lives, or worked for but $30 a month. Factories, railroads and farms produced and handled many times their former quota. This in the face of millions of men abroad fighting. More, and at the same time, America had quantities of reserve labor, either totally idle or engaged in personal pursuits. But of such is concentrated effort always. Always greater production, despite thousands of men away fighting. In the Civil War and the Spanish-American War, the same condition existed. An impromptu, if necessary, activity, gave rise to a phase of "prosperity," which later was added to by the tremendous public zest for the automobile, radio, moving pictures, etc. To-day there are more automobiles in use in the United States than there are telephones. Only, and alas, in the case of so many of these recent and remarkable inventions, we cannot now consume as many as we make: automobiles, radios, phonographs, telephones, moving pictures, plays, etc., because the people who make them have no money to buy them.

But what of all this? Has it increased happiness? Has it

safeguarded prosperity or insured to any but a minor percentage the economic and social necessities which so much activity would suggest? One has only to go over America and see! The corporations, banks, holding companies and the like grow stronger while the individual grows weaker, mentally as well as economically. He is drilled in his schools to salute the flag and swear to a one hundred per cent patriotism which he may not feel; is spied upon as to his morals; dragooned as to his educational as well as social views and pleasure. Indeed, during the last war, powerful groups of radicals, as well as individuals, indicated that this very economic boom which the war created, would lead to more pseudo-prosperity that would result in injury to the individual; enrich the trust, but weaken the economic strength as well as the insight of the minor individual. And exactly this has happened. Chain organizations of every kind and description, including banks and factories, in which clerks and imported managers now function and where formerly the local individual looked upon himself as one who, by a small business, could insure himself of at least old-age security, to-day he is dependent on a corporation which cares nothing for his later day. More, he is liable to discharge at any moment, and will remain so. His gray hair and the after years of labor are against him and spell and insure his fate. And no Government aid for him; only for the corporations who exploit him. In short, neither the great trusts and money groups, nor the Government that fosters them, owes the individual anything. He is handed over to the devil of misery.

Of the 117,000,000 people in this country shortly after the World War, 14,000,000 were foreign-born, and 21,000,000 of foreign parentage. The War interrupted their comfortable or at least busy new lives, to strike them with such definite realities as the Germans slaying the Belgians; the Russians, French and English fighting the Germans; the Austrians, Italians and Balkan nationalities clashing, etc. Yet in America had been the much lauded thought of Americanizing the immigrants by providing them with equal opportunity and liberty, the melting pot! Yet behold that war sweeping that all away. The melting pot? A foolish, discarded sentimentalism. Liberty? No liberty unless your country's whim permits it. War measures against free speech emasculating opinion. Later immigrants debarred so strictly as to make it all but impossible for husbands to bring their families to America. So Americanization became a failure. And hardboiled business and money, long the Wall Street gauge, became the order of the day. And these their banks and corporations controlling. The strongest phases of our new American philosophy, an emanation, by the way, of this new bank and trust supremacy, are the desire for enormous business, more wealth and less liberty, more despotism and less freedom of education, which always accompanies the absolute rule of the few. Oligarchy!

But against these, there are now struggling millions of laborers insecure, underpaid, and in many cases illy-treated and fed. Among them are those individuals whom I have mentioned as being against capitalistic wars; also those foreigners turned race-conscious by the War, who now look hopefully upon the recent economic solutions of their homeland governments— i.e., Sovietism in Russia—with the possibility of applying it as a cudgel against the ever aggressively selfish corporations here. More, nowadays workers are beginning to awaken to the fact that wars are for the capitalist. For obviously so it is. And he who through his government declares them, in order that he may either protect endangered profits or realize them (fabulous profits) as often out of his own people as out of foreign lands, begins to stand out more clearly for what he is—a buccaneer—an international pirate. (Consider only our own wars—from that of 1812 on.) And so to-day the laborer and the farmer, as well, are beginning to believe that wars and preparedness are of no benefit to them—only an expense, and a gory one—and in consequence are joining to take issue against the capitalist.

Yet the banks and trusts of the United States are reaching out to finance and possibly even start war in every part of

the world where capitalism stands endangered. Thus, South
and Central America are certainly being revolutionized in order
to further such industrialism on the part of American capitalists. And banks like that of J. P. Morgan & Co. operate now
in every part of the world from Asia to South America. To
protect their money and that of their largest creditors, American banks and corporations now indirectly through the government "beat up" natives almost anywhere they choose, or they
loan their money to some capitalistic country or its dictator who
desires so to do. I call your attention to Cuba and its dictator—
Machado—and the American financiers and industrialists who
sustain him in enslaving the three million starving citizens of
that land, with their huts and their bare larders. These poor
creatures there are rebelling to-day for no reason other than that
their misery is more than any human being can stand. Yet our
American financiers and industrialists take over the customs or
even coerce the government of a sovereign state, and so virtually
make a protectorate of it. Or through our State Department,
they send ultimatums sharpened by delivery under the aim of
battleship guns. This is actual imperialism—as witness just recently in Panama—the same brand as that used by the British
and the Germans. It is a policy abhorrent to every class of
Americans other than the capitalistic class, yet a policy always
fostered by that kind of conservatism which emphasizes the need
of armaments and the protection of our citizens abroad, the
while Wall Street imperialism at home increases.

And now to-day, not only is American money invested all over
the world, but fortunes, amassed for the most part in the United
States, are now being spread to the ends of the earth, as gifts,
the while millions of Americans continue to starve. I think of
such gifts as those made by John D. Rockefeller, amounting
to hundreds of millions, to Tokio, Paris, China. And this same
wealth become a family affair, held and directed, in order, if
possible, to lull the worries of the magnates' more or less incompetent children. One girl, for instance, with eight hundred
million dollars, amuses herself as best she may, while another

slaves for six or eight dollars a week. Or take a man like the
late Russell Sage who, not knowing what to do with his millions, left them all to his equally incompetent (sociologically
speaking) wife, who, herself not knowing what to do with them,
turned them over to the Russell Sage Foundation, which is doing
such asinine things as Mr. Rockefeller, Mr. Harkness, Mr. This,
Mr. That, are doing. Or heirs build ridiculous palaces on equally
ridiculous estates, only to leave them to be quarreled over by
their various heirs in many courts. Witness only the doings of the
Thaw family in connection with their paranoic son! And to what
constructive end, all this? Any?

The deep trouble with America to-day is that the gifted and
strong individual, however self-centered and selfish and wholly
unsocial, is supposed nevertheless, to remain uncurbed because
he is part of a presumably wholly social state which was organized to guarantee the right of equal opportunity for all. But
equal opportunity for all cannot possibly and by the very same
phrase mean unlimited license for the cunning and the greedy
who take advantage of that equal opportunity to establish
special or, in other words, unlimited individual privileges, and
the power that goes with the same, the while the remaining
ninety to ninety-five per cent of the citizens of this land trudge
in comparative want. And yet, that is exactly what has happened. The cunning and the strong have made great use of the
land of real opportunity. They have, from the very beginning,
seized upon its great perquisites as private to themselves. (I am
thinking of not only millions of acres of the actual land donated
to the influential, but the natural resources of the same: lumber,
minerals, oils. Also of the various types of franchises, railroads,
telegraph, express, lighting and the like, which have been given
or stolen and now, through the wealth and power brought by
the same and the private control that goes with them, have
proceeded to direct the Government itself which—due to the
phrase "equal opportunity for all"—has permitted them to obtain
that special and private control.)

But this is something which cannot cumulatively proceed for-

ever. The end is almost here and now. For we have proceeded
from the original point where one shrewd individual could gather
many millions, and even hundreds of millions, of dollars, to
himself, and reinvest and direct it, to the further point where
to-day not he alone but others like him join with him to form
and control banks, trade, corporations and the like, through
which (and without nearly as much trouble to themselves as
formerly) they now direct the Government itself. For what
else is heard to-day, in Congress or out, in the states or their
cities and towns, but the voice of the trust, its banks and its
hirelings? These now, through their combined means—the politicians, police, courts, lawyers, and what not whom they employ
and direct, are now able to safeguard not only their combined
millions or billions, but to add to them and more, in so doing,
legally or illegally, but always with Government sanction, you
will note, use the same not only to destroy all competition but
to compel the Government or people under whose eye and by
whose ignorance or indifference or both, they have grown to
such great strength, to help them so to do. Need I point to the
Standard Oil Company, the United States Steel Company, or to
the great railroads, banks and service corporations generally,
which now tax and rob and underpay the very Government and
people which originally, and ignorantly, perhaps, permitted them
their selfish and now wolfish rise?

But not satisfied with individual supremacy (under a Government which was never supposed to tolerate any such thing),
we now have not only class but family supremacy—the supremacy of the lords of money, the Morgans, Rockefellers,
du Ponts, plus the social and economic supremacy of their heirs
and assigns—their children who never created or developed
anything but who, because of inherited means and names, now
step forward to say who shall be first and who last in social
and financial economy. At one and the same time, the expansion of the capitalists' families to almost an almighty
station in life, the while through the destructive power of low
wages, and lack of employment, the worker families are falling

proportionately lower and lower—a distinct characteristic of capitalism in its decaying stage in this country. In short, the great quarrel to-day in America is between wealth and poverty —whether an individual, however small or poor, shall retain his self-respect and his life, or whether a commercial oligarchy shall at last and finally take charge and tell all the others— some 125,000,000 strong now—how they shall do and what they shall think and how little (not how much) they may live on, the while a few others (the strong and cunning) exercise their will and their pleasure as they choose. That is the war that is coming!

But now as to the method of these individuals and their corporations, who through privileged laws have so solidly entrenched themselves and are now proceeding to dictate to all and sundry, what they are to believe, how they are to vote as well as work, and for how much, how they are to think, etc. In fact, by now it is such an old story that I feel I scarcely need recite how Presidential campaigns are organized in favor of the trusts and banks, how State politics are arranged to favor these money organizations and large corporations behind them; and how education, publication, religion, public speech and the like must march to the tune of those who have power and constantly seek to enlarge and perpetuate it. The fatal human fact that is back of all this is that the majority of men and women are never as wise or cunning and unscrupulous as those who seek to use and rule and profit by them. They are nearly always credulous and believe in what they hear, until some form of slavery awakens them, usually too late. Actually an oligarchical group of lords in America is to-day seeking to enslave this great people. And, for that purpose, first seeking to debase it mentally. It is for that reason, and that reason alone, that I have deemed it necessary to share in this contest.

It is interesting, though, to watch the processes employed. For a while, it was actually assumed that religion (a hurrah in regard to the need of faith) would bow in humble obeisance before any and every form of might and power. That now ap-

pears to be not true. For in America, it is the religionist, his
minister, his priest, his bishop or his cardinal who, side by side
with the money lord, is seeking power—and even power over the
money lord himself, his government and his slaves. So much so
that in thousands of American papers and magazines to-day
are to be found inspired articles and editorials boosting the
value and comfort of religion. And among these are to be found
the handwriting as well as the subtle propaganda of the Catholic Church, the strongest and slyest and most devastating of
all! But always with its dream of supreme power for itself,
and itself alone. But as to that, more later.

In the present clashes of capital vs. people, of government vs.
people and of church vs. people, education and public opinion
are not only directed for the benefit of the trust and the church
but in so doing education is stunted. It is stunted because it
cannot speak the truth and hence cannot even seek understanding.

Meanwhile, it may be pointed out that our present-day owners
and masters, the capitalists, demand all sorts of unscrupulous
and selfish means of handling profits and they, along with the
banks, grow fat on the speculative phases of their stocks and
bonds which now destroy others. Watered stock! Dividends of
forty or fifty per cent. And so a profit of many thousands of
per cent on the original stock. And not only that, but manipulation, by giving three shares of stock, say, at a no par value,
for each former one hundred dollar share. So that when companies make tremendous profits, not daring to declare huge
dividends, they may reinvest that money. Yet if, in turn, dividends cannot be earned on this reinvestment (which stockholders
weren't entitled to before as dividends) it becomes, in so far
as the Government and its rate-making are concerned, confiscation of property! And these privileges all flourish for only a
small inside group. Thus Commonwealth Edison, one of our
flourishing American corporations, voted to issue millions of
dollars worth of stock for which the old stockholders were to
have "rights" to purchase at $15.65 a share less, a total gift

of $22,000,000, and for no other reason than that they were the old shareholders. But that is the way of keeping a few in control.

Too, other directors in other companies—many, many of them—have proceeded to swell the firm or original corporation's capitalization to almost unbelievable size. Thus, to take one single instance, the Philadelphia Electric Company now earns eight per cent on four times its real value. Yet while it earns this profit on a valuation set by the Utility Commission at $428,000,000, it pays taxes on $113,000,000, a valuation determined by a—shall we say kindly-minded board of tax appraisers? But to come by the first figure, no basis for earnings is either too sly or dishonest for these corporate executives to insist upon as real: increased value of surrounding property, growth of the town, or natural decreased purchasing power of the dollar. In fact, to-day quite all American corporations are trying to make the courts of this land treat patronage, business, and even prospective income as "property" which cannot be tampered with. In other words, to hold all that they can upon imaginary "property," to keep others from confiscating an as yet non-existing thing. And already our most powerful courts have permitted reconstruction costs to be allowed in establishing a corporation's valuation for rate-making purposes. Yet private economic or cost valuating companies called in as experts in these matters, have differed in their estimates of these reconstruction costs by as much as a hundred million dollars.

And yet, what evils in connection with money-making has not this induced! For it is that kind of economic hypocrisy which is at this hour inciting the average man to hate. To illustrate, one manufacturer in Niagara Falls, New York, has asked Congress for a tariff, saying that he could no longer make a profit because of the exorbitant rate for power in comparison with the low rate charged across the river in Canada. Then there came the résumé of the same situation by Floyd L. Carlisle, head of the Niagara-Hudson Power Corporation, who insisted that his firm was charging less for industrial power than the Ontario Commission was charging across the border.

To me, as I have said, one of the most acute and deplorable evils in this situation, is the corporation greed for profits. Marx's concept, *cash value,* generally the final standard of effete capitalism, has now become realized in actual practice. Otherwise, why a $11,000,000 suit by the Government against the Bethlehem Shipbuilding Company for alleged excess war profits? The Bethlehem Shipbuilding Company justifies a twenty-one per cent profit by saying that the U. S. Steel Corporation was piling up a fifty per cent profit. This is a typical example of the profits obtained from the operations of corporate business. A large profit is recognized in America as being a necessary accompaniment to the functions of corporations. Although this may not be considered a large profit comparatively, still it constitutes a sample of the inside workings of corporation business.

But think of utility income, which grows to new heights while men who burn their electricity, gas, etc., walk around the streets looking for work! Receipts of utilities companies for the first six months of 1930 were $1,191,000,000, an increase of five per cent over the same period of 1929. Such profits as these give a power which I here denounce as unwarranted. For George F. Baker, former chairman of the First National Bank, and now deceased, testified before the Pujo Committee in 1913 that he and J. P. Morgan had to approve any large financial enterprise for it to be a success—for which power over life and industry neither he nor Mr. Morgan could be held to account. And true, I answer, because of their power! For not because of any legal rights were Baker and Morgan beyond the arm of the law. Rather, Baker, knowing this eighteen years ago, admitted the situation was not "comfortable" for the country and argued that mergers should cease. But have they? To this hour, more and more concentration of money, in the hope, I presume, that greater combination of capital leads to personal fame or the world in some creditable direction. But just where? And just what will this issue bring? If not a financial dictatorship by one person—a financial Cæsar, as it were, then its only possible alternative, the antithesis of the same: a people's central committee as in Russia, with full power over all construction and execution, and with the interests of all the people, and not one special group, as its first and only concern. One or the other will be the result of this present struggle of the masses against the oligarchs. This issue grows out of the present tendencies of clash and disaster, an understanding of which will be discovered. And what there is to this issue is what constitutes the subject matter of this book, and written for those alone who have the patience and desire and will to learn the drift if not the present-day meaning of American life.

CHAPTER II

I HAD heard much and studied much of present-day living conditions, but I also wanted to see for myself certain definite examples of life under our present economic régime. Therefore in June, 1931, I visited the western Pennsylvania miners' zone where a strike was then going on, and there I found unbelievable misery. Miners receiving wages of but from $14 to $24 for two weeks' work. Yet paying $25 a month for a shabby four-room house. The company store charging enormous prices for goods, which amounts were deducted from the miner's pay before he received what was left, if any. And many miners thus kept in debt for years. Their food of the poorest; I studied their menus. One of their main foods at that time was dandelion weeds.

Yet when men strike against these uncivilized conditions, what happens? The coal operators, who own the mine and the town as well as the schools, churches and jails (and who issue their own money and hire their own police) are also friends with the judges. For instance, Judge H. H. Rowland, of Pittsburgh, issued an order against picketing at the Butler Consolidated Coal Company, and because of that, police fired on the miners and killed one, wounded nineteen, and arrested thirty-eight. And up to that time a total of 550 miners had been arrested, two killed and nineteen wounded,—and this despite the fact that the miners, throughout the strike, had been unarmed. More, over 2,000 persons in this section had been gassed or ridden down and clubbed, at the hands of State or private police. Yet despite this state of affairs, Sheriff Robert V. Cain, of Allegheny County, showed me a letter from Governor Pinchot, insisting that miners were entitled to picket and to induce, if they could,

14

"scabs" to strike. But did this fact influence, let alone control Sheriff Cain or the Pennsylvania State Mounted Police? I saw State police escort "scabs" to and from the mines, but the protection Governor Pinchot demanded as legal due for the striking miners was denied.

These company-owned towns exist in industry the length and breadth of America.

Again, in my investigation of living conditions, I chose to visit Passaic, New Jersey, because I believe it to be a fairly representative small industrial city—accurate in reproduction of living conditions of towns of the same caliber throughout America—no better and no worse. In fact there are scores of other towns just like it. Yet a certain banker whom I know and met there said that since conditions are as bad and the masses so disturbed, no propaganda should be written or it might make trouble or uprising. I replied that I did not consider faithful reporting of the facts as propaganda.

When I arrived in Passaic in April, 1931, I walked out Dayton Avenue, past the Botany Worsted Mills. I learned later that this mill owns some twenty-five acres of land, on which are erected many houses which are rented to the workers. Also, the Forstmann and Huffman woolen mills there rent some sixty-four houses. I also noticed that all of the houses were similar, most of them dark, shabby, two-story flats, placed so close together that a driveway or a garage was not to be thought of. Later I learned that most of the mill-workers could not afford automobiles; also that the "bosses" live in the more fashionable Montclair. At that time, many houses stood vacant; and I noticed signs reading "For Rent—New Jersey Dress Manufacturing Co." The number of vacant houses was especially noticeable in the east side section and in the Fourth Ward, east of the Erie tracks, for the eviction process had ousted scores of families. A local minister also told me of instances of eight and ten persons living in one or two rooms. A Communist leader whom I chanced to meet made the same statement. The minister also told me of many cases of unemployment for over a year; in particular he mentioned one woman who, trying to earn a living for her family (the husband out of work) by making artificial flowers at the rate of 15 cents for 24 flowers, could not possibly earn more than 90 cents a day. The Communist leader I talked to emphasized the underfed condition of many of the unemployed, and I could well believe it after walking through the Third Street area.

The Salvation Army, the main source of charity here, aids all it can, but since its help is of a limited nature, many have to resort to the Poormaster, who gives them two or three dollars for groceries. But he cannot help them in the matter of their water, light and gas, which in many cases have been shut off. The water rate there was $20 per year, and recently the price had been raised to $28. A telephone, with a limit of thirty outgoing calls, costs the subscriber $2.75 monthly. The Railway Express Agency (run by the Government for the enrichment of a few individuals) charged 62 cents to carry a 50-pound package only two miles out to Paterson.

These were but a few of the facts as well as cases that I heard about:

Frank Tuma, a painter, of 2 Belmont Avenue, Garfield, an adjoining suburb, who had been out of work for five months, asked help from a hospital. Since he had no money to pay for the operation—he already owed $300 in grocery bills—his proposition to the hospital was that if it would operate on his son, who needed surgical attention, he would work for it. The proposition, in this instance, thanks be, was accepted. Yet the failure of the Red Cross to meet its quota in Passaic is an indication of the state of affairs there. Many of the members of trade unions, as I found, had been out of work or on part time, for some time, and could not even afford their dues. More, on January 3, 1931, James Golden, aged 50, an unemployed tinsmith, went into a bakery at 247 Monroe Street, and asked for something to eat. As Rosenberg, the proprietor, reached for a loaf of bread, Golden fell to the floor and died. The Passaic police reported that they had, on several occasions, given him a bed in a cell at police headquarters, but nothing more. Then there was John Pitak, 43, of 183 High Avenue, who committed suicide, leaving a wife and three children, because he could not find work.

In short, Passaic, a town of 63,000, is reported by the American Federation of Labor as having 7,000 jobless, and by the Communist leader as having 10,000 jobless. Since the 1920 census listed 18,000 as the average number of wage-earners, (although the population has decreased 5,000 since then), that leaves more than one-third out of a job. About the only way a man may get work there, I learned, was for him to take much lower wages on a job from which some one has just been laid off.

On the day of my arrival, I rambled about until I came to the home of Mrs. O.S. to which I had been referred. This kindly German soul rented me a room, with every home-like comfort, even to a thin, rose-covered featherbed. It was her parlor, and the last room to be rented, for without so renting it, as she said, she could not make out. And thereupon she and her husband were compelled to sleep in an attic room, home-partitioned from the rest. She also stated that she was renting her rooms because her husband, who had been with the Botany Mills for thirty-one years, was told more than a year before that, though able-bodied at the age of sixty-two and as I saw, he was then too old to work. More, he had been discharged with no pension. Yet the way they met their plight brought to my mind John Newman's words: "Lead, kindly light, amid th' encircling gloom." The old man seemed to find some consolation in the evenings spent in the immaculate blue and white kitchen, listening to the zither playing and singing of their fresh, young German roomers.

Mrs. O.S. told me that even as they were doing then—renting quite all of their rooms and slaving over the care of them— they couldn't keep up with their bills; for one thing, there were taxes for the year amounting to $225. Thus it appeared that although a mill foreman, over a period of years, might succeed in buying a house (even such a simple one as this), the city or

state would charge him enough in taxes to keep him in debt—
$4.73 on every $100.

And yet nothing ever brought to me more pointedly the insecurity of the workers than their persistent and independent
joining together over a period of years in order to aid each
other in sickness, since they well knew that in times of trouble
there was no help to be obtained from the Government, and
but very little from the factories, although some of these have
small insurance. Thus, Mrs. O.S. told me, among other things,
that she had been a depositor in a local sickness society for
twenty years. And a conscientious member she was, as I can
testify, since because she had been unable to bring in more
than a few new members, she held herself to blame for the organization's slow growth during its first five years. More, numbers of these workers here, as I also found, were united in
groups or clubs, some for men, others for women: German, Hun-
garian, Polish, Russian, Ukrainian, Italian; and some with as
many as 300 members; the purpose being to save enough money
out of the 65-cent monthly dues (and occasional card parties,
dances and suppers) to pay to any sick member the sum of $10 a
week for sickness during his first month's illness, then $5, and
finally $2.50, with a final total or closing bonus, as it were, of
$100 at death.

In addition to this some of the workers carry insurance
through the mills, such as it is. This valuable insurance is supposedly assured by company policies, but in many instances the
amount so assured cannot possibly meet the exigencies they are
supposed or devised to meet. And even for these, the worker must
submit to a deduction from each pay check. The Botany Mills, for
instance, pays $7.50 to $12.50 weekly for sickness, and, in case
of death (even by accident in the mill) only from $750 to $1,250.
Forstmann and Huffman, another woolen mill, had no sickness
plan, but for death, the widow is awarded a monthly allowance
for a year until she can find work or rehabilitate herself in some
other way. The United Piece Dye Works, in Lodi, a suburb of
Passaic, sponsors a system of insurance payable at death—

$1,000. The Doherty Silk Mills of this same area, and despite the standard of living forced on the people there, provides insurance at death of only $500. The Manhattan Rubber Company has a sickness plan run by the employees, and the U. S. Rubber merely a burial plan which guarantees $1,000 at death. Ponder the predicament of a man whose lot holds no more financial assurance than this!

Since I wanted to examine industrial health conditions, I went to the General Hospital, where I was told that many cases of lead poisoning come up from time to time; this in a number of cases means death, and quite often autopsies show it as a contributing cause of death. Dyes infect open wounds, although these cases are rare. A great danger of lead poisoning exists in the large rubber industry here, however, and at A. L. Prescott & Co., makers of stove and other polishes, who employ 500, the possibility is the same. Yet a company doctor would give no information on these cases which the General Hospital said often came up. Dr. Ryan, head of the Passaic Board of Health, said that no cases of lead poisoning were reported to his office. None the less, I believe that the industries seek to keep these cases secret, for when I mentioned tuberculosis, Dr. Ryan said: "Now there's something we want to tell you about. Passaic has the best record in the section." Yet the work in the mills does injure the lungs. Tuberculosis clinics are held weekly in the suburbs, and some 300 active cases exist in Passaic alone.

What I have said about general living conditions in Passaic can hardly be comprehended, however, until the reason for them— low wages—is shown. Here is exactly what people receive when they work. Botany Mills, employing 3,000, 60 per cent of whom are women, pay their expert help as follows: spinners, $35 a week; weavers, $25; finishers and dyers, $21.60; laborers, $19.20. But it must be remembered that most of these employees are not expert, and in consequence receive the lowest wage. I talked with a girl from Botany who, having formerly run a twisting machine at $25 weekly, now receives only $17 for keeping two machines running, which is not only hard work, but almost impossible.

Samuel Hird, another mill with about 1,000 employees (where personal contact worked so well that this mill did not join with the others in the big strike six years ago) pays about the same wages. Forstmann and Huffman, with 1,000 women and 15,000 men employees, reward their experts as follows: weavers, $40 weekly; spinners, $35; finishers and laborers, $24. Doherty Silk Mills, employing 300, pays weavers $30 weekly, warpers $35, loom fixers $45, and winders and pickers (women) $16. In the same way, and with the same exception as to those who are not expert, United Piece Dye Works, with 4,500 employees, gives their machinists $35 weekly, while the dye house workers and common help receive from $21.16 to $31.20. The 3,000 employees at the U. S. Rubber Plant and 1,500 at the Manhattan Rubber, fare alike as to wages: $35 for skilled labor and $21.60 for common labor. And it must be considered that these wages are constantly coming down. All of these plants and mills operated under the 48 hour week, although later, in August, 1931, I learned that many shifts at Botany Mills are now working 9 hours and 40 minutes a day. These low wages make it necessary for all members of the family to work, thus breaking up the family, lowering their living conditions and squelching development of any kind whatsoever.

In 1920, of about 729 children employed in Passaic, 512 worked in industry. Now about 700 between the ages of 14 and 18 go to a continuation school and work at the mills for about $10 a week or less. Although I heard of a number of cases of mill-workers' children going to college, all were working their way, a movement encouraged by the local Y.M.C.A.'s. So here (neglecting the distribution of money so that the masses may not acquire it) we find a type of labor and ambition which can only produce poverty, permanent unemployment, and worse, aggravate the child labor dilemma. In proof of this, witness this: In order to install new and better labor-saving devices, they scrap so much old machinery here in Passaic that foundries now exist there to melt and mold the old machines into decorative ornaments, toys, etc. Yet children are employed while men are laid off. Then Botany has just entered upon an enormous remechanization of its plant. A contract has just been let by it for 360 new *automatic* looms, which will keep Crompton and Knowles, of Worcester, Massachusetts, their makers, busy for a year. Of the 1,304 old handlooms now being discarded, 306 dress-goods looms have already been demolished, and not so long before this, Botany Mills had given out the statement that the new machinery being installed would bring about "greater speed and lower production cost." But whereas Botany employed 7,000 before the war, now it requires but 3,000. And with these advanced machines, now entering, what may be forecast for the working class still seeking employment here—or almost anywhere else—for that matter?

In 1925, though, 16,000 mill workers struck against all this. But to what end? No money, no honest or effective labor organizations to fight for them—no understanding, let alone sympathetic public, either to strengthen or uphold them—for such is the general attitude toward the worker in this land of the individual and his opportunity. Yet imagine the distress that must have caused this and, more pathetically, in a great year of "prosperity"! All of the woolen mills were tied up except Samuel Hird. The specific cause was a ten per cent wage cut at Botany. Lasting fourteen months, it not only caused great suffering among the workers, but is reputed to have cost Botany $5,000,000. And how much better it would have been to pay that out in wages. Albert Weisbord, a Harvard Law School graduate, and said to have led a strike against a factory of his father's, came to Passaic and commanded a terrific Communist following. An American Federation of Labor union among these textile workers, to which they paid 35 cents weekly dues, participated. Yet despite an heroic class struggle, the strike was lost. Months of suffering, tear gas and fire-hose used to break up their gatherings, and trouble at the strikers' food relief station, brought surrender.

But at this point, I should like to say that I hold that all police used to supervise strike conditions anywhere on such occasions should be directed by our national Government only, and receive all orders from it. For the public and private abuse of individuals, and more particularly laborers, at the hands of corporation-controlled police in towns and states, is much too brutal and so obvious. Aided and abetted by the courts, and yet directed by private organizations, these labor disputes become mere shambles for workers in which they are beaten and slain. And who does not know that? As I was walking past this same Botany one day, I noticed an officer in uniform. On his cap were metal letters "BWM." Of course, that stood for Botany Worsted Mills. I wanted to make sure this man was a policeman, and did. At the next gate I saw a man wearing the same kind of cap; the badge on his chest read "Police." I believe, and have the best of legal opinion to confirm that belief that these special officers, if paid by Botany, should be prosecuted for enforcing the public law under private salary, and if imbursed by the State, for serving private interests under public pay.

But what is the reason that people working for immense corporations, with the most amazing and money-saving devices the world has ever known and dividends that are handed in the form of shares and bonuses to the more fortunate of the insiders, still have so little that they are forced to strike for a livelihood? Obviously it is not that the mills, under the stress of competition, cannot make money. For although Botany has paid-in capital of only $3,600,000, the reproductive value, less depreciation, of the plant which has been improved out of profits, is $14,400,000. And from 1911 to 1923, its dividends averaged fifteen per cent; then in February, 1925, and May, 1926,—the latter the year of the strike—dividends of only $4 a year were paid on Class A stock, but with a par value of only $50. Though there have been no dividends since, accumulated dividends on Class A stock to December, 1929, reached $1,400,000, or the equivalent of $14 a share, I believe. Despite the fact that ninety-nine per cent of the stock is owned by Botany Consolidated Mills, Stohr, who owns 36 mills in Germany, controls the whole thing.

Data on Forstmann's, Samuel Hird's and Doherty's are un-

available. The United Piece Dye Works has been formed by
merging at different times the Alexander Dye Works, the Boett-
ger Piece Dye Works, American Silk Dyeing and Finishing
Company, and the Lehigh Silk Dyeing Co. Dividends have
reached $1.62 quarterly, right up to January 2, 1931. An in-
complete record on common stock dividends shows $10 a share
in 1923, $12 for 1924, $12.50 for 1925 and $18 each for 1926
and 1927. On December 31, 1927, the capital stock, which consisted of 100,000 shares of common at no par value, was changed
to 450,000 shares of no par common and $7,500,000 in six and
one-half per cent cumulative preferred with a par value of $100.

Three shares of preferred and 18 shares of common were
given for each 4 shares of old common. Then, in 1928, these
450,000 shares of common earned a dividend of $4 each. In 1929,
it was voted to double the shares of common, making 900,000,
and each stockholder received free the number he already held.
Altogether stock gifts of more than 800% to the owners.
In 1929, and 1930, dividends amounting to $2 at least were paid
on each of these 900,000. Still the firm pays its labor $20-$25
weekly.

The nature of corporate business, the sole executive management of which functions in the interest of those who own the
money rather than those who do the work, has induced such
extensive methods of stock split-ups, stock gifts, investments of
profits to enlarge the business, etc., that the high percentage to
the financiers has come to seem to them almost the order of
nature, and intended so by God, as it were. Yet there is not
enough real wisdom among the possessors of wealth to warrant the placing of such immense sums in their hands. Still, our
capitalists are not satisfied with their profits. Ever greater and
greater returns to themselves is the cry of to-day with, in consequence, unescapable enslavement for the less informed classes.
Mill owners in the North as in the South (where labor averages
about $10 weekly below the wages cited for Passaic) continue
and even enlarge this hard and reasonless differentiation. In
other words, everything for the strong man who is sure he can

lead and plan perfectly, and almost nothing for those who can only serve to carry out his vaulting ambitions.

Yet here in Passaic, as in quite all of America, the newspapers voice the thoughts of the industrial executives, and only *their* thoughts. The Passaic *Daily Herald,* for instance, has a three-fourths page business review of advertisements weekly, also a long feature story booming Passaic business. And every week, to quote the words of one employee, 15,000 copies of this story are sent all over the country to chambers of commerce and rotary clubs, and at the expense of the *Daily Herald.* Yet who pays the *Daily Herald* for this? The business interests with their wars against all their commercial enemies who advertise in it? Or the people who read the *Herald* and buy what is advertised in it? Or both? Surely both, with, perhaps, the general public contributing the greater percentage toward the paper's costs and profits. Yet helping the manufacturers in this way is done not only by the papers but by the Chamber of Commerce, which wanted, as I learned while I was there, the suburb of Clifton to hire a public relations counsel. The two Passaic newspapers, the *Herald* and the *News,* (controlled by the same men to keep out competition) are owned by James H. Waldon, who made his money selling textile machinery, and by Dow H. Drukker, ex-Congressman, officer of the People's Bank and Trust, and a contractor under the firm name: Union Building and Construction Company. But neither has any alliance with labor, which has no money to speak of and this is the case with most newspaper owners.

Now not only as you can see from this do those who order public opinion in the press belong to the same class as the owners of the mills, but this is also true of those in local as well as other government positions. Passaic and its suburbs have a Taxpayers' and Manufacturers' League. And this Taxpayers' and Manufacturers' League, as I here wish to emphasize, is not composed of laborers or mill hands. For out of 10,000 rented and 3,000 owned homes, the 3,000 owned (at the time of the last census) were not the property of either semi-skilled mill hands or laborers. Hence it becomes obvious, I think, that this League of Taxpayers and Manufacturers and the same actively supported by the local Chamber of Commerce, must be closer to the property owners and the manufacturers, than to the rank and file of the workers there. At any rate, since the city has the Commission form of government, and the Taxpayers' and Manufacturers' League in alliance with the local Chamber of Commerce have, in all elections, their own ticket, and have also, as the records show, elected the same, it was interesting to me to see how these superminds of the community functioned as stewards or caretakers of the affairs of the majority, whose state I have just been describing. Well, just after I was there, an election of City Commissioners was just around the corner. And the Taxpayers' and Manufacturers', together with the Chamber of Commerce, had their own candidates or "ticket." By the way, a petition signed by only 50 citizens nominates a candidate. And the candidates or ticket of the above bodies, as I saw afterwards, won. And then, I noted that the Taxpayers' and Manufacturers' League, exercising considerable influence in city government, asked for a *private* audit of the city departments, its *public* affairs, whereupon the vote on the next year's budget was postponed for two weeks—a postponement which suggested to me that this government by this and that superior body was not so different to our old-time money-controlled boss system. It just had a nicer name.

More, and despite the assurance of Public Safety Director Benjamin Turner that "the city is clean," I heard of the following allegations: that policemen assaulted young girls, that the cost of garbage and ash removal is the same in summer as in winter, although fewer ashes exist in summer; that an offer had been made whereby garbage could be collected for $50,000 a year less, yet was rejected or ignored; that $1,100 yearly was spent on ice water for the Police and Fire Departments; that six per cent was paid on tax revenue notes when the city could as well have paid five per cent and saved $30,000, and that Pettersen's Engineering Bureau worked for other people on city time. At any rate, neglect or mismanagement must have something to do with the fact that the Botany section of Passaic was, at the time I was there, asking the Board of Education for a new school to eliminate part-time conditions at Schools Nos. 7 and 12. One other fact which I observed in connection with the compatibility between the government and money-owners was that although the Grand Jury returned a presentment declaring that the $40,000 fee paid by the Passaic Valley Water Commission to Arthur S. Corbin as special counsel was "not only questionable but illegal" still, the Grand Jury later smoothed the matter over and said this action was all a terrible mistake. Yes?

Indeed, in New Jersey as elsewhere, and in Passaic as well as in other parts of New Jersey, I noticed and still do, for that matter, that editorially in the local newspapers, Big Business and Big Business alone, sounded the trumpet call. One editorial in Passaic, for instance, rejoiced in Senator Reed's statement that "this is a billion dollar country." This with Passaic's people half starving.

And in Passaic, while I was there, editorials from other cities relative to President Hoover's veto of the Muscle Shoals bill calling upon the Government to operate the plants, were copied with approval in all of the local papers. Thus one editorial read: "He is to be commended for having enunciated a policy in accord with American ideals." And another: "The Government muffed its chance when Henry Ford showed a willingness to lease and operate the plants." Then, too, the doctrine taught by the numerous and influential pastors is a quiescent one, urging all to make the best of present conditions. One minister, while I was there, preached on "Faith"; another on "Obedience." One minister alone, young and well-informed, disapproved of the capitalistic system. He has denounced the uneven division of profits, from his pulpit, and has been reprimanded for it by some of the members of his congregation.

And lastly, kindly give your attention to the activities and

statements of Colonel Johnson, President of the Botany Worsted
Mills, of Passaic, for alliance of corporation and government
continues in local affairs as well as higher up. Colonel Johnson,
manufacturing adviser to the wool and mohair division of the
Federal Farm Board, stated, and that not so long ago, that
whereas the Botany Mills used to have as much as $8,000,000
worth of wool on their inventory, the present action of the
Farm Board *controls the price* with such comparative certainty
that only three weeks' supply is ordered in advance. In other
words, the great manufacturers do not need to compete in connection with this business of prices any more. The Government
obviates all that sad work for them. Next, of the last tariff bill,
Colonel Johnson, in discussing the remechanization of the Botany
Mill, said: "When the tariff was passed, giving us full protection,
we felt safe to go ahead with our program." These tariffs, as
you see, completely assuring the industrialist his profit, make
him easy in his mind. He is a Government pet. But what about
the farmers who for the last fifty years have suffered by this
tariff price fixing? And who does anything for the laborers and
mill hands in Passaic whose state I have just described? Why,
by God, they don't even give them a decent city government—
one that would be fair to them, let alone a state or national one.

Because Paterson, New Jersey, is a kind of sister town to
Passaic, I went there also at the time, and now want to outline
some of the recent outgrowths of similar economic conditions
there. (This is as of July, 1931.) At that time, the silk workers
there were carrying on a strike in some 150 mills and shops. The
American Federation of Labor claimed 6,783 strikers and the
Communists 5,000. These doubtless overlap. The Communists
demanded as follows:

1. 8-hour day
2. No wage cuts
3. Wage increases
4. Minimum wage scales
5. No speed-up
6. No women at night work

7. Withdrawal of all injunctions
8. Equal pay for equal work
9. No race or sex discrimination
10. The right to organize and strike

In late July, 33 laborers were arrested for picketing at the mills controlled by Henry Doherty, the largest in Paterson. The *Women's Wear Daily,* a publication for the textile executives, stated in July that 20 Federal agents had been sent to check up on aliens and deport them. In other words our national Government immediately stepped in to help its pet manufacturers to break the strike. It is the way of our Government in these days. But almost any excuse will do to arrest a striker. Anything to intimidate him with the power of the law, and so restrain him from effective striking! Thus in early August, 54 strikers were arrested for not walking ten paces apart near the Colt Dye Mills, where wages had been cut twenty per cent. Others have since been arrested for "loitering" and for distributing hand bills. Also, 67 pickets were arrested at the Streng Dye Shop for disorderly conduct. And now the Taxpayers' League (and probably the Manufacturers' League also) is protesting that motion picture news reels of these police attacks upon strikers is giving Paterson adverse publicity. They are not protesting, as you can see for yourself, because these police attacks constitute an abuse of the workingman! On the contrary, and only because the reels were giving Paterson "adverse publicity."

In 1926, during the great strike in Passaic, Albert Weisbord, the leader who first preached there the Russian slogan, "Solidarity of all races," to the six or seven nationalities in Passaic, on strike against the bosses, so electrified the community that masses of strikers were for months doing the least bidding of the leader, and those who hated Jews were calling him "little Jesus." Despite his almost evangelical following, however, the strike was lost. Now the Communists have a small textile union there of about 100 members, called the National Textile Workers' Union. But these members, as well as all other Communists, are put in jail for distributing literature—although not for possessing it, as I understand. The Communists are nominating their own following for the coming city election of commissioners. And the editor of the *Daily Herald* told me that although Weisbord's battle cry of "solidarity" once influenced elections, two candidates of different nationality are being put up to split the workers' vote.

So you see—Passaic, a typical American mill town—is an illustration of what I look upon as complete Government failure in America. For where in it anywhere is equity, decency, any social harmony, beauty of peace? Can you or any one show me? And yet, on the other hand, wealth, wealth and power. And the pride and even arrogance of power. Imagine, in a local strike there—our National Government sending 20 Federal men to check up on possible aliens among the strikers and so deport them. A fine picture of "Of the People, by the People, for the People."

More, what has forty years of Government regulation of financial combinations done for the people of Passaic? The situation there is graphic proof of the failure of reform. And as long as the Government functions in the way it does now our country will be dotted with just such spectacles as this!

CHAPTER III

I MAINTAIN that American business, in the large, is and always has been carried on by force. I decry the entire system as far too backward for present needs, and far too uncivilized for the present-day stage of organized society. To-day's capitalistic method of conducting society is by no means the only way, and I am convinced that it is not the best way. The fundamental principle—that all of the necessities resulting from the comparatively advanced stage of invention which has been attained should be given to all people equitably for their services or labor—has been, in the main, disregarded.

But from the beginning of this country, though those with influence in our American legislative spheres have gobbled up America's natural resources, and with the coming of the railroads and the development of means of transportation in every direction, plus the consequent changes made possible for industry, the business of exploiting natural resources grew still more rapidly, so much so that to-day the immensely concentrated wealth resulting therefrom is controlled by only a few men. And these men, or their heirs and assigns, now direct the actions, if not the spirit, of the country. So much so that even now, in the near distance, a dictator looms as a possibility. But that man is not Herbert Hoover.

I will start at the beginning, so that a comprehensive view of America may be had. The earliest capitalists here—those gentlemen who began the private exploitation of public domain—dealt in land. The land company was the way to pioneer riches. Congress, in 1792, enacted a law giving the Ohio Land Company 100,000 acres. Then this same company possessed the influence to buy additional land—very good land, indeed—for almost nothing. One of its purchases was 892,900 acres for $642,856. This type of road to private enrichment was common in that day. Indeed, the Georgia Legislature of 1795 sold millions of acres to four land companies. Although another legislature in 1796 annulled the sale, because the former legislature had been accused of being under "improper influence," the Supreme Court of the United States, implying that the fraud made no difference, called the sale a good one. It was a good one, all right! And again when, in 1796, a law was passed to give the little man an opportunity to obtain property on credit, the big companies grabbed endless tracts through "dummy" holders, which tracts (the companies holding them on credit and tax free) they sold for all they could get from individual farmers whom the law had been supposed to benefit.

Again, under the Stone and Timber Act of 1878 and 1892, there was even more startling business chicanery, because these land companies were thereby enabled to trade in the public domain, reserving the lumber for themselves. Yet no little man was to get the benefit of that wealth, because even then, the financial vultures of that day descended upon him, and by reason of strength and numbers as well as laws made by their friends, enforced their vulture demands. Again, the Cash Sales Act of 1876 made possible the sale of great quantities of land to one person or company for only $1.25 an acre, providing it was a cash deal. By this means, rich mineral properties were secured for private exploitation. Still a little later, the Land Exchange Law, its supposed purpose the making of national forests, opened the way for these same sharpers to trade poor land for valuable property and so again enriched the cunning. This law would not appear so suspicious if great companies hadn't taken advantage of it to improve the value of their holdings.

Next, I want to bring out the point that most of the railroads in America were built on land grants from the public domain and on loans of public money, most of which never was paid for or returned. Some detail is necessary to prove this point.

It has been admirably made plain by Gustavus Myers in his "History of Great American Fortunes," and since his researches among Government papers have been so extensive and so accurate, I am saving time at this point as I have elsewhere in this book on historical finance and economics, by taking facts from his work.

Myers states in his book: "Practically every railroad corporation in the country stood indebted for immense sums of public money, little of which was ever paid back." Between the years 1850 and 1872 alone, Congress enacted laws giving 155,504,994 acres of land to railroad companies. In just one year (1856) Myers says that at least thirty laws effecting this were passed. Definite figures covering actual money loans are available. In one State (New York), $40,000,000 of taxpayers' money was loaned to the railroads of said State, and only one-fourth was paid back. A present of $30,000,000! And in those days $30,000,000 was an exorbitant figure and could command limitless quantities of material and labor. Yet think now of the tremendous valuations forced on these same railroads by private individuals, and the high rates every member of society must pay to these individuals! Myers quotes from Parson, who said that "land grants to railroads in Minnesota would make two States the size of Massachusetts; in Kansas, two States the size of Connecticut and New Jersey; in Montana and Washington, the grants of each were as large as all of Maryland, New Jersey and Massachusetts put together," etc.

But let us revert back in this connection, to the early financiers on the Coast; Leland Stanford, Collis P. Huntington, Charles Crocker and Mark Hopkins. These men, banded together to start a railroad company, were able to raise only $200,000. No figure to build a railroad on, as you can guess, but enough to carry on the work of getting the legislatures to make them generous gifts of public wealth! And here's what $200,000 and their efforts brought them!—$400,000 from the City of Sacramento; $550,000 from Placer County; $2,100,000 from California; $25,000,000 and 4,500,000 acres of land from Congress for the Central

Pacific Railroad. Also, according to Myers, the Pacific Railway Commission of 1887 said that these four financiers charged $75,000,000 for building 1,171 miles of this railroad which really cost them only about $25,000,000. This same Commission, in re the Southern Pacific Railroad, said: "A large portion of $4,800,000 was used for the purpose of influencing legislation . . . and elections." Again, the Wilson Committee of the Senate said that the Union Pacific, after receiving huge donations from Congress, spent $436,000 to bring about a supplementary act of 1864 granting them $16,000 to $48,000 for *every mile* of railroad (*figurez vous!*) and alternate sections forty miles wide as land grants. And after the older Vanderbilt had united road after road in New York State (built out of public funds), and had enlarged his system to obtain a through route from New York to Chicago, his son, William H. Vanderbilt, in 1880, obtained the great Chicago and Northwestern rail system, a 4,000 mile road created mostly by means of public property; land and taxpayers' money!

More, Jay Gould, open-faced Jack Cade of the middle of the last century, who sacked the Erie Railroad (built out of public funds, almost none of which were ever returned) was another of our great financial founders, exemplars and leaders. He played upon public opinion, which at that time was becoming enraged at the actions of that invincible giant, Vanderbilt. Claiming to be a friend of the people in preventing Vanderbilt from securing a monopoly, he put a black mask over his eyes and went to work. In this guise, he advanced until a railroad constructed and equipped for the most part by public money had become his own private property. It was the Erie. Having put this over, Gould and other Erie directors, according to the New York State Investigating Committee of 1873, lavished over $1,000,000 in only one year (1868) on "extra and legal services," it being "their custom from year to year to spend large sums of money to control elections and influence legislation." Indeed, Gould, in order to "legalize" his outrageous activities between 1868 and 1872, joined interests with "Boss"

Tweed, the infamous and corrupt leader of a band of political and financial thieves of the day and the City of New York, and then told the New York State Assembly Investigating Committee of 1873 that he had given Tweed funds and disbursed cash all over New York State to influence nominations so many times that it would be as difficult for him to remember them as it would be to remember "the number of freight cars over the Erie"!

Just a few more examples, if you please, so as to get a more rounded picture of our American railroads and of our financial forefathers and founders—the men who made the tradition as well as the pace, financially speaking, which now we look on as *American* and all right! Gould and Sage, working together so successfully as they did when it came to corruption and greed, gained, among their many systems, the Missouri Pacific Railroad. This road was made up of many little roads, the construction of which the State of Missouri had aided to the extent of $25,000,000. About this time, though, the United States Interstate Commerce Commission found that Gould, with his many railroads in the West, had, by means of "dummy" title holders and driving rightful owners off their land, obtained for himself nearly all of the coal lands of Wyoming, Utah and Oklahoma. But was anything done to him for that? No! Did he suffer any loss of any kind? No. And isn't he to-day one of our great and admirable figures of what are now known as "those good old buccaneer days"? Yes, he is. You know he is, as are Commodore Vanderbilt, Jim Fiske, Russell Sage, J. P. Morgan, and a score of others.

But this exploitation of public property was so widespread and universal that it is actually impossible to touch upon it all. John Work Garrett and Johns Hopkins, masters of the Baltimore & Ohio, in an earlier day, had, by 1876, inveigled legislatures, courts and common councils in Maryland, Virginia, West Virginia and Pennsylvania to loan them public money, cancel obligations to pay it back, and make possible watered stock and no taxation on $88,000,000 worth of property. And as an illustration of how these financiers looked upon their obligations to the Government which gave them so much, the financier, John Insley Blair of Blairstown, New Jersey, when he sold the Sioux City and Pacific to the Chicago and Northwestern, made an agreement to the effect that all debts, except that to the Government, were to be taken over by the latter railroad. Yet for every mile of the railroad, the Government had given 100 sections of land and $16,000 in Government bonds. Not only that, but according to testimony before the Pacific Railway Commission, Blair charged at least four times as much as should have been charged for construction. But so it was all over America in those days and I must move on with my subject.

I think it might be of interest, and what's more, might correct certain delusions subsequently forced on the public (historically and otherwise) as to our financial and other origins, moral, religious, etc., if I were to outline briefly the methods by which our American financiers of early and later days really did get their start. The common picture of them is of men saving their pennies until they got enough to build a railroad; in other words, the Pluck and Luck, Work and Win theory of achievement. But the truth is different! The first of these financiers, Commodore Cornelius Vanderbilt, started as a worker on a small ferryboat; then became owner of one, and finally had a fleet powerful enough to start a competing steamship line to California, for the stopping or dropping of which he was able, by the power of his wealth and to his ability to compete and destroy, to collect $480,000 and finally $612,000 a year as graft from rival companies whom, had he operated his proposed line, he hoped to destroy. By these means (see Myers' "History of Great American Fortunes") he made enough to start railroad deals. Also at about this time, and at an early age in their own lives, both Gould and Sage entered into questionable business deals which netted them much cash; Gould in the tannery business with New York City partners, and Sage in the produce business. Sage, operating in Troy, New York, became an alderman there, and later Treasurer of Rensselaer

County, of which Troy is a part. False to the public trust in him as a public official, he promptly and dishonestly influenced the city of Troy to sell to him cheaply a small railroad built out of public funds, which railroad he had already contracted to sell privately to the New York Central at a great profit to himself. And from then on he rose, as I will show. But let us leave him here for the present.

On the other hand, and unlike these others, the revered J. P. Morgan of those good old buccaneer days, was the son of a millionaire banker, Junius S. Morgan. Yet he, too, banker's son or no banker's son, laid the foundation of his later great success in a deal like the following:

It was around the opening of the Civil War and, of course, guns were a very marketable thing. Somewhere, in some armory in New York City, I believe, the Government had stored a number of old and condemned guns, said to be so dangerous as to blow soldiers' thumbs off. Of these, just the same, Morgan by paying $17,486 for the lot, bought 5,000. A little later, though, he sold the very same guns to the Government as *new* for $109,912. The Government, having got on to the deal, wouldn't pay for them. Therefore, Morgan brought suit and eventually obtained a court award of $55,550 for these guns, said to be old and very dangerous. In other words, more than two hundred per cent profit from the transaction! But by no means stopping with that, he went further, and eventually won, with his partner, $58,175 *additional* payment. The facts are from Myers' "History of Great American Fortunes."

I have also stated, and here I shall prove, that the methods of these and all our financiers, who actually have ruled or now do rule American business, were and are lawless, and might be described as lawless force. And one phase of this force should be characterized as conspiracy within the law, although it is so much like criminal conspiracy according to the law as to be of the same effect. Thus, Gould, for instance, used the profits of his railroad frauds to buy up large quantities of gold in order to control the gold supply needed by bankers and manufacturers. And because, from the effects of his trickery, they feared that gold would command higher prices, they were literally compelled to buy quantities from Gould at his highest prices and this just before "Black Friday" the crash of which, stocks and all prices falling, carried so many to ruin—his gold buyers among them. Yet even Gould, while he made great profits by selling gold and everything else high, was himself trapped, in part at least, by the necessity incidental to the panic created by him of his buying and also making many contracts to buy. Had he been compelled to fulfill these contracts, as he quickly saw, all of his handsome profits would have been lost. So in one day he secured twelve injunctions and orders from his complaisant judges, enjoining him, said Gould (mind you!) from fulfilling these contracts to buy! The Congressional Committee of 1870 stated that by this outrage, Gould saved himself or made, rather, $11,000,000.

Other examples which I look upon as conspiracies to make others pay exorbitantly, yet are within the law as that law is arranged for the time being, are out of the life book of the elder Vanderbilt, the Commodore. Thus, once upon a time a group of politicians, bankers and brokers of his day were in on the news (and possibly news created by himself) that his, Vanderbilt's, street car franchise to his New York and Harlem Railroad Station was to be voided by a decision at law. Had it been so voided, it would, of course, have made the stock of the road go down; and believing that it would be so voided, these bankers, politicians and brokers contracted to sell quantities of New York and Harlem stock to be delivered in one month, for they knew, or thought they knew, that after the court decision, but before the time of delivery to the vendee, they could buy it for much less. On the other hand, Vanderbilt, "learning" this —although it has been said he knew all the time—he himself having engineered the rumors, bought all of these offerings of stock that he could. Then when the time came for these brokers, bankers and politicians to deliver the stock which they had contracted to sell at $90 they had to come to Vanderbilt himself, or his brokers, to get enough to fulfill their obligations. And when they so came, Vanderbilt was there with his exorbitant price, and cleaned up millions, and in one week!

A similar trick was repeated by him in connection with a New York State legislative action, only this time Vanderbilt soaked them for fair: $285 a share for stock which they had figured to sell at a profit. American business is full of such conspiracies.

Another almost universal American business practice of this force order relates to running one business in order to advance another or to buy it for a song—a process which has so often frozen out the small unsuspecting investor who has thereby lost his all. An example of "By force" in this sense concerns some of our big railroads and their schemes to get control of the rich coal mines in their area, mainly by charging such preposterous freight rates to independent coal operators as to make it impossible for them to compete with other companies. In lawsuits afterwards, it has been brought out that these independent companies could not fulfill their contracts because the railroads claimed there were no cars available in which to ship their coal. Of course, this was not true. Later, these same railroads or some subsidiary of theirs, bought out these defrauded independents. They were defrauded of a national right too—transportation— and it should be criminal to withhold that right. So, many of our railroad executives should really be serving years in the penitentiary.

Another illustration of wealth by force was (about 1900) the Morgan-Vanderbilt attack upon the Philadelphia and Reading Railroad, which owned great coal deposits. At that time, our American money kings were interested in swallowing coal lands, and Morgan and Vanderbilt made one attack after another on this railroad's credit. Their favorite method was to circulate reports of imminent adverse legislation. This forced down the stock, so that it could no longer be used as collateral for loans. When it was very low, of course, Morgan and Vanderbilt bought a great interest in it and divided this between themselves.

Once Morgan and Vanderbilt obtained coal deposits, much of this coal land was held by separate companies, but under their control, because the Constitution of the State of Pennsylvania prohibited railroads from owning coal mines. Just the same as having railroads own coal companies however. Yet in this matter of interlocking directorates the partisan American law does not even presume influence upon one company because of control of another contracting with it. But what did this control mean to the average man? How did it affect the American citizen who was not a coal trust organizer or a financier? In the first place, the price of hard coal was raised $1.30 a ton. Following that, and rapidly, in the first few years of the twentieth century, came further increases in price until finally people who used coal were forced to pay seven times as much as it had cost the trust to mine and ship it. In fact, about this time, our national American House Committee on Interstate Commerce declared that these men who controlled coal had deliberately limited production in order to increase the price.

More of the same is the following: Gould and Sage, two of our royal buccaneers of the 70's and 80's, constructed a telegraph line alongside the Union Pacific tracks in order to force Vanderbilt to buy their line or to sell them his Western Union. And by strong competition, they finally forced him to buy their American Union Telegraph Company for $10,000,000. Yet only a little later, after Gould, by manipulation, forced down the Vanderbilt telegraph stock, he was able to buy or wrenched control of both companies from him.

In Mr. John D. Rockefeller's early days, there was The Tidewater Pipe Line, an independent oil transporting company, which threatened his scheme of complete oil monopoly. This company was then vigorously attacked, of course, and harassed and embarrassed in every conceivable way; its credit assailed here and in Europe, the refineries which it supplied bought up by Rockefeller interests and so ended or declared a public nuisance and forced to move. Finally, when Tidewater's financial state was desperate, Rockefeller bought heavily of its stock and thus forced it to terms.

But not only the publicly owned railroads of the day, but also some privately owned but held by rivals, were crippled by financiers of the Gould, Sage and Hill type, who thus by force gained control for themselves. In the unnatural course of events which brought this about, officials were bribed to lease them for a fraction of their value, or freight and passenger service was cut off or led over other railroads until stock fell so that control could be bought for little, or bankruptcy permitted buying it for a song. These business methods must be understood for they operate as much to-day as at any other time. Another method of our buccaneer financiers of those (as some of our numbskull Americans now see it) glorious days was to charge so much for building a railroad that it went into bankruptcy. Then these same financial Captain Kidds bought it in for very, very little. Sage did this with the Minnesota and Pacific Railroad. The Northern Pacific, forced into bankruptcy, was thus secured by James J. Hill, another of our great rail magnates. Any number of oil refineries, subjected to powerful attacks by the Rockefeller companies, were finally bankrupted and bought up by Standard Oil. In fact, these were the methods of our railroad and other leaders all over the country and at a time when our American voters were annually or quadrennially voting for as trashy a crew of grafting misrepresentatives as has functioned officially anywhere. The value of the ballot!

The next phase of raw force in American business was, and still is, contract by collusion. This means one group or person fraudulently playing into the hands of another group or person. For instance: a man cannot make a contract with himself which will be sustained by law. It is void and unenforceable. Yet the directors of one corporation can make a lawful contract with another corporation of which they are also directors. This is because the law now considers all of our corporations, regardless of this really lawless interlocking directorate system, as separate and honestly competitive. Imagine! Yet this can and does lead to the greatest frauds. For directors can and do contract with themselves, but in the name of the corporation only, and so manage to pay or charge exorbitant prices for whatever they choose in order that the public via its rate payments or tax bureau may be made to pay on expenses or bear losses on this or that that never really were. Indeed, this has always been, and now is, a way for our corporations to get rich quickly, and a way of which they always take advantage.

One example of this was furnished by William H. Vanderbilt, heir to the lawless Commodore, who, controlling the New York Central Railroad, troubled to organize a construction company to build the South Pennsylvania line, a branch of the main line. By so doing, he was able to contract with himself in such a way as to get $30,000,000 in securities. And the dear and by now financially sainted Russell Sage did practically the same thing with the Minnesota and Pacific Railroad. More, Gould and Sage, controlling the Kansas Pacific, the Denver, South Park and Pacific and some others, as well as the Union Pacific, sold the former to the latter—or from themselves to themselves —thus taking a secret profit of $20,000,000. Indeed, this particular law which permits one interlocked company or corporation to deal with another interlocked company as a separate and independent thing, so privileges the corporations as to cost the American people (and most of whom cannot pay without severe deprivation to themselves) untold billions. In fact, this above group up to 1887, had issued $84,000,000 worth of watered stock.

But think of this as a robber assessment upon the public, and over such a brief period of years! And of it, the minority report of the Pacific Railway Commission, which afterwards investigated these transactions, stated that "the Union Pacific Company had, during the last eighteen years, received $176,294,793 in surplus earnings and land sales, and if its stock had been fully paid, as Congress required that it should be, and as its officers certified under oath that it was, nearly all of that money would to-day be applicable to the payment of the Government debt. But the company has paid out $28,650,770 in dividends and $82,742,850 in interest on bonds, nearly all of which was distributed to shareholders without consideration. It has sunk over $10,000,000 in Denver, South Park and Pacific; it paid out $10,000,000 to Jay Gould and his associates for branch lines and other investments which were worthless." But did any one go to jail, or pay back anything? No one went to jail or paid back anything.

It was about 1900 that J. P. Morgan, the sainted, bought the Pennsylvania Coal Company; then he sold it to the Erie Railroad, which he controlled, for the exorbitant figure of $37,000,-000. This outrage of contracting with oneself through controlled corporations is just another of those business practices by force which, as I am trying in this book to show, are the very basis of corporate business to-day, and in full use by all of our interlocking monopolies.

Another method of business exploitation by force is via size and power as well as ownership,—the power of a big body to glare at and drive off a little one—right or no right. And how this unscrupulous force has been brought to bear in America! Many of our large manufacturing concerns, by reason of weight and so force of business (the size of the same) were and still are able to threaten and force railroads or other corporations in this way: i.e. by saying that unless preferential freight rates are granted them, they will ship over other systems. John D. Rockefeller, by threats amounting to coercion, once made a contract with the Lake Shore and New York Central at a rate so much lower than his competitors in Cleveland received, that he was the only one who could make any money.

Yet probably never up to that time had this rule by force of size been more drastically enforced than when the Southern Improvement Company, controlled by the Standard Oil, was formed in 1872. By means of this company, to which I will refer frequently in this chapter, Rockefeller brought to a peak his theory of rebates. The whole idea of his Southern Improvement Company was the uniting of many oil companies to make fabulous profits from railroad rebates. The Southern Improvement Company, a secret monopoly, had contracts with J. Edgar Thompson, President of the Pennsylvania Railroad, Vanderbilt of the New York Central, and Gould of the Erie, to give them a rebate of $1.06 on the usual freight charge of $2.50. And not only did Rockefeller's competitors have to pay $2.50, but $1.06 of the charge thus paid by competitors went to Rockefeller. Not only that, but this also gave Rockefeller information as to the who, when and where of his competitors and the exact extent of their business. And one competitor, Alexander Scofield & Company, asking the railroads why he could not receive rebates, was told that he did not ship as much as the Standard Oil. Under this unscrupulous agreement as to rebates, Rockefeller was able to crush this Scofield firm.

More, and by virtue of this Southern Improvement Company, Rockefeller was able to inform Hanna, Baslington & Company, a small rival oil company, that since Standard Oil had the facilities, its rivals would be wiped out. Yet finally (out of the goodness of its heart, I assume), the Standard chose to pay $45,000 for this Hanna plant, which had cost $75,000. And whereas before this Southern Improvement Company deal to receive rebates, Rockefeller had 26 rivals in Cleveland alone, later, or within only three short months thereafter, 21 of these had been forced to sell to the Standard, thus increasing the Rockefeller oil capacity from 1,500 to 10,000 barrels of crude oil per day.

Yet with even these vicious commercial methods of agreement, the Southern Improvement Company could not rule forever. For in spite of all efforts to suppress it, the truth came out. Some one hostile to or beaten by Rockefeller laid the whole thing bare. And although in those days it was almost too preposterous a story for the people to believe—they were so innocent in regard to all this rushing financial stuff—they did finally become enraged, and thereafter—and very soon—was formed by the independent oil well owners the Petroleum Producers' Union, which led public opinion in a fight which abrogated the secret rebates and established open rates. Also it brought about through the Pennsylvania Legislature the withdrawal of the charter of the Southern Im provement Company, and later a national investigation which declared it a "gigantic and daring conspiracy." But was any one punished? No one was punished.

But even so, Rockefeller couldn't be held down. He had by then an organization big enough to win by force, and he was bent on making it more powerful. Within three or four weeks after his rebate scheme had been demolished, he had forced another rebate on the railroads operating between Cleveland and New York. In other words, although one practical monopoly had just been broken up, after a few months he was able to bring about another: the National Refiners' Association.

At this point in his career, though, here is how Rockefeller, by outrageous treatment of his competitors, became a greater and greater force. After having beaten competitors in Cleveland and elsewhere, he decided to attack Pittsburgh, Philadelphia and New York City, where were many large and flourishing refineries. And victory for him sprang from his ability to show one company in each town what enormous gains would come to it from merging with the Standard, which meant that the others would be left out in the cold and to die. And when, by secret agreement, any one of these companies did this, the Standard put through a rebate for it. Since competition could not possibly hold out under this onslaught, the others sold out to the Standard so fast that as early as 1875, Rockefeller had ninety-five per cent of all of the oil refineries in the United States. Yet only business methods, of raw force,—that is, outside the law because there was no law to cover such deals.

But now let us once more consider the pipe line, previously referred to. This was not a Rockefeller invention, for by 1869 a certain Charles Hatch had developed it. Yet when the Petroleum Producers' Union of that day tried to put through a free pipe line, that is, one that would accept and transfer anybody's oil, and at the same rate—i.e. a common carrier,—the Pennsylvania Railroad prevented it. In other words, illegal corporate force was used to block it! For in its stead, the Pennsylvania Railroad came forward with a duplicate or substitute, i.e. the

Empire Transportation Company which it controlled and which, owning pipe lines and refineries, obtained this pipe line business for the Pennsylvania Railroad. But because Dr. Rockefeller wanted all the pipe lines and refineries for himself, he ordered the Empire to be liquidated. And when his command to this independent company was not obeyed, he ceased shipping oil over the Pennsylvania Railroad, *and* his was sixty per cent of its oil traffic! Hence, the sale of the Empire to Rockefeller. In other words, one large vulture descended upon a smaller one and drove it away from the kill. And, as I keep saying, by *raw force*, that is, ungoverned by law. Indeed the thing which has built up the great organizations of our day and now permits them to rule everything and tell the rest of us where to get off, is just that raw force beyond the scope of the law.

About this time, though, Rockefeller, ungoverned and not bounded by any realms of law, had extorted such stupendous rebates from the Pennsylvania Railroad that while the open rate to the non-trustified oil producer running a little oil well on his own was $1.90, Rockefeller's for a like shipment was $.80. Ditto, practically, with all of the other railroads! But at the same time, and like the Pennsylvania before him, he was fighting pipe lines, and by all means possible. Also he or his Standard Oil as well as the railroads, saw to it that the proposed bill against rebates did not (in 1875) get through Congress. He wasn't quite ready for that as yet, you see. But by 1877, having combined all of these pipe lines under himself as the United Pipe Lines Company, he was then ready for this rebate law. For by then, you see, it might be passed or it might not. For owning the pipe lines he could pump his oil to wherever he chose, and no rebates were needed. And more, in 1887, when it no longer made any difference to him, the Interstate Commerce Law declared rebates illegal.

By now, though, Rockefeller's size, gained by raw force, had made and was making for him so much profit that he was able to have the advantage of more tanks for storage, more railroad cars, more pipes, and also the money wherewith to develop the new oil fields of Illinois, Kansas and Oklahoma, than anybody or everybody else together. He was an oil Goliath, as it were. And this permitted him to continue his rule by force. Hence, Standard could and did cripple its competitors by not furnishing them with the railroad tank cars that the roads owned, but the use of which Mr. Rockefeller directed. So bruising was Rockefeller's force or whip that by 1888, not only did he refuse to let his competitors ship in the Standard Oil tank cars, but he forced the railroads to raise the rates on all oil shipped in barrels—which his competitors were by then forced to use!

But to go on. Although pipe lines—even those he owned— were by law common carriers which must take everybody's oil, still by reason of his ownership of a pipe line system 35,000 miles long, he was able to say to oil well owners who supplied independent refineries that unless they stopped this selling to a Standard Oil rival the pipe lines serving them would be torn up and removed, or his lines would just refuse to send oil when it was destined for an independent refinery.

Also, while Standard was able to ship oil through its pipes from the oil fields to New York for 11 cents a barrel, it "soaked" all of its competitors 60 cents a barrel! But of course, according to our American business standards of the time and since, the Pennsylvania Railroad was really entitled to graft on oil shipped over Rockefeller's pipe lines, and took it. In other words, it was a little stronger than the crude oil producers and so could exact a little more! Big dog eat little dog but not medium-sized dog!

But now, for a change, I want to give an example of what a banker can command by the force of his resources. Examples are endless throughout American history up to the present day, but here is a good one: J. P. Morgan, through the power of the money he controlled, brought about the Steel Trust, with its iron deposits of about 600,000,000 tons and its coal fields of approximately 2,000,000,000 tons, together with various plants covering every branch of the steel industry as such. And for organizing that, Morgan received a hundred million dollars worth of its stock. Yet even so, and outside the new trust, remained the Tennessee Coal and Iron Company, with considerable resources—enough to disturb the United States Steel, at least at the beginning of the twentieth century. At that time, though, due to American panic conditions of the hour (always in the offing in this "prosperous" land), the Trust Company of America, a New York financial institution, was holding quantities of Tennessee Coal and Iron stock as security for some loans. And when it, the Trust Company of America, suddenly needed money, it went to J. P. Morgan. So there was his opportunity to do up, or in, as the English say, this dear independent Tennessee Coal & Iron Company. And did he do it in? Well, knowing the Trust Company of America was holding this Tennessee Coal and Iron stock as collateral for loans, he proceeded at once to demand the same or no help for the Trust Company of America! And did the Trust Company of America give up that stock? It did. For what else could a poor honest Trust Company do? For else Morgan would have let it, as well as a large string of other banks, in which it was interested, fail. And so and at once, it turned over the stock to him, Morgan obtaining the same at such a low price that the saving amounted to six or seven hundred million dollars for U. S. Steel. And so passed the Tennessee Coal & Iron. It had to become a humble subsidiary.

Yet long before this, though—a small final comment, this—this same Steel Trust had resolved formally not to contract with labor unions for work of any kind (no dictation from labor, you see!) and by its size and power it was able by force to carry this out to the letter, so much so that right up to the present date, U. S. Steel is non-union. No independent unionization at all.

So as you see, and when necessary, little corporations are ruled by bigger ones, and by force, law or no law!

But now a further word as to Mr. Rockefeller and his pipe line. It concerns the period during which some independent pipe lines—not so many—were attempting to compete with Mr. Rockefeller and at which time, as I will now show, a state of open force existed. For when any of these independents tried to lay their pipes underneath the tracks of the big railroads, these same railroads time and time again tore up such pipes. And so brutal and consistent was this opposition to them—right though they were in their efforts so to do—that in order for any of these independents to get any pipe line at all, they had to set up camps at the point where their line (legally laid, of course) crossed or proposed to cross under the railroad in order to guard the same night and day. Otherwise, no pipe line crossing. And as for law, or recourse to law? Toot! Toot! What was law as against the will or desire of a great railroad! And so these pipe crossings had to be guarded for months as against the forces of these supposedly honest, law-abiding railroads (which, as you well know, were always in the courts demanding justice or the law on some one else—their competitors or some badly injured employee who didn't like the fellow-servant law which shut him from any compensation for any injury that he received); in fact, many of these railroads sent men, even hundreds of men, to attack these pipe line independents at their crossing work. Open civil war, as you see. And there were fights, and lots of them, and ultimately, of course, enforcements by one side or the other of their will, but by violence. In other words, raw, illegal force.

But now, and finally, the following will serve to illustrate my "by force, law notwithstanding!"—the basis of all our American wealth and present day financial grandeur. For to-day we are the heirs of all that and do not flatter yourself that we are not. Our trusts and giant banks and our great and lawless money lords are the true children of all of these who went before. In 1896, a fair bill on pipe lines was before the New Jersey State Legislature. Four days before the legislative session was over, the senator acting as champion for the bill disappeared with the bill and all of the papers thereto appertaining. Kidnaping charges were made; Standard Oil and the railroads were blamed. But the law was not passed.

And here is another. When some English stockholders in the Erie Railroad, representing considerable of its holdings, wanted to shape its policy, Gould and his directors were voted out. Although Gould obtained an injunction against them, they took the Erie office and books by force and were never punished by law for so doing.

And so coercion, and to this day, Government vigilance (if there is such) to the contrary notwithstanding. Thus, for a long time, some of our American bankers were wont to exchange paper money for gold at our United States Treasury and then hold this gold in order to force the Government to borrow it back from them, thus multiplying the bankers' profits. The late J. P. Morgan, father of the present one, was the chief exponent of this nifty system. And so expertly was it worked that before it was stopped—this was back in 1895—not a few millions were filched from the Government, and no questions asked. Thus, in 1894, two bond issues of $50,000,000 each and another of $62,000,000 were forced by the bankers on the Government. By these, of course, the banks, Mr. Morgan's among them, made millions in profits. And this despite the fact that our Government officials of that day had previous knowledge of the gold hoarding, its purpose and probable result.

But to go back to that dear Standard Oil Company—our exemplar of trust methods and their honesty—it once maintained (and still does, for all I know) a regular army of hired information gatherers. In this way, all kinds of data concerning a rival's business were obtained. Some of it, for instance, checked and rechecked daily by Standard Oil men and covering all rival oil shipments over railroads. And sometimes also the railroads were forced to supply Rockefeller regularly with this data in order that he could use his army elsewhere. If the necessary information was not to be extracted in any other way, then employees (bookkeepers) of rival firms were bribed to furnish the data to the Standard Oil interests.

And these unfair business methods in the matter of rate discrimination did not end even with the Interstate Commerce Law of 1887 against them. Rather, as Ida Tarbell, the historian of Standard Oil, and the commentator *par excellence* on Rockefeller, wrote in 1903: "There is no independent refiner who doesn't meet incessant discouragement and freight rate discrimination. Rates are made more favorable to Standard refining points, and switching and dock charges are multiplied for outsiders. Loading and unloading facilities are refused, payments on small amounts must be paid in advance," etc.

In other words, money, in American business, has always been and at the present time as I either have shown or will show, has been used lawlessly to force the other fellow to do or not to do such things as meant either profit or loss to the one with the most money. In fact, as early as the middle of the last century, Lawrence Stone & Company, of Boston and New York, in order to have the duties on woolen and dye products lowered, disbursed bribes amounting to $87,000. Yet so widely was this type of thing practiced by the affluent members of our dominant commercial class, that our history as a nation is most disagreeably colored thereby. Indeed, by 1850, money was being so extensively used to bribe Government officials to lower import duties that our Congress of that day reported that 2,062 cases of lawless under-valuating for Boston, New York, Philadelphia and New Orleans were on record.

How's that for an honest, kind and true country of presumably democratic and yet wholly—as it would appear—individualistic and better still, corporate, and better still imperial, or in other words, financially tyrannical leanings? How?

CHAPTER IV

OUR BANKS AND CORPORATIONS AS GOVERNMENT

THE tremendous trusts and holding companies bear down hard on every American. Afflicted at times to the point of realization of the economic, political and legal skullduggery that is at the bottom of this, the average movie and baseball addict of this country, as well as the petty tradesman and worker, squirms to loosen himself, even protests here and there in meeting, only to discover that the subtle and powerful banks and corporations rule and defeat him. Yet just how far, as yet even he is not prepared to say. And more, if he does discover, even in part, afraid is he in these days to protest, lest additional ills, corporation-instigated and promoted, may descend on him: a custom of the country, as it were!

Twenty years ago, laborers dreamed of a halcyon machine age, with six or seven hours' work a day. Yet to-day, with machinery at almost the perfection point, they are beggars, receivers of charity, while 40,000 millionaires bestride the land. To go beyond the present economic fiasco of this year of our Lord 1931, labor now senses that overbearing banks and trusts buy their own laws and elect their own officials. These have the time, background and "polish" to consort and argue with and persuade senators and judges. In fact, the small American, once so free and glorious in his own mind—to-day, although not exactly elsewhere—is no more than a drilled and dragooned member of one or another of our corporations' chain gangs.

But while some are aware of this, others are not; a large number not. For Americans, so genuinely clever with machinery and at sports, are, in the matter of economics, perhaps the dullest people in the world. They do not know what it is all about, and unless severely pressed, as in the present situation, do not care. ("Oh, let's go to the ball game!"!) But in the present situation, and in certain places or lines of work, they cannot now afford to go to the ball game, and are beginning to sense, and in spots actually to see, that their government now belongs to the above said banks and trusts, and more, are beginning to fight them. But far from successfully, as you will see. Just the same, in such States as Oregon, Washington, Massachusetts, Pennsylvania and New York, the people, in elections, have supported public ownership of utility projects. A mild protest which I hope is far deeper in the hearts of the people. Yet mainly, as I will show, the people have already lost self-government. They are already driven and are afraid to protest. Yet that these lost liberties are to be regained without drastic storms of many kinds, I question.

John Dewey, one of our outstanding American thinkers, says of the trust movement in the United States that it cannot now be arrested by legislation. And I think, of course, he is right. Our corporations have grown to such an extent (130 of them controlling $55,000,000,000) that they are by now far beyond all former business developments and even concepts of the human mind, and the banks that represent and in many cases control and manipulate them have reached the stage of such tremendous profits and power ensuing therefrom, that regulation of them by the Government is a dead failure. They can easily parry such regulation, because they are themselves the Government.

The size of these corporations can hardly be imagined. It means almost nothing for them to write a check for seventy-five or a hundred million dollars, or to buy up hundreds of companies in which are deposited the savings of thousands of individuals. I do not myself even know how to grasp, let alone state, the immensity of these things. But I did look at a map of the Pennsylvania Railroad the other day. At most points across Pennsylvania, Ohio, Indiana and other States, four or five lines, maybe a hundred miles apart, running parallel east and west, and all controlled by it. And not only have hundreds of short branches been acquired by it, but also longer ones to such faraway points as Louisville, Vincennes, Sodus Point, the northerly Mackinaw City, and far down the peninsula which on the east forms Chesapeake Bay. Three different lines run into Cincinnati, two into Chicago, and three out Long Island. Yet if a Pennsylvania train, or only one of its engines, is derailed for a short distance, several thousand dollars worth of damage is done to the track and roadbed. This illustrates, in a small way, how valuable is a single American railroad; and there are so many of them.

But let us turn to the insurance companies, and imagine, if you can, insurance policies aggregating hundreds of billions of dollars. Such immensity cannot be visualized, even by the individuals who control the companies. It is more like an immense dynamo which is started and stopped by a button. The bankers actually know more about the button than about anything else. As to resources, the New York Life Insurance Company alone has about $700,000,000 in bonds, public utilities and all kinds of industries, besides $600,000,000 invested in real estate, if you can imagine such sums or their import!

So large are these corporations, so large the banks which finance and control them, that one passes into the land of dreams in trying to visualize their immensity. Not only by enormous rewards from business, but also by a system by which bankers throughout the United States prey on hundreds of municipal governments to whom more loans are made than the people can ever pay back and over whom laws are forced by financial influence in legislatures, do their resources grow. And from the pockets of those workers who must buy or use what the business houses offer as well as pay taxes for loans which these bank-ridden cities have obtained, come the dollars, dimes and pennies which swell these great central wells of money. In short, these banks all over the country have become so large that by now the Bankers Trust Company of New York has total assets of $800,000,000, and even larger is the Guaranty Trust, with $1,800,000,000, and even more powerful the National City

Bank of New York, which itself is not the largest, having less than the Chase National Bank, which, ever since its merger with the Equitable Trust Company, stands as the largest bank in the world. I hesitate to bother you with these mentally quite meaningless sums.

The more clearly to realize the power of these banks and corporations, though, let me briefly analyze their profits. In 1930, the year of most drastic depression, the Standard Oil of New York earned $40,000,000, almost the equivalent of ten per cent, on the 17,800,000 shares of outstanding capital stock. The income of the Radio-Keith Orpheum Corporation so increased as to make its earnings rise one hundred and three per cent. In the same year, America witnessed the astounding spectacle of one individual, Henry Ford (and his son, Edsel), receiving profits of $44,000,000 or $257 per share. Profits per share, not the market quotation of the share! There isn't any such thing! And in 1929, Ford's earnings were nearly twice as great. (What would even a portion of this wealth accomplish in relieving the millions suffering for food and necessities?) But how ridiculous that any constructive force, no matter how amazing, should, under any government, pilfer from the poor. In the large, an analysis of 407 representative corporations in 20 different industries (according to Ernst & Ernst, accountants) shows an earning of six and one-half per cent in 1930 on capital investment.

As to profits in the large banking concerns, those with loans and investments over $10,000,000 outside New York City made four and one-half per cent, and those in New York City, three per cent. Tremendous profits indeed, when you consider that they are on the total capital funds of these banking concerns! And as if in proof of this, Rockefeller's National City Bank has in the last few years acquired bank after bank. Indeed, the ease with which it has taken over one and another of the various metropolitan banks, with some ten or twenty branches, has been one of the wonders of our recent American economic years. The National City itself now operates 43 branches in

New York and 99 throughout the world. This very plainly
suggests, I think, how easily one or a few of the dextrous and
ingenious manipulators of these great institutions may and do
pull strings which effect enormous results everywhere. Yet for
this long time now, the American Government has been unable
to control its own Federal Reserve system. Not only that, but
the prestige of these great New York banks and their subsidiaries—the actual money which they command and direct
—makes the Government itself take a back seat, appear what
it really has come to be: financially not important! You have
an illustration of what is meant when you see, say, the Mexican
Minister of Finance, as happened recently, going to J. P.
Morgan Company for the engineering of the terms and agreements governing nearly $1,000,000,000 worth of bonds which
the Mexican Government was offering as collateral for a loan.
It was not the Federal Government to which he resorted, but
an American private bank!

And yet, more and more favors to our American capitalists
and financiers! All of the inner stockholders in the National
City Bank have, ever since 1920, received at least sixteen per
cent in dividends. In January, 1929, the National City split
its $100 par stock into five shares each of a par value of $20,
merely to conceal the market value of the $100 share, which
was selling at $800 or over. Again, in July, 1929, the National
City paid a dividend of $7 a share. The high and low for the
year was $585 and $180. But how ridiculous for a government
of all the people (supposedly) to permit a type of insane
speculation which will cause a $20 stock to swing between
these figures!

Or, a certain utilities company gave away to its old shareholders of the parent company $25,000,000 worth of rights in
its new stock issues, or more, even outright gifts of stock in a
new and, of course, underlying company. These industrial profits
are, of course, so manipulated that a few men gain and control
all. As an illustration of what I mean—eight persons in Pittsburgh, for instance, and at this time, each have incomes of

$5,000,000 a year. But as to the laborer's pay in the industries which yield this, or the security of his job, that is another matter and to be dealt with later.

But let us look still further at these bankers' profits. Thus, for merely floating the German reparation bonds, the bankers will eventually receive $40,000,000 for themselves. Such great amounts of money as this, placed in the hands of special interests, would naturally—would you not think?—give rise to the use of at least a portion of it to promulgate ideas agreeable to them and their interests, which are money-making and not necessarily for the betterment of the country at large or the minor individuals who work to create this wealth. And so it really is. For, for the most part, these capitalists find themselves resisting, ideologically, all theories and movements which tend in any direction other than toward their own private welfare. Hence, our American capitalist, by reason of greed or love of power, or the fame, or even name, of having money or being "on top," most viciously and wholly enthusiastically wars on labor, communism, etc.; in short, any theory or action which tends to expose or weaken his powers and private ambitions; and by the same token, is ready and willing to spend really enormous sums—in politics, through the newspapers, over the radio, and where not else—endless forms of bureau propaganda—to see circularized and, if possible, popularized such beliefs and theories as will tend to popularize him and his methods among the people who, not understanding his methods or ambitions, are the very ones and the very first to be ignored by him. (If you doubt this, read the career of the late Thomas F. Ryan.) For propaganda in regard to finance is not so very different from propaganda in regard to religious or political theories. The rank and file may not, in most cases, understand, but they, as we all know, can become so very positive, so exceedingly faithful, and no one knows this better than the present money rulers of America!

Now all this is done through hundreds of highly-paid advisers and counsels on public relations, who write books and pamphlets and disseminate material to the press. All corporations and factories of any size to-day in America have them: Rockefeller, the Standard Oil, the Pennsylvania Railroad, the utilities, etc., etc. And their purpose, of course, is to influence public opinion in their favor. The more clearly to sense the scope of this raid on the minds of the people, let me take the case of a few of our great utilities.

In 1927, the National Electric Light Association and the American Gas Association formed the National Utility Association, an organization representing the great privately owned utility companies and intended to campaign from the inside against Government ownership of gas and electric companies— the biggest publicity bureau ever under and in favor of private control of public wealth and of the national resources of the country. This organization aimed at national, State and local influence—from national politics right down to control through contacts of its little power houses and of their employees. Employees alone number 250,986 in the electric light and power industry, 262,725 in the electric railway industry and 75,285 in the gas industry.

And more, upon Government investigation of the same, it was found that this joint committee maintained shrewd and highly-paid directors in every section of the United States. And not only that, but for the $28,000,000 which they spent annually for hundreds of small ads in newspapers all over the country, they expected (and in most cases were successful) the editors of papers approached by them to print as *straight news* these specially prepared utility write-ups, most unfavorable to Government ownership and, of course, favorable to private control, yet supposedly non-partisan. According to letters later discovered (a Government investigation is the authority for all this), these utilities boasted that such good work had been done in this field, that of 250 newspapers in Georgia, only four would print anything favoring Government ownership. And one W. P. Strandburg, the utilities' director in Oregon, stated that of 270 papers, only three said anything unpleasant. The Ohio director got 20,000 inches of news items published each year; the Illinois director got 60,000; and the Florida director 900 a month. The *United States Daily,* which had a $200,000 per year contract for utility advertising, wrote to the Committee: "The *United States Daily* is held in high esteem because it is a fact newspaper containing no editorials and no interpretations of its own, and being absolutely non-partisan, it has an extraordinary amount of prestige and influence." In fact, all of these people courted the favor of editors, and yet J. B. Sheridan, director in Missouri, wrote of editors: "All of them are God's fools, grateful for the smallest and most insignificant courtesy." And so, most valuable to the trusts and corporations, as any one can see!

But to continue with this pretty picture of paid propaganda and its agreeable results. Bernard J. Mullins, the bureau's director in Illinois, said: "Jog each editor's memory from time to time in a friendly, personal way." The director in New York said that though no one ad or news story would do much, material persistently and continually sent and printed would shape public opinion. S. E. Bowery, director in the Carolinas, and at the same time working for the Associated Press, sent the identical utility items as news over A. P. circuits! Likewise, he got Governor McLeod, Senator Stewart and Colonel Dawson to sign articles which but for minor changes he himself had written. He then wrote to all the editors suggesting that they comment editorially on these very important views of distinguished individuals! Still more, George Okley, General Publicity Director of the National Electric Light Association, wrote not to tell anybody that the ideas of Haley Fiske's article, of which millions were circulated, came from the National Electric Light Association. This same Haley Fiske, President of the Metropolitan Life Insurance Company, wrote to 3,000,000 policy-holders: "The Metropolitan owns over $75,000,000 worth of securities of electric light and power companies." And yet nearly everybody in America is of the opinion, or was, that insurance companies invest only in safe real estate and Government bonds! Well, Fiske went on to say that "when one of these companies is *unfairly* treated," it is the policyholders' savings that will be depleted, and he warned them that when Federal ownership came up for local consideration or decision, they should think of this. It is thus that our corporations put people in their places in regard to said corporations' welfare. They get the people coming and going!

Again, the utilities above mentioned established a Syndicate Public Service, which staged 200 campaigns (imagine, campaigns, and 200 of them!) and spent over $100,000 investigating municipal plants. These investigations, written up as sponsored by individual inquiry, were always presented as unfavorable to said plants and their results to the municipality. As you can see, the power of money stops at no pettiness or deception to achieve its distant, and yet, in the main, wholly ridiculous and futile, ends. Power and show for a few! And with the masses tramping the world in misery! Again, utilities financed such news agencies as Hoffer & Sons, which furnished news items favoring private ownership to 14,000 country newspapers in 48 States.

In order to have strong material in their literature against Government ownership, prominent individuals were and are still solicited and given contracts. Richard Washburn Child, former U. S. Ambassador to Italy, was paid $7,500 by this utility group to write an unsigned pamphlet against national development of Boulder Dam. The law firm of Meechem & Vellacott, of Albuquerque, New Mexico, for $500, wrote up a governors' conference on Boulder Dam, at which Merritt Meechem sat officially to represent the interests of the State of New Mexico, but he wrote it as the utilities wanted it written. Under the title of "Aladdin, U. S. A.," more propaganda, published by Harper's, cost them an initial fee of $5,000 to Ernest Greenwood, former American agent of the League of Nations Labor Office. And so it goes, and to this hour!

Again, and in connection with education in America, I want to say, odd sums of from $50 to $15,000 were used to line up, and did so line up various teachers and college professors! And not only that, but there being some advocates of Government ownership among the teachers and professors of certain Illinois schools and institutions, the Illinois Committee of the utilities got the superintendents and boards of these same schools and institutions to discharge these advocates, and that without any trouble. Then, here is what they prepared for school children—quotation: "Adverse criticism of the utility advertises the entire community as a poor place in which to live and tends to retard its growth." God, no wonder education is a failure.

More, certain professors who were of the proper mind and temperament—willing, if not necessarily anxious, to see the corporation viewpoint—were duly furnished with material for a number of anti-government ownership books which the utilities got published for them. And more, a certain Professor Grayson, under pay from the National Electric Light Association, lectured at the Wharton School of Finance of the University of Pennsylvania in Philadelphia. Also, Dean Rugby, of the Ohio State University, was employed by the National Electric Light Association at $15,000 a year to hold conferences of college professors to investigate the introduction of utility courses in universities! And to shape the student mind in the proper direction, a committee of this conference bought hundreds of books favorable to the private operation of public utilities and presented them to the libraries!

The utilities gave a $90,000 three year endowment to Harvard University to "be used for an investigation of regulation and also for the establishment of a case system dealing with that subject..." because a university public-utility relations text-book "would better appear under academic auspices than as a publication of this (National Electric Light) Association." Then "The fund for Northwestern University will be devoted to consideration of Government ownership of every sort." Of course that is only nominally. The utilities see that it favors them. Before awarding a fellowship, the committee examined the student to "scrutinize his natural leanings."

Now don't go away yet, for there is still more. Thus, utility committees in Illinois and Missouri (and before the Government investigation of their action, of course) had completed a study of high school and college textbooks. Those favoring capitalism were labeled "good" and those mentioning injunction of monopoly or political corruption or watered stocks were termed "bad." (This book will probably be called "bad.") In fact the Iowa Committee circulated the statement that "there is no such thing . . . as . . . 'watered stock' . . . in a utility company." Imagine! Among the books which they blackballed were "American Citizenship" by the Beards; "Our Government," by James, and "City, State and Nation," by Nida. Are these in your library? Not if the corporations know it! And they not only tried to get schools to remove such books, but also to have authors and publishers change them. A letter from the General Manager of the St. Joseph Gas Company to the Missouri director reads: "I have your letter of September 8th in regard to the revision of the textbooks on civics, economics, and civil government, so as to give a fair statement of the case of the utilities. I think this is a very good work, but great care must be taken to avoid going too far, since if the public were to get the idea that textbooks were being used as propaganda for utility companies, the reaction would be worse than the original misinformation." Jack Levin of the Research Staff, People's Legislative Service, in Washington, said in his book, *Power Ethics,* "With fabulous sums of wealth at their disposal, such 'public utility information committees' . . . render impossible an honest dissemination of complete and impartial information on all sides of controversial public questions."

In short, the banks and corporations not only spend enormous sums of money to keep down developments in government to aid the people in general, but when one such movement arises anywhere, they use any outrageous form of political or financial coercion—brute force, really—to smash it. In illustration of this let us take the case of the North Dakota Nonpartisan League, formed in 1915. Their program to promote the State's agriculture and commerce was to have North Dakota found banks, build grain elevators and flour mills, manufacture many farm products and sell them where and how they wished; also to create a housing department. Interestingly enough when one considers the American mind—its apathy in regard to all things economic, and more especially, things radically economic—this frank socialism gained a following powerful enough in 1918 to elect the State Governor and control both houses of the State Legislature. Not only that, but two years later the Non-Partisan League had 200,000 members in 13 States. *Voilà!* And some of its proposed activities were actually entered upon by the League. Thus, a bank created by law for deposits of the State and its municipalities and townships. Not only that, but other industries were organized under the State, and the flotation of State bonds necessary for financing the plan, proposed. Whereupon, however, the same was blocked by bankers who could, and did, do everything possible to garble the cause. For by then the corporations had decided that the existence, and more, the activity, of this particular organization was to be forced to run the gamut of the courts. And so it came about that very presently the League had to prove that so enormous and so decidedly a socialistic program was not opposed to the American tradition of free competition and "hands off" on the part of the Government in so far as private business was concerned. Although finally its projects were held constitutional by the Supreme Court, still it ended a long and arduous fight.

But, as to this financial interference, outrageous, said the League's members and others! By what right do they block the flotation of well-secured Government bonds? Well, the answer being that money, in America, is stronger than the Government itself, after the next election, the capitalists, having regained political control, succeeded in having a law passed taking not only all Government deposits away from the bank referred to above, but also confining it to merely rural credits. A run on the bank was thereby brought about and it was then pronounced a failure. With these facts in hand—but later, of course—some sappy professor whose article I read had the thickness of wit, or the cold nerve, as you will, to attribute this particular bank's failure to the inability of the Government to manage business efficiently. And such facts actually do prove that Government ownership, or Communism, or whatever name you give it, must cover the whole country in order to be a success. Otherwise, the private bankers and capitalists can and do harass and ruin it.

But not only brute force under cover, as in this instance, but our corporations and their financial leaders suffuse business with a despotism which the Government appears powerless at this time to avert. To illustrate further what I mean, let me outline briefly the general trend of business here. The stock market, for instance, and hence all employment, proceeds by cycles. Thus, betimes, stocks are active, yet selling at a reasonable figure, and at that time there is very little unemployment. But business increasing, stocks rise, and then new issues are floated. That at once inspires, as easy money always does, hundreds of factories and building projects. Men work overtime, and for a while that brings in a return, though stocks at such times quite invariably sell several hundred per cent above their actual value. Yet, more and more business. It leaps! Manufacturers and new speculative enterprises of all kinds borrow large sums from the banks, but with these high-priced and highly watered stocks as securities. And the banks at such times permit borrowing and borrowing and borrowing to every one, and in addition, millions to brokers dealing in stocks known to be highly speculative. The result, of course—as in 1873, 1891, 1907 and 1928 and subsequently—is violent inflation and also, of course, the inevitable crash. For during these periods of inflation, manufactures are doubled, profits soar, everybody buys. Production is doubled and tripled. The general public feels rich, and in that sense, is. World distribution becomes —as always here—the aim of every growing corporation. Hundred dollar stocks go to five and six hundred on the stock exchange.

At such times, banks, because of inside information, are in a position to discount all this far in advance, to gorge the people with stocks and a little later swindle them to the limit. For, of course, the thousands of cars and millions of dollars of manufactured goods, radios and such, forced into the retail market at such times, do not sell. And so, by degrees, as in the last crisis—yet before its public evidence—men are laid off, there comes the break in stocks, skyey prosperity falls to the ground, business cannot meet its loans at the banks, and so it loses the stocks which at high "prosperity" figures were its security. Sometimes the banks, unable to collect loans, fail. Then with rock bottom prices for securities which would otherwise be good collateral for a loan no one can borrow any money with which to continue business. And, of course, no one can buy. And so, unemployment, which must continue a year, or two, or three, before money, and the demand that comes with it, gets stable enough so that corporations again hire men.

But this system—which the capitalists would have us believe to be the work of sheer fate, utterly fortuitous—is actually no more and no less than the absolutely planned and executed method by which the banks (with high loans and the ready financing of lesser corporations for no other purpose than this hurry of over-production) bring on a state of prosperity for only one per cent of the people. For there is no one person or thing, government or corporation, to guide all this. It is individualism armed with capital and corporate power and laws run mad. As for the average individual anywhere, American or what you will, he appears most completely to misunderstand this prosperity, its intrinsic and evil nature—who receives it and when—and so in due time pays in poverty, hunger and death. But the method and its results are not at all unknown to our financiers, and are even counted upon by them to create great fotrunes out of the savings, and, of course, the losses, of the little men in these crises. If you doubt this, talk to those among the powerful who are willing to see the underdog starve or survive as he may!

Not only that, but during the present depression of 1931, manufacturers, editors, and all capitalistic attachés are most busy making the laborer's lot seem not only much less wretched than it is, but really as though it possessed phases of comfort, and even well-being. A most insidious form of lying! In truth, they seek to and do pull layer after layer of wool over the public's eyes until it cannot even see the light of day, let alone the truth. And while stringing the workers along and starving them, they themselves await a slow revival, their acquired holdings in their pockets. Let me illustrate.

Here in America, for instance, are newspaper headlines which read that "75,000 auto workers return to their jobs" at the River Rouge plant of the Ford Motor Company. Or that this or that other giant corporation is taking on more men, or at best not reducing wages. But does that actually mean what it says? The public must really read to the very end of the article (which it rarely ever does) in order to find that in this case of the Ford Company, the majority of these men employed, or reëmployed, work only three days a week, not the old-time full week. Or as at Youngstown, Ohio, and elsewhere—everywhere, in fact—men by the thousands are working under this starvation or "stagger" system, as it is called. And yet our Colonel Woods, industrial adviser to the President and the supposed saviour and redeemer of the unemployed, not long since sent to 65,000 manufacturers bulletins explaining and encouraging stagger systems even more cruel!

That our American capitalists want, and so help, to bring about these depressions in order to cut the wages of employees and hence enlarge stockholders' profits, particularly by low wages during the next era of prosperity, is almost obvious from what one sees going on after every panic, the working formula of which has just been described. Thus, even now, West Virginia miners receive only 21 cents a ton for coal mined instead of the former 67 cents. And is not that worth a panic? Wage cuts of 40 per cent to 75 per cent have already been forced on miners in general throughout this country, and more are promised or desired. And not only that, but the wages of laborers in most industries in America have decreased between 40 per cent and 50 per cent. Yet in all the front offices of our immense manufacturing concerns you will hear the statement that no wage cuts are desired or intended, and the newspapers print that! Yet our bankers are now advocating wage reductions! But what will this recognized cutting be like? Already workers have lost wages amounting to billions of dollars, while our corporations, financiers and banks actually hold and wait to loan anywhere—here or abroad—their gains!

Chairman Wiggin, of the Chase National Bank of New York City, recently said that high wages do not make prosperity, but rather that prosperity makes high wages. I rise to show differently. I say that not even prosperity makes really high wages. During the height of the business boom, the average factory worker in New York State made $29.99 weekly, *but only when he worked,* and it is the same the country over for the laborer. This while $3,600,000 in bonuses was given by Bethlehem Steel to its executives! So, as you see, the worker never really achieves prosperity, be business flourishing or dull.

On the other hand, the owners of money never have anything short of prosperity. In 1930, the year of the most acute depression, the rich had $1,000,000,000 loose to add to their $14,000,000,000 already invested abroad. And during the first half of 1930, dividends (the income of the rich) increased over those of 1929 by $350,000,000, while wages (the pittance of the poor) decreased by $700,000,000. And only one per cent of these stocks are owned by the workers, including office managers and executives. Not only that, but less than one per cent of the total population of America trades on the stock exchange. But to that one per cent, and that one per cent alone, comes prosperity, and that all at the beck and will of the banks and corporation executives who are that less than one per cent of the total population! And so it is that these, profiting periodically by these financial swells and recessions over scores of years now in America, are so much stronger than the Government which has tried in some vain ways to arrest the cycle movement but at the present time seems to be incapable of doing anything more than look on. In fact, it frankly announces that it can do nothing. The rank and file must help each other, said Hoover. And not only that, but any and every effort or bill or movement tending to check this cycle system meets up with bank or corporation machinery opposed to such interference.

And does any one really think that even the highest of our American dignitaries are more than rubber stamps or pushers for corporation activities? A Morgan and a Rockefeller need a Calvin Coolidge and a Herbert Hoover to go through the supposedly democratic ceremonial of approval of their deeds. If you doubt this, look to the big contracts affecting millions of people but which bring profit and power to the few alone, or the big "deals" here in America. Two van Sweringen Brothers of Cleveland, Ohio; a Daniel Willard of Baltimore; a Crowley and an Atterbury of New York and Pennsylvania, and not one of them a Government official, but rather all railroad magnates—these five, and these five alone, can and do decide who is to have a certain railroad, and then they, and they alone, tell the Government. And a Herbert Hoover, so hearing, then, and then only apparently, tells the members of the Interstate Commerce Commission who are in office (and so remain at his behest) that he favors approval of this certain arrangement. He practically tells them what to do. And this in the face of the fact that this same Commission is supposed to *order* (railroad) consolidations, supervise security issues, etc. . . .

In fact Government action which the financial lords want is encouraged and usually brought about aided by the efforts of Government officials like Andrew Mellon, Secretary of the Treasury, who is himself a money lord. It was Mellon who went to Europe in the summer of '31 and saw that European financial conditions were so bad that German reparation debts to the U. S. must be canceled for a year. But underneath, this is protecting private American bankers' loans in Europe. Now reparation cancellation for this year comes out as President Hoover's plan and it will probably come about. So clever is their publicity that people feel as though they have cancellation already and hence will not be opposed to it when it comes.

Then Hoover in a speech at the Pan-American Conference on October 8, 1931, said:

"The sole function of government is to bring about a condition of affairs favorable to the beneficial development of private enterprise."

And private enterprise is no longer the individual's but rather the corporate money lord's.

Never, in short, is one important step taken by the Government without the approval of a John D. Rockefeller, Jr., a Walter Teagle, a Charles Schwab, an Owen D. Young, a William Loeb, a Walter S. Gifford, or his employers and superiors. And it is these men—not the Government—who actually rule. Do you wonder then that the regulation of capitalism is a failure? And that the banks and corporations are not going to and do not intend to either regulate or check themselves? As one of them once said to me, and that so blandly: "Who's to stop us?"

And I rise to inquire: "Who?"

CHAPTER V

OUR BANKS AND CORPORATIONS AS GOVERNMENT

(Continued)

HERE is a situation: the banks and corporations of America functioning as Government. How was this alliance of Government and commercial enterprise built up and affirmed? Well, for example, the first Vanderbilt, at the height of his career (1870), forced, by corruption, of course, the State of New York not only to pass an act making New York City pay one-half the expense of lowering his street car tracks on Fourth Avenue, but also to slip in a clause or phrase whereby his franchise was made to last forever, and whereby in connection with all this, he was released from taxation forever. (Too bad he couldn't have lived forever!) Again, in 1868, when Vanderbilt and Gould were fighting each other for control of the Erie, each was trying to outdo the other in the matter of bribes, the one to prevent the passing of a bill legalizing a stock issue by Gould, the other to make sure that it would be passed. And later, a committee investigating this, found that one senator had taken not one but two bribes, one for $75,000 from Vanderbilt and another of $100,000 from Gould. And although the expensive and cautious senator retained both, still he voted for Gould—a soupçon of honor which, for the life of me, I cannot properly allocate, although I assume that the long since lamented Dr. Gould could. Maybe! During this fight, though, Gould himself took a half million dollars to Albany with which (the illegal force of money, you see!) he terminated the contest in his favor.

Now flash a moment to what magnates of this nature were at the same time doing to labor. One incident. About this time a Federal Judge, sitting in Milwaukee, issued an injunction which ordained that a man could not even advise his own son to quit the Northern Pacific without going to jail for it. The injunction is the sharpest implement yet devised and now is constantly used against the workers—a legal weapon which for a long time now has caused the greatest terror and hence revolt among the workers.

The bankers and corporations are Government because they have taken over the Government by secret corruption, and with their corrupted Government have passed laws in *the name of the people*. What I want to show in this connection is that corporate practices as they are known to-day and as they function right now are based largely upon corrupt law and unfair court decisions.

To illustrate why I say this, let me point out some laws and their results, and then ask should such laws or their results be respected. To be sure, by this time, to unscramble some of the vile financial omelettes that have been concocted would be impossible. They and their powers can only be taken over by the government and operated for the benefit of all or they will ravage the more acutely. But to respect them or their originators or beneficiaries or the courts and laws that sustain them, that is not possible. To illustrate—Cornelius Vanderbilt, the first, in order to carry out his expensive schemes in connection with the early New York Central, got innumerable bills passed at Albany. His privileged laws gave him the right to water his stock and to charge exorbitant rates to the people, the while he stood exempt of paying a due share of the taxes with these people. (Taxes on Vanderbilt's projects were reduced to almost nothing.) Concerning this period of inequitable laws between 1853 and 1867, the Treasurer of the New York Central testified before the New York State Convention Committee that his railroad spent hundreds of thousands of dollars to influence legislation. But not only were Vanderbilt's improper laws continued unmolested, but at Albany on May 20, 1869, was passed a law giving Vanderbilt not only his franchises *free* but the power to merge railroads and more—and better—more of his old but insidious right to water stock as much as he pleased. Whereupon he immediately issued $44,000,000 worth of watered stock—so highly watered, in fact, that in 1879, a lawyer, Simon Sterne, declared to the Hepburn Committee sitting in Washington, D. C., that this $44,000,000 represented no labor at all—just water, or $44,000,000 cold cash for Mr. Vanderbilt! In fact, Vanderbilt's whole system was built up just like this, i.e., the Lake Shore & Michigan Railroad, the capital stock of which, as early as 1871 was one-half water!

But of course and after all, it wasn't just Vanderbilt who was busy building up our American oligarchy. For by then the method was general or national. In proof of which we have the minority report of the Pacific Railway Commission, which, in discussing Gould's activities with western railroads, said "hundreds of thousands of dollars have been disbursed at our state and national capitals for the purpose of influencing legislation." But behind Rockefeller, the Standard Oil, Gould, Sage and all others was inequitable law, the result not only of bribery— it wasn't always bribery but really an inequitable way of thinking on all subjects relative to getting on in this world which seems to have infected almost every type of American political and professional mind at the time. For consider here John D. Rockefeller's first "trust," the notorious Southern Improvement Company of 1872, which, shrouded with the utmost secrecy, as the name shows, was planned by clever lawyers no doubt and passed by mentally and morally agreeable legislators who saw in it little more, I am sure, than the individualistic right of a strong, shrewd man to devise and execute as many clever traps for his commercial rivals of the time as he could think of. In other words, it was really the custom of the country. Yet this particular company had for its legal base a charter giving it unreasonably wide privileges unheard of and denounced in those days but similar to the present holding company. (And think of the number and scope of holding companies at this writing. And their significance!) Although the charter of the Southern Improvement Company was later repealed, still it survived in other forms and has at last become the model for heaven only knows how many trap organizations since.

For during the period from 1862 to 1882, Rockefeller's business had increased 14,000 times—that is, from a $4,000 to a $55,000,000 concern. Also by 1882 and in order to have all his various interests under his personal control in the future, he was compelled to form the Standard Oil Trust of 14 old companies and 26 more. And this needed, as he saw it, some such holding company as this Southern Company for him to manage it all properly. Later, though, or after this trust, due to the decision of an Ohio court, was dissolved, the corporation law of the State of New Jersey was studied and finally changed to admit of the wider privileges of just such a corporation as this. Also, to attract interests similar to those of Mr. Rockefeller. And accordingly, in June, 1899, the Standard Oil of New Jersey was formed, the same acting as a holding company for all the rest of Mr. Rockefeller's companies. And while, in 1911, this Standard Oil Company of New Jersey was dissolved, it was not because it was illegal under the corporate law of New Jersey (that was still existing and permitting hundreds of such companies and their copies in several states to write "of New Jersey" under their names), but because the Standard Oil Company was itself illegal under the national Sherman Anti-Trust Law. I have shown, though, that this Sherman Anti-Trust Law is seldom looked to, let alone dusted off, and when it is, holding companies that are most obviously monopolies in restraint of trade, like the United States Steel Company, are not always declared illegal. So true is this that I really can't see why it was ever invoked against the Standard Oil Company.

Before the Standard Oil was prosecuted, however, under this usually defeated Sherman Anti-Trust Law, there was almost frantic popular disapproval of Standard Oil as such. Its ways were too rough. Too many men and lives had been frustrated by it—their heirs and assigns. At any rate, it was Standard and almost Standard only that was dissolved under this law and because it was an illegal trust. But was the Standard Oil dis-

solved in more than appearance only? It was not! Rather it was
the companies composing the Standard Oil Company and not
their united owners who were separated. The owners, as you
may well guess, were still allowed to function together. And
still do. For example, the following shares of stock were, in 1915,
owned by the President of the Standard Oil of New Jersey:
6,000 in his own company, 4,575 in the Standard Oil of New
York; 300 shares in Atlantic Refining; 1,858 in Standard Oil of
Indiana, and 1,100 in Prairie Oil & Gas Company. In fact, the
same owners controlled all of the companies, and so under the
same management, and after the parent company's dissolution,
all of the Standard Oil companies continued to function, and
with the same monopolistic abuses as before. In fact, in 1923,
Senator LaFollette of Wisconsin made a report to Congress
showing all this to be true, because even at that date, the
Standard companies still continued almost completely to control
the prices of crude petroleum as well as the products manufactured therefrom. And so I say again that in so far as either
reform or government regulation of our American trusts and
monopolies is concerned, neither our national laws nor the department nor yet the elected or appointed individuals supposed
to enforce them, amount to anything at all, and are certainly
not worthy of respect.

But with this onslaught of industry on Government, contrast
those whom it ruins—their cries and methods of retaliation! In
America, a favoring tariff has always been for the manufacturer
or his present master, the corporation and the bank—never for
the little man. In recent years, in this respect, the East—New
England, New York, etc.—has given its farmers such a short
run that together with competition from Western farmers, the
New England, New York and Pennsylvania farmers have been
completely broken. They are through. And it has been industry,
which has been against the farmer, with industry benefited by
every tariff and the farmer starved, which has done it! Meanwhile, the American farmer, politically and economically too dull
or weak to grasp what is being done to him and fight, drifts the

while this same tariff, because of its effect on other lands, induces a feeling of revolt against America everywhere abroad. Even in Switzerland, when the data concerning our latest tariff were given out, 15,000 people gathered and with uplifted hands swore to purchase no American articles! Five days after this same Hawley-Smoot tariff was signed by President Hoover, Italy placed a duty of more than $1,000 per car on automobiles of the Ford and Chevrolet class. I have referred before to American imperialism. This is more evidence of its reality, and what is more, the violent desire of foreign nations to repel it. In Latin America, for instance, where twenty per cent of our exports are or were sold, tariff rates have recently been very greatly increased. And Canada, which consumed fifteen per cent of our exports and has been our greatest single market, has raised its tariff on merchandise sent there in large quantities. This makes for a fierce and open international competition in trade which cannot but do harm here. In short, this tyranny of a really imperialistic tariff only hastens an international strife and probably war, thus further dragooning individuals here and elsewhere already dragooned by the cause of the said war.

As for the American people in general our trusts and monopolies are now so strong as to be able to enforce their own prices and profits—and so greedily, viciously and unescapably as to outrival the greed and oppression of any monarch or tyrant anywhere. I call your attention to the mounting charges of the American Telegraph and Telephone Company—now dominant in the United States and the world for that matter and which in the twenty years just past has trebled and quadrupled its charges to the American public so that by now it is exacting charges so outrageous as to make a telephone as expensive as light or heat, or in some instances both, to the American consumer. And without the slightest hope of redress on his part, since courts, legislatures, bureaus, commissions and what not, wherever functioning, all do the bidding of this shameless and bandit corporation. Even the railroads are no greater grafters or stick-up-men. Yet its methods, daring and success are bedded in the crimes of the past—for from the beginning it is plain that in the American individualistic plan monopoly was to succeed royalty in power and domination.

Thus Rockefeller's purpose from the first in connection with Standard Oil was to own all the refineries, regulate their production, and, by so doing, keep the price of refined oil artificially and hence extortionately high. There has long been in America, from the early days of oil development in Pennsylvania to the present Governor "Alfalfa Bill's" shut-down on petroleum output in Oklahoma, a fatal overproduction of oil, which, of course, has tended to cause the price to fall. For in their first anger at Rockefeller's monopoly scheme, the independent well owners of his day combined as the Petroleum Producers' Agency in order to get a monopoly of, and thus control the price of, crude oil. Purchasing crude oil from the individual anywhere and everywhere this agency sought to keep up the price, just as Rockefeller was doing. The temptation to take all the traffic would bear was too great! And in this connection, the Producers' Agency made a contract with Rockefeller to sell oil to him at $3.25 a barrel. But in a short time, though, so great was overproduction, that Rockefeller quit the contract, thereby causing the death of the Producers' Agency.

During these 70's also, the Standard Oil was striding to greater and greater monopoly. And by 1877 its position was so strong as to permit it to control export oil. Also because of his monopoly, and by 1877, Rockefeller had forced the price of oil so high as to be able to pay (and in 1879 he did pay) $3,150,000 in dividends, the while his total capitalization was only $3,500,000. More, monopoly was bringing him such luscious fruits of profits (no matter by what vicious means) as to cause many independents to desire to get in with him. It made the marketing of their product so much easier. So true was this that when Scofield, Schurmer and Teagle, of Cleveland, who had been making a profit of 34 cents a barrel, went in with Rockefeller, their profits rose, between 1876 and 1877, to $2.25 per barrel! The power to tax as you see!

Also, between the years 1879 and 1904, Rockefeller always controlled at least eighty per cent of American oil. And during that time and since, he has held up the price so that improvements such as that of pipe lines, bringing about, as they did, a great cost reduction to him, benefited the people not at all. He would not permit any natural let alone any unnatural decline in the price of oil. Even the prices of crude oil did not proportionately follow the prices of refined oil. For by then he had agents all over America. And as soon as any retailers of oil began to buy from independents—that is, those not in Rockefeller's monopoly—(and Rockefeller always knew whose oil was going to whom, as I have heretofore shown), the Standard's employees told these retailers that the Standard would lower the price so much in that town that nobody would buy independent oil. Usually this threat worked. Yet on other occasions Standard had to undersell, but it was always strong enough to do this here and there because it had already made wide conquests elsewhere—in other and more profitable fields. (This is also the principle of the chain store to-day: to undersell till it runs every individual merchant out of business and then recoup by raising prices on its larger volume of business.)

To prove that this is what the Standard did, let me state that in 1897, in regions where competition was extinct, the people were forced to pay twenty-five per cent or thirty per cent more than where rivalry existed. With its control of export oil, the Standard was also powerful enough to lower prices to fight off competition in the great foreign markets. Also in America, by 1915, Standard was free to, and did, divide the whole country into 11 marketing territories—its States over which it ruled, as it were. And in consequence, where there was no competition, high prices ruled, and the consumer paid as much as 8 cents a gallon more than he would have had to pay had there been present in the field a competitor. Where there was competition he paid less. In short, like a monarch, Rockefeller or the Standard, as you will, was taxing some provinces this and other provinces that and just as it chose. Even so late as 1927, when the

now-deposed government in Spain tried to buy the Standard and
Royal Dutch stations, and the companies were refusing to sell
at the price bid, they, in order to force Spain to buy at their
price, cut off the oil supply until finally, Spain, being at their
mercy, agreed upon the company's price. We will teach these
upstart nations, what?

More recent facts in regard to the oil industry seem to me to
disprove the allegation that Standard is losing its place in the
oil world. It is my opinion that she is not losing it, even inap-
preciably. For in the Federal Trade Commission report of 1915,
quite accurate data on the Standard is available, and this shows
that between 1914 and 1915, the demand for gasoline increased
thirty-eight per cent; the price was put up seventy-five to eighty-
five per cent, the while the gasoline became inferior in grade.
And this, although I doubt if you know it, made the following
peak profits for the several Standard companies or divisions: 7
companies over twenty per cent; the Standard Oil of Indiana
thirty-six per cent on net investment; the Standard Oil of Nebraska thirty-seven per cent; Continental Oil thirty-four per
cent; and all other Standard companies examined (11) over
ten per cent. The same Commission making several tests found
that the price charged, whether judged by the cost of gasoline
per gallon or by the by-products method cost per gallon of gas,
or by the cost of all by-products per gallon of crude oil, was outrageous. In short, Standard was able to keep up its rates because, firstly, it had a monopoly of refined oil, and secondly,
because by 1915, having changed policy, it controlled, either
by direct ownership or by shipping through its own pipe lines,
seventy per cent of the crude oil of the country. And it did it
all illegally—by crude, raw, brutal force—the thing that has
placed all our American monopolies in the position where to-
day, they say to the Government, go, and it goes, or come, and
it comes. And the people not only may be, but are damned. And
if you don't believe this, ask any Government official not—
as yet—directly in the employ of one or another of these great
industries.

Now if you think that this power of the corporations to tax the people by high prices—as if they themselves were openly the Government,—if you think this corporate power to tax is merely by chance, kindly examine into the Standard Oil's Government. Here is a little evidence which has come to public attention, although it was never meant to. In the main it concerns that distinguished giant and financial robber of these same earlier days, John A. Archbold, another of the high officers of Standard Oil, whose activities are, to a certain extent at least, known, and some of which may as well here and now be set forth. Archbold was wise, diplomatic, cynical and ruthless—also a charming letter writer, and although not as important as some of the others, still what he said, did and wrote serve as a good criterion of the politics by force (the force of money) at that time and now. For through Archbold, apparently, and by means of short loans from the Standard Oil Company, whose officers testified that they were never paid back, and more, were not supposed to be returned, and so were soon written off the books under "profit and loss" funds were furnished to various politicians of the day for this and that. Thus, one J. W. Bailey, in his day a distinguished Senator from Texas, was shown, just before the close of his career, to have received thousands of dollars for preserving the Standard Oil of Texas from prosecutions. To achieve this, certain untruths had been or were indulged in; also money borrowed by him from Standard Oil was apparently never returned. Also, one Senator J. W. Foraker, of Ohio, very much talked-of and once considered distinguished for his mind as well as his honor was, in January, 1902, "loaned" by the Standard Oil Company, the sum of $50,000. Afterwards, the Senator asserted that he had paid this large sum back, but he was not generally believed. (He was, as you see, a Senator Fall of his day.) Later, or about this time, Archbold gave John Lowndes McLaurin, a Senator from one of the Carolinas, I believe, funds for his election campaign. What the distinguished Senator did for that I cannot learn. Some little thing, you may be sure. Yet when Archbold donated $100,000 toward the election of Theodore Roosevelt, he promptly asked that Roosevelt be made cognizant of this fact. In short, Archbold knew the particular type of politician whom, by this method, he sought to convert to the idea of government by Standard Oil rather than by the people—also, to some extent, at least, how to convert him. For example, in letters to McLaurin, Archbold proceeded to flatter him, most directly commenting on his intelligent views and calling one Ben Tillman, McLaurin's opponent and an opponent of the Standard Oil Company and its ways, a rank demagogue. Well, Tillman was that, but he was not bribable.

And now here is a letter from a Standard Oil executive of twenty years ago to a Governor of that day. To my knowledge, nothing equal to this has ever gotten out:

"I am sure you will pardon any seeming presumption on my part in writing you on a subject in which both personally and on behalf of my Company, I am greatly interested. It is to urge the appointment of Judge Morrison, of McKean, to the Supreme Court bench, *vice* Mitchell, deceased. Judge Morrison's character for ability and integrity needs no words at my hands, but aside from these great considerations, his familiarity with all that pertains to the great industries of oil and gas, in the important relations they bear to the interests of the western part of the State, makes him especially desirable as a member of the Court from that section." (Quoted from *Living Age,* May 20, 1911.)

But Archbold, of Standard Oil, worked as cleverly, and by the use of force of money, of course, with the press as he did with politicians. Such publications as the Pittsburgh *Times* (if any city isn't "bought up" to-day, I'm sure it isn't Pittsburgh!), the *Southern Farm Magazine* and the *Manufacturer's Record* were all strongly subsidized before 1902. And during the period of years in which Rockefeller was struggling in every way possible against the outraged independent oil producers, great sections of the rural press, as well as the city press, not only antagonized, but by such other processes as were legally available, fought pipe lines that might have reduced oil prices for the people and most certainly would have reduced the power of the Standard Oil Company.

Again, Archbold also patronized a certain *Professor Gunton's Magazine*—a monthly publication—very heavy and dull, I thought, which used to be on most of the newsstands between 1895 and 1900 or thereabouts. It was a publication devoted to economics of the sort most useful to monopoly and, to keep it going, Standard Oil contributed $15,000 a year, but fruitlessly, I think. For if that magazine ever converted anybody I would like to have a look at that person. Dull! God! The Company also gave Gunton about $250,000, not only for his magazine, but for speakers on economic matters, and you may guess for yourself exactly what kind of speech-making this was!

More, Standard Oil also worked closely with such notorious corporate politicians as Mark Hanna and Stephen B. Elkins—men whose records and connections speak for themselves; I do not need to say that they were unscrupulous. And like all the rest, the J. P. Morgan previously mentioned in this chapter, bought, forcefully or by money, which is the sense in which "force" is used in this chapter, such political aid or alliance as he deemed most valuable. Thus, among other sums, he gave to George W. Cortelyou, then the organizer of the Cleveland Campaign which was to end in the election of Cleveland and the appointment of Cortelyou as Secretary of the Treasury, $150,000—for the purpose of electing Cleveland of course who appointed Cortelyou. It was called then and is to-day, a campaign contribution. But afterwards, Cortelyou, as Secretary of the Treasury, permitted Morgan to borrow $25,000,000 in gold from the Treasury at two per cent, which sum Morgan immediately reloaned to banks and business houses in need of cash *gold* at six per cent. But could there be anything wrong with that, I ask you? Again, Morgan helped financially to put in office the very Republicans who voted a $10,000,000 mail contract to some of his steamship lines.

So that is the way bankers and corporate directors handle

the Government for themselves. But for a side light on the law these days and how these very same magnates impose upon men working for their corporations or those in which they have "interests" let me add something concerning "the Yellow Dog Contract." This is a weapon devised, you may be sure, by some corporation legal sharp or "slicker" as they say in California, and used to this day by American corporations generally, and under Supreme Court sanction, you may be sure (and which the Anti-Injunction Bill, if it is ever passed will abolish), to terrorize labor in general. It is an enforced or "take it or leave it" agreement which any worker seeking or accepting work with most large corporations which he is compelled to sign or no work, and which reads that in so signing he binds himself not to become a member of any union other than such a union as may have been organized and is controlled by the company itself. But these "yellow dog contracts" are innately void, and should not need any Congressional enactment to say so, because (1) they are without consideration; that is, the worker receives no benefit or money by contracting to stay outside his own or any labor union; (2) they are made under coercion. The laborer does not agree that he wants to stay out of a union, and yet he must bind himself so to do or else starve. Again, (3) these contracts are against public policy, for right of contract is a property right, and deprivation of that right without due process of law is unconstitutional.

Yet by this time American labor understands that wealth has been leveled in Russia and that the laborer there is receiving his just share of its returns. They see that Russia's Five Year Plan has made and is making scores of modernized cities for workers, with clean, new apartments, with nurseries, cooks, and hence no household drudgery, and they yearn for this better form of life.

But now let me, and most interesting it will prove, too, show how some—most, you may be sure—of Rockefeller's small stockholders were made to fare from time to time by the prosecutions which the Government from time to time and by reason of public uproar was really compelled to institute against some, not all, of his trusts. Thus, when in 1892, the Ohio Courts decreed that the Standard Oil of Ohio could no longer be in the Standard Oil Trust, and the latter was broken up by ratably disbursing the stock of each company in the Trust to their stockholders according to the amount of certificates of the Trust previously held, all that the little stockholders got was 50,000/972,500ths of a share. And when, in 1911, the Standard Oil Company was dissolved into thirty-four parts by the United States Supreme Court, the same method of freezing out the little man was used. For example, a small stockholder received 7,143/983,383rds of a share in the Washington Oil Company. But the Supreme Court had already declared, mind you, that no stockholder with less than one full share of stock could vote. So in that case, it was necessary to have 1,400 shares of the old Standard Oil stock in order to get one full share of Washington Oil in this dissolution—nearly 100 old for 1 new Standard Oil of Indiana share, etc. And in the first instance quoted, it was necessary in order to be able to vote at all, for the holder of one of these 50,000/972,500ths of a share, say, to buy 922,500ths of a share more. Only there were very few if any such shares for sale and their call was very high for they were very profitable.

In several of the separate companies into which the Standard Oil Company was dissolved, eighty per cent of the old stockholders were, by this method of reorganization, altogether deprived of their right to vote, so you see how well the little middle class American who believes so strongly in capitalism and its leading giants or ogres fares at their hands. They eat him up.

Yet all corporations heads I am sure will deny that this oligarchical rule of the few is true. They will produce proof that thousands of people own stock in their concerns. Yet this is merely to pull the wool over the eyes of the people, for frequently portions of that stock are non-voting and, almost always the controlling stock ownership is held under the management of the oligarchy.

But here consider what this oligarchy has done to the average

man, yourself, perhaps, or your relatives, friends or acquaint-
ances.

Are you a grocer or small dealer of any condition or state?
Then please note that corporations in America, by every shabby
device thinkable or available to the end of collecting wholesale
produce cheaply, are permitted to undersell, and hence put out
of business, every small dealer in every town in the country.
And more, when Robert Gordon Duncan, of Portland, Oregon,
assailed the chain systems of that city and elsewhere, declaring
that they short-weighted and short-changed their customers, he
(not the corporation) was clapped into jail on the extraneous
and petty charge of using the radio to defame honest merchants.
And not only that, but the franchise of the radio which he was
permitted to use was also revoked.

But to demonstrate the poor chance of the average individual
in America becoming anything more than a petty salesman or
clerk, one need only look at the growth of the chain system as a
whole: oil station, hotel, garage, newspaper, barber shop, department store, drug store, bank, bakery, milk station, clothing
store, haberdashery, restaurant, taxi company, bus company,
and their compliments and equivalents in a dozen other lines
also. Already one private telephone company has all the telephone stations in the land, and taxes all. Ditto the Western
Union and the Postal Telegraph, as well as the new International Radio Corporation. So that any one may see what to-day
it is that is left for the little man: a clerkship, or at best, a
managership, and a nomadic one at that! He is born a clerk or
agent and will die one, from now on though he still believes, the
dub, that he is going to become a corporation giant—or has a
chance to become. Well, that chance is just about $\frac{1}{125,000,000}$
of that.

In this chapter, as you have seen, I have brought forward
out of our present-day American life such important facts as
seem to me to present, in every economic as well as sociologic
sense, the failure of capitalism sprung from a too free and

untrammeled competition of the strong with the weak—which has resulted in the monopoly of quite everything by and for the few—and have tried to show what has brought this about. In the subsequent phases of this analysis, I will show the relation of present-day American reform to our present economic system and the failure of said reform. My facts and experience I interpret as meaning not only that this is the decadent stage of capitalism, but also that any and all reform is now, in the large, vain. In sum, it is, as I see it, much too late for any really workable capitalistic or bank and corporation reform. What must now come is something that will synthetize all forms of human effort, but not with the view of making the individual too powerful, and certainly not with the view of making him exorbitantly and ridiculously comfortable and showy and intractable, and that at the expense of the millions who make his pride and his utter intractability possible. The rich are too rich; the poor are too poor. And the hour has come when some form of equitable sharing in the means of living—shall not only have to be considered but wisely and truly enforced.

CHAPTER VI

In the early stages of any branch of transportation, the Government always starts out grandly to give: land, loans, rates, subsidies. Though some of these are justified, many enrich a small and particular class. Just as air and mail routes are now aided by the Government, so in the beginning the Government gave to the railroads as if they were children, deeding them tremendous areas of land, little thinking that these children when grown would bleed the fond old parent of his funds! The Union Pacific once sold outright all of 7,000,000 acres of valuable coal lands, which land it had fraudulently appropriated, since it did not even have a patent for them from the Government. The Southern Pacific, through other railroads which it owned, once controlled 10,000,000,000 feet of the finest timber for a 600-mile stretch between Portland and Sacramento. You need not ask by what outrageous political connivances such gains as these were won. And to this day the railroads still roll up millions in surplus by lands awarded to them for little or nothing. They think of and execute all kinds of schemes, like the organizing by the Texas & Pacific of a subsidiary company to develop oil. Before the present action, this railroad had the land and the oil; now it has the land and the oil as well as millions of dollars from the sale of stock in the oil development company, which still remains its company, and the land from which the oil is taken still remains its property also to use for whatsoever other purposes it will. For it retains fifty-one per cent of all stock rights and the public does the paying for all improvements, in the hope—not the surety—of getting six per cent on its money.

But giving land—hence wealth—was not the only aid to growing railroads in the old days. Money was loaned to them by the various States, mostly by reason of political jobbery—one of our leading American industries. The Boston, Hartford and Erie Railroads, for instance, borrowed money from the State of Massachusetts, and almost every railroad has had a similar beginning. Even the counties must have sympathized with the railroads in the old days, for County Treasurer John Scin, of Indiana, was once tried for raising money by taxation to buy stock in the Cincinnati, Richmond & Fort Wayne Railroad. But this then was not unusual, but rather a common practice.

But do you think that those good old days are really over in that sense? Wake up! The railroads at this hour, and as an additional Government favor, receive such exorbitant rates for carrying the mails as constitute little less than downright robbery of the millions who are compelled to patronize the postal service. And this money swells railroad profits, not for the general public good, as they so persistently claim, but for the benefit of a mere few—first the great lords of the industry who hold the great blocks of stocks as well as the underlying bonds, and after them the thousands of stockholders (some 840,000 all told, according to one Dr. Splawn's recent Government report) who are counted upon to give the appearance or feeling of a general distribution to the remaining 121,000,000 Americans who have no stocks or bonds of any kind. For there are 122,000,000 persons in the United States, and so for every one person who is benefited by the fat incomes of the railroads, 122 people get nothing. Besides, the proportion of ownership in this stock must be considered.

For who really owns the railroads which own railroads? Figures show that 14 groups control eighty-five per cent of the total mileage of Class I railroads. Of these, 32 railroads with a mileage of 47,000 (total United States mileage, 240,000) are the property, for the most part, of one or a few interests. The two Van Sweringen Brothers, of Cleveland, for instance, with their 32 corporations (holding companies) control 28,411

only the New York Central and the Pennsylvania of the 160 Class I railroads received together in 1927 as much as $22,000,-000 annually from the Government for mails.

But then, in addition, if you will believe it, the Supreme Court, in February, 1929, gave the New York Central rate increases in mail transportation for which it had asked in 1921. And the amazing part of this is that the Supreme Court held that the increase should date from 1921, eight years back! Such a refund has never been made to any private person or minor corporation, as I will show later in this book. In short, millions of dollars in back payment and as a gift! This seems to me one of the most reprehensible of all railroad decisions. For the Court held that not only should the new rate be retroactive, but it should be so because the railroads could refuse to carry mails at confiscatory rates. But the railroads had not refused, and the old rates were not confiscatory in any sense of the word.

And what is the result of this corporate dickering with and drain upon the Government? The United States Post Office Department is now faced with annual gross deficits: $86,000,000 in 1929, $98,000,000 in 1930 and $150,000,000 for the fiscal year ending June 30, 1931. Running behind only a little more every year. Yet Postmaster General Brown recommends that postage be raised one-half cent—a gain of $66,000,000 annually —or one cent—$130,000,000. Sums far over what's needed every year, just so they'll have vaster subsidies to railroads. Congress, doubtlessly, won't vote postage increase this year before election but it will come and with added difficulties to individuals, more millions to the railroads.

But no practice or discrimination has ever been considered too shady or too unfair by the railroads when it comes to the matter of profits. In 1910, the Portland Cement Company was charged 92 cents a ton freight on its coal, while that of mines controlled by a certain bankers' clique was being sent a greater distance for 55 cents a ton. I also recall that out in Nebraska, in order to develop railroad business, they charged so much more for local freight there than for long-distance freight passing into as well as through the State, that Omaha products were undersold by imported Chicago and St. Louis produce. These "class rates," as they are called, made a citizen of Nebraska pay as much to send anything a hundred miles as the St. Louis shipper paid to send the same thing almost five hundred miles.

Not only that, but either Henry Ford is wrong or rates in many cases and on many railroads are too high. For if all of the first-class railroads in the country had the same rate per ton per mile as has his road, over $2,000,000,000 a year would come to the public in lower rates. Also, as you may discover for yourself, if you wish, there are always scores of cases of citizens, towns and companies protesting in the courts against excessive railroad fares and rates, since after nearly a hundred years of rate discrimination and rate regulation, so called, the same cruel and greedy abuses as ever exist, only now sanctioned by the Government and hence, theoretically, by the people.

One of the worst forms of this rate abuse, however, is the practice of our national Interstate Commerce Commission of making particular, and often discriminating, rates according to section and condition of the country through which a certain road runs. The general tendency of this is to make for the poverty of one railroad as against the exorbitant profits and so success of another, the reason being that one road may have trans-sectional traffic and another only local, or there may be differences in the number of people living along a given line or in the articles which the inhabitants consume and produce. Yet the Commission, by its practice of making general rates high enough to carry the lame duck roads, swings money into the pockets of the larger and more successful railroads, and so taxes the public most unfairly. Yet Congress and its Commission still persist in thinking that this is the only way. To prove it, Senator Cummins in 1922, quoting the Santa Fe as having an operating income of $4,000 per mile, the Union Pacific $7,000, and the Chicago, Rock Island & Pacific, $2,000, asked what would become of the latter railroad under reduced rates. My reply to the Senator would have been that the rates on a lame duck railroad should have been higher than other rates in the section, providing it was not the competitor of a more profitable railroad. In the case of the strong competitors, excess profits from freight should be paid by the strong railroad to the weak one.

But now I want to discuss the Commerce Commission's latest effort at rate-making. On July 8, 1930, the Interstate Commerce Commission gave the railroads in the Middle West a freight rate increase equivalent to $12,000,000 annually, a most generous bonus, since at the time business was greatly depressed and people were already barely able to sustain themselves. But the only sop thrown to the public was the statement that prosperity would soon return and this rate increase would help bring that about. Yet in 1931 there was, as we have seen, greater rather than less unemployment, less economic activity, and larger and more impatient bread lines. This the Commission must have known would be the case, or at least they might have known had they troubled to examine the several business indices open to them. (Business and Government executives, despite their knowing quite accurately the immediate future of business, always plead, with seeming innocence, its uncertainty.) And yet at this very time, wheat was at its lowest price in sixteen years and other grain markets were equally depressed. But did that open the eyes of the Government or its Commission? Conditions now should speak for themselves. Yet what a help it would have been to the farmers of that region to have had the rates lowered instead of raised! Even Commissioner Porter, who did not favor the decision of his group, said that in some cases this increase would make farmers and shippers pay twice the old freight rate, and in many cases they would be crowded out of business altogether. None the less, from extortions like this, and at this very time, the railroads are growing richer while the many (their patrons when they have the money) approach beggary or worse. And the Government suggests in addition that they help each other—neither the Government nor the corporations being able to do much of anything, all being so poor and hard-pressed!

But our American railroads have from the very beginning taken advantage of every opportunity, equitable or otherwise, to better their financial condition at the expense of everybody, hard times or good times. If you doubt it, look back over the panic periods of America from 1871 on and see what, if anything, the railroads ever did to help out in those periods. Not just practically nothing, but nothing! And their action following the great World War was only a more recent example of this same thing. Thus, although the general private impression was that all of our American railroads had been bettered, not injured, by public operation (since the same officials, only under Government direction, were in charge during as well as after the War), still after the War, the roads seized every possible avenue of publicity to complain that their lines had been not only greatly injured but all but ruined (and that by the very railroad men who had always been running them, only under Government direction, and but slight direction at that), and that it was therefore the duty of the nation to give them more money as well as permit higher rate charges in every direction in order that they might rehabilitate themselves. And was this done? Yes, it was done! They got $100,000,000 from the Government for the purpose of building and rebuilding 300,000 freight cars. At the same time, no sooner were their own officials once more officially acknowledged as in charge than they persuaded a complaisant Government to permit them to add one-half of the regular Pullman charge to the old fare, thus adding $35,000,000 annually to their so greatly depleted income—which had never really been depleted at all. And to the public, taxes. And this was supposed to put them on their feet, repay them, in part, for the damage done by the Government. Actually, though, it was all cut and dried profit. Their lines had not been injured. They had not suffered major losses. And not only this, but the Interstate Commerce Commission immediately raised their rates. And this in spite of the fact that the Government in wartime had operated the railroads successfully without so doing. So you see that not even the railroad magnates, who term themselves vastly superior to Government officials in business acumen, could run the rails on the fares and charges made by the Government! Yet they were dishonest enough to propagandize afterwards to the effect that wartime operation of the rails by the Government was the height of business inefficiency.

Don't forget, though, that in addition to all this they also took every advantage of the supposed post-war depression to reduce wages. For did the railroads, with all the money mentioned above as extracted from the Government, pay their employees the same wages as the Government had paid? You know they would not! They would not be corporation-owned and controlled railroads if they did. On the contrary, on July 1, 1921, they secured, through the Interstate Commerce Commission, which fixes all such things in America, a wage reduction of twelve and one-half per cent, which meant a saving to them of $1,000,000,000 a year, a saving which competent economists have declared was entirely "blue sky profits." Yet this $1,000,000,000 yearly saving for the stockholders. This enormous amount in the face of the fact that the total value of the railroads, mind you, according to their own tax figures, is only $18,000,000,000. So now tell me is the average American being robbed for the benefit of his corporations, or is he not?

After the War again, however, and when the railroads were returned to their private owners, the Government, seeking to regulate them further than had or could the Anti-Trust Act up to that time, passed the Transportation Act of 1920, stating that as to income if the railroads made over six per cent profit, that profit was to be divided equally with the Government. But here is what happened to that law! In 1921, railroad profits were enormous, and in 1922 they were even greater. Then and there was the people's chance, if ever. And the railroads, by some sudden and surprising development of our Government's conscience, were asked for the surplus due the Government.

And at once, of course, the poor, poverty-stricken railroads began to make a poor mouth, to cry "confiscation," and with that as a slogan, to declare that it was unconstitutional to confiscate private property and that they would fight—in the Courts, of course! And so, the anger of the people (only a few of the people, say a dozen or so, for the others were at the ball game!) was eventually diverted to other channels, and by the cry, if you please, that the prosperity of the railroads spells the prosperity of America! And, of course, you see how that is now. For the railroads are not starving, while some fourteen million of the rest of us are! But why bring that up, eh?

But before leaving this subject, I want to dwell still further on the methods by which the railroads succeeded in this connection. In the first place, they made reports showing five and three-quarters per cent earnings, just within the law, while at the same time the common stock earned ten per cent! Magic, that must have been! Or at any rate, it must have taken some clever accounting to arrive at such results. None the less, since then profits have soared even higher. For one thing, a ten per cent wage cut during the next five years added to the gain. Next, consolidations speeded up the money-making, and by 1928, just before the crash, the Pennsylvania Railroad was making $15 on every $100 invested (as investment is reckoned); the Union Pacific was earning nearly $20 a share on common stock; and the Santa Fe was hoarding a $1,000,000,000 surplus. Yet our poor, poor railroads even now are crying that they cannot even attract capital for improvement, because of the wretchedly low rates still forced upon them by this corporation-hating and skinflint Government of ours!

But now we come to 1929. During this year the dividends paid were eleven per cent higher than in 1920. (And in that year Congress decided that the Government must have half of everything over six per cent!) And for the first four months of 1930, two-thirds of the $90,000,000 increase in railroad income was clear profit. In sum, after the railroads had paid all of their expenses out of their income, every year they had

$1,000,000,000 left over—but not to be divided with the Government, as you have seen! Of course, now that hard times are here, here is a new cry. The busses and trucks on the roads are killing all business for our railroads, and therefore must be taxed higher and higher in order that the passengers and freight in these fields may yet be driven back into the cars of our railroads, in order to save them! And if the railroads have their way, will be! Only by now they have developed a still larger and brighter idea. And that is, first, to get the Government or the States or counties of America—all of them—to tax the various bus and truck lines to the point where they will be glad to sell out to the poor railroads. Whereupon said bus and truck lines being in their possession, the rates on the same will be raised, the taxes by the Government wiped off as confiscatory, and presto, the same old railroad crowd in charge of everything! And with but one remaining bright idea, and that will be to collect all the traffic will bear. And the bus and truck lines are now being so purchased and joined up, as very presently you will see—only do be a little patient, please!

CHAPTER VII

OUR AMERICAN RAILWAYS—THEIR PROFITS AND GREED

(Continued)

To go on with this pitiable tale of our undernourished railways, I would like to add that as an indirect means of regulating the control of profits, the Transportation Act of 1920 declared that a man could not be a director on the board of more than one railroad without the consent of the Interstate Commerce Commission. Yet now after eleven years, during which period the Commission has had ample time to arrange and regulate under the powers duly accorded it, *now,* mind you, there are 391 railroads on whose boards the directors of other railroads serve, not counting railroad subsidiaries. That railroad directors do not have time for studied execution of their duties is evident from the fact that 219 rail directors of 15 of the big roads also fill 2,298 extra posts on the boards of other corporations in various fields, not including subsidiary companies. One Charles Hayden holds 64 directorships; A. J. County and E. J. Berwind each 47; and W. A. Harriman 44. Of the 2,298 outside positions, 336 directorships represent bank and trust companies, 210 investment trusts, 284 industrial corporations, and 192 mining, lumber and oil. Corporations and banks do not run this country? No?

The same Transportation Act empowered the Interstate Commerce Commission to regulate security issues in whole or in part. Yet this, too, has been most artfully, or blatantly, as you choose, evaded by the railroads, which with their complexity of control of companies can easily manage this. For what need they fear of a people that is almost wholly interested in ball games, golf, tennis, prize fights, the movies, flag-waving and bootlegging?

And more, the holding company, a contrivance which Mr. Rockefeller practically used in the 70's, now permits almost anything under cover, it being a separate entity, though not a separate control from the railroad company proper. And to date it has remained immune from regulation. In fact, the present-day railroad holding company exists with but one main purpose, and that is the issuing of securities and the controlling of other railroad properties which are not possible under the Transportation Act. It was created to evade, and does evade, Federal law.

But think you that is all of the evil involved in the rail holding company idea? Tush! Properties of a railroad are acquired and controlled through pyramided companies which control a road by owning only a small percentage of the total capitalization of that particular railway. And stocks in these holding companies being frequently non-voting (think of the fundamental equity in this established principle of corporate law, now autocratically denied the people!), they grant no power of direction to those who hold them. The giants at the top are not willing to jeopardize their control or dictatorship. You cannot gain any power by holding the stock of any subsidiary or "held" company. If you doubt it, buy its stocks! The rail holding company also makes possible the holding (more or less intact and without danger of assault) of large personal fortunes by an estate.

Aside from the financial upset of the workings of the Transportation Act, as caused by the holding company, this invention stands responsible for much of the failure of that law in the matter of consolidations. The Pennsylvania Railroad gained control of a large percentage of stock in the Wabash and also in the Lehigh. When the Interstate Commerce Commission ordered Pennsylvania's holding company to sell this stock, the railroad is reported to have said that it would fight it "to the last legal ditch." The railroads argue that the holding company (a separate organization) cannot be regulated as a railroad by the Commission, and that even if it could be, this enforcement of the law, and hence all financial regulation, is contrary to the Con-

stitutional guarantee against confiscation of property. And so the
fact remains that the Pennsylvania has made no move to divest
itself of either Wabash or Lehigh properties. A similar command
by the Commission to the Baltimore & Ohio to sell their Western
Maryland and Nickel Plate stock has to date been met with the
same disregard and inaction. So what better proof can be asked
that regulation of our railroads is, if not impossible, at least
nonexistent?

Yet regulation is constantly talked of and as constantly and
effectively resisted, a result which is responsible for much of the
legal and financial confusion of to-day and by reason of which
the autocrats of money hold their own. Yet although so unsuc-
cessful, as you have seen, our Interstate Commerce Commission
is reported to have eight anti-trust suits against several railroads
in process of adjudication. Yes? Well, isn't that just too interesting for words? Probably the relationship of the Pennsylvania
to the Boston & Maine, New Haven, Pittsburgh & West Virginia; Detroit, Toledo & Ironton, and the Norfolk & Western
will be assailed! Probably! But let us not be too hopeful. For
disorder, and even defeat, is quite certain to arise, since although
the railways may and doubtless will be prosecuted for consoli-
dating to lessen competition, the Interstate Commerce Commission, as ordered by the Transportation Act, is supposed not to
thus lessen consolidation but to direct the consolidation of all
railroads for more efficiency into a very few systems, to be
regulated by the Federal Commission. So you see it comes to
the same thing as saying yes and no, or do and don't; blowing
hot and cold out of the same mouth. More, the railroads have
always balked, and apparently always will, at any plans for
any through transcontinental systems which might make for a
considerable saving to the public; they are one and all for the
larger profits which now accrue from separate lines and the
changing of the public from one to the other, regardless, of
course, of the convenience of the public.

But please do not go away! There is still more legal as well as
national hokum. Lots of it! At the present time, for instance,

the Interstate Commerce Commission is considering an application made to it by eastern railroads seeking to have the Commission let them merge into four great systems, but asking it at the same time to decide ("in the public interest," of course) to permit them to keep those very controls of other lines which would be denied them through the proposed anti-trust prosecutions previously mentioned. In other words, it is more and more railroads which they wish to be permitted to buy and control. Ownership is what is desired, of quite everything in the way of transportation—but not to be regulated in any way by the Government. In fact, a stronger defense against government interference in any form is what is desired—that is, interference in behalf of the public. Interference in behalf of the railroads is quite a different matter, for all they aim at is the substitution of their power for that of the Government in as many directions and fields as possible. But that, as any one should be able to see, can only result, in the long run, in a miasma of disorder. For either our original form of government is to endure, or it is to abdicate. And abdication in favor of the trusts and holding companies—their owners and directors—is now the order of the day. We are nearly trust ruled already and will be completely so in the very shortest of periods unless some portions of our American body politic choose to bestir themselves on behalf of the public at large. But will they?

The proposed eastern consolidation scheme offers another problem in connection with our national industrialization process. For with the union of such roads—all roads, in fact, under private control—it is proposed to release a program of electrification in connection with these several great systems which will then have no need for thousands of locomotive firemen now employed. Also that would unite stations and offices in many cities now employing thousands. In fact, the jobs of 580,000 employees would be directly concerned. Though it is almost a truism that mergers do away with the need of many workmen (railroad consolidations have already caused the dismissal of over 200,000 in various fields), still not one Crowley, or Atterbury, or Van Sweringen, has made any contract or promise to labor. Rather they offer only lofty, crafty, insolent silence. Of all of them, it was Daniel Willard, President of the Baltimore & Ohio, alone who said that in any mergers affecting his railroad he would keep all men on the payroll until they could fill all the places of those who just naturally died or dropped off. And he offered this as a complete solution! Yet of course, as any one can see, it is no solution at all, because the railroads would not be hiring thousands during the long period of this natural shrinkage.

Not only that, but experts in economics have already publicly charged large railroad systems in the West with manipulated bookkeeping and excessive maintenance charges in order to conceal their real incomes, the purpose being to keep freight rates high. Also that the bankers who are behind these railroad activities can and do make either a small or a large valuation, as they choose. But what amazes me is that these bankers and their railroads can get away with one valuation for taxes and another upon which railroad earnings are figured in percentage. For experts tell me that the latter is padded to the extent of probably $10,000,000,000. A blow indeed, in view of the fact that the total United States railroad valuation is about $30,000,000,000, I believe. It is for this reason that I keep insisting that the railroads have done and still do everything in order to get profits for themselves, and without let or hindrance on the part of the people or their government. Thus, the late E. H. Harriman added $60,000,000 to his railroad liabilities and our national Interstate Commerce Commission of that day found that not a dollar of this represented additional investment.

Also, all stock is and long has been watered. In 1929, for instance, after the Pennsylvania Railroad had paid all the dividends and extra dividends which it reasonably could to its very limited group of stocks and bondholders, were their mental resources as to what to do with their exorbitant profits at an end? They were not! The first thing they thought of was to make a special or extra stock allotment of from ten per cent to fifteen

per cent. And to themselves, of course! Next, twelve other roads
with much the same thought in mind, and in order to get additional profits, of course, violated a regulation of Congress by
farming out work to concerns where the laborers employed did
not have the protection and safeguards required by the railroad
laws, and where they were paid lower wages, of course. The New
York Central, for one, which has broken this particular law
many times, lent, in 1921, 400 electrical workers to the Western
Union at $50 a month less than they were entitled by the unions
to receive. The Michigan Central, too, and the Big Four also
contracted for enormous quantities of shop work, but in nonunion
shops. Also, both the New York Central and the Pennsylvania
made and do still make millions for themselves by forming and
controlling subsidiary repair companies, which, of course, eliminate all the profits of the possible individual owners of the same.
Yet because the railroads want their net earnings to seem as
small as possible, immense sums are paid to these supposedly
independent repair companies and these are then counted as
railroad outgo. Yet in the long run, of course, the railroads
receive the outlandish profits of the repair companies, too.

To motivate the more surely, and to direct the more clearly,
these various money returns, the railroads possessing the power
in America have so bought into or seized upon other railroads
unable to help themselves. So much so that by now an immense
intermingling of railroad-owned rails exists. In fact, upon close
study, the data before me show that some eight or ten of our
principal railroads own or control 33 per cent of the mileage of
other railroads. Thus, the Pennsylvania, owning shares valued
at several hundred millions of dollars in other rails with, in many
cases, a 50 per cent or 75 per cent control, has a sure interest
and, in some cases, full ownership of twelve railroads; the New
York Central dictates, by right of property, eight rails; the
Baltimore & Ohio, ten; and the Southern, nine. It is the elimina-
tion of the small roads which has built such immense systems as
the Pennsylvania, with assets of $2,000,000,000, and which after

conquering more than a hundred rivals, now extends through eight states.

In this way also the railroads rule for profits, despite the fact that they have not improved their service one whit in the last ten or fifteen years: no increase in speed, no greater comfort, no added conveniences. Start across the country on any one of the best transcontinental roads, say the Santa Fe. Through Kansas, New Mexico and Arizona, over the level plains and plateau, its trains still creep along at thirty-five miles an hour, a speed attained fifty years ago! Also there are railroad officials who have told me that their roadbeds would not endure fast traffic! If such is the case, then under any other than this present corporation and profit-minded government, they would and should be publicly charged with mismanagement, in that they have poured out dividends to their shareholders for scores of years when instead they should have been improving their roadbeds!

Not only that, but consider that after nearly a hundred years of railroading in this country, discomfort and dirt still prevail, and at prices per mile entirely out of proportion to the present-day economic purse of the country. Ride on the Pennsylvania fifteen minutes from New York out on Long Island for sixty-five cents! Ride two or three times as long for a nickel on the subway, built at much greater expense. And while the automobile road and its very superior automobiles, busses and trucks, has come, and the air is now freighted with airplanes winging from coast to coast in as little time as twenty-four hours, the railroads are still considering thirty-five to sixty miles an hour as the ultimate of railroad perfection. And the service! One William D. Cameron, of Yonkers, New York, a lawyer whose business is that of legally defending automobile, bus and truck lines from the envious and determined attacks of the railroads (who seeing in them the transportation masters of the future, are determined upon either owning or, by a complaisant scheme of taxation on the part of Congress and the various State legislative and more pliable city and town administrators, destroying them, thus compelling the traveling public to use the railroads again) has this to say, and over his own signature:

"Consider the matter of speed alone. For as long as I can remember, I have been making one trip of about 350 miles. I used always to make it by rail. I still do sometimes. And when I do, it takes me by rail just as long as it did when I was a youngster. About fifteen years ago I made it for the first time by auto, and my running time by auto to-day is less than one-half of what it was when I took the first trip fifteen years ago. In other words, the automobile has improved while the railroad has stood still. Of course, any railroad man will immediately point out to me that my improved running time is due to improved roads. To a large extent, this is true, but will he not admit that the improvement in the speed and reliability of the auto in that period has been out of all proportion to that of the railroad? Then too, if civil engineers have been able to improve roadways to such an extent that vastly increased speed has been made possible, why have not railroad engineers been able to make better road-beds in the same period?"

He goes on to show that whereas both bus and airplane are much better lighted, ventilated and cushioned than the average railroad car, the latter remains about as it was twenty years ago. Windows are still hard to open, and made as irritating as possible by cross-sashes mainly at eye level, and dust and cinders are by no means done away with. And, in so far as sleeping accommodations are concerned, they are the worst in the world, far behind those furnished to passengers (and for less money) in Europe, Asia and elsewhere.

Well, this is certainly a fair indictment, and, in the face of the enormous returns and general favoritism exacted and secured by the railroads, an intolerable state of affairs. Yet not content with fighting the general travelers' use of the bus and automobile, they are making a savage war on the truck. The plan of the railroads is for the Government to tax the truck as well as the bus, in order that it will be cheaper for helpless passengers to ship or travel by rail. But to do that would simply be to penalize the public for the slothfulness and greed of the railroad owners. For neither the bus nor the truck will pay the tax, of course. The traveler or shipper will do that. Yet the enfranchised bus or truck is as much entitled, as a matter of law and fair play, to a fair return on its investment as any railroad or telephone or express company. And besides, to-day it gives more to the public. Still, the railroads, stuffed with Government and State legislative favoritism, and armed to the teeth with legal, economic, propaganda and other departments the business of which is not only to protect them against any interference or encroachment but to fight to the death any natural and superior development which they cannot control, are out to either gain control of all busses and trucks, and so to charge the public as much as they please, or to destroy them. And if you choose to watch your Congress and your State legislature, as well as your city hall, you will see how admirably, in many instances, they are succeeding. For already the airplane is being tied up with the railroad. Also the bus. And wherever possible, bus and railroad and truck fares or rates are the same. Where the bus, truck and airplane are independent, there is already an economic struggle to get control, at first by hampering and bedeviling them with all sorts of ills; next, when the struggle can no longer be maintained by truck, bus or airplane, by buying them up and fixing the rates according to the desires of our never satisfied and wholly unscrupulous and economically brutal Czars.

But to return to another phase of all this. What about labor's plight during this long period of railway profits? In the South a few years ago, one Gregor, a white man, leading a strike against a twenty-per-cent wage cut by the Missouri & Northern Arkansas, was routed out of his home, strung up by the neck and hanged by an irate mob of three hundred citizens. But why? Well, here is a phase of the American temperament which you will have to study and meditate on for yourself. For obviously we are, as yet at least, a surfacey and unthinking people who take our political, social and economic notions from any one who gets to us first with the biggest lie or noise or show or bluff or pretense. And since our American corporations, no matter how ridiculous or inequitable or brutal they may be, have the money and hence, in America at least, the power to pay the press, the pulpit, the politicians and the jobholders everywhere, you have the spectacle of the rawest and most cruel and brutal phases of propaganda and pressure swaying masses of people everywhere to the most savage attacks on those who can in any way be made to seem to be interfering with *business,* and hence the financial well-being or even the starvation wages of those who depend on any form of robber-business enterprise for their miserable existence. And so the mobbing and hanging of a man who felt that a twenty-per-cent cut by the Missouri & Arkansas was unfair and tried to bring about a strike in order to prevent it!

But why mob and hang him for the benefit of a wage-cutting railroad? And at the hands of the poverty-stricken citizenry of his own region? Well, if not propaganda of the sort I have described, what else? Is there any one who will rise and sensibly rationalize the whole business? If not, and regardless of whether or not, the fact remains, or so it is alleged, that hill-billies (poor whites of the territory adjacent to the place in which the lynching occurred) were imported into the town on company trains and made drunk on company moonshine. And it was this mob which perpetrated the crime. The strike apparently had been pictured to them as unlawful insurrection, the strike-leader a radical or socialist or communist intent on undermining the social welfare of the supposedly perfectly happy Americans of the region! Well, were the hill-billies paid or merely propagandized? Who really knows? And did the other people of this region rise and protest? No! For so great is economic fear in America that almost every living American kneels and begs at the thought of losing his job. And since now mostly he is an employee of one corporation or another and told daily how much he owes to that corporation for being kept at work, and how dreadful will be the state of America, and hence himself, in case that corporation fails to make as much as it desires, all thought of independence, let alone courage, is beyond him. What, fight a corporation? Stand up for one's right or fair play against a great trust or bank? Me? You? Why, the corporation will get you, blacklist you, follow you from city to city and town to town! More, through its legal or spy department, it will look up your record and see what, if any, crimes or sins you have committed. Your neighbors and former friends, even, may be warned against you. For you are a trouble-maker, not a true-blooded, one-hundred-per-cent American! You don't love your flag; are against the welfare of your country! Oh . . . !

And so it has actually come about in America—in this my native land—that the people, due to corporation propaganda, as in this instance—are moved to look upon lawful strikes as insurrections, and to act accordingly. And our laborers, whatever their ills, rarely receive any credit for the order and peace which most usually they do maintain during strikes. Instead, our corporation-controlled and propaganda-stuffed Americans say, as they said in the great Pullman strike of years ago, that it was the immense number of police who kept order. Yet half of the money lost in that strike and others meant butter and eggs to thousands of scuffed-under-heel workmen who maintained order, too. But no credit for that! None! The corporation-controlled police got the credit for that!

In America also, as I see it now, our people mentally bite off their own noses to spite their faces, because, as I have said, the railroads, with their efficient public relations counsels, like Ivy Lee, the lawyers' propaganda bureaus and what not, propagandize in the truest sense of the word, the while labor, led by its misleaders who are as truly controlled by the corporations as any of the other of their employers (I am referring to the officers and leaders of the American Federation of Labor), remains unacquainted as well as unaffiliated with the great news periodicals, and although having immense sums of money at its service, fails to present the interests or values of its workers to the public, and in consequence evokes far less sympathy than it might. For one thing, our big railroads argue that because the poor roads among them cannot pay big wages, none of them need to do so. But an efficient and honest union of labor in America would soon dispel that lie. And although an Atterbury and a Willard might, as they now do, state that they want free sailing in order that they may conduct the railroads as a business and not as a charity, they would be called to an honest accounting of their stewardship. And their high wages to a few and low wages to many others, disguised as workers in outside companies, would soon be exposed for the fraud that it is. But the American workers have as yet no real leaders anywhere. They are led by the Greens and the Wolls whose business it appears to be to reconcile them to the rule and almost the charity of Big Business; to persuade them into acquiescence. And elsewhere in my 1931 argument with President Green of the American Federation of Labor I have proved this. He could make no intelligible or respectable reply. Meanwhile, the Interstate Commerce Commission, in order to help the railroads, said that in 1929 passenger revenue was \$414,000,000 less than in 1920. But why should this have so much weight? The Interstate Commerce Commission must also consider that they reported freight revenue to be \$498,000,000 more in 1929 than in 1920.

The railways have always endorsed the policy of asking for relief from what they term or deem economically unjustified forms of competition, most especially competitive forms of transportation—and also in hard times. Yet if busses can more cheaply take people to where they want to go, why not busses, and these independent of the railroads? Why not? Although the railroads fire back that busses are taxed only 5 per cent and railroads $6\frac{1}{2}$ per cent on their gross earnings, I have found, upon investigation, that bus taxation is adequate. They pay all that they should pay, and give better service. Yet the railroads cry that motor busses since 1920 have increased more than 800 per cent. And that busses are undermining them. Well, what of that? Is not the bus the real local transit service of the future? I think so. So the ethics of the railroad argument come down to this: a plea to Government and people to come and help them keep their profits up the while the people suffer for it!

But is this argument used by the railroads made in good faith? For who owns the busses? The rails! 67 railroads operate motor busses themselves or through subsidiary companies. The Boston & Maine Railroad runs busses over 1,200 miles of road; the Reading has 11 lines; and the New York, New Haven & Hartford, 50 lines.

But in this as in many other things, the Pennsylvania Railroad is the worst offender. (No wonder Mr. Atterbury is always recounting his difficulties!) Here is an example of its activity. The Greyhound and the Pickwick bus lines are the greatest systems in America. On January 1, 1929, the Pickwick Corporation, which controlled the stock of many bus companies, merged with the Motor Transit Corporation (this name was later changed to Greyhound Corporation) to form the Pacific Transportation Securities, Inc. Besides this interest of Greyhound, it had a substantial interest in the Pickwick-Greyhound lines, the Northland Greyhound, the Southland Greyhound, and the Eastern Greyhound. And why such complexity of manipulation? The pursuit of power on the part of the railroad interests, as I will show! The Pennsylvania Railroad provided their franchises over routes in Indiana and Pennsylvania which were used by the Greyhound busses, and in November, 1930, the Pennsylvania Railroad and the Greyhound Corporation executed a merger to form the Pennsylvania Greyhound Lines, Inc. Nine subsidiaries of the two companies figured in the merger. And now, the Pennsylvania Railroad and the Greyhound Corporation each hold 50 per cent of the stock of the new company. Their busses run over 7,000 miles of territory, with some of the largest cities on the schedule, including half the population of this country.

To me, the rankest instance of all their propaganda is their recent allusions to some Government-operated barge lines on the Mississippi and Warrior Rivers. They claim that these are subsidized by the Government and compete with the private railroads. But this is not so, or if so, then Rockefeller subsidized the Standard Oil Company. The Inland Waterways, running this barge line, is an independent corporation, which, although capitalized originally from the United States Treasury, functions as such. Yet because of this original $5,000,000 capitalization, they insist that the Government must be paying the Inland Waterway's annual deficits. But this statement is contrary to fact. The Inland Waterways is at present a paying business. Started in 1924, because the Government after having spent great sums to improve waterways found that private capital was not attracted to them, it made such profits (and with only the $5,000,000 from the Government) as to reach a book value of $19,700,000 in five years. Thus, the capitalization was raised to $15,000,000, and this additional stock is now held by the United States Treasury. (Now say that the corporate method does not make for excessive profits!) Yet rates on this slower transit agency are only very mildly competitive. The Government does not venture so far afield as to discipline the railroads, as the latter would have the public believe.

In the large, then, our Government, due to the influence of industry (our corporations and banks) rather than the will of the people, now entertains the firm view that business should be encouraged to make limitless wealth, the while business itself, by some mental kink or downright meanness, feels that merely enough to live on if so much—and usually not so much—is all that is due labor. And this relationship between our political and labor leaders and our employers makes for a power that for the present at least appears to be unshakable. For business, through politics, certainly dominates in America to-day, and we all walk accordingly and pay and pay, to the railroads, the milk trust, the beef trust, the telephone monopoly, the lighting and gas corporations, and what not else. Only I have not the space here to reveal all of the subtle connections as well as sympathies between railroads and these other corporations and the Government. It is too large and too long a story. Yet consider only, if you will, the railroad attorneys alone who have served on the Supreme Court bench. Also that J. R. McNutt, Treasurer of the Republican Party, as well as one of the Van Sweringen group of railway men, are also promoting the four-system railroad merger.

And speaking of yet another phase of this unfair alliance between Government and corporations—rail and others—made for the purpose of unfair profits and privileges in special cases, let me cite that when freight rates were increased in the Atlanta, Birmingham & Atlantic case so that this railroad (three times in the hands of the receiver in ten years) could earn a profit on $25,000,000 plus its actual valuation, this same privilege was automatically extended to all the other railroads in the South, so that they also were permitted to rob thousands of needy people in order to enrich their rail systems.

In short, our Government, as you must well know by now, keeps very close to all corporations—their woes, their demands, their analysis of any or all of their issues—not those of the general public at large, since it is always supposed to profit—in these days at least—by all that the corporations gain. Yet does it? At any rate, it comes about that the Government is not greatly concerned when, say, its Labor Board in 1921 decreased wages twelve and one-half per cent (unreasonabe pay and hence illegal) and thus violated the provisions under which it was lawfully created. The corporations wanted a reduction and got it— illegally. More, the Government then stood ready to go to any extremes to carry this order through. And in the great Pennsylvania's shopmen strike of 1922, the loss of which was partly modified by the New York Central's higher wages which the Pennsylvania finally adopted, a Dougherty injunction backed by Federal troops was used by W. W. Atterbury, the notorious strike buster, to intimidate and finally defeat the strikers. In other words, it was the Government, plus the corporation, who won this victory!

In conclusion let me say that every one of these regulatory measures has contributed to the colossal failure of our whole American political and economic régime, which is now no longer in keeping with the ideals of the republic, which in the first instance had the public interest at heart. More, they have caused to be placed first and foremost the principles of competition under which this régime of capitalism, now rotten and corrupt, has flourished. Most of them were brought to an issue and won by the railroads and other corporations. In fact, in the very recent O'Fallon case, the Supreme Court decreed that present costs of railroad reproduction now must be a factor in all rate-making in the future. In other words, increased fares and rates out of the pockets of the already overburdened masses!

In this chapter I have presented, I believe, sufficient facts to show clearly the complete failure of the Interstate Commerce Commission in its attempts at any form of regulation. Yet in final proof I now offer the following. That body, demoralized and done for as it really is, proposes to Congress that that section of the Transportation Act ordering that half of all railroad earnings beyond five and three-quarters per cent revert to the Government, should be repealed. In other words, ten years of effort comes to this! Also, this same Commission now proposes that consideration of the industrial conditions of the country and the economic needs of the railroads be allowed in rate-fixing. A way to get high rates during depression! An open door for endless railroad arguments before the courts and their maintenance by those same courts. Yet the railroads, not satisfied with the joke they have made of governmental regulation, are not even satisfied with these lenient recommendations. For more recently still, the Association of Railway Executives openly voiced its unqualified opposition to all of the proposals of the Interstate Commerce Commission looking toward arbitrary rules for rate-making. They do not want arbitrary rules of any kind unless they make them! Also, this same Association now takes the stand that railroads should have complete freedom in rate-making, even going so far as to say that the lowering of rates anywhere is confiscation of their private property and therefore unconstitutional. And more, to-day, all American railroads are demanding a 15 per cent freight rate increase. And the National Security, a patriotic organization (paid for by whom?) is telling over radio station WABC that the rails should get the increase because so much stock is owned by insurance companies, etc. The same old bunk widely and endlessly circulated.

A Gordian knot, and all because of false motives shabbily and deceitfully sustained in our Courts; no honest or worth-while labor leadership in America; politics and legislative bodies aiding and abetting the few at the expense of the many, and so making for loss, confusion, and as we see now, even national as well as financial futility.

CHAPTER VIII

WHAT is the present express company system in America? A private monopoly? Certainly! And this despite the fact that the American Railway Express is run by the Government, which exists theoretically that it may care for all men alike. But how did that come about? What of all the enormous old companies? Neither these nor their heirs and assigns in the American Railway Express of to-day can be understood without consideration of yesterday's salient features of development. Upon the past is built the present rapacity of Government operation for private profit. The true story is absolutely unknown to the general public. I offer the data in regard to it, and for the first time, I am sure, here and now.

Although express companies originated because of an actual need, as was shown in the early part of the last century by the personal hand valise express for valuables organized between Boston and New York City by William F. Harnden, America's first express company, the railroads themselves could have attended to these matters. Yet in accordance with the American financial policy of having a large corporation own or control, and hence obtain large profits from, small companies with whom it does business, a separate express service has always been carried on. The express companies, which almost as soon as the railroads, at first enlarged their service by using and even owning stagecoach lines. In the fifties, a rider and a horse carrying the sign "Wells Fargo Express" on the saddle, with old-time haversacks and saddle-bags, comprised the equipment and personnel.

113

Even in these embryo years for express companies, the men
who faithfully watched the old offices from dawn until the
arrival and departure of a 9.30 train at night (the same frequently arriving as late as 10 or 10.15)—mostly men who had
a fondness for and romanticized the companies because of their
far-flung ramifications (the enchantment of distance)—were
content to receive but $25 or $35 a month, the while, even at
that time, a few families were drawing to themselves unprecedented millions from their services. Only the workers didn't
know that. Again, in an era long before popular knowledge
or disapproval of watered stock, the United States Express
Company, between 1854 and 1876, increased its number of
shares fourteen times or 14 for 1. No records remain to show
by what probably dark and dubious methods this was accomplished. But so it was. And a little later, but still during
this early period, the Adams Express Company was also already
indicating the future tendencies of corporations. For in 1866,
this company, which had but 12,000 shares at the time, allotted
free and pro rata 100,000 additional shares to its stockholders
as their ratable portion of its excess profits to that date. For,
as you must know, I hope, the capitalist has always considered
himself entitled to such increases, regardless. And this, even
under our so easily distended Constitution, could never be interpreted as confiscation of private property or confiscation of
money rightly returnable to the people, because the capitalists
were on top at that time, and their colleagues were interpreting what was confiscation of property and what was not.
Also, at about this time, or in 1868 to be exact, the American
Express Company, whose whole valuation at that time was only
$1,000,000, had amassed as much as $3,000,000 in securities
and real estate. In other words, investment from profits! And in
its faltering immaturity! But this practice was consistently followed thereafter by all the companies. They had learned how.
In fact, during the first part of the twentieth century, the
Adams Express Company gave away to its stockholders 20,000
additional shares and $36,000,000 in bonds. This and other

similar transactions were characteristic of that era. And only think how since then the idea has grown! The "melons" that have been cut! The billions, collectively, that they represent!

Also, in those days, as seems obvious from the above profits, the express companies charged all that the traffic would suffer. Under a rate of $1.00 per 100 pounds, the agent would receive 40 cents for a 10-pound package, and unfairly, even $2.00 for a 60-pound package. Another system, that of charging by a 5-, 7-, or 10-pound scale limit, made, say, an 8-pound package go at the 10-pound rate, thus compelling the consumer to pay for two pounds he did not send. Yet these high rates did not appear to better the service any even in those days, for it is written that the claims for lost and broken goods were excessive. And with these various long-distance packages going through possibly five or six companies, setting the blame wasn't easy. Besides, the inconvenience and delay of routing parcels over several systems was enormous. Also, the simple equipment of those early days did not lend itself to particularly efficient service. Once, down in Texas, a turkey broke out of its cage and rode rakishly on top of the train for several miles until one station operator telegraphed another farther down the line.

For the first sixty years of their existence, though, the express companies struck forth on their course absolutely independently and altogether unregulated by the Government, apparently. No utterance of disrepute or hindrance was offered by the American statecraft of that day—a statecraft always devoted to the concept that it was equitable for a small group of financial aristocrats to organize such a package transportation system in a country growing by leaps and bounds in population and commerce and charge all that the people, who must patronize them or go unaccommodated, could bear and forbear. Furthermore, no State legislature sought for scores of years, with any thoroughness or efficiency, at least, to regulate these companies. Indeed, before 1890, there are no reliable figures which show anywhere near accurately the amount of business done or the income from the same. Rather, as late as

1912, only a few of the thirty-five States which had any laws relative to tariffs or unfair discrimination, regulated or even sought to regulate the accounting systems and securities of these companies. Indeed, so inadequate were State laws concerning these interstate transactions that they were looked upon by the various companies as practically negligible.

Finally, though, the hidden qualities of these companies, always in disaccord with the general well-being of the nation, inevitably rose to the fore, so that Congress was compelled to curb the already wild activities of express companies. In 1906, for instance, the national Hepburn Act, establishing a uniform system of accounting, gave the Interstate Commerce Commission access to all books and records and permitted it to fix rates upon complaint. Yet even so, it was not until the Mann-Elkins Act of 1910, four years later, which threw the burden of proof on express companies in rate cases, that the Commission was given sufficient power to initiate rate proceedings against the companies.

But to continue. Business doubled and tripled! A score of great companies became enormously large. Thus, the Wells Fargo, enjoying as it did the traffic between large and rapidly growing cities of the caliber of St. Louis, early scored profits and properties totaling hundreds of millions. And this and other companies, by contracts with steamship lines running all over the world, increased their service enormously. Soon, the Wells Fargo was shipping to British Columbia, to Central and South America, Hawaii, Alaska, in which latter place it even ran a dog team to Seward. Besides that, as transportation improved, every possible device—even the amusing old trackless trolleys of California in 1913, with their double feed-wires above two wispy, awkward and rebellious poles—was utilized to get and deliver business.

By this period, though, the express companies were exchanging checks and money orders in quite all of the commercial countries and ports of the world. For instance, Wells Fargo and the American Express Company were already becoming recognized as financial institutions. About this time also, the great companies were being reduced by mergers and competition to five: Adams, American, Southern, United States, and Wells Fargo, each with a mileage of about 35,000.

But by this time also they had gobbled up many others. Thus, in 1907, the Adams Express was already a holding company for the Dodd & Childs, Dunlap's, Earle & Prews, Morris European & America, New England, New York and Boston, Southern, United States companies. And during the next years, or from 1909 to 1912, profits leaped from seventeen to sixty-five per cent! More, there were special dividends of from $100 to $200 a share, also gifts of bonds, but all given away to the stockholders of record and to none others. And already scores of millions invested by these same express companies in outside securities. In fact, in 1907, the total mileage of these various express companies aggregated 235,000. Yet by what trickeries and manipulations assembled! And power, the possession of the wealthy, already erecting itself into great fortunes, the while the lesser fry—our far-flung American rank and file—retained their spirits only.

And so at last Government attention—the problem of these corporations as opposed to the general welfare of the general public to be considered and legislated upon. Yet it was these conditions that the Government, when later it took over these companies—yet for their private and by no means the public's gain, as it turned out—sought, ostensibly, to alleviate.

Firstly, however, these express companies, as it was well shown at the time, had been secretly working with the railroads all of the time. That is, while the express companies owned $20,000,000 worth of rail stocks and many millions in bonds, thirty or forty per cent of the express company capitalization was in the hands of the railroads. In short, a profitable intermingling of resources by those who executed that they themselves might derive! Particularly, the New York Central held stock in the American; the Southern Pacific in the Wells Fargo; the Adams was allied with the Pennsylvania Railroad; and

the famous flyer on the Erie, No. 14, carried exclusively Wells
Fargo perishable foodstuffs into New York City. But by 1909,
the railroads and the express companies were so interconnected
that of seven directors of the Adams Express Company, four
were directors of railroads; of seven of the Pacific Express, six
were on railroads; and of thirteen on Wells Fargo, ten sat on
railroad boards. More, by 1918, more than half of the directors
of the four large express companies dictated rail policies. No
wonder, don't you think, that the railroads were interested!
They received *as transportation charges* about one-half of the
entire income of the express companies.

Yet even before the Government went into the express business, and because of the convenience and money-saving values
of the same, some slight efficiency (in several cases, because
of mandatory legislation, and in others spontaneously) had been
introduced by the companies. For instance, in 1912, the Interstate Commerce Commission compelled the institution of a uniform method of way-billing and labeling among all companies.
Next, in 1915, an enormous and systematic plan regulating
definitely the period of time for which records of 250 specific
items must be retained, was introduced and enforced. In addition to this, delivery of packages over larger and larger urban
areas was also insisted upon, though not without proper compensation. Yet some of these compulsions, seemingly bent on
efficiency, actually served to abuse people the more, since although Wells Fargo delivered free of charge all over such
enormous areas as the city of Chicago, yet if a patron brought
to or called for his package at the express office, no reduction
in transportation rates was made, and to this day this practice
survives. Even as late as 1918, these various companies, servicing only 307,000 miles of railroad, lacked the efficiency of the
then only six-year-old parcel post, which was doing business
along 1,300,000 miles! And yet Government operation is always
harped upon as a failure by all our large and most decidedly
outlaw corporations; the railroads the loudest harpers (I had
almost said "harpies") of them all!

But add to this, absolutely exorbitant rates, plus starvation wages—resulting, of course, in enormous profits—and you have a picture of the old express companies at their best. Finally, as I have said, though, conditions drew public criticism and hence Government attention, and the Interstate Commerce Commission eventually found (in 1914, to be exact) that the express rates, always fifty per cent to one hundred and fifty per cent higher than first-class freight charges of the day, were exorbitant. And hence the good Interstate Commerce Commission finally reduced them by sixteen per cent! *Get that!* At the same time, though, 79,000 employees were receiving only $39,000,000 a year, or about $10 a week. Also at that same time, express profits reached $76,000,000 yearly, nearly twice as much as the amount paid out in wages. And it went to people who did nothing to earn that much. Worse, these returns of $76,000,000 a year were enormously out of proportion to the primary minute investments of about $9,000,000, which by then, though, had been over-capitalized in the sum of $200,-000,000! To be sure, the Interstate Commerce Commission, on several occasions at least, asserted that the profits of one company—the Wells Fargo—were excessive. For this company, by 1910, had not only grown to a capital stock increase of from $8,000,000 to $24,000,000, but it had profits enough for a three hundred per cent dividend or "melon"! Also, its income by then had been additionally and most greatly swelled by business with other tremendous corporations, such as Sears, Roebuck and Montgomery Ward, in whose buildings Wells Fargo maintained their own offices.

What the Government actually did with these express companies in 1918 was not so much to take over their business as to do all their work for them and let them take the profits. And I do not lie! Wait and see for yourself! For on March 28, 1919, the United States Railroad Administration announced that the American Railway Express was to do all the actual express business for the Adams, Wells Fargo, Southern, and American Express Companies. The exact nature of this agreement between the Government and the express companies was that the Government, through a company—the American Railway Express, in which the four large old companies took stock —was to carry on the express business and use the express property. But the Government added that it was going to *control* express companies. Yet when financiers take control of an industry, they own it, do they not? In this case, however, the ownership of these companies still remained with the stockholders of these old companies. In other words, the old express business was not bought out by the Government, but rather, like the Government's control of the railroads during the War, it was to be conducted for them. The only thing that was done was to fix the capital stock of the new company at only $30,000,000, evidently no over-capitalization there. Only don't think that this bought out or disposed of the old companies in any way, because it did not, as you will see. But the contract originating this new company, which the Government was to supervise if not ultimately control, read that if possible dividends of five per cent were to be paid, also that all profits in excess of that were to be divided with the Government.

About this time, however, the rates, in accordance with the War prices of the day, were raised nineteen per cent, the only increase since the sixteen per cent reduction of 1912. And the Federal Labor Board, a body functioning in connection with war labor, then also under Government control, began to cooperate with the railroad administration board as organized by the Government, and each began playing with the other. Thus, in 1920, the Federal Railway Labor Board announced a wage increase for 90,000 express employees of about $30,000,-000 yearly. Later, in 1925, to offset this, rates were increased in the east and reduced in the west, 53 railroads, still swinging a powerful arm in express company matters, mostly of the western mountain and Pacific group, tried to obtain an injunction against putting into effect the lower western rates.

Just the same, the American Railway Express, then as now practically run by the Government (but for its private owners), has for the past six or seven years carried on a booming business. There were, for instance, notable increases and changes in the size of articles shipped. Whereas in 1895, say, a heavy express shipment was no more than the comparatively light farm machinery of the time, to-day boilers weighing from 2,000 to 7,000 pounds are taken as express and so shipped. And statistics also show that the actual *average* package weight of these several companies now functioning as one and as Government also, increased from 60 to 80 pounds.

For another thing also, and since this Government management of the express companies has been in force, the transporting of money has been so much extended that to-day a fleet of armored money trucks (these same put to work in March, 1922) function everywhere. And these cars, with only one entrance, bullet-proof glass and all-bronze gratings, carry money to and fro among the banks of all our big cities. And though not so long after this business came into being, the Federal Reserve Bank of New York brought suit against the armored money truck branch of the American Railway Express business because of the excessive rates exacted, the Government declared the charges reasonable. And since the money trucks are owned by a subsidiary company of the monopoly of which I am writing, these profits go to the private owners of the same, or to private individuals.

Just the same, the new régime, in some ways at least, appears to have brought greater efficiency. For under the consolidation, it has become possible to run cars direct to distant points. Also traffic men are now sometimes able to map out quicker and less expensive routes. Also, by reason of more careful packing (everywhere insisted upon under the new arrangement) there has been less damage to and less loss of goods shipped. More than that, Government inspectors have been and are being sent into the fields during the boxing of such perishables as celery, etc., to see that no unclean material gets in. This wars against decay. Again, in connection with these matters, the Government has issued bulletins. And naturally, a decrease in claims for loss and damage has resulted, there being now but two and thirty-nine hundredths per cent of claims to every 1,000 shipments. But by reason of the wisdom of the private stockholders for whom the Government does the work? You think so? More, loss is now prevented by the use of hundreds of all-steel express cars. And further efficiency has come with a faster express service over the various roads, so much so that the chain store systems with anywhere from 500 to 5,000 groceries and meat markets, depend and can depend on express service to supply perishable fruits and vegetables, and even bread, to stores hundreds of miles apart. And not only speed, but new devices such as the enormous package chutes in various offices, have served to shorten time and lessen labor.

Yet at that, too much of the country still remains entirely without express lines. And lately when because of bus competition, railroads were discontinued, express service (since no contracts were made with bus lines to carry packages) automatically stopped. So that to date, a large percentage of the 25,000,000 rural residents of this country are still without express service. It seems incredible, doesn't it?

But say that despite abuses, tincup holding, and being actually run by the Government for private profit, the American Railway Express does good work. All right! Now what about this company financially? You are not to forget here that under this new arrangement, the Government was to share fifty-fifty in all profits over five per cent to the stockholders. The stockholders first and always. Yet has the Government received any profit? Well, let us see. Though a vast business is carried on by the Government for these combined private companies, the expenditures thus far, presumably at least, have used up almost all of the tremendous revenue derived, and the Government has gotten almost nothing. Thus, in 1925, the operating income was given as $294,000,000 and the expenditures $292,000,000. And from 1921 to 1927, our American Railway Express paid only an annual dividend of six per cent, amounting to $2,087,520 each year. Yet the governing theory of this new combined Government service being that the company was to be managed in such a way as to have no enormous profits, one is puzzled by the fact that its investments, mostly in United States Government bonds, amounted in 1924 to only $28,000,000. But the American Railway Express, of course, out of its enormous financial turn-over pays the big bill of the business; that is, transportation charges to the railroads, which also, in part, own the underlying express companies. So you can see for yourself for whom, exactly, the Government is working. Not for itself, most certainly!

But to show how the Government is really running the express companies for the private profit of the old stockholders, I must point out what became of the old privately run companies which merged in 1918 to make this American Railway Express. Since the latter was formed by the Adams, Southern, Wells Fargo and American, naturally these, it would seem, should be non-existent now. But that isn't the way this proposition was handled. For and although Adams, Southern, Wells Fargo and American did and do no work, they continue to exist to receive the profits. In other words, they remain as trust or security companies, whose business it now is to invest their fabulous earnings of the past, as well as such sums as they now receive, in such a way as to further swell their old holdings and create new ones.

Thus, the Adams Express Company, which by 1922 and maybe earlier, had the old Southern Express as a subsidiary, by 1923 had nearly ten shares of stock for every dollar invested in property and equipment. And on every share of this, and for years since, the Adams has made over $9 annually and paid dividends of $6. No wonder, then, that between 1923 and 1924, its surplus increased from $3,000,000 to $5,000,000, an amount equal to one-half of its entire capitalization! And by the next year, its surplus had increased another $1,500,000! Yet its income was and still is derived chiefly from dividends of the American Railway Express stock which it owns, although it obtains sums from other securities also. In fact, during 1922, the Adams received from the American Railway Express five payments of one and one-half per cent on the 103,103 shares of regular stock and two dividends of six per cent on 15,940 shares of qualified stock owned by it. And by 1925, its income was three times as large as its expenditures! Two-thirds profit! Yet if you will recall, the American Railway Express balance sheet came out almost even—balanced nearly perfectly!

And although by 1927, the Adams Express had increased its shares by twenty per cent, still its surplus was accumulating by the millions.

But this concerning the Adams and its subsidiary, the Southern, represents but two of the former great express companies which formed the American Railway Express under our Government management. The other two, Wells Fargo and the American Express, came to what, did what? Since 1915, the American has controlled the Wells Fargo Express. Well, let us see as to that. Though the youngster of to-day considers the American Express as a company which only arranges trips around the world and takes care of mail for people and issues travelers' checks and the like, this same American Express is that which started here in the United States about four generations ago in the express business. And this is the same company which joined the Adams, Southern and Wells Fargo in 1918 to make the American Railway Express. Thus, since 1925, only the Adams and the American of the then four joining companies have existed independently. The others are merged in them. But then on March 1, 1929, when the express business of the American Railway Express was transferred to the Railway Express Agency, Inc., the great *American Express Company,* with its enormous amount of foreign and other activities, severed all relations with the actual express business and sold its stock in the American Railway Express to the Adams Express Company.

So now, sole empress of the express business, yet serviced by the Government for quite nothing at all, stands the Adams!

For in March, 1929, it already owned as much as seventy-six
per cent of the American Railway Express stock, on November
29, 1929, it acquired the net assets of the new company, recently
renamed.

The Adams also owned on December 31, 1929:

5,000	shares	of	Brooklyn & Queens Transit, Inc.
9,000	"	"	General Realty & Utilities Corp.
22,000	"	"	Thompson Starrett Corp.
20,000	"	"	Atlantic, Gulf & West Indies S.S. Lines.
10,000	"	"	Continental Diamond.
10,000	"	"	Continental Oil.
23,000	"	"	Curtis Wright.
43,000	"	"	Electric Steamships.
27,000	"	"	International Cement.
24,000	"	"	Mack Trucks.
16,000	"	"	Petroleum Corporation of America.
20,000	"	"	Chicago & Northwestern Railroad.
17,000	"	"	Lackawanna Railroad.
15,000	"	"	New York Central Railroad.
16,000	"	"	Pennsylvania Railroad.
10,000	"	"	Philadelphia & Reading Railroad.
15,000	"	"	Southern Pacific Railroad.

The Adams Express Company, which represents all the combined earnings of the great, old, private express companies and
receives the consummate profits from every source of the express
business to-day, is now like a tremendous investment organization. All it does is take care of the money it has accumulated.
Not a bit of work is executed now in the express business. The
entire company merely holds stocks and invests the past profits
to make a lavish income of eight dollars a share. This in the
face of the fact that the government is doing all the work and
had to, because the private companies couldn't turn the trick
and because people were denouncing private express profit.
Yet now, as you see, it is still private profit. And these profits
have been and are paid to Adams' stockholders.

But now despite its great wealth and the vast sums that
through the Government's kindly direction of its affairs come

to it, what of labor's share or its privileges as labor? Well, during the last economic boom period of extremely high profits, its union, the Brotherhood of Railway and Steamship Clerks No. 2,525, whose members do the express business in metropolitan terminals for their big boss, the American Railway Express, Inc., was contending with the officers of the American Federation of Labor, which controls their union, because the latter had just made express drivers join a separate union and hence had prevented the union of all express workers in one solid demand for better wages, if not hours, which as they saw it were acutely needed.

The wages of the business in 1928 were:

Clerks	$31.25	weekly
Assorters	33.86	"
Office clerks	30.37	"
Stenographers	29.80	"

But when these wages had to be spent in New York City, a vicinity where rents and food prices mount higher than anywhere else in the country, and when the economic period in which they were earned was encouraging the most inflated of prices for everything, these wages were practically nothing. And hence, on October 9, 1929, these express workers struck for a $3 weekly increase and recognition of their union, which union, or the membership of the same, affected the Hoboken and New York City terminals of the Erie, Lackawanna, West Shore and Jersey Central, New York Central, and New York, New Haven & Hartford Railroads. At once also, and true to its policy of selling out labor to the corporation, and at every turn, the American Federation of Labor outlawed the strike. Lunacy? Corruption? Or what? And then, of course, the Teamsters' Union, which the express drivers had been ordered to join and by which they were separated from the sorters and clerks, was ordered by the American Federation of Labor to keep all the express trucks running else (and this an official A. F. of L. threat) scabs would be called in! And all this for the good of a corporation—the Adams—which was already bursting with its ill-gotten• gains! So by this iron-handed betrayal of labor by the A. F. of L. were all of the express company trucks kept running!

Nevertheless, a terrific strike swirled about for some two or three days; the union claimed that 7,500 men were striking. Then meetings, cajolings, and at the end of that time these leaders of labor sent their men back to work, but under a promise of future arbitration, which was in accordance with the Railway Labor Act that ordered or agreed that both parties should let things stay as they were until mediation could be had. The company, however, did not keep to its side of this agreement. On the contrary, and immediately and before any settlement, this corporation openly set out to find the workers who agitated the strike in order to discharge them. And the two men most active in the strike were suspended. About this time, too, the President of the Brotherhood of Railway and Steamship Clerks announced that although a mediation council was about to be held, the matter of the $3 wage increase (to me such a pathetic trifle, and so sorely needed) would not be asked for or brought up in the arbitration conference. Wonderful! Then several weeks of supposed labor-capital conferences. Imagine! And with such stuffed money-bags at one end and these $30 a week laborers at the other! Even here the company threatened, in case of a future strike, to take away workers' seniority rights, and finally, after more waiting, a settlement was declared which granted, so it was said (no details being printed), every demand of the workers, including recognition of the union. But no pay increase. Not a dime! Just the usual hokum in regard to recognition of the union, the same to be treated, as you may well guess, as the fat corporation should in the future see fit and as was evidenced by their particular acts in this instance. Yes indeed, all the demands granted, when the one great hope of the men—a modest pay increase—was not even mentioned!

And all of this from an organization with the reserves and profits from these reserves above mentioned!

In fact, a menacing economic development and influence— millions in profits for no production or service whatsoever. And these profits, all of them, to a little handful of stockholders! And recall, please, and if you will, those free allotments of hundreds of thousands of shares of this fat stock to the few original stockholders, their heirs and assigns! And not only that, but only a year later, or in November, 1929, another 4-to-1 split-up of stock for the benefit of the insiders! But as for those men and their $3.00 wage increase, not so! The express company could not see that. It was probably looked upon as *confiscatory!*

CHAPTER IX

OUR Supreme Court! The Honorable the Supreme Court of the United States! What part has it played in the game of changing America from a democracy into an oligarchy?

I propose, by outlining its decisions of the past and of to-day, to get at its merits as well as its flagrancy. Yet since the actions of a Court cannot be interpreted without going into the environmental influence and characteristics of the judges themselves—that is, the individuals comprising the court—I propose to tell something of these justices, not merely those now sitting but the many who have sat in that court in the past.

The first shall be Curtis, who resigned, as have many others, from the Supreme Court bench in 1857 because the money to be made in private practice was his standard rather than the responsibility and honor attending the interpretation of the final law of the land. As proof of his wealth (for his time) he made about $700,000 in law practice for corporations. How deeply sympathetic to the cause of labor he must have been when he was a justice! But so it was with almost every Supreme Court Judge of that time.

Next after him I choose to select for consideration Salmon P. Chase, Chief Justice of the United States Supreme Court (1808-1873). Before his appointment he was a lawyer for the bankers. At that time $76,000,000 disappeared from the United States Bank and another $30,000,000 from it was loaned to Congressmen, newspapermen and politicians, and Nicholas Biddle, of Philadelphia, President of that Bank, paid out more than $1,000,000 of the bank's funds with nothing to show where it went; also $130,000 was paid as bribes to the Pennsylvania

Legislature for banking laws. Chase, at the same time, was willing to defend banking scoundrels before the bar. Working thus closely to corruption would necessarily eat into a man's mind, I think, accustoming it psychologically to subservience, and therefore once so influenced, could the mind of a Salmon P. Chase see the sponsors of corruption in any save an apologetic light or perhaps even as creative geniuses to be legally aided?

In fact, our justices have been, and still are, allied with corporations in a closeness and mutuality that can scarcely be separated, let alone beaten. There was Bradley (1813-1892) who before he became a Supreme Court justice, conducted many cases at law by which the New Jersey railroads were able to merge and charge exorbitant rates. I claim that with these trends of thought, the state of the workingman, laboring twelve or fifteen hours a day for $1.50 or $2.00, could not possibly be visualized. Persons of the temperament and influence which surrounded such a man as Bradley could never intellectually comprehend or realize the laborer's needs.

Waite (1816-1888), who later became Chief Justice of the Supreme Court, was formerly attorney for the Southern Michigan Railroad. Here is a sample of his insidious arguments. A train on the defendant railroad, going through Toledo at a speed of more than twenty-five miles an hour, and without blowing its whistle at the crossing (both against the law) killed one Veronica Muhl. Her child received a verdict of $5,000 damages, but in a lower court. What defense did Waite make in a higher court? That the child must be proved legitimate in order to be awarded damages! Do I need to say anything more as to that?

Something of Justice Gray's (1828-1902) natural reaction to the laboring-man may be gained from one of his remarks to a witness who appeared in the courtroom in his shirt sleeves. "I direct you to go home and put yourself in the proper garb for the humble part you are to take in the affairs of this august tribunal!" Is it not reasonable to assume that a judge who instinctively thinks of a workingman as a member of an unprivileged class, would naturally tend to grant the assistance of the law to those who in his estimation stood high above the unprivileged laborer? I would think so. And yet Gray was once one of our Supreme Court justices.

And again, while on the Supreme Court bench, one Justice Field (1816-1899) was wont to pal around with Leland Stanford, western railroad magnate, and once decreed that this friend need not answer questions concerning a certain $4,000,000 which a certain Pacific Railway Commission of that day alleged had been fraudently spent to bribe legislators. These natural friendships, in a country where class differences are now as strong as ever they were in the heyday of European nobility and underdog peasantry, develop so easily from private school to college, and later, dominant positions for both being the most engaging and effective of factors in this social and ideological relationship, naturally close any inroad for labor, or even common justice. Most certainly, our once Chief Justice Field was an illustration of that.

Next, to show the recurrency of these abuses, I will mention Chief Justice Fuller (1833-1910), who previous to becoming a Chief Justice was counsel for a railroad, and with an income of $20,000 a year.

This same Fuller, once arguing for his railroad against one Samuel Warner, who had lost an arm through the negligence of his client railroad company, had Warner's case thrown out of Court, and without a nickel in the form of compensation, because he (Fuller) successfully argued that the loss of Warner's arm did not infer bodily pain!

A new form of physiology, but strictly for corporation use!

And next comes Justice Peckham (1838-1909), at that time merely a Supreme Court justice-to-be but at the moment also a trustee of the Mutual Life Insurance Company at a time when $20,000,000 was being spent by said insurance company,

with others, to bribe certain New York legislators and at the
same time maintain a certain "house of mirth," where a number
of these legislators were lavishly entertained and even lived
free. Yet he became a Supreme Court justice! You may well
ask how could a man who countenanced any such illegal plots
and snares become a Supreme Court justice. If he had been
aware of schemes so insidious, even illegal, it is certainly fair
to assume that he would use any means to win a point for a
powerful corporation.

And now we come to the Court of to-day and the justices
sitting on its bench. To begin with, there is Chief Justice
Hughes, most certainly a corporation bulwark. Let us go into
his views. He holds the interesting view that the bigger the trust,
the more power it should have. The ramifications of this idea
suggest that the feelings, desires and burdens of the masses
may be totally lost sight of. To the thinker of such a thought,
they may well become merely beasts of burden to pull and
slave. The following are the words of Justice Hughes. They are
in the opinion he wrote on the Chicago Bell Telephone Company
case, very recently passed on by the Supreme Court. "It is evident we are not dealing with an ordinary public utility company,
but with one that is part of a large system" (A. T. & T.)
"organized for the purpose of maintaining the credit of the
constituent companies and securing their economical and efficient
management." Since this was a rate case in which Chicago
sought to obviate a telephone rate rise, one may see how Justice
Hughes thinks. These have long been the pet arguments of the
corporations. In other cases, but of a related nature, he argued
that the fares on the Interborough Rapid Transit (New York
subway) should be increased; that a radio license granted by
the Government lasts forever; that the Government cannot restrain corporations, oil transportation and production, etc.

May I pause here to meditate that never has a lawyer who has
led labor to victory (there haven't been many—which is a fair
indictment of American equity) served on the Supreme Court

bench. It may be argued, of course, that neither labor nor corporation, but rather nonpartisan lawyers, should sit there, and
that is true. But the fact remains that by the mere logic of
present-day American, but corporation-controlled, life it is the
most natural thing in the world that a majority of these presumably nonpartisan gentlemen are always corporation attorneys.
Thus, prior to his appointment as Chief Justice of the Supreme
Court, Chief Justice Hughes acted as a lawyer for the Wabash
Railroad, the Piedmont & Northern Railway, the General Elec-
tric, Anaconda Copper, Standard Asphalt & Rubber Company,
Aetna Insurance Company, Benefit Life Insurance Company,
Hanover Fire Insurance Company, and the Salt Lake Railroad
Company.

Yet as opposed to Hughes by way of antithesis, say, there is
the ninety-year-old Holmes, in my opinion, the most liberal and
kindly man on the bench, and probably the most intelligent as a
leader, more nearly directing the people how to reach what they
want.

But in the matter of land-grabbing, railroad-scrambling, trust-
conniving, etc., how do these judges stand? For instance, how
do they stand now on the troublesome demands of the railroads
and utilities for more and more power and means, and especially
where these so directly affect every individual in this country?
Are they responsible for the failure of democracy? Are they
honestly in favor of the new oligarchy that is now functioning
here? What are we in for? Are we, through them and their
decisions, facing an economic revolution? America had one when
it contended for a ten-hour day as opposed to the day in which
even children eight and ten years old had to work twelve hours a
day, and for not enough pay to keep them from starving, and
when at the same period this country had to go to work and
free the Negroes. Does the present situation augur another
revolution?

In my chapters on the railroads and their looting of the
Government, I dealt with the early important facts adequately.
They did so loot the Government. Yet never would that have been

possible, as I wish here to insist, without the aid of the Supreme
Court in magically transforming fraud into *law*. To begin with, to
build the Union Pacific, a land grant of 12,000,000 acres and a
loan of $27,000,000 was bribed through Congress. Although the
total cost of the railroad was only $50,000,000, the Credit
Mobilizer Company, organized to construct it, charged $93,-
000,000. And the Supreme Court later held that by its action
Congress desired to aid transportation. Yet the $43,000,000
profit—equal to almost the full cost of the railroad—could
scarcely have seemed less than extraordinary in those days, particularly in the light of the loan and land grant. Yet if one talks
to any one with knowledge and memory of that era, it will soon
be evident that people in those days, even the lawyers not engaged in furthering the aims and games of the great constructing
companies, considered that the railroads were just starting and
needed to be protected and encouraged. Just the same, this
lenient attitude of the public toward all this was due to vigorous
propaganda indulged in by the promoters and politicians who
were also heavy stockholders. And even at that time the railroads were capitalized at $15,000,000,000 and had an average
income of $600,000,000. Their trains killed 10,000 and injured
100,000 persons a year. To say the least, they were plethoric
beneficiaries of a very amiable mood on the part of the American
people.

But here is what the railroads, under the guidance of the
Supreme Court, did about the above startling number of accidents. I will take the case of Chauncey A. Dixon, a fireman on
an extra train, who was killed in a head-on collision because of
a telegraph operator's forgetfulness. The Northern Pacific, on
which this occurred, contended, through its lawyer, that this
telegraph operator was just a fellow-servant with the fireman,
and for that reason the railroad was in no way liable. The railroad won the case, too, on that! And eventually the Supreme
Court confirmed the decision! The outrageous "fellow servant"
precedent has plagued labor for years!

By this time, as a result of the economic growth of these

various corporations, and therefore their increase in power, the
United States Supreme Court was thoroughly controlled by the
railroads. At that time, all but two of the judges on the bench
had been previously either active railroad attorneys, heavy
stockholders, directors, or lobbyists for railroad legislation. Both
as attorney and judges, Fuller, Day (1849-1923) and Shiras
(1832-1924) put all American laws through a sausage-grinder
for their clients, the railroads. The railroads even tried to get the
politicians to change the number of judges on the Supreme Court
bench so that justices favoring the railroads could sit. And they
did succeed in doing that! Several times!

Our magnates of that day, in a frenzy of profit-making, consolidated and enlarged their railroads into tremendous systems.
Pools, combines, trusts! How little even then did the voters sense
what was happening! Back in 1870, already pools were being
formed for the partitioning of traffic and maintaining of rates, as
in the cases of the Southern Railway Association and the Western
Freight Association. At the same time, rail corporations, suddenly grown powerful, were already rampaging, cheating and
squeezing money out of such other railroads and industries as
they were strong enough to order and control. Business men
generally were thrown out of their individual business. Read
any fair history of John D. Rockefeller or the late Andrew
Carnegie. Freezing out competitors, underselling till the rival
lost enormous sums, unfair discrimination and price pools and
rebates, were the order of the day.

Finally, in 1890, the American voters of that day, enraged (if
you can believe it of any American voter), by such practices,
stirred and bellowed, and in that year the Sherman Anti-Trust
Law was passed. And our good citizens of that day thought that
this would end monopolies. But, as we shall see, they believed
foolishly in believing that the Supreme Court of the United
States would interpret this law as they intended it to be interpreted.

True, there was one notable case, but only one in that day, in
which this great Court interpreted a monopoly as a monopoly!

There were numerous cases, of course, but they were never prosecuted. But in this particular case, J. P. Morgan, Sr., and his lackeys had formed the Northern Securities Company, with a capitalization sufficient to control the stock of two great railroads: Great Northern and Northern Pacific. Object, monopoly; the privilege of taxing the people! In due time, but owing to numerous complaints, the Government finally proceeded to prosecute them under this new monopoly law, and (believe it or not!) successfully, at least to the extent that these two railroad systems were no longer joined in control of the same company. Yet I am compelled to report that the Government even in this one case did not enforce the law. The Sherman Anti-Trust Act made monopoly a crime, as it had been in England for hundreds of years, and this crime was punishable by fines and imprisonment. But were the originators and propagators of this scheme fined and thrown into jail? Would you think so? Then you do not know your Supreme Court! Remember, the person in question here was Morgan, J. P. Morgan, a sacred person if ever there was one in America! And fine or jail for him? No one would have dreamed of that! Certainly least of all the judges of the Supreme Court! Yet had the people really and determinedly insisted upon it (which they did not), some catspaw of Morgan's would have been allowed to serve for him. It is a way we have.

But do not go away. We are not nearly through with our Supreme Court. There was an early case of the United Hatters, of Danbury, Connecticut, some 200 members of a labor union. A labor union formed for the purpose of protecting wages and other interests, not a trust or a monopoly! But fought as a trust and a monopoly! Yet in that case, the Federal District Court of Connecticut boldly and flagrantly held that this labor union was a combination in restraint of trade under the Sherman Anti-Trust Act. The Court even fined this handful of men the exorbitant sum of $222,000. Imagine! Fines for workingmen's unions, which were never meant to come under the Act, the while, for Morgan and his corporation, at which the law was aimed, none! And with this astonishing case as a precedent, and as you may well guess, it was easy to proceed against any number of other labor unions; for instance, the Workingmen's Amalgamated Council of New Orleans, assailed by no less an organization than the United States itself! You see at that time it was thought that the unions might be done away with altogether. And they nearly were.

In other words, here you had a law—the Sherman Anti-Trust Act—passed by the laborers and farmers of America to keep the capitalists from swallowing them up, and the purpose of which was plainly indicated by its very name, yet not so used by our Supreme Court; in other words, switched about so as to apply to the laborer! And the nine dictators on the United States Supreme Court bench, as calm about it as though it were the acme of justice! And yet, among the fundamentals of law is this: one must interpret the intention of the words. Besides, any one who knows anything about law, or even pretends to, knows that each case is different, and that therefore the law has to be interpreted in the sense of its general meaning, working, and purpose to suit the particular situation. And in this particular case, how plain it was that these labor unions, by actual legislation in many jurisdictions and by various protective laws in all, had a right to exist as such! Yet and although this Sherman Anti-Trust Law was not intended to apply to them, and although it was only by a trick that it was made to apply, still it was made so to apply! Grossly and willfully made so to do!

But how? What was the public excuse? Well, here it is. Section I of this very law, reads: "Every contract, combination in the form of trust, or conspiracy in restraint of trade." And the labor union, fighting not so much for its life as the lives of its members, was a "combination in restraint of trade." And our good Supreme Court said that! Yet every good lawyer knows that such an essential phrase could not be considered apart from the meaning of the law as a whole. And the meaning of the law as a whole was clear as day. Yet not to the members of that

Supreme Court. They had to find a way to strike at the unions, and they did.

But if you doubt me as to this, read Section II of the Sherman Act: "Every person who shall monopolize or combine or conspire with any other person or persons to monopolize any part of the trade or commerce between States or with foreign nations," etc. . . . According to this then, these 200 members of this labor union had to be combining or conspiring *to monopolize trade or commerce*. But were they? Could they have been? Is a labor union a conspiracy to monopolize trade? Yet to this day our corporations' lawyers do not, or rather let me say *will* not, read and our Courts (our Supreme Court included) will not heed the water-clear language of the law which they are supposed to be interpreting. Though the latter most definitely makes plain that it is the financial monopoly and not any minor trade union with 200 members that it is aiming at, still the United States Supreme Court has repeatedly held, *and still does so hold,* that a labor union is a conspiracy in restraint of trade. In consequence, and because of these decisions and their effectiveness, the law students of our colleges, together with the law professors of the same, are compelled to hold (with these decisions as precedents) that the law was actually made forty years ago to restrain labor. And in one sense it may have been—that is, secretly and deceitfully.

So with this first outrage successfully achieved, our Supreme Court was ready to serve the actual monopolies in restraint of trade. And here is an instance demonstrating their reasoning in connection with this. In United States *v.* E. C. Knight, the following facts were before the Supreme Court. The American Sugar Company, under its controlling magnate of the time, Havemeyer, incorporated in New Jersey and controlling sixty-eight per cent of the sugar of the country (that a monopoly in itself!) bought four more concerns: E. C. Knight Company, Spreckles Sugar Refining Company, Delaware Sugar House, and Franklin Sugar Company, which together produced thirty per cent of the total sugar refined in this country. This meant ninety-eight per cent of the entire output under single control. A monopoly? Perfect! And our Supreme Court, you might think, would have to go some to fix that up for Havemeyer. But the Supreme Court, being an "august tribunal" and capable of the most scholarly conduct, did wonders! Mr. Justice Fuller, who was on the bench at the time, handed down the opinion of the Court, saying: "The Sherman Law pertains to restraints of interstate trade, but this is a monopoly on a necessity of life." In other words, the fact that sugar came under a "staff of life" category made the monopoly not all the worse, or if worse, still immune! For while the Court admitted the monopoly, it also decided that it could do nothing. For and although the monopoly had succeeded in suppressing interstate trade instead of merely restraining it, still Mr. Justice Fuller added that this was really not a true legal restraint of trade because the companies that had sold out to the American Sugar Company—thus establishing it as a monopoly—could, if they chose, still proceed to engage in business anew, although as any one not a Supreme Court justice could easily see, the American Sugar Refining Company would certainly be in an ideal position to push any new competitor off the map; and having just bought out these same rivals, would it not be in a perfect mood so to do? I think so! I know I would be! But the Court, intentionally or otherwise, was using the English common law, which said that a man selling his business may sign a contract not to compete in the same immediate vicinity, but if he contracts not to compete at all anywhere, the contract is void because it restrains trade. But the English common law is not the Sherman Anti-Trust Act, and the former should most certainly not have been invoked as against the specific American law which contradicts it. The Sherman Anti-Trust Act reads that general restraints are void and monopoly is a crime.

In the case at hand, though, and because Congress, under the power given it in the Constitution to regulate interstate commerce, had made the Sherman Law, the Supreme Court proceeded to interpret the law, not by deciding first whether the

American Sugar Refining Company exercised a monopoly, but whether it was engaged in interstate commerce, which if not sly, and even crooked, is certainly dumb! Yet Justice Fuller continued with his bungling by adding that the manufacturing which the American Sugar did was something entirely different from interstate commerce; the latter was only secondary, indirect and incidental! And I say, isn't this a marvelous illustration of how, in the law, words may wash away facts? Why, declared Dr. Fuller, the manufacturing company never moves out of the State! (of its incorporation). (What do you know about that?) And more, it even made its sales, not in New Jersey where it was incorporated but in Philadelphia, no less. Its offices were there. It contributed to the sale of ninety-eight per cent of the sugar for the entire country, fully controlled, by railroad shipment from the same city. Of course, such a company would have no influence—so the Court seemed to think!—on the other 47 States! Or, if any, that would be secondary, indirect and incidental to 47 States oppressed by an illegal monopoly!

In this same sugar trust case decision, Justice Fuller continued: "Congress did not attempt in the Sherman Act to assert the power to deal with monopolies directly as such." No? Well, I think that the people who elected their Congressmen to Congress certainly thought that that was exactly what Congress was doing when it was passing the Sherman Anti-Trust Law, Mr. Justice Fuller to the contrary notwithstanding. Yet Mr. Justice Fuller continues with this, if you please: "Congress, too, in the phrasing of the law, did not want to limit and restrict the rights of corporations created by the States in the acquisition, control or disposition of property." No? Just the same, I challenge the Court, for the law was made because the States could no longer handle the corporations, and in order to enforce this Sherman Act, the law expressly gives the Courts power to take property away from the monopolies. But Mr. Justice Fuller continues still further with: "Congress did not intend to make criminal the acts of persons to acquire and control property which the State of their residence permits." Yet this is false, as I know, because the law again makes a monopoly a criminal offense, punishable by fine and imprisonment. Of course, the State creates corporations, and being created, they acquire property. But I would like to ask the Supreme Court if they understand who is governing monopolies; that is, the larger phases of that acquisition of property. The Federal Government or the States? And certainly our Civil War decided for the Federal Government and not the States!

But Justice Fuller went on with more of this outrageous tush: "Nevertheless, it does not follow that an actual monopoly is an attempt to monopolize commerce." But why not, I beg to ask, and I think there are many others who will ask the same question. And more, I ask what relation has this to a sensible interpretation of the law, which would be: Is producing and controlling ninety-eight per cent of all sugar a monopoly? And if not, why not? And therefore why should Justice Fuller assert that: "There was nothing in the proofs to indicate any intention to put a restraint upon trade or commerce," when any good lawyer knows that intention to break a law, when the facts show a violation of law as clear as day, has absolutely nothing to do with it? Yet Justice Fuller wound up his opinion by saying that the Sherman Law "does not contemplate interference *in advance* with commerce which may be in one State or may be interstate." But wasn't this monopolized sugar being shipped then and there all over the United States? Not in the future, but then! And how strange that Justice Fuller and his fellows on the bench, trying so hard to see what the law contemplated, could not possibly understand that it was a monopolistic control of an entire industry or product that was under discussion! Yet so it was. And was this monopoly ever again prosecuted or even questioned? No, it was not!

Yet this same sugar company, not having been previously sufficiently ruthless in its profit connivance, and possibly—I do not say actually—encouraged by the very kindly opinion of our highest court, afterwards cheated the Government, by underweighing, out of millions of dollars in customs, so that when the matter was discovered, Havemeyer, the head of the sugar trust, paid the Government $2,000,000 just to hush things up. Yet to date this case under the Sherman Law has been only so slightly over-ruled by the Supreme Court as to make negligible the change. In short, the tremendous effort of the common people to make monopoly—but more particularly its abuses—a crime in this country was annulled and made void by the decision of our Supreme Court—that same Supreme Court that to-day is the only tribunal to which the people can, and even must, resort when they would flee the ills and crimes of monopoly and unbridled power.

But what follows will, I think, show that our railroads and corporations can and do have decreed what they desire decreed under the "interstate commerce" clause of the Sherman Anti-Trust Act. For there is another national law which says that in interstate commerce (Congress had to insert this phrase because they made the law under their constitutional power to regulate interstate commerce), corporations should be liable to employees injured because of other employees' negligence. But this meant, you see, that a very considerable personal injury burden might fall on any corporation or organization engaged in interstate commerce. And that would not do. It would be expensive. So we have the spectacle of this our same Supreme Court ruling, in an interstate commerce injury and so damage case, that a man working on a railroad in one State is not to be considered as being engaged in interstate commerce. So here then you have the remarkable spectacle of a sugar monopoly selling to all the States, yet not thereby indulging in interstate commerce, the while a man who works on some State division of an interstate railroad corporation—the same carrying mainly, and in some cases almost entirely, interstate commerce—is none the less not entitled to the benefits of this interstate commerce responsibility. In other words, decisions diametrically opposed, yet both made by the same Court. And all for the corporations! None the less, is it not plain that all commerce national in character should be termed interstate commerce?

In the case of the Standard Oil¹ and its monopoly, which also was interpreted by the Court as a monopoly, we have still another type of decision. For in this instance, although the monopoly was dissolved, still it was not; in other words, "hocus pocus, abra-ca-dabra!" This Supreme Court of ours, you know! It was this way. A certain group of men, with John D. Rockefeller as the big stockholder, previously owned the stock of the Standard Oil, which controlled a great many companies. The bad effects, as charged in the indictment, were due to the control of the industry by so few men. And after due consideration by the Court, the monopoly was "broken up." But how? Well, now let me tell you! Watch closely! By the simple process of giving each stockholder his proportionate share in every company controlled by the Standard Oil! Thus, as many companies as ever under the same control; as many pleased stockholders as before; as much power as before! The chimera of corporation dissolution! (Will somebody kindly page Mr. Houdini?)

Yet in the face of all this, the American workers' unions have been outraged and their real rights voided by being called "combinations in restraint of trade," and that under the very law which they had passed in order to protect themselves from the immense monopolies. In protest against this, though, the unions have had passed the Clayton Act, which says that "No labor organization or its members shall be deemed conspiracies or conspirators or combinations in restraint of trade under the anti-trust laws." But even after thus putting that thought or wish into words, it was not long before the Supreme Court held that the International Machinists' strike did not come under the Clayton Act, but did come under the Sherman Law. In other words, America's highest court again completely ignored the express correction of the law. And the following year, the Supreme Court, under the Sherman Law, held that the United Mine Workers were a conspiracy in restraint of trade and fined them three times the amount of damages which the law provided and meant for those who originated monopolies. Theodore Havemeyer, however, as you may recall, never received any such punishment. He could not have persuaded our Supreme Court, I think, to say that his sugar trust was a monopoly if he had wanted to! And most certainly in its decisions the Supreme Court has shown that it considers our American voters as mere boneheads, who never follow up the laws which they have passed in Congress. And as to that, the Court is about right!

But throughout the whole of its history, the American Supreme Court has consistently held to the doctrines that have facilitated the march of a small favored class to the control of the great industries and needs of this country. So effectively has the Court combated the anti-trust feeling for the last forty years that practically nothing has been done in the way of prosecution of scores of cases deserving it. Great systems like the Pennsylvania Railroad, New York Central, General Electric, and the American Telephone & Telegraph, have been allowed to grow up, step by step, as if a score of their contracts did not give rise to an action and as if a Sherman Anti-Trust Act never existed.

The Van Sweringen Brothers, as I have before indicated, have been permitted only recently to build up a railroad system for themselves consisting of twenty-four railroads. Think of two men controlling more than one-tenth of the railroads in the United States! This is not an example of the old Vanderbilt and Gould type of control of an earlier day, but is going on to-day, 1931! And what about the control of the Missouri Pacific system, the Chicago & Eastern Illinois, the Wheeling & Lake Erie, and others?

But now that the corporations and the Government have succeeded in making a joke of the law, it is to be the butt of a fierce revision drive next year. The American Bar Association is now to offer a bill to make mergers easier! The Chambers of Commerce of the United States, it is also indicated, will support a law to make possible combinations to end trade abuses, which can easily be interpreted to end what they term destructive competition. And the Congress of Industries, said to represent 550,000 individual units and 130 industries, will fight to the end that the Federal Trade Commission be empowered to "accept trade agreements and give quick relief"—a speed-up of mergers! In other words, we are to have fewer great groups to control production, distribution and price. In other words, we are going to grow more, not less, monopolistic.

Another reform, which, like the anti-trust legislation, hit at the greatest abuse of American industrial and business life, was the Transportation Act of 1920. What was the Transportation Act? It promised a close consideration of the small man's needs. Yet the Interstate Commerce Commission, which was and is supposed to enforce this law, did nothing—and itself is now crumbled, or at best completely demoralized. An important cause of this was and is that the Supreme Court, rather than support the Commerce Commission in its extremely difficult task, backed up the corporations instead. The Commission, charged with the duty of recapturing for the Government one-half of all excessive railroad profits, improperly withheld by the railroads everywhere, ordered the St. Louis & O'Fallon Railroad to pay $1,700,-000 to the Government for 1922 and 1923. In answer to this, of course the Supreme Court flagrantly held that the railroad did not have to do so because it was entitled to earn profits on a valuation which considered the costs of reproducing the railroad itself. But how many times as much would it cost to build the railroads now as it did at first? Well, said the Court, the Interstate Commerce Commission would have to find out as to that and prove it. Next, such reproduction costs must figure in any valuation which anticipated a recapture order from the court, no matter how great the profits which are or were made or how far removed from confiscation such profits might show the railroad to be. Next, said the most kindly minded Court, recapture of excess earnings could not depend on any prior establishment of rate level. Now if that isn't leaving the Commerce Commission holding the bag, what is?

And with these few rulings to contend with, of course the case was lost. In fact, the loss of this case so smashed the power of the Transportation Act that until quite recently (April 21,

1931) no final order of this kind was entered against any major railroad. On that date, however (after eleven years of the statute), one was finally entered against the Richmond, Fredericksburg & Potomac, but for only $800,000, a minute sum compared with what was asked for. But even so, the O'Fallon decision started a controversy that is likely to mean the depowering of the Interstate Commerce Commission in so far as this Transportation Act is concerned. Indeed, the actual depowering has already been accomplished, for the Commission, trying to strike a basis on which the corporations, protected by the Supreme Court, will let them work, not only proposes to have this recapture clause repealed, but to consider, in rate-making, the present and future needs of the country for railroads, the capital to be attracted for these improvements, and the general economic condition of the country. Imagine! And yet the railroads, taking advantage of the fiasco caused by the Supreme Court decision in the O'Fallon case, now want to break the force of the whole thing by establishing that it is unconstitutional for the Government to *"confiscate"* (get that!) *any* private property by regulating rates in any way! ("Of the people, by the people, for the people!")

The same corrupt disintegration from within, due to the autocratic powers of a few judges, is likely to face the Federal Power Commission, not so long since created to regulate the Power Trust. Although this Commission, under the Federal Power Act, is supposed to base rates on the actual valuation in States having no commission, last winter the Senate Interstate and Foreign Commerce Committee found that in not one instance did the Federal Power Commission base the electric rate charged to the public on the actual investment. Indeed, despite the fact that they could not, or at least have not, done any better than this, the Commission ordered that the Clarion River Company, which claimed a valuation of about $11,000,000 but had a real investment of only $4,000,000 (less than half as much as its desired valuation for rates) base its rates on $4,000,000. But the utility, determined not to obey this, has carried its demand to the Courts, not on the ground that its investment is actually $11,000,000, but on the ground that the Federal Power Commission cannot establish the net investment on which to base rates. And this right comes before the District of Columbia Supreme Court under the power of Attorney General Mitchell, who not only granted the Appalachian Company, with 80,000 horse-power, a "minor part" license (a designation in law for a little plant of not more than 200 horse-power) but who also considers the Federal Power Act unconstitutional. But if the Commission doesn't get smashed here, depend on it, the Supreme Court of the United States will have its opportunity!

On the other hand, failure of the laws of the United States to protect the common people as they should be protected is never the occasion for any regret, let alone denunciation, by the United States Supreme Court. On the contrary! On May 18, 1931, our great Court decided that the Atlantic Coast Line Railroad was not liable for the death of one Powe, a switchman who was killed by a semaphore put up by the railroad just within the minimum distance away from the track as required by law. Yet certainly it killed the man, and obviously the law was inadequate. So, too, the Court never expresses any sorrow that it must decide cases according to laws designed to defeat rights which the people should have and would have but for these tricks. On March 23, 1931, this same Supreme Court decided that the New York, New Haven & Hartford Railroad did not need to pay a certain Edward Flynn's widow any damages for negligently causing his death, because the law says that after two years' lapse of time, this kind of a suit cannot be brought. He was injured on December 4, 1923. And even the fact that he did not die until September 1, 1928, availed his widow and children nothing.

More, many of the laws which the States of late years have tried to make to regulate the corporations have been punctured by the United States Supreme Court; i.e., the Western Union Telegraph Company *v.* Kansas, and the Pullman Company *v.* Kansas, declaring it unconstitutional for a State to tax property outside the State, meaning corporations existing by the law of another State. Virginia law which says that any company doing express business between points in that State would have to give way to the great Railway Express Company (the huge private express monopoly, incorporated in Delaware and run by the Government for the benefit of a select few private individuals) is constitutional.

Other important present elements of valuation upon which corporations can charge rates high enough to earn a profit should be here included to fully comprehend how the Supreme Court makes lawful most of the inflations Wall Street can think of. Back in 1906 or 1907, the United States Supreme Court denied a large sum for "good will" in the valuation for rates of the Consolidated Gas Company in New York. So thereafter Wall Street began entitling this "good will" as "going value" or "going concern value," and we will see what this change has netted them since.

But first let me tell you how this same Supreme Court aided the Consolidated Gas back in 1922. At that time, it held that the rate of 80 cents per 1,000 cubic feet of gas was confiscatory. The New York State Public Service Commission, thus forced to raise the Gas Company's rate, or rather to permit it to raise its own rate, said that it could not exceed $1.15. On the strength of this, though, the Gas Company changed its capitalization from $125,000,000, with par value of the stock $100, to 2,500,000 shares of no par stock, and each stockholder got two shares of the new stock instead of one share of the old. Then again, in December, 1922, the number of shares was increased to 3,000,000. The people, justly furious, had, on June 2, 1923, a law passed in the New York State Legislature saying that in New York City the Gas Company could not charge more than $1.00 per 1,000 cubic feet. Yet the Consolidated Gas, knowing its power, increased its stock, in December, 1923, to 3,600,000 shares. After that, dividends of five per cent (how much would that be on old stock?) were regular. And on December 31, 1924, this stock was valued at $217,999,236 and the average market value for September, 1925, was $325,000,000. In 1924, the Consolidated Gas earned a net income of twenty-six per cent on the cost of its property and thirteen per cent on the replacement value, according to figures in the testimony of Walter Addicks, a vice-president of the Consolidated Gas on June 17, 1924. Despite this glorious financial status of the company, the United States Supreme Court, on November 29, 1926, declared that the New York State law limiting the rate to $1.00 per 1,000 cubic feet was unconstitutionally *confiscating* the property of these noble stockholders! Besides, in this decision the Court allowed the Gas Company $9,000,000 for its "going concern" value—the old illegal "good will" but now disguised under a new name!

In connection with all American street railway lines, the Supreme Court holds, and has held, that rates producing a profit of less than 7.44 per cent are unconstitutional. Just why less than 7.44 per cent should be so illegal unless we want our corporations to tax us to the limit, I don't know. I can't make that in *my* investments, but so it is! And on January 6, 1930, it ruled, for the Baltimore Street Railway Company, that a profit to that company of 6.26 per cent on its various holdings was confiscatory, and in mitigation of that allowed it to add $5,000,000 to its rate valuation as the value of franchises granted to it by the city for almost nothing. I might easily cite other cases, but this will do, I think. Look up others for yourself!

But now what about the latest anti-trust law cases? Monopolies seem to be closing in all around us! On March 1, 1920, the United States Supreme Court declared that the United States Steel Company was not a monopoly in restraint of trade. Yet here are the facts. In 1901, United States Steel was formed as a holding company for twelve concerns, each of which had a monopoly in its own line; i.e., American Steel & Wire Company, American Tin Plate Company, American Sheet Steel Company, American Steel Hoop Company, National Tube Company, and American Bridge Company. They controlled vast natural resources of ore, pig iron, and ingots for its own use. And in this case the facts proved that before the merger a general competitive situation, with low and uneven prices, existed, but that afterwards or on its completion, prices rose and remained at a higher level. Monopoly in restraint of trade? Of course! Not only that, but anticipating the profits of prices certain to be, because of monopoly, artificially high, $100,000,000 in stock went to J. P. Morgan, the promoter. As of December 31, 1913, there were, in round numbers:

Total assets	$1,800,000,000
Outstanding capital	800,000,000
Surplus	151,000,000
Cash	75,000,000

Yet the $75,000,000 in cash on hand was more money than any one of their remaining competitors was even *capitalized* for. Yet the Supreme Court afterwards held that the fact that this enormous concern's competitors *"voluntarily"* follow its prices (those of U. S. Steel) did not prove any unlawful restraint of trade or prices. And it was even brazen enough to add that U. S. Steel was not only not a monopoly but also did not restrain trade. But to me, as to any other sane person, I hope, this interpretation seems a ruthless interpretation of facts.

And now another case, please, and under this same Clayton Anti-Trust Act, but this time one governed by a clause of that Act which said that where competition was to be eliminated or greatly hurt and trade is restrained by the purchase by one company of the stock of another, such stock might not be purchased. Well, in New England were the International Shoe Company and the McElvain Company, two of the greatest shoe manufacturers in America. The McElvain's specialty was dress shoes for men. In this line they were running the International's shoes right off the market. For by 1920, McElvain's sales were more than $33,000,000, whereas International's shoes had dropped to only $2,500,000 in this line—a fact which caused International Shoes to buy out the McElvain Company and eliminate its competition. . . . Yet when a suit under this Clayton Act was brought to test the legality of this, the United States

Supreme Court held that in buying the McElvain Company, the International Shoe Company did not restrain competition or trade because previously both companies sold to different distributors. Yet and just the same, there had been, among these distributors who sold to the retailer, the severest competition, which by the merger had been eliminated. But, and just the same, so held our Supreme Court. And so, in connection with these corporation and merger matters, is the mind of our supreme judicial body. It is always looking in back of and never in the face of the very plain facts, where they chance to be anticorporate.

But just one more, and then I am done with this. It concerns a recent Standard Oil case decided April 13, 1931. As you may or may not know, when gasoline first became so popular, the oil companies wanted an easier method of manufacturing it, of course. Finally, a better way, termed the "cracking" process, was developed. The basic idea of this "cracking," as it appeared, every one understood, and more, there were no patents covering it. Yet the Standard Oil of Indiana (more progressive than the rest, maybe), made it, by 1913, a commercial success, and from then until January, 1931, at which time this case came up, it had made $15,000,000 in royalties from other firms for the use of the devices, and also by this time other companies had been finding methods of doing this and using them. Then the Standard Oils of Indiana and New Jersey and the Texas Company got into a quarrel over alleged patents of their own and went to court. And then, in order to settle this, these three companies entered a contract whereby each was to receive a portion of these royalties from these several processes or "patents" used. But the Government's suit against these oil companies was based on the allegation that these quarrels were not honest quarrels at all, since the so-called "patents" claimed by each were not patents but mere claims intended to frighten off other companies who might wish and really were free to use them but who, by this method—a suit before the Supreme Court and a decision by that body in favor of the respective claims of these three companies

—might be driven off or made to pay royalty. And in substantiation of this the Government showed that these three companies owned, or claimed to, and licensed fifty-five per cent of the total "cracking" capacity, but without real right. Lastly, the Government showed that because of these so called "patents," these three companies had suceeded in controlling the price and supply of "cracked" gas, and the most flagrant abuse brought out in this whole case was the discovery that while all of the independent companies were most unjustly charged burdensome royalties, still these three companies not only did not have to pay any royalty but received as clear profit the royalties put upon the other fellows for a commonly known process. None the less, the Supreme Court saw no monopoly or restraint of trade here. On the contrary, it upheld the claims or "patents" of the three companies then before it. This patent stuff is a new kind of Rockefeller trust. Recall the radio trust to which I'll again refer.

In view of all this, I call the Supreme Court of the United States a thoroughly corporation- and trust-minded body. It seems to lack a willingness to understand or appreciate the needs of the great masses of the people. This is perhaps natural when we consider the sources of supply of the members of that body. Its members for the most part had been corporation servants. They had earned or at least had received enormous fees for serving special corporate interests. Long training imbued them with the corporate point of view. A lawyer, who for years has guided a corporation through the mazes of the law to various and successful raids upon the public treasury, cannot be expected in the later years of his life entirely to dissociate himself from all the influences that surrounded him. He is appointed to the bench; he has become a judge, but he is still a lawyer; his lifetime habits of thought do not change overnight.

But in the wider view of our economic life here, what is the meaning and significance of this reactionary rule of the Supreme Court? Out of the French Revolutionary era, which destroyed the domineering French nobility, came those ideas of personal freedom, live and let live, make something for yourself and let the other fellow make something for himself, which furnished this country at least some of its governing principles. Time, however, as is always the case, has changed all this from a vigorous effort on the part of everybody to compete and possess (but not to the end of enslaving or destroying any class), to the present system of the gross ownership of all by a few: the banks and corporations who now try to and do ravish the multitudes in order to increase their own wealth and power. And herein lies the failure of our entire American capitalistic system. And this was feared in the United States forty years ago, at the time the Sherman Law was passed. And even before that, had not attempt after attempt at reform been made? But the spirit of the land has not been toward maintaining anything like equity in this matter of competition. Rather, and from the very first, the strong and selfish have been encouraged and lauded the while the lesser fry have been cheated and ignored. And leading in this matter of strengthening the strong and defeating the weak has been our Supreme Court, for by its successive decisions has it sought to make all of capitalism a failure. Law after law—like the Child Labor Law—for the masses has been broken, and by that Court! But there is one consolation. The more conservative and tightened becomes the judicial rule, the more quickly will the failure of our senile capitalism reach a climax!

CHAPTER X

THE CONSTITUTION AS A SCRAP OF PAPER

FACTS alone may portray the liberality or non-liberality toward all of such a document as our American Constitution, and from this liberality or its opposite shines forth the degree of its worth.

The further to comprehend the forces which conditioned the drafting of the American Constitution, and give weight to its setting in the thought and life of that day, one must return at least a little way in modern history. In seventeenth century Europe, as we all know, the great wars of religion were fought. And by the time the American Constitution was being drawn, religion, on the European continent at least, was still occupying quite the foremost place in the minds, motives and actions of its governments and peoples. Catholicism, entrenched in the South, and Protestantism in the North, wrangled to such a degree that liberty, although Montesquieu, Turgot, Voltaire, Rousseau and Lessing had written or were then writing of toleration and humaneness, was but dawning. This dominance of religion and its abuses, so trenchantly and bitterly assailed by Voltaire, existed in a day when kings, as we know, ruled by the direct will of God. And this assertion, due to the mental humbleness of those who can be led by dogmatic religion was too noble, as well as too sacred, to be questioned. Yet but a little while after all this was laughable to us here in America, as we also know. But now when we see how corporation despotism, bolstered by propaganda, can triumph, it does not seem so laughable. Dishonest and entrenched wealth is becoming sacred here; and those who question its rights and powers are not so different to the "possessed" and the "heretics" of a former day.

The first modern political revolt, as we all know, occurred in England (1640). Charles I was beheaded, and for treason. But not treason against God—the divine appointer of kings on the continent—but rather against the people of England, who, according to the very advanced thought of the radicals of that day and country, ruled by the wish and favor of the people of that country, and none other. They had come to believe, apparently, that the Lord checks up on kings. Their great thinker of the time, John Locke, expounded these conceptions of theirs so clearly that subsequently they, among other things, became strong, motivating factors in the production of the daring and noble, and yet inevitable, French Revolution. But despite this radical defiance and the subsequent superiority of Parliamentary power over the monarch, still the House of Lords remained— a forceful voice of the aristocracy,—while the commoners were either appointed by magnates or chosen from the electorate of less than one-tenth of the men of England. The idea of extending the franchise to the mass of the people of that day was not yet thought of. And of course the aristocrats of Spain, France and the German countries, as well as the nobility of Russia and Poland, considered themselves infinitely more lofty than the masses.

During the seventeenth century, however, those radical churchmen, the Calvinists, electrified Europe by stating that all men in the church were equal in the sight of God. Naturally, this did not "get much of a hand" from the nobility, and most particularly when it was hinted at or broached as a political doctrine. Only Cromwell, with his army, asserting that all men, equal in the state, should be the source of governmental authority, came near to establishing such democracy as could then be established which was little enough. But he and his army also passed. They were quenched like a light, and their ideas vanished or became a dusty and neglected philosophy. Yet in 1748, Montesquieu wrote that men are born equal (a figment of the mind); and Voltaire believed that men should possess equal rights before the law (which is not so true as that they should have equal consideration); and Rousseau would sacrifice even liberty to gain utter equality.

Although these warm radical breezes blew on and fluttered all that they touched, the nobility of that time, making light of them, was wholly preoccupied by such supposedly critical matters as the growth of Russia, the Austrian policies of the time, and the plunder of Poland. Yet by a certain few, the radical movement was looked upon as perhaps a natural but not a momentous matter. No one dreamed of a complete transference of power from kings and courts to the people. Yet with no more background ideologically than this, the English colonies in America a little later declared their independence and asserted that "all men are created free and equal."

It was not until eleven years later, during which time these same ideas, and these alone were propounded, that the United States Constitution was written. The imminent French Revolution, which was to make Kant, the dignified professor and philosopher, weep for joy, had not even occurred. No other democracy existed. Americans in 1787 blazed out a unanimously willed democracy—a Russian Communism of that day.

But now to contrast the Constitution with what had gone before in this country. Pre-independence times here saw charter, proprietary and royal government. Massachusetts, Rhode Island, Pennsylvania and Delaware were overlorded by proprietors; New Hampshire, New York, New Jersey, Virginia and Georgia were directly subject to the English Crown. Under the new and wonderfully progressive (and by that I mean better balanced) Constitution, representatives of the people, elected by them, were to raise all revenues, regulate commerce with foreign nations and between States, and declare war. In lieu of the prevailing religious intolerance abroad, with its strife and death, and motivated by what idiotic superstitions and brought to bear by what former regulations, the first Constitutional amendment, adopted in 1791, guaranteed freedom of religious belief and the practice thereof. Instead of a distant and infallible British government impossible of approach by the people—an example of which was the English Governor Berkeley of Virginia, who said: "Thank God there are no free schools nor printing presses here"—there was granted the constitutional right to criticize by speech or through the press, and to freely assemble and petition the government to mitigate any abuse. In short, freedom after the severely repressive laws of the earlier day! And if their severity be doubted, recall that in New England colonial life, twelve offenses were punished by death, and in Virginia, seventeen!

Yet all of the class differences conditioning the British nobility and the British proletariat existed in Colonial America. Only the gentility here in America were permitted to use the prefix "Mr." or "Mrs." Others above the rank of servant were honored by being addressed as "goodman" and "goodwife." Catalogues of Yale and Harvard were arranged according to the rank of the student's families. One whose estate did not amount to £200 or more, could not wear gold or silver lace. And it was the aristocrat and the aristocrat alone, who could wear calf-skin shoes, flowered silk, or gay-colored embroidered velvet suits with wide ruffles of gold or silver lace, or have a cane-head and snuff-box of gold or silver. The farmer and laborer must venture to no better than a homespun shirt, neat's leather (cow-hide) shoes, enhanced on Sundays by buckles, and leather breeches, greased and blacked for occasions. Yet in spite of this actual practice of British class difference, the Constitution verbally lessened the whole business of class distinctions by prohibiting titles.

People now laud our American Constitution as a great document that has kept up with the times. Yet what does that mean? That the Constitution has given free sway to a corporate oligarchy which its framers never contemplated, or to a capitalistic unionism so dominant of the people as to exercise an undue power against them and frustrate their every guarantee? Of course, 2,000,000 Colonists who didn't as yet have a single daily newspaper, whose largest city was Philadelphia (William Penn's "fair greene country town"), of 25,000 inhabitants, and who were so excited about a stagecoach line established in 1766 and making the unprecedented time of two days between New York and Philadelphia, that they called the stages "flying machines," could not foretell the capitalism which now motivates and dominates the American life. The American government to-day is not so much government in the sense of managing for the many as it is in licensing for and to the few—the corporate interests, no less—and with the privilege of getting all they can for their private purposes. The strongest and final hold of capitalism to-day in the Constitution is its guarantee of private property. And in framing this clause, the Constitution-makers, thinking of real estate and personal property in terms of that day, never dreamed or imagined, let alone contemplated, the vast industrialism that later was to come and hold as personal property, not only unimaginably large amounts of stocks and bonds in holding companies, trusts and corporations, but the same in their entirety and in perpetuity. Most of the great fortunes of to-day which carry with them crucial power are personalty of this nature. And only a little while ago, the late George F. Baker, Chairman of the First National Bank of New York, died leaving hundreds of millions of dollars worth of this personal property in the form of tens of thousands of railroad, bank, etc., shares and bonds.

But now, with this change in the times, our financiers and corporation and bank-heads finding such dominance and control to their liking, have not only fought and in the main prohibited all natural and needed additions to this freedom, but have tightened and limited that naturally acquired by the Constitution nearly one hundred and fifty years ago. They have not welcomed and have not intended, if by such ways as they could devise they could frustrate it—a government of and by the people.

During the long one hundred and fifty years which have passed since the Constitution was drafted, our industrialists, and this almost unanimously (read Gustavus Myers' "History of Great American Fortunes"), have used every means in their

power—money, government and the influence of connection—
to filch one liberty and another from the layman. Of course,
I take account of the fact that many petty regulations of olden
days which mattered not to industry have disappeared. They are
as nothing. Also, I pay due homage to the fact that the Constitution was drawn up by wealthy landowners, who did not
intend all powers to be conferred upon the even then somewhat
distrusted masses. In the large trend of affairs, however, my
contention as to the primary liberality of that document is sound.

If this is doubted, an examination of the liberties of the individual citizen of to-day as contrasted with those the Constitution intended and those the corporations, who now control the
Government which is supposed to abide by and enforce that
Constitution, are willing to grant him, will, I think, command
support for me and as only facts can.

Firstly, any scientific or cultural learning which will loosen
customs or free the mind of industrial shackles, is suppressed.
Free speech, free press? Our radio, public schools, colleges, pulpits? One needs only to scan the current American scene to
know what already has happened as well as is now happening.
If you will recall, in the chapter on Our Banks and Corporations
as Government, I outlined the propaganda program in regard to
private versus public ownership, and how schools and colleges, as
well as newspapers and their editorial sanctums were invaded and
suborned or betrayed. And to-day, if you investigate any factory,
college, radio concern, newspaper office, moving picture company, library, or any other source of public information, its
distribution or clarification for the masses, you will find out
how quickly money—the present oligarchic program for the elevation of the few and the domination and suppression of the
many—has invaded all these fields, and is saying what and how
and where and why anything shall be said, and ruling always
in its own interests. And that directly in the face of the line
and letter of our American Constitution which guarantees the
freedom or use of these to all.

But let us see now if this is not so. Students at a Brooklyn college were forbade to hear Norman Thomas, socialist leader, speak. Then at the University of Pittsburgh only recently, the Student Liberal Club of that School, prohibited from holding a meeting on the campus, assembled off the college grounds to listen to Professor Harry Elmer Barnes, of Smith College, speak on the Mooney-Billings case. For this, and this alone, one Fred Woltman, who taught philosophy, and two students were dismissed from the University. In other words, a nationally and legally acknowledged injustice to labor closed to comment in an American college. But at whose orders or wish? And next, in March, 1929, a sex questionnaire, distributed among students by psychologists and sociologists at the University of Missouri, resulted in the suspension of Professor Max F. Meyer, for many years a member of the faculty, and the dismissal of two other men. Yet the questionnaire in question had already been deemed entirely proper by scientific students of the subject at other schools as well as by the American Association of University Professors. Then why the suppression? The answer, as I took it from the mouths of some of the faculty itself, was this. The faculty itself is subject to a board of trustees. The trustees, in themselves not too highly informed, and highly conventional, publicly speaking, individuals of the moneyed and professional classes of the State, and looking to the State as well as individuals of wealth for endowments and funds, were determined not only to please these, but to see to it that their university conformed in every way, morally and otherwise, to the local as well as (as they assumed) generally current and therefore conventional notions of what a university should or should not teach and do in America. And hence the ban, which has fallen in well enough with the general feelings of our corporations, commercial and religious, which is that the less education, apart from things technical and financial (by no means political or sociologic) the better!

I sum the matter of dictation by all to the professor as to what he is to teach, in this way. A writer writes as he sees fit, a lawyer interprets the law and an educator should educate, unhampered.

But one of the most daring and subtle of all the attempts *so far* to undermine the right of free speech and, by the natural and obvious extension of the same, the right to a free press (defeated in the Supreme Court of the United States on June 1, 1931, and that after a two-year fight), began in Minneapolis in 1927, and came to be known as the Minnesota Gag Law Case. This concerned a weekly newspaper in Minneapolis: *The Saturday Press,* in which, in late September, 1927, there was printed an attack on not only one Barnett, a gangster operating gambling and vice houses in Minneapolis, but also on one Brunskill, the Chief of Police of that city, for accepting graft. Also, one Davis, of the Law Enforcement League, and Leach, the Mayor, were included. Because H. A. Guilford, who, with J. M. Near, ran the *Saturday Press,* was shot, though not killed by gangsters when the first issue of this exposure came out, I have a suspicion that most of the charges were true. At any rate, among the statutes of the State of Minneapolis at this time was one which declared that any newspaper repeatedly publishing "scandalous, malicious and defamatory" matter, could be declared a nuisance and on that ground, suppressed. Exactly how that statute came to be there (although the why of it is obvious) is yet to be explained. Nevertheless, by virtue of the authority of that, the local individuals so attacked, and through their lawyers and the police, clamped this suppression power down on this publication and ended it. Then the usual thing— the gangsters tried to force these editors to their side by offering them a share of the gambling and illicit profits. The paper, however, to be thoroughly wiped out. And for three years, or until it was, by a vote of 5 to 4 only (note the 5 to 4) voided by our Supreme Court, it ran the gamut of the State courts. And the gag law was sustained by them. And nearly so, as you see, by the Supreme Court of the United States. And that in the face of the plain mandate of the Constitution itself which says that the rights of a free press are not to be abridged.

But consider the implication of all this; the fact that a sovereign State in America should pass such a law and, next, that its Supreme Court should uphold it. And that three years had to elapse before any final decision of any kind could be reached! For under that power, assuming it had been sustained (and consider the vote 5 to 4), the government, if it chose, could have stopped any publication on any such trumped up charges, and this in the face of the question as to whether or not there existed evidence that the statements circulated were libelous or true! Or if this law had been held Constitutional, like legislation in other states would have been able also to muzzle the press.

In short, it doomed the individual, regardless of his rightness or wrongness, not only as to editorial expression of his ideas, but subjected him to financial loss as well. And this was upheld in the Courts of the State of Minnesota and enforced there until three years later, until, via funds furnished, I believe, by the American Newspaper Publishers' Association, and others, it was set aside by the Supreme Court. But even so, there were those who, editorially and in court, argued that because England has practically the same thing, it would be equitable here. But in England, total suppression, as was so decidedly effected in Minnesota, is not possible. Besides, England does not have a constitutional guarantee of freedom of the press, whereas we do. Yet this sinister attempt to dictate to and actually control the American press got as far as I have indicated.

But let me turn to a related phase: that of the power of our Government to deny at any time the use of the mails to any individual, firm or publication. This on the strength of the laws which relate to obscenity and sedition. But in practice, to-day, how does it work? You can imagine! Is there anything political or anti-corporation or anti-social as a religionist or a trust sees it? If so, and quickly, the mails are closed, and perhaps proceedings of a different character started: examinations, prosecutions, etc., on the part of the Department of Justice. No need to mention anything Communistic. Although there is nothing in the

Constitution which should prevent a widespread study and discussion of that new economic theory, attempt to do that through the mails! It has not been long since several publications dealing with the new Eastern economic theory have been suppressed, and with scarcely a protest from any but the Communists. And yet labor, antagonistic to the corporations, fares no better, or very little. I cite two cases. First the booklet: "Smash the Gastonia Frame-up!"—a sharp comment on the Gastonia, N. C., labor war, which was held improper for the mails because it reflected on the State of North Carolina! And next, a second booklet, "Justice, California Style," was decreed by the New York Court of Appeals in March, 1930, as fit for the mails because the law does not contemplate libel against a State. To me, since libel is a tort, a private, civil, uncontractual wrong to an individual, the latter is the better case. But all this is just the gravy; here is the roast! Even in peace time, the Postmaster General may exclude *future* issues of a newspaper which has published nonmailable material. Our United States Supreme Court has so decided. But is the Postmaster General a sorcerer or a wizard, that he can know beforehand what is to be printed in the future issues of a newspaper, or is it merely a way for him to save himself time and trouble?

Although arbitrary suppression by the Government is an outrage, that of a *corporation* to evade the Constitutional guarantee of free speech is infinitely worse. Yet now comes radio censorship, the worst because no legal action may be taken. The corporations who want to sell radios to the tomfoolery-seekers and half-baked people who would not dare to know anything, will sign all kinds of contracts for "Madame Distingué" to tell how sub-debs with black hair and green eyes, brown hair and blue eyes, yellow hair and brown eyes, should dress, or with "Amos and Andy" for years of service, but let more serious matters be suggested, how different! Last year, for instance, in December, the National Broadcasting Company refused to broadcast speeches of the National Birth Control Congress in New York on the ground that they were evil—although the Church of England does not now appear to think so. And again, in Pittsburgh, KQV canceled, for the alleged reason of "conflicting programs" a talk by Patrick Fagan in which he berated the "coal and iron police."

Now turn to the Negro situation for a moment, and his place and rights under the Constitution. As I see his problem, it is like this: Though the Constitution freed him and gave him (and now to-day his wife and daughter) the right to vote, this right in ten States to-day, flagrantly and directly in opposition to the law, is interfered with. More, our high courts in thirty States now hold that the State laws of those States prohibiting intermarriage of whites and blacks, and in seventeen States segregating the Negroes in schools and public conveyances, do not conflict with the Constitutional amendments that freed them and gave them the right to vote. Yet directly under the judge's eyes, does it not say in the Constitution that *the enumeration of certain rights does not disparage others retained by the people?* It would seem to me that constitutionally, at least, the Negroes have the right to marry whom they please and to ride in all conveyances. Why? Because by the Constitution and by gaining citizenship, all of their privileges are protected. This 14th Amendment, though, by which a State may now pass these crotchety or credulous acts if only they "protect" all equally by them, is a hoax, because all of the Negroes aren't all of the people.

More, the Negro, fast being absorbed by industry, is to-day, under our individualistic and capitalistic approach, being put to the meanest labor and suffering abuse involving a loss of Constitutional privileges. For it is the Negro and the Negro alone to-day who must sweat all night in the gas-filled, nauseating and hence enervating checker-chamber of a steel mill, or crawl into underground sewers or repair red-hot furnaces. Much work of other kinds does not go to him. And in the steel mill at Sparrow's Point, Maryland, common Negro labor is paid but 25 or 30 cents a day for 12 hours work. Again, at the Allegheny Steel Company, near Pittsburgh, Pennsylvania, Ne-

groes labor fourteen hours a day. Yet one word of protest on
their part, and all of their Constitutional privileges in this
matter are blotted out, as I will show in my chapter on labor.
Our Negroes, likewise, are the first to be laid off. What happens
then? They have to go back to the country. Yet back in the
country again, these same Negroes as tenant farmers become
practically the slaves of landlords, who assume actually—not
theoretically—the power of slave owners, and before whom, because of local coöperation, these Negroes are helpless. (You will
meet up with them again in the chapter on The Abuse of the Individual.) Though the crops raised on this tenant-farmer basis
are supposed to be shared fifty-fifty between the landlord and
tenant, the landlord who sells the crop and receives the money,
keeps all he can. If a Negro protests, the landlord can, and does,
have him arrested on the ground that the ignorant and unknowing Negro still owes him money, and sentenced. Or perhaps he
is lynched, or just shot down in cold blood—a conclusion which
is locally if not legally, passed upon as justifiable homicide. And
when in 1919, Negro tenant farmers of eastern Arkansas organized to obtain a fair price for their cotton, they held a meeting, which they had a right to do under the Constitution. But
upon so doing, the henchmen of local landowners fired upon the
gathering and the landowners had the local militia come and kill
scores of these Negroes. In cases of this nature, the local government of Arkansas then forced evidence adverse to the Negroes for use at their trial by torturing Negro witnesses on an
electric chair which shocked them until they said such things as
there and then transcribed could later be used against them.

But not only is the individual, black or white, misused and
suppressed in this way in America, but our Government officials
once they are not just duly, but, rather, swindlingly elected,
and that in the face of the intentions of the individual when
voting, and once inducted in office, and vested with some
power, then they proceed not only to interpret the law for
themselves or according to the wishes of some corporation, but
they themselves proceed to grant to others authority which was

never delegated to them by the Constitution or the people. And mostly this arbitrary and unconstitutional power in office is exercised to help corporations as against the public at large. Thus, the legal authorities of any given State, or the United States Government itself, via its charter or franchise-granting powers, will allow a corporation to set up a town or city within a State and give it authority to make and enforce rules and regulations for the inhabitants of said town or city which are no part of any law of the State, the while and at the same time, the same corporation thus governing a city is allowed to refuse to the State, via the franchise granted it, the right to make the corporation obey it not only in police, but other matters. In other words, elected or appointed officials, without any constitutional authority for what they do, set corporations above the State and the government itself in order that the corporation, for such favors as it may be willing to do them, can the more closely and drastically regulate those who work for it. Also, it is in such illegal and purely corporation created towns that the corporation may say what newspapers shall or shall not be read, what store or stores dealt with, what rents paid, social or mental actions indulged in, and the like. And if you doubt this, you need only recall Cœur d'Alene in Idaho, Carnegie in Pennsylvania, and Gary and other towns in Indiana and elsewhere.

In fact, in any matter relating to the American corporation to-day—its assumed rights, privileges, its power to tax, destroy, suborn, suppress, even enslave (as in the case of the chain and camp gangs in the South and elsewhere) or to imprison and otherwise abuse the individual who in any way protests or seeks to annul or frustrate its arbitrary abuses as in the case of Tom Mooney,—the Constitution and its various guarantees as to all this is as nothing. The courts, where the corporations and their interests are concerned, are no longer willing to hear the individual, let alone aid him. Concerning this case, may I quote a capitalist who said: "Practically all I know is that he has a pretty clear record of being a bad actor and is a party who would probably start this same thing all over again if he were out of jail." I could cite cases, not by the dozen but the hundreds, I am sure, but just to prove roughly that I am not talking without the machine guns of fact at my elbow, I will list these (and please read them):

1. Lochner *v.* New York, 1904. This case came to the United States Supreme Court because a Utica bakery contested the constitutionality of the New York State law *limiting* the employment of help in bakeries to ten hours a day. Our highest court held the statute *unconstitutional* on the ground that it denied "equal protection of the laws to all." In other words, it denied sufficient protection to the corporation, although incidentally it was denying *all* protection to labor. Not only that, but the majority opinion of the court proceeded to call the law a "meddlesome interference" with liberty, property and *the right to contract* (the individual's right to contract to work 14 hours a day or more if by poverty he was forced so to do, is what is meant here) guaranteed by the 14th Amendment! But what about the liberty and property and right to contract of the laborer? It is stingingly minimized.

In this case, the court would not in any way limit the right to contract, because, although the law protected the laborer from abuse, it inconvenienced the employer. I believe this is a sound statement, because the same United States Supreme Court had not hesitated to limit contracts before.

Thus, in many instances, the Government has not hesitated to limit the people's right to contract. For one example, when a municipal or state government grants a franchise, it limits the people's right to contract in this way: You and I have a right to buy a house from this company or the other, and theoretically, you and I have the right to contract with this, that, or the other gas company for gas. But when a franchise is granted, one company has a monopoly on gas. Thus, if any one wants gas, he must take it from this company or go without. The people's right to contract for gas is limited to this one company.

2. Hammer *v.* Dagenhart, 1918.

Our National Child Labor Law prohibited the interstate transportation of goods made by children. Child labor was thus regulated because Congress, under its constitutional privilege as well as duty in regard to interstate commerce, the regulation of the same, so ordered. Many consider that law as protecting health, etc. Questions similar to this protection of health, however, deal with police power, and police power is held by the States according to the Constitution.

Yet this National Child Labor Law was declared unconstitutional by a 5-4 Supreme Court decision, on the ground that the subject matter of this law—that is, regulating the ages at which children can work—is really a police power. But many preëminent justices agree with me that this law definitely concerned the regulation of interstate commerce. Yet the court cast aside this right of Congress as if it was nothing. The very same court, though, had previously held that the right of Congress to regulate interstate commerce was more important and came before the right of the States to exercise police power. So there you have it. Now a thing is wrong and now it is right—but all according, apparently, to who is seeking to know. In this case, obviously, it was much to the advantage of capital to have this law declared unconstitutional. Then it could hire hundreds of thousands of children for practically nothing. And in declaring this law unconstitutional, the court even went against its own principles and past decision; because previously, it had held interstate commerce more important than police powers. Because of this and because the decision obviously favored capital in preference to labor, it is most clear that this decision was made to favor capital rather than to protect police power. And in going against its principles, the court cast aside as nothing, the constitutional privilege of Congress to regulate interstate commerce.

3. Adair *v.* United States, 1907. One section of the Federal Erdman Act (resulting from the great railroad strike of 1894) to promote arbitration between labor and capital, prohibited discrimination against employees who belonged to unions. This

section of the law was declared unconstitutional by the Supreme
Court in this case on the grounds that it denied liberty to the
individual to contract—of course, actual liberty for the boss to
hire, fire and keep whom he pleased. (A court decision on the
subject of labor *v.* capital has never been made for labor on
the grounds of his liberty, etc.) Personally, though, I see no
liberty with the power to discriminate lawfully. Yet the court
was "hipped" on this idea. It said: "No government can legally
justify such legislation in a free land." Actually, what this
court decision legalizes is this: the bosses are free by law to
unite into corporations, powerful enough to fight all labor, and
so united, do oppose all labor, but labor is not free to unite,
because this decision gives the bosses power to discriminate
against unionized labor. The liberty of contract in this instance
was held to be the liberty of the employers to enforce their
demands—not liberty of both parties to agree, a supposedly
necessary mutuality if any contract is to be held as good law.

When it comes to the individual, who is not protected by a
union or some organization of some kind, there is still another
story to tell. Thus, in many of the Southern States, like Florida
and Alabama, where laws exist saying that a man who owes
his employer money cannot leave his job until the debt is made
up, individuals are forced to sign notes and other evidences of
debt, until in some cases men are kept working all their lives
at the most inadequate wages.

More, in this same area, men arrested on petty charges are
victims of a virtual press gang system which runs counter to the
very essence of the American Constitution. The old custom of the
press gang master—getting an affable sailor drunk in order to
shanghai him, and then forcing him to slave as a sailor without
pay—had at least more of preliminary affability about it than
which now operates against the unemployed man, in the South
or West. For alleged vagrancy, the mere necessity of passing
from one region to another in search of work the unemployed
man of this hour is seized, jailed and then hired out as part of
a prison or chain gang to work under a private contractor who

makes the money. All of which is described in "Abuse to the Individual."

The chief ill of most of these abuses all over the United States is that usually they fall to individuals impotent because they are single-handed and uninformed. In this complex society of ours, with its government now almost wholly privately controlled, I have traced them either to our dominant corporations and their allied interests, or to the influence of their example now so widely known of all. For naturally, in a country where private powers able to coerce the government, and strong enough, as are our corporations, to resist regulation exist, this abuse of the individual is sure to arise. For who is he to ask of any one anything, or to complain when he considers himself abused? Was this not so long ago the land of slavery, par excellence? And has not the general and brutal attitude of our corporations and financiers since encouraged this wholesale abuse of the individual? And since that desire for slaves on the part of some in the South appears never to have died we have what we have, now. For our corporations do seek, via wealth, for themselves and poverty for all others, to enslave. And this they still seek, mainly by making reform in any and all of its phases anywhere in America a failure—and always in the teeth of the Constitution and with the aid and consent of the higher courts.

But how do corporations and our Government in aiding them (and when it is caught in so doing) get out of their jam? I will show you. There is an antiquated Constitutional privilege which says that an individual does not have to testify or answer questions which even *tend* to incriminate him. (Recall how the common man is forced by 3rd degree violence to testify.) In other words, because a man has committed a crime, he doesn't need to tell anything about it. Thus, when the proper Government officials set out to investigate something, they cannot force those who know the most about it to disclose anything, and hence they cannot obtain enough evidence even to take the case to court. Thus, in the matter of the investigation of the disgusting New York milk graft, as well as the investigation—by public prosecutors after public exposure, of course—of graft in connection with the State census of the building and equipping of public school buildings, hospitals, sewers, etc., these same were either blocked in part or thwarted entirely by this legal hocus pocus in regard to your testimony tending to incriminate or degrade you. The State officials could not answer, because, etc. Again, it was illustrated in connection with those New York judges and various prominent New York City officials who, having stolen this or that, or winked at the same for what there was in it for them, were freed because of this Constitutional privilege to sit back and while still holding their jobs, mockingly evade these investigators and their questions. Yet these same Government officials, since they had openly and publicly accepted a public trust by taking a position of trust, were certainly answerable to the people for everything except private matters. And in so far as any public matters were concerned, these officials should not have been permitted to use this so-called immunity privilege. Accepting a government office, as I see it, at least, should carry with it in law a pledge not to take advantage of this Constitutional right. And although some lawyers say that this would be unconstitutional (forcing a man to give up his Constitutional rights) I say, and I am supported by distinguished legal opinion, that this would not be forcing him because no man is compelled to take office unless he wants to.

But be that as it may, the entire business is not only shameful but outrageously and brazenly dishonest. All of the rest of the everyday living methods of the common American citizen is not based on any such immunity idea. If a lay individual does something to be accounted for, most members of society ask him: "What about it?" "How do you explain this?" And it is natural and just that he should answer for his deeds, whether he incriminates himself or not.

The other legal hoax preventing Government investigations comes from a hazy law, used hundreds of years ago in the trials by combat and torment. And its proper place, to-day, is not among national or legal principles but among those of our corporations. And this legal hoax reads that no person "shall be twice put in jeopardy of his life for the same offense." But those who want to oppose Government investigation use this to keep what witnesses tell the Grand Jury from being admitted as evidence against them in any trial which may follow. But this is dishonest—a mere subterfuge—for even according to this legal jargon, a man isn't actually "in jeopardy" until he is actually put to trial. And when he is before a Grand Jury most certainly he is not on trial. None the less, this obviously dishonest loophole is now used in this way to free crooks who might be punished. And worse, not one American out of a thousand who would not permit, let alone sanction, this knows anything about it. It is too new a piece of legal legerdemain. Yet how often does a judge, veiled in the mystery of learning, rule out such evidence! And how many Government officials thus fix things for corporations!

Indeed, our corporations aided by "influenced" government, not only unscrupulously get out of predicaments by the misuse of these Constitutional rights, but in any labor issue and in order that they themselves may win at the workingman's expense, do flatly renounce them, thus doubly penalizing the little man for his littleness. Indeed, these denials of these privileges to labor come about through heartless wrong to the workers in the first instance. They are, at such times as the corporations choose, and regardless of past profits earned by the corporation at mainly their expense, forced to accept a 10 per cent, or 15 per cent or even 25 per cent wage cut in pay that permits as it is, for the worker, only the barest needs; or, for instance, as at the American Woolen Company in Lawrence, Massachusetts, a single worker who used to operate two combs must speed his body unduly so as to run nine combs. These conditions the wage-earner cannot meet, but against these outrages he is not supposed to do a thing. As proof, I offer the data for 1930 arrests: at strikes, 1,037; at unemployment demonstrations, 1,598; at open and shop-gate meetings, 644; for distributing leaflets, 962; miscellaneous, 1,598; a total of 5,935! And this in a country where strikes are lawful and where freedom of assembly, of the press, and presentation of grievances to the Government, are Constitutional sacraments!

But to show by facts that corporations are arbitrarily helped by the courts in labor disputes, I wish to cite that injunctions have been, and are still being, issued forbidding union leaders to ask laborers to join workers' organizations or ordering labor leaders to call no strikes, and worse, to pay for no necessities of life for the striking workman, and so aiding in breaking any strike. And not only that, but the courts have even issued injunctions to prevent legal proceedings in behalf of workers! But then, you may ask, are the courts in this country to be denied the underdog? Can he not be protected as to his guaranteed rights? The answer is no, he cannot! Meetings and parades in the present depressing state of unemployment are arbitrarily prevented, despite the freedom of assembly guaranteed by the Constitution. Again, the circulation of newspapers and pamphlets is forbidden, as though a free press were no longer a valuable or valued thing and one especially needed and craved by the workers, if not by the corporations. Any of our American judges to-day can, or at least does, decide to and then does issue these injunctions on affidavit that life or property require protection; or that peace requires to be maintained; also that the Sherman Anti-Trust Act (meant only for conspirators restraining trade by monopoly and not for labor) is being interfered with. In other words, our American Constitution is now a scrap of paper to the rich and powerful, but by no means such to the poor. For this is the day of the corporation judge and the corporation land. Our judges now not only establish what social regulations they see fit, under the argument of protection to property which would probably never be damaged (and so do in violation of the United States Constitution) but simultaneously they exercise partisan favor. For the workers in America are not even given a hearing before the judge, who previous to his decision and issuance of such preliminary and restraining order as are asked for by corporations and which usually hold for a long time before any hearings whatsoever, is supposed to be interested to know what they, the workers, have to say. But is he? Not he! And the little man takes his loss and goes his way. More, a reform injunction measure cannot even now be gotten through Congress. And if it could, our all powerful corporations, legally so well armed, would evade its purpose by some divergent and underground channel of the law. A capitalistic failure? Certainly. And what is to be done about it? That is yet to be seen.

Not only that, though, but our corporations and our Government likewise use any—even the most despicable—legal loopholes to smash any but an extremely reactionary political analysis, and this in violation of the fundamental rights relating to thought, assembly, address, publication, distribution, written into the Constitution. Thus, the National Espionage Act, passed during the World War for purposes of that war only and to suppress sedition supposedly, is now being invoked again, and for the first time in ten years. But for what? Thus far, to keep from the mails the following Communist newspaper publications: *Revolutionary Age, Young Worker, Young Pioneer, Vida Obrera* and *Labor Sports Monthly*. And this on the ground that violence was advocated in them. But there is one point connected with this legal interpretation of this advocacy of violence that I want to make very clear. Always in America, as well as in its mother country, England,—that even more conservative country from whence came the Common Law upon which America's entire legal structure is built—advocacy of a violence which is not a clear and present threat does *not* constitute sedition. Yet the most graphic proof that the present Government is waging a campaign against all political interpretation which is not reactionary—in other words, against Communists—is that even during the War, sedition under the Espionage Act had to be advocacy of a clear and immediate violence. Yet in none of the recent Communist publications has there been any specific incitement to violence. None the less in their case, certainly freedom of the press had disappeared like frost on a warmed pane. And this when for generations, the assassination of British kings—but not a specific king, like the present King George—could be advocated. Yet all that the Communist literature in this country is guilty of is the use of such words as "fight," "militant," "revolution" and "war," which in Webster's Dictionary, as well as in common use, have meanings like "a fight or war of any kind" and "revolution signifying a complete change." And these listed not only as *prior* meanings, but naturally connoting such in the mind of the reader.

But what mention is made, if any, of the advocacy by conservatives of violence against such enormous groups as Communists, labor leaders, strikers, and Negroes? Lynchings, turning machine guns on strikers, etc. No law is passed to prohibit that! Scarcely any attempt to minimize it, even. But to return to sedition—sedition being discontent with the government. As official interpretation—arbitrary or legal—runs now in America, the people, who are supposed merely to entrust or delegate their power to their elected officials, have now no longer the right to express discontent over phases of current statecraft or action. They are to take these interpretations and acts of their elected officials, whatsoever their nature, as legal, just and in the interest of all, or suffer the consequences. Yet sedition with no definite act committed, only words "tending to treason" (a vagueness which makes for poor law, and already is at variance with any reputable law relating to crimes) has become a criminal offense, subject to extremely long imprisonment. But unless interpreted in the traditional, definite way, i.e., as words containing a clear and immediate threat to the Government of the United States, our sedition law is nothing more than an illegal and arbitrary denial to a specific group, and at the behest of their enemies, of an inherent Constitutional right and, as such, subject to all the abuses that usually accompany such an arbitrary denial. And that is exactly what is occurring in America to-day.

Not only that, but our various State sedition laws meet with an even more hazy interpretation than does the Federal Espionage Act. In Woodlawn, Pennsylvania, for instance, where stands the Jones & Laughlin Steel Works, holding relations with 2,528 families of the 2,928 in the town, and paying its laborers but 40 to 50 cents an hour on the 12-hour system, three Communists who not only disavowed even belief in the overthrow of the Government, let alone a desire to bring it about, and who had never attempted in any way so to do, were sentenced to five years in the Allegheny County Workhouse because they had in their possession some Communistic literature—not guns and ammunition—and had tried to organize a Communistic group which had almost no followers. They had not attempted or argued military revolt or siege, but were alleged to have made certain utterances.

Laws similar to this Pennsylvania Sedition Act have been passed, since 1917, in 33 states. Get that! Then conceive of a statute like California's Criminal Syndicalism law—but no worse than the others—being used against the workers in this land where all men are by no means free or equal in or out of the sight of the law—and used to jail them for years. Thus, six men, together with others, were charged under this statute on three counts: first, membership in the Communist Party (political views, a crime, would you!); second, advocacy of violence by speech and printed matter; and third, conspiracy to advocate these matters—this last in substance the same as the first count and hence an unjust addition to the duration of the sentence. The State's evidence against them consisted of Communist literature found in their possession, plus statements alleged to have been made that mass picketing and violence, such as carrying "pop" bottles (not revolvers) and the tearing up of cantaloupe vines as well as railroad trains and bridges, would be resorted to in case of a strike. Yet all of these statements relative to the advocacy of violence, etc., were testified to only by stool-pigeons (spy detectives in the union) who admitted at the trial that they had urged the workers to fight with "pop" bottles and who when asked by the defense, "Did you or did you not say to...that you had to provoke these Communists and that you were fixing the testimony to get a conviction?"

hesitated until under furious objections by the prosecution, they answered "No." And although this embodies every important phase of their trial, none the less these six men are now serving sentences of from three to forty-two years—an undue variation in length of time or servitude which can keep these men locked up for a lifetime! And yet actually for no other reason than being Communists and having Communist literature in their possession.

Yet in America—or according to its Constitution at least— that is no crime, but rather an individual and guaranteed right. That it is now being so severely punished by an especial American exile system introduced into this land of ours is due to the growth and self-entrenchment and now would-be self-perpetuating money power, which for daring, cruelty and downright Neronic despotism is not to be rivaled anywhere. But now wanting to forfend itself against the rise of a rival and more equitable economic system in the East, it is prepared to indulge in such tactics as we have seen;—to battle and drive men who are no longer satisfied with its methods;—in short, to make a memory of the American equality idea and of America's Constitution a scrap of paper, which by now it really is.

CHAPTER XI

THE POSITION OF LABOR

THE very fact that labor has to organize against the savage financial pursuit of corporations who hire labor's large groups, points to the very core of capitalism's failure. The trouble all started about one hundred and fifty years ago, when England, swiftest to industrial development, began building factories employing great numbers of weavers, these employees being robbed simultaneously of freedom, fair competition, and profits. England's Chartist movement of the nineteenth century definitely showed Karl Marx that capitalism would eventually evolve to failure. His prediction, based on a most scholarly study of economics, has come true. The gulf between capital and labor grows wider. The labor groups have failed in almost every major way.

In the first place, the organization forced upon labor by capital is in itself now effete. The existing American Federation of Labor, with no educational or economic goal for the workers, amounts to just nothing at all. Only about 10 per cent of labor in America is organized, while in Germany the proportion is 75 per cent and in England 65 per cent. More, and worse, there is almost no independent organization in such fundamental industries as iron and steel, rubber, automobiles, oil, electrical manufacturing, etc. The labor groups lack power because of decentralization. On the other hand the German Federation of Labor has 5,000,000 members in 38 unions, while the American Federation of Labor scatters its 3,000,000 followers throughout 120 unions. The latter insists upon many, weak unions which make labor gains impossible. The Federation figures for 1930, with a total membership of only 2,961,096, probably are padded.

178

They list their United Mine Workers group as having 400,000 members in the United States and Canada, but the United States Bureau of Mines reports that while the United Mine Workers in 1920 had 467,172 members, 1929 (and this despite the 400,000 claimed) showed a total of only 156,978 bituminous and anthracite members in the United States and Canada.

The policy of the American Federation of Labor—and a most reprehensible one it is—is, in the event of a strike, to play the skilled unions off against the great mass of loyal unskilled workers, and to secure wage raises from the bosses for those few at the expense of the many. Under this really evil and obviously corporation-favoring leadership, the skilled are foolishly led to believe that they are far above and infinitely more intelligent than the unskilled and hence worthy of greater pay, and the unskilled worthy of nothing. More, the Federation, disregarding the tremendous differences between employers and laborers characteristic of all capitalistic countries, and in themselves the actual reason for the existence of labor unions, believes that capitalism is all right. Hence the fundamental maldirection of that organization, which instead of widening its activities so as ultimately to encompass and embrace all phases of labor's need, excludes workers by limiting membership and setting the union initiation fee at almost, for most, prohibitive figures; in some instances as high as $100 or $150. Thus, these highly skilled workers' unions leave thousands of laborers out in the cold. In fact, only five per cent of the textile workers of America are organized, and even less in the metal trades. And as for individual concerns and companies that defy the unions and remain unorganized, these are very many. Consider, for one, the Childs Restaurant Company with its 9,000 non-unionized workers, who recently had to accept a large wage cut—ten per cent, I believe.

More, the workers who should take the offensive in their struggles, and keep it (something they have never done) are so wretchedly and even crookedly directed by their present organization and its leaders as to seem not to know even the value of such initiative. They have been so often betrayed as to be afraid, and as for these wretched leaders of theirs, rather than hire a good labor lawyer—who would prepare, before a strike, injunction papers protecting the workers' civil liberties and warrants to be used against the police, who arrest and assail workers without warrant—the conservative trade unions, led by cabbage-heads, think that the injunction should not be used by labor. None the less, I think that labor should at least use it while it exists. But as yet the injunction remains capital's first resort against the worker. And almost always our striking laborers have been totally undirected legally, and so left to be herded off the streets and beaten up by corporation police.

Yet a good labor lawyer could certainly and easily instruct workers on how to arrest, see that papers were served and all cases prosecuted and given publicity. In these cases concerning civil liberties—free speech, assembly, etc.—if they were ever brought to court as they should be, it could be argued that during a strike, as well as at any other time, a man is entitled to all of them within the law. If the courts denied these Constitutional privileges, they would at least thus definitely and publicly ally themselves with capitalists. Labor should prosecute the Government police by enjoining the use of public money to protect private interests; and it should prosecute such as the "coal and iron police," hired by corporations, for being public officers under private pay. During a strike, any raid on workers' food supplies is absolutely illegal, and aggressiveness on the part of labor in the courts could put a stop to that. The right to hold meetings is also a Constitutional property right, of which the workers should take advantage. If permits for meetings were not given, a writ of mandamus could be brought in order to force the town or city officials to grant such permits, or the District Attorney could be solicited in order to impeach the offending town official. Our American workers, though, not properly or legally advised, permit their gatherings to be interfered with by a sheriff's proclamation prohibiting disorderly meetings, interpreted by the police to include every gathering, and this when a sheriff's proclamation is not the law. Picketing, likewise, should be properly carried on. In all these matters, a cracker-jack lawyer and publicity man for the workers should take the lead. Yet the American Federation of Labor has never taken the offensive in a law court by starting a case to restrain the corporations from depriving labor of its rights.

Instead, our reactionary American union leaders, leaving the general mass of workers helpless, cater to the corporations and their capitalists by endorsing their issues, such as the quondam income tax revision, unfavorable to the poor man but good for the rich one; also by honoring with membership such men as Mayor Hylan, Presidents Roosevelt, McKinley, Taft and Wilson, all of them outstanding individualists. (Taft, whom they so honored, did not even consider a strike lawful.) And by accepting political jobs so easily directed or controlled by Wall Street, and where knowingly or unknowingly they can be used for capital's programs, they are actually frustrating their own aims. E. E. Clark, of the Railroad Conductors, later of the Interstate Commerce Commission; W. B. Wilson, first of the Miners' Union and later Secretary of Labor; J. M. Lynch, first head of the Typographical Union and later the New York Commissioner of Labor, are illustrations of what I mean. In these higher political jobs, they do less, not more, for labor. In their outcome, if not their proved planning, these are all capitalistic devices for drawing the worker away from his class-conscious state, and more, converting him to the money side. One such device is that of selling stock in the corporation for which he works. Workers should never enter on capitalistic ventures, for capitalists, as you may be sure, either by selling non-voting stock or else limiting what each worker can buy, intend to and do keep control of all large ventures for themselves. They do not intend to improve the real condition of the workers by any such device. And in proof of this I offer that only one per cent of the total stock of all companies or corporations is at this time either owned or controlled by the worker, including managers and executives. One one-hundredth! And during times of depression this proportion decreases, as in the case of United States Steel in 1921, when the stock held by its employees decreased from forty-two to sixteen per cent. Yet to make workers believe themselves to be capitalists is not a bad thing as the bosses see it, and, actually and hypocritically, even the reactionary labor leaders think the same. As a matter of fact, it is only a way of making the workers more content with their unfortunate lot.

Thus, while the Brotherhod of Locomotive Engineers was neglecting any improvement for labor in general—and by that I mean those ignored and increasingly unskilled classes whom the unions never trouble to unionize—its President, W. B. Prenter, said: "It is the Brotherhood's aim in its financial enterprises to show its members and workers generally how they may become capitalists as well as workers." Imagine! And what a brainless economic analysis! The enterprises undertaken by the Locomotive Engineers (probably the most extensive of all labor union projects) consisted of $100,000,000 worth of investments in labor banks, in apartment house and office building real estate, coal mines, and an enormous tract of land in Florida, the value of which went with the failure of Florida. In sum, the management of these up to 1927 was so bungling and rash that $30,000,000 of the savings and contributions of locomotive engineers was lost; $12,000,000 in Florida, $1,350,000 on one apartment house, etc., etc. And to cover this, the 60,000 engineers of the Brotherhood were later taxed $5 a month besides the regular dues and insurance, which frequently came to $35 monthly!

But labor union management in America has developed, and still develops, endless corrupton. Any one familiar with the history of American labor will recall "Umbrella Mike" Boyle, of the Electrical Workers in Chicago, who used to receive graft by hooking his umbrella on the bar in saloons, for builders to drop their money in as they drank beer. In trial it was learned that Boyle had accepted a bribe of $20,000 from the Chicago Telephone Company to prevent strikes. And one Brindell, President of the Dock Builders, not only accepted a $5,000 bribe, for which he was convicted but, like many other labor leaders, bled his union by a $35,000 yearly salary. A grand success, he, in doing something for the $3 a day man! Then also, Brindell, President of the Building Trades Council and the Dock Builders' Union, carried out an agreement to work for the Building Trades Employers' Association if they would shut out everybody else and employ only Brindell men. His graft was $42,000 from Todd Iron and Robertson, $25,000 from A. Hershkovitz, $17,120 from the G. A. Northern Wrecking Company, $25,000 from the Gotham National Bank Building, etc. Hugh F. Robertson paid Brindell $32,000 to prevent strikes during the erection of the Cunard building and docks, according to testimony before the New York State Lockwood Committee to investigate housing costs in 1920. Finally Brindell was sent to the penitentiary for extortion. And A. E. Barker, Grand President of a railroad union, spent $220,000 entirely unauthorized by the workers. The most recent case concerned the New York Clothing Cutters Union, Local 4, on which Supreme Court Justice Untermyer declared that allegations that $47,863 of the local's unemployment fund disappeared were not denied.

These conservative and typically American labor unions are scarcely superior to the present-day corporation or company union, itself an insult to the already thoroughly injured American workers. The company union is a travesty and a joke on the rights and needs of labor. I charge the American Federation of Labor with being so uninfluential, so small and so in sympathy with the employers' greedy interests, as to permit its followers to become so demoralized as to stand for these company unions. More, I believe that, consciously or unconsciously, the American Federation of Labor, by its flimsy policy of co-operating with the employers (which always works out in practice that the workers get little or less) is rapidly destroying the independent labor movement in America.

In their manual to train-workers, the American Cast Iron Pipe Company, of Birmingham, Alabama, with its idea of coöperating with the worker and letting him help run the business said: "The Golden Rule and the teachings of Jesus Christ are to be made the controlling principles of business." But recall that in wage matters, etc., these doctrines are waived by the corporation managers, who actually run the business for themselves. They consider their own intelligence as far above a simple maxim like the Golden Rule. These company unions grant a thousand futile favors, while any genuinely beneficial thing, like high wages, is tactfully evaded by the appointment of committees which gradually squelch the issue. In the last analysis, of course, the company alone has knowledge of the firm's real financial status, and concerning this status any deluding and false explanation suffices so long as labor's just demands are quelled. Lawyers, accountants and statisticians are employed by the companies, and these in turn fix everything for the firm, which seems to make huge gains from the laborers' work despite high salaries to these serviceable lawyers, etc. But the laborers in the company union do not even have the independence of a treasury, let alone any national or international connection for aid or publicity, so what chance has a strike?

And company unions have regularly recently been organized in the strongest industries: the Rockefeller interests and their like; steel, textile, railroads, electrical, packing, lumber and other industries. And, of course, such great corporations as Bethlehem Steel, Pennsylvania Railroad, Westinghouse, International Harvester, Pacific Textile Mills, Western Union, etc., take the bull by the horns and organize their men as they please. There are 814 such company unions, all unfavorable to the true interests of labor.

Or else corporations employ strike-breakers of the following character: The Standard Oil of New York and the American Can in 1929 employed Peter De Vito, of Queens, to break strikes. He received $250,000 from Standard Oil, it is understood, says the New York *Times*. In the Standard strike there occurred shootings and stabbings. De Vito stood in with police. The workers lost.

For as in Russia before the revolution, the employers, for their own personal gain and even ruthless greed, not only wish to but do hold the worker to a mean state of existence. They want him to be ignorant of anything which might better his state. They pay such low wages that sixty-three per cent of Connecticut working children leave school at the age of fourteen to help support the family. (In other words, America's halcyon universal education!) And only two-thirds of the States (whose legislatures are usually corporation-stacked) require children to go through the sixth grade before leaving school at the age of fourteen. The rest don't even ask that little. Then, too, in the Southern mill villages, the corporation, which hires the teacher and the preacher, says just what education and thought for laborers should be. Yet by what right other than that of greedy power is the learning and beauty of the world kept from these thousands of unfortunates?

In North Carolina, where one-fourth of the 119 schools for village children are owned and run by mills, only one-fifth of the pupils go beyond the fifth grade and another one-fifth are illiterate. It is obvious that efforts to improve upon a situation like this might and probably would be met with opposition by the employers. And the preachers (their training constitutes practically the only ideas open to these people) naturally penetrate to the very heart and bone of these people, as is evident from such remarks as these to social workers: "We mustn't concern ourselves with earthly things; it's all in God's hands." "A labor union may be a good thing, but my mind is all on the world to come." Or: "Seems like us mill hands jes' work harder and gits poorer, but then as our parson says, 'the Lord chasteneth those He loveth.'" Do you wonder that the representatives of banks and corporations give liberally to all religions, regardless?

And may I say here that there can be no worthy society without some understanding that is based on knowledge of the facts that govern exchange of all kinds? An appreciation of the fact that organized society means doing something for the person who does something for you; in other words, a reasonable return to all for labor performed and an alertness looking to this balance being kept. Yet any such full conception as this the laborer is not allowed to have. Otherwise, why would one of them, when asked by a union organizer if he wouldn't like an eight-hour day, reply: "No, I can't make ends meet workin' ten." And the General Silk Corporation, for example, has any number of small plants in six different States in which they keep the worker ignorant so that he won't know their power and wealth and hence demand wage increases. Yet despite this sly way of deceiving the laborer and robbing him of his due, our capitalism of to-day is not free of trouble nor sure of success. In the South, therefore, as well as in the carefully scattered mills of Pennsylvania, but all this entirely apart from any effort on the part of the American Federation of Labor, these devices are meeting the same opposition as arose and broke in Paterson, New Jersey, a few years ago. So that this attempt to evade the issue is merely delayed for a short period.

But with low wages in the South, due to the spirit of greed among employers, and the inefficiency and worse indifference and even corruption of most of our American labor leaders, the youngsters have nothing to look forward to but the ignorance of mill life, from which they cannot escape no matter how much they long to do so. One girl, with her heart set on becoming a "swell stenographer," ended in the city as a five-and-ten-cent store clerk. A mill lad saved for fourteen years from his $8 weekly wages to take a $90 correspondence course, but could never make it. A social worker who has interviewed hundreds of these workers, said: "Three-quarters of these silk workers are dissatisfied." For naturally, children of the workingman should have a decent technical school system, with the necessary cultural and hence ideological phases thereto appertaining. They should not be deliberately kept dumb. And for that reason I prefer the Russian system—which, and regardless of a heavy percentage of failure, does all that it can to strengthen the weak, stir desire for betterment and so change, in them— to the dull routine of our American schools. Think of the thousands of future grade school-teachers in our normal schools all over the country, as well as and even our college professors, studying during but one summer in Columbia University perhaps, and learning word for word, and not with their minds at all, just what to tell students, and do so tell them—the same old antiquated jargon year after year. In Russia at least they teach by questions. For instance, cotton—"what is this?" Each pupil answers differently. "It's a string." "It's cotton." "It's thread rolled together." Then the teacher discusses its practical as well as physical, chemical and esthetic qualities; that is, how it looks to the eye, how it comes to be, the work done on it by man, how it is raised and manufactured into thread. For so comes interest. And under this system school-teachers have to be more than mere numskulls. They must have a wider, more practical, scientific, and æsthetic conception than most American teachers have or are allowed to have.

Not only that but I insist that child labor, if not a main cause, is at least a strong contributing cause of the ignorance among our working people. But though Congress some years ago stopped (or at least supposedly did so) by law all child labor, there is still no national law actually prohibiting child labor to-day. For our Supreme Court has said that the law is unconstitutional. Hence, the general estimate of the real meaning of our Supreme Court, which is that it is here to prevent Congress from seriously bothering capital! The actual facts are that these American poor children to-day, as well as all other employees, slave for long hours. Southern States allow 10- or 10½-hour working days. (The bosses have time for golf, motoring, bathing, dressing, dining and reading any or every business day.) The textile mills, automobile factories and others drive their men during "prosperity" to twelve and thirteen hours of work per day. And this only to be thrown out of a job the next year during depression! But is this overtime legal? What's the difference to the employers? They get away with it! And so often these workers do not receive overtime payment. In agriculture—lettuce and melons in California, cotton in the South, and grain and fruit in the North—if the boss says a 14-hour day, a 14-hour day it is! But the equitable thing would be two shifts of seven hours each, or at least time and half-time for all hours over seven hours' work in one day, and a nine-hour deadline for all.

In connection with this matter of long hours, I note also that women and children in many of our States work all night. State laws are no barrier. Twenty-one violations of child night-work in Connecticut factories! In New Jersey, where law prohibits night shifts for women, they work them nights regardless. In the South also, thousands of women and children work constantly day and night for practically nothing, while in the North scores of employment agencies are herding families out the door because nothing can be found for them to do. And these conditions make a mountain of opposition on the part of labor which capital does anything and everything to resist. But, and although, the issue to-day is sharp and raw, there appear to be almost no leaders sufficiently informed, courageous, and powerful to direct labor. But just a moment. . . .

Factories burn electric lights and have their machinery running day and night. But what does it mean? Overproduction! Then American manufacturers have to look to foreign markets, and when there aren't any! In silk, for instance, the whole of Europe was generations ahead of America in this now competitive foreign market. Oriental mills send silk all over the world. And then, too, overproduction in automobiles! In the spring of 1927, Dodge worked its men 13 and 14 hours a day; Hudson 12, Briggs Body 10 to 14. So many cars were built up to 1929 that the world market was glutted with a huge surplus. So true was this that dealers could have sold stones just as easily. Not only that, but the machinery installed to make these automobiles, as well as other things for the steel and textile industries, has a much greater capacity than the real need of the country under normal conditions warrants. Hence, if foreign markets are wanting, a consequent depression is sure. Despite this, however, witness the scores of factories now undergoing an almost complete remechanization. Our capitalists, thinking only of private and underhand gain—how much

cheaper they can produce with better machinery and less labor—
only aggravate the ills already put on America by planning a
laborless and so more destructive competition. Yet to relieve overproduction a really new system is needed in this country. Not
Communism or Socialism, necessarily, but something similar and
suited to the American temperament and certainly not with the
money lords directly or indirectly reaping the profits. The present conditions are not inevitable or necessary, as capitalists
would have the worker believe.

As it is now, though, overproduction comes about and finally
causes lay-offs, and this means the wolf at the worker's door
while the employer, glad of the opportunity to save money by
wage-cuts, plans to invest all of the profits which he made during
the speculation concurrent with prosperity, in stocks which
have fallen to the bottom but are certain to rise in two or
three years to two or three times their "depression" value. And
he can wait, the while the laborer starves. Right now—August
1, 1931—three per cent of the entire population of the New
York suburbs is out of work; three per cent are unemployed in
certain States like Michigan and California; and six per cent of
the entire population of Georgia, Alabama and Oklahoma is jobless! And the Industrial Aid Society of America states that one-
half of the job-seekers have families with an average of three
children! Then the 1930 survey of families seeking employment in New York City shows an average income per person of
$10 a week—an impossible level for the metropolitan prices. Yet
in April, 1931, it dropped to $5 a week and the week of May
4th to $4. Applicants for jobs had been out of work an average
of 16 weeks.

The treatment of capitalistic overproduction here proposed
would make unemployment negligible, because when there were
two persons for one job, the work would be divided into two
jobs, and the increased facilities for labor to meet its needs
would be devised. Also, as I see it, a system of Federal employment exchanges would help, because they would furnish labor
to local branches everywhere. In addition, an unemployment in-

surance law is necessary. But the American Government does not want that, despite the fact that most of the European nations have it. The corporations, however, seeing the agitation in this direction, are taking the initiative by drawing up insurance plans before the Government does it, making them lenient for themselves and providing that Congress need pass no law enforcing this on all corporations because it is already being widely observed. And the American Federation of Labor is helping the corporations save money on this. The General Electric Company already insures its employees against unemployment. But how? It is based, so it says, on contributions by employer and employee. But in time of emergency (the only time money is needed), the fund is maintained by employees only, not the company, and by those who are earning fifty per cent and over of their average full-time pay; maximum help to unemployed, $20 a week. But it says nothing as to what the employer gives in time of need. For as this plan works now, the corporations will have unemployment insurance and yet be out scarcely a nickel for it, the laborers paying the whole bill for their hard luck. And will they pay? They certainly will, unless all kinds of demonstrations by workers are made against this abuse, and in fact, against these depressions so regularly and cleverly repeated. For they are repeated, and that consciously and shrewdly, I am sure, and so many times as to be not only an established principle of modern capitalism and finance but an established fact, one of the new and shrewd and terrible menaces of capitalism. Yet capitalism is not the only system of civilization, as any one can now see, and one day may be regarded as being as primitive as feudalism.

The position of labor to-day is such, though, that in view of the encroaching power of the machine to displace it, and the increasing power of the owner of the machine—the capitalist —to misuse, ignore and even defy and defeat the employed as well as the unemployed, it becomes imperative for those who are interested in seeing a land not made up of lords and slaves to look sharply to the means at present available to protect themselves. And in connection with that thought, it is my opinion that labor itself, through its committees, contact and publicity men—and when I say labor I am not thinking of such a recreant and uninspired body as that now labeling itself the American Federation of Labor—should be not only contentious about unemployment due to depression but also combative toward permanent unemployment caused by improved machinery. For as it actually stands now, automobile plants are using a machine for pressed steel frames which makes six frames a minute, and thus one man performs the work of 175 men. And where before a laborer used to grind 21 cylinders a day, now with cleverly devised machines, one man does 170. More, the belt carrying automobile frames on which each worker puts a wheel or mud-guard or some such piece, now travels 13 feet a minute whereas formerly it moved but 3 feet. The new cigarette machine now makes 160,000 cigarettes a day, while the old method produced only 2,200. Too, in steel mills with the mechanical puddler, 150 men turn out 500 tons more iron in a given time than 400 men could formerly. In other words, the worker, like the machine, is being speeded. But not for his particular benefit. For when he is worn out physically or reduced in capacity, he is through. A younger and speedier man takes his place. But can he coldly be asked to die or starve or, like the worn-out machine, be thrown on the scrap-heap to rust away, while the owners of the corporations running the machines flourish in ease? I know that he can be, but should he be asked or forced so to be?

In other industries, especially in shipping, the introduction of oil-burning engines is crowding men out almost altogether. The Cunard Line alone now uses 240 less men, and the Scandinavian-American Line has developed a new Diesel oil-burning engine which requires only one man. But what of the laborers thrown out of work? Must they starve, or will we have birth control? And on an all-electric ship now, the captain, using the automatic steering gear and gyroscopic compass which steers better than a man, handles the whole ship from a switchboard and does not need engineers even to start the Diesel motors. Again, in the matter of ship repairing, rust is now chipped off with automatic hammers, and a whole ship is gun-sprayed with paint in twenty-four hours. Longshoremen carrying loads to boats are almost part of early American folk-lore, for now conveyors are so successfully used for loading and unloading that many ships with huge cargoes are loaded and discharged entirely by machine. Not only that, but hundreds of thousands of men have already been thrown out of skilled jobs on railroads, in newspaper telegraph offices, and in cigarette factories. With the new typesetting machines, for instance, one person can automatically set type in a great number of places at once, whereas previously and in each instance, a man was needed. In other words, this is what happens when the corporations are out to make money for themselves rather than for the workers. But has it added anything to the peace or happiness of the masses, given them even a trifle of health, security, leisure in their old age? Need one call to witness the present situation throughout the world as well as here in America?

It should be added here, though, that the country presently will get, no doubt, from the radio and electric business—something of a labor stimulation comparable to the activity which followed the sudden rise in automobile manufacture from 425 cars in 1901 to 4,000,000 a year to-day. For radio and electricity and the aëroplane are still in their infancy.

On the other hand, and as it is at present, with this speed-up and these improved machines, injuries double and triple. Among coal miners, the death rate from 1927 to 1928 increased five per cent. And in the automobile industry, 2 deaths, 40 permanent disabilities and 270 temporary disabilities occur for every 10,000 workers. Every few days men on oil tankers on the Great Lakes or in New York harbor are killed because of explosions due to careless methods. I could name case after case that is never printed. Only laborers killed! But if it had been Calvin Coolidge! Then in New York, during the year ending June 20, 1928, the construction industry was the source of 370 demolition and 740 excavation accidents. And there are practically no demolition laws in any of the States. Altogether in the United States, accidental deaths in industry total 30,000 a year, and the National Safety Council places non-fatal industrial injuries at 3,000,000. But laws to cover this? Well, they are scanty, haphazard and incomplete. Reform? Oh, surely, but scanty, haphazard and incomplete reform is all that is ever gained. Five States of the South furnish women no compensation for injury. And in reading over the statutes of the year in each State on this question, the only action I see is to increase the salary of safety inspectors.

Yet there is an organization which could have, and by now should have, done much to obviate or aid in all of these matters. I refer to the American Federation of Labor, the supposed leader, guide and defender of labor. But has it been all this? As I look around to-day, it seems to me the most inefficient of all labor leadership, the kind of numskull or parasitic, or even frankly feeble, direction that, as in the capitalistic world itself, has looked more to the prosperity and notoriety of its leaders than to the development and welfare of the men led. I call your attention to the leadership of the United Mine Workers of America—a subsidiary of the American Federation of Labor—which in West Virginia in 1921 had a paid up membership of nearly 50,000, almost half of the miners of the State. In the winter of 1920-21 and the summer of 1921, the great West Virginia strike was lost through not having McDowell and Mercer Counties support Mingo County. (No training in class fight, and hence need of wide mass fight.) In the national strike of 1922, the bituminous miners of the United Mine Workers wanted, instead of reduced wage scales, the old wage, shorter hours and other concessions. The United Mine Workers sent miners in Kentucky and Tennessee back to work under the old wage before strikers in other sections had won this, thus breaking their mass strength. And when 100,000 unorganized miners in Somerset and Connellsville Counties in Pennsylvania went out on strike, the United Mine Workers, instead of helping these men, made agreements for their union miners to go back to work and sent them back long before struggling and more or less loosely organized strikers returned to work, mostly under "yellow dog" contracts.

I mention the increasing weakness of the United Mine Workers, which could not hold their employers to the wage contract of 1924, a three-year agreement. During the very next year, wage-cutting by the great corporations began, and in 1925 alone, 110 mines in Pennsylvania and 50 in West Virginia broke with the union. The great strike of 1927 was lost by divided support as directed by the union. And in 1928, the United Mine Workers of the American Federation of Labor ordered local settlements at reduced wages instead of interstate settlement at the old wage for which the miners had been fighting. This succession of failures reduced the number of union bituminous miners from 386,000 in 1920 to a mere 80,000 in 1929.

Again, the American Federation of Labor has neither an economic nor an educational nor yet a political program looking to the uplift of its followers. It talks much of this and that reform, but refuses to enter politics. But why? And it has no classes or schools looking to the economic and social enlightenment of its members. But why? Always there is talk, but of a *gentle* reform. Always it must conform to the capitalistic method: "Nothing hasty, nothing unproven," which has little meaning except to keep the masses down. I assert, and without fear of contradiction, that the American Federation of Labor has not even lived up to its own wishy-washy policy of leadership, for if it had, it certainly could have driven in at least a few of the political and economic spikes that from time to time have been prepared by those who have labor's true interests at heart. But, no! The actual facts are that to-day our American workers are really more insecure than similar groups in any other highly developed country.

But I insist that this American Federation of Labor should be disestablished—the leadership of American workers taken over by others. Has it, I wish to ask here, encouraged or brought

about a national social insurance law? It has not! Yet a law of
this nature went into effect in France on July 1, 1930. And it
applies to men and women in industry, commerce, and even
in farming and domestic service. But nothing like that exists
here, where only a small percentage in industry and commerce are insured, and none in agriculture and domestic
service. Again, this French law insures the worker with a
modest wage against old age, sickness, and premature inca-
pacity. Also it includes compensation during maternity periods
and free medical services to all. This insurance is also kept up
by the worker (unless he is involuntarily unemployed) but also
with the joint aid of the employer and the State. And Belgium
has an old-age pension for all wage-earners, contributed to by
employee, employer and State. As yet there is no national law in
this country to cover the situation. On the contrary, it appears to
be much too advanced for most of our great industrial American
States. They consider it Socialistic, Communistic, "Red," and
almost anarchistic! And again, although England has had unemployment insurance ever since the Act of 1920, the idea is
"radical" in this country. In Germany children cannot be employed in mines, factories or workshops, although our children
are duly enslaved and by a legal figment—the fate of the Child
Labor Law! But European insurance debases living standards.

Since these things, supposedly, constitute the aims of the
American Federation of Labor, I see no unfairness in charging
them with failure. Most of all I can charge them with the failure of active and due protest or encouragement. Their flabby,
half-hearted leadership has not only destroyed all possibility
of their doing anything really constructive but is also rendering
them effete. Not that they aren't loud enough, but that they
work with no force.

Yet while the American Federation of Labor leaders smoke
cigars without a care in the world, or one leech extends to
another laudation and encomiums on their grand program of
"Do nothing!", the developing machine age speeds, reduces and
discards men, the while the particular machines which constitute

its man- or machine-power injure thousands upon thousands, as do a hundred other pagan and merciless conditions under which men work. Breathing asbestos dust causes disease—pulmonary fibrosis, recognized by yellow foreign bodies in the sputum and lungs. Use of the pneumatic drill and sandpapering in automobile factories causes tuberculosis, because of inhaled dust. And the Metropolitan Life Insurance Company, I notice, says that death from tuberculosis is eighteen per cent greater among industrial workers in youth and three and one-half times greater in old age as contrasted with other occupations. Well, reckon this in the light of millions of people in industry! And our scientists have listed 600 such hazards from present industrial methods. But do any of our 48 American legislatures know this or act on it? Or the American Federation of Labor? Or if it does, has it done anything in particular? It does not even know the nature of many of these diseases. Lead, which in some cases acutely poisons workers until they die from insanity, and which affects 150 occupations, should be abolished. But has it been? It has not! And benzol, a coal tar product, causes many deaths, as does radium for watch dials, killing by slow torture those who work with it. Yet are they illegal? They are not! Then, too, there is a disease, pellagra, caused by undernourishment, from which thousands suffer. A worker may count on merely natural illness nine days out of every year, since this is the average. But is he properly safeguarded against this by insurance or capable medical attendance? You know he is not, not in America to-day! In fact, 3,000,000 are sick more than thirty days, and a quarter of a million more than six months each year. The achieved betterment of health so loudly extolled by capital's puppets—the charity, religious and other organizations and societies always busy smoothing the public's fur—means practically nothing. Salaries to the all too practical charity workers and inspectors, (but that is about all!) the while the industries that should carry sickness insurance for their workers and be made to hire doctors who would render free service, do not. If you doubt this, undertake an extensive examination of labor, and see!

But with all these abuses and chances which workmen take in the matter of overtime, speeding, unemployment, accidental injury, or danger to health, insecurity as to work, how much does labor make? To cite a few examples: men in airplane plants average $32 a week and women $17. In Portland Cement, men $31 and women $20; in machine shops and foundries, men $31 and women $20. And those are "prosperity" wages. They are, in the main, for the few, those who are especially skilled and work rapidly and well. As for the others, who in many cases do the heaviest work, they receive from ten per cent to forty per cent less. Common labor, by far the greatest in numbers, receives, as a whole, from $18 to $25 a week, and this not always, allowing for the cycle of employment and non-employment. Yet what kind of a family can a man support on $20 a week, or a woman, when forced to, on $10, $15 or $18? Yet one sees the same thing in every business or line of work to-day—women taking on the work of men at half or three-quarters of the pay, while the men walk the streets looking for jobs. The silk mills which dot Pennsylvania and New Jersey are put in those towns for the specific purpose, according to the capitalists, of taking as workers the wives of foundrymen and miners already there. So you see, manufacturers scheme together and prearrange matters in order to double their profits. They are not missing many bets! The only organization of any power that could do something is the American Federation of Labor, and it misses nearly all! One of its greatest campaigns, one would think, would be equal pay for equal work. But is there such a campaign on its part? Investigate and see!

Then, too, one would think it would demand higher pay for every laborer to-day—an obvious need and sound practice in the light of present-day exorbitant prices and profits. But is there any such demand for any save the most skilled? In the Associated Dyeing & Printing Corporation, although profits have doubled within the last four years, the workers still receive the same pay of 25 cents an hour (data more than a year old). Du Pont, in which an investment six years ago brought over one thousand per cent profit to the capitalist, has a surplus which would double the wages of 50,000 workers (data more than a year old). The Tubize Silk Company, which publishes a record showing eight times as much assets as liabilities, pays an average annual wage of $617. But how ridiculous such a commentary on American prosperity, let alone its freedom and self-government! The sad fact is that labor's share in every large industry—iron, steel, textiles, oil, clothing manufacture, etc.—has decreased. No higher wages for those who really deserve them! Instead has come a really furious war for lower wages in every line.

In substantiation of all this, let me point to the alien who is now bootlegged into this country by the thousands by corporations, since he will work for less pay than the native Americans who cannot and will not accept the pittance handed these aliens. The latest case is the arrest of 19 persons who smuggled 8,000 aliens, according to Federal authorities, from Canada and Mexico at $100 to $5,000 a head. A month before 11 steamship agents and government officials were arrested as a ring, charged with illegally smuggling in 100,000 aliens in the last ten years. Yet later, should any of these aliens complain or strike, there is another advantage. They can be promptly put in jail for evading the immigration laws and deported. But not so the trusts that want them in, nor can they be fined! For the courts are theirs! So by the thousands they come across the Mexican border, with families and their possessions in the old flivver! And our railroad and farm labor contractors fix it with our authorities. Thousands of Filipinos, Italians, Syrians and Poles crowd in through corporation tactics. Most of these, like the 35,000 Filipinos in California, go to work for about $65 a month. The result is a wage war between races, like the Mexicans and the Filipinos. By the time they have sliced off half their wages by underbidding each other, though, what wage does the white laborer receive, on the great California truck farms, say?

Yet workers do exist on these low wages. But how? At the Tubize Silk Company, for instance, girls live with mind-breaking and dull regularity: they must eat at the company cafeteria, register in and out of the company dormitories, where no male guests are allowed and where morals are most meticulously guarded; and must clean their rooms and make their beds before work. Not only that, but entertainment consists of such inane and useless diversions as the company offers: "Our Girls' Corner," for instance, or company baseball games. In the South, the mills, by hiring their own preachers, sheriffs and school-teachers, run the towns, disenfranchise the people, because there the corporations do not even make these communities into villages but keep them as mere collections of humans without political status of any kind. Thus they take away the right of the people to vote on all local matters of street improvement, parks, bridges, health, etc.... In fact, mill-hands aren't supposed to have money for or need these things! And in consequence, of course, the mill towns there are an outrage. Also mining company-owned towns! Recently the United States Coal Commission found that of 713 mining towns examined, only 2 had a decent water and sewerage system. Yet has the American Federation of Labor ever led a powerful, nation-wide attack on the company town?

In a "prosperity" survey of Ford workers (supposedly the most handsomely and deferentially treated workers in the world, and whose minimum wage is $7 a day or at least was) each laborer pays about $30 a month rent—a sum which fails to command any reasonably worth-while house in Detroit, as I know—and about $1.50 a day for food for four persons. Yet 12 cents a meal is not enough! Not only this, but more than half of Ford's families do not even have a central heating system in their homes. Reports everywhere show men making only half as much as social workers say it takes to live only decently.

Yet these wages, as any one can see, create paupers and men forced to resort to charity. Yet how nobly our capitalists "do good" by giving to charity! And as if labor should be compelled to accept it! Yet one Boston débutante may spend $125,000 on her coming-out party the while thousands of laborers, having slaved for almost no pay, agonize over the belittlement of having, as the churches put it, to ask for "something for nothing"! Yet didn't this Boston débutante receive thousands of times as much for nothing as the laborer will ever get from charity? And is that right? Yes, as this brainy world of ours sees it to-day, it is! And so, it comes about that Paterson, New Jersey, a city of 130,000 and many, many mills, has on the books of its local charity associations 8,000 needy families—not individuals, but families, mind you!—and this more or less permanent record cannot be, in the main, due to general unemployment because of the present depression. Yet with labor in this distress, and actually becoming no better off these many years, the American Federation of Labor, the grand publicity agent of labor, actually unites with the capitalists to undermine its followers and strengthen capital.

For if the National Civic Federation, organized in 1900, and which two years later came under the leadership of the notorious Mark Hanna (and of which Morgan, du Pont, Willard, Guggenheim, Dodge, Speyer and others of the past and present are or before their deaths were members, and of which Samuel Gompers was first Vice President) and the purpose of which was to combine the labor leaders of its day under the direction of the employers, was not a combination of capital and labor, what could be? The National Civic Federation arranges for meetings of leaders in strikes, and so possibly influences wages. Thus, it dictates the economic policy, and this economic trend for many years now shows that this policy is not to the benefit of labor. For one of the Federation's first moves was to carry on a campaign against the Socialism of that day; later it made an investigation of Government ownership, and its reports of this investigation so juggled and obscured the facts as to give the impression that the Government was constantly enlarging its management of business. More, it denounced the failure of the Government in its operation of telephone and telegraph systems; and pointed out the "inefficiency" of Government control of railroads. But what other interpretation could be expected from an organization whose prominent members included Frederick P. Fish, President of the American Telephone & Telegraph Company from 1901 to 1907; Lucius Tuttle, former President of the Boston & Maine Railroad; and Frederick D. Underwood, former President of the Erie Railroad?

Besides, is not the present American Federation of Labor Vice President, Matthew Woll, now acting President of the National Civic Federation? And fighting against unemployment insurance, recognition of the Soviet Union (the only economic system which as yet has sought, and wisely, I think, to establish society at large on its proper economic, social, political and educational basis), etc., etc.?

And can you not understand then why it is that I insist that without a fundamental change in our Government, the rights and needs and just desires of the laborer can never be met? For how can any good come of the present situation: the employer or corporation absorbing nearly all of the profits and deliberately degrading labor in order to do it? For as it is now, the living wage of the average laborer—not the Brotherhood of Railroad Engineers, for instance, or the masons, plasterers, and this and that other union, but the rank and file of workers in general— is so scanty as to be under the minimum necessary for decent existence. Nor can this situation—because of the power of those in the upper ranks—now be bettered one iota without a fundamental change. For the bosses are already too powerful and appear not to be willing to compromise. And as I have said before, they *are* the Government, and hence can say what the nature of that government is to be. Yet such a fundamental change as is here contemplated would not do away with any of the good features of capitalism (organization, constructive direction, efficiency, etc.), but on the other hand would add immeasurably to the strength and peace of the masses, from whom much good has already come and will come in the future.

CHAPTER XII

THE GROWTH OF THE POLICE POWER

In this connection I recall a remark made to me in 1907 by a Wall Street lawyer, who said that corporations must devise ways of increasing the police power in America for corporate benefits as opposed to labor interests. Upon investigation I find that this increase has been effected, and in those subtle ways by which capital usually works.

The growth has been along three lines: one, the private detective system; two, the State Police; and three, the commissioning by the Government of police hired and directed by the corporations.

Pinkerton was the first detective who realized and took advantage of the scope in industry for the spy. His detectives first started industrial espionage on the old Knights of Labor. And since his day hundreds of these detective agencies have come into existence—a development which should indicate to the layman the growth of this movement or idea. The legal and legislative paths for these same have been blazed somehow—fields always under capitalist control. Private detectives and their agencies are licensed by State law or by a court or some other official government source. This, of course, has been made possible through politicians and their methods. And a law licensing detectives in Wisconsin was recently declared constitutional. All of this has a political footing.

The purpose of private detectives is, of course, secretly to observe and obtain evidence for criminal or civil proceedings. The facts show that all too often what they do is to *create* evidence in an underhanded and illegal way. And since they operate secretly, their conduct *in toto* is by no means on the table. Coach, an industrial detective of Cleveland, said that there is more money for detectives in industry than there ever was in crime. These detectives, operating in the guise of employees or union members, obtain information for the employers and definitely influence the workers' policy in the union; they have been discovered in New England, New York, New Jersey, Pennsylvania, Ohio, Illinois, Colorado, Minnesota and California. Of course, only a slight percentage of the total number is ever caught.

Pinkerton's early hunch has been of such benefit to capital against labor that now the Pinkerton National Detective Agency has 35 offices; the William J. Burns Agency 35 offices, and there exist also many other such huge concerns. Bergoff Brothers & Wadell in New York City boast that they can raise 10,000 strike-breakers in seventy-two hours (an accomplishment of merit and distinction!); the great Corporations' Auxiliary Company and the Baldwin Felts supply machine guns to fight labor unions. If you think that machine guns are not a common corporation adjunct against labor, study any of the big industrial strikes. In the present miners' strike in the central eastern section of the country, machine guns are playing a prominent part. The Thiel Detective Service is said to be the worst offender in this direction, although the Sherman Service, Inc., also publicizes on industrial harmony. In addition, there are: The Gorton National Agency, Dun's National Detective Agency, Schindler, Inc., International Auxiliary Company, Industrial Service Company, and the Foster Service Company of New York City, which guarantees to control the unions. All are most serviceable in labor matters.

These industrial spies have infested the railroad, steel, textile, and probably many other industries. The corporations themselves, having a secret service department to arrange for these things, actually make a business of it. The railroads, U. S. Steel, Western Union, etc., function in this manner. The employers, through their National Erectors' Association, their National Manufacturers' Association, their National Founders' Association, etc., manage industrial detection. And industrial detection means just what? Detectives work by a variety of means. Thus, these agencies or their men frequently agitate disorder for which others are arrested. In short, they do anything to reduce labor's opportunities, to put labor in disrepute and weaken its force. Coach, the industrial detective of Cleveland, said that he owned every labor union in his town. This probably meant through their officials, who so often betray them. And detectives have been discovered as union officers, even. In order to carry out his policy, Coach even bought *The Columbus Labor News* and edited it.

The writings of Charles A. Siringo, for twenty-two years a Pinkerton detective, give an idea of the lengths to which these men will go in their corporation activities. He states that the Pinkerton Agency helped "fix" the jury in a trial of the Colorado Fuel & Iron Company. Also that the corporation owned the sheriffs and court officials of southern Colorado. (Rockefeller rules quite as powerfully there as elsewhere.)

The State Police is yet another enormous system which has been evoked to no negligible extent to exploit labor. One may see its effects in western Pennsylvania, where, and so recently, and although paid by the State to keep order as between corporation and striking employees, it has actually functioned as a corporation tool, the attitude of the individual State policeman toward the striking employee being that of a soldier to an enemy. I personally saw this with my own eyes. The purpose of the State policeman appeared to be to insult, threaten and otherwise irritate the striking and often starving miner in order that he might be able to arrest, injure, and in some cases even kill him.

And for that reason I have always advocated the abolishment of all forms of State police. They do not or are not permitted to function fairly or wisely. In fact, the American Federation of Labor and the Communist Party roundly oppose them. Their violence and lawlessness against industrial workers of the country, viciously instigated and propagated by Crœsus corporations too powerful to be checked, is fully recorded in many State and Federal Reports. Yet who knows anything in detail of these official investigations? Who knows the actual facts? Few, other than the victims! The reading public is too indifferent, or where feebly interested, as in this devil-take-the-hindmost American world is too often the case, has the wool pulled over its eyes by sly suggestions and in some instances deliberate omission of important facts by the press. In other words, our corporations—their industrial heads—put our editors and publishers, and hence the reading public, in their place, as the magnates see that place! So much so that to-day I am sure most people think quite favorably of the State Police, their idea of them being that they are engaged in putting down or holding in check vicious, disorderly and un-American (and very likely anarchistic) persons whose secret intention is to undermine this kind and happy land! Well, I know that these persons do not know anything of what is really going on, so cleverly and smoothly have the real facts been glossed. But issues have been and are now being raised. It is all a part of the struggle of the worker against the corporation, its financial directors and banks. And already labor has fought and abolished the Colorado State Police. And I am hoping that they will do it elsewhere, and for the following reasons:

State troopers work for the corporations who command them and are parties to their lawlessness, whether troopers themselves see labor's rights or not. The corporations (their functioning officers and directing owners, the capitalists) even furnish them with luxuries in order to influence them, consciously or unconsciously, to favor the corporations. Thus the "coal and iron police" *are* the hired men of corporations, in many cases actually receiving their pay from them, and that they do beat up laborers at the command of corporations is true. In fact, there now exists a widespread practice of issuing police commissions to any kind of men, often the most lawless and brutal, whom the industries can discover and hire, and for the above purpose. And if, perchance, the policemen do not have a mind for such lawlessness, they are further candied into acquiescence by actions like that of Stuyvesant Peabody, of the Peabody Coal Company, who announced some time ago a fund of $50,000 to provide these "guards" with athletics, dinners, dances and medals. Pin a medal on a policeman, a public servant; honor him with a big banquet and see if he will not serve you. And with cruelty and brutality to others where necessary. It is the uninstructed state of the masses in regard to organized society and their part in it which permits this.

But more vicious still is the fact that at the least sign of disturbance at any of the apexes of the coal and iron industries, State troopers are, by means of railroad fares paid by the corporations, imported to and housed upon the corporation's property and provided with guns, machine guns and what not. Now if that doesn't make clear that the State police is a corporation institution, present on the scene solely to fight labor and help the capitalist, what does? But the following case reported by John P. Guyer, a Pennsylvania State Commissioner assigned to investigate conditions a few years ago, will substantiate, I believe, the truth of the above.

At Jerome, Pennsylvania, John Hess, a striker, was arrested on the street by State police and, as per the usual practice, taken to a hotel room (who paid for that?), where he was severely beaten by these policemen. In this hotel room, during the outrage, there was a witness (and most likely as a director), one John Gibson, a coal operator. Though he testified under oath that the State police attack on Hess was not severe, he later admitted to a Mr. Uhl, connected with the Hillman Coal & Coke Company, that Hess had been terribly beaten.

The first duty of the corporation State Police force, apparently, is to break up all gatherings of strikers. That these laborers may be acting peaceably, or that the United States Supreme Court declares workers' meetings lawful, means nothing. In Vintondale, Pennsylvania, during the strike of 1922 (now forgotten by America's indifferent luxury-lovers, of course) free speech and free assemblage were denied. At Export, Pennsylvania, in the Westmoreland coal region, where labor unions are outlawed as anarchistic (any theory of action against the meager standards of living imposed on the laborer by the corporation is interpreted as anarchy), the State police, in April, 1922, after asking the leader to disband a meeting of workers which the leader declared was lawful, reared their horses into the crowd, clubbing and chasing the men up the surrounding hills. At Crucible, Pennsylvania, in the same year, State police rode down miners assembled in public.

Then there is the case of some miners who, with their wives and children, on August 22, 1920, were holding a picnic in an apple orchard on the Gadje farm near Pittsburgh to protest against the deaths of Sacco and Vanzetti. The State police, armed with clubs and revolvers, burst in on them and drenched the crowd with tear gas. Women and children were ridden down and clubbed. Yet do you know of any law against protesting if it does not disturb the peace? Would you even consider such a law valuable, assuming that there were earnest, thoughtful speeches concerning the protest?

Another phase of this pursuit of labor by such police is illustrated by the following facts from Texas. Some Mexican labor agitators down there were trying to get out of the country to join a revolution against capitalism in Mexico. Why any particular American should wish to stop interested Mexicans from going to Mexico, unless American corporate interests in Mexico were to be affected by them, I cannot see. Yet the police, urged to do this by some one or many, did, with the result that Silvestre Loma, one of the strikers, was shot down by them and killed. There followed, of course, anger, intrigue and fighting, which was about to end in the lynching of these Mexicans, when the United States Cavalry rode up and interfered.

That frame-ups between corporations and police are frequent is perfectly clear. The corporations have it in for the bravest, most militant leaders among strikers, of course, and send these State troopers out to hunt them down. For instance, there was Brobb, a striking miner in West Virginia, who picketed every day during the strike. Of course, the bosses, running a scab coal mine, hated him. On May 15, 1929, as he was returning home from a visit to friends, he was captured by State Trooper E. W.

Mazingo and trounced and drubbed until he was senseless. Why? The answer is: in order to make him confess to participation in the dynamiting of some company property. For previous to this Mazingo had charged and testified that he had found Brobb with dynamite in his possession. Yet Brobb, for denying this, and without further evidence, was beaten until for a long time he could not even walk unassisted. The trooper testified that Brobb said the dynamite was his, but of course such testimony without further evidence was of little weight. Hence the beating! The National Miners' Committee believed that Brobb was drugged and taken to where the dynamite was stored.

Again, and as the corporations see it, the first duty of the police is to "get" the leaders of labor. Thus, on September 8, 1930, Lee Mason, Negro Communist candidate for Congress from Chicago's South Side, died after three months' illness due to wounds from a police beating after an anti-lynching rally. He was just a Negro, and (such was the question of the beaters) what business had he in Congress? His murderers appear to have answered that question with the word "none"!

Then on March 14, 1930, in Chicago, the police, making a raid against the Communists and their activities, burst in upon all those in a local Russo-Coöperative Reading Room. The men there who were playing checkers or reading were clubbed, kicked and thrown downstairs; books were torn and thrown away; furniture and pictures smashed—and all without a warrant! And, except as a rebuke to Communism, purposeless, for only one arrest was made, and that a camouflage, it being for vagrancy only and at once dismissed. In addition, though, I may add that although I am in a position to cite case after case of State troopers raiding workers' homes without warrants and, on finding Communist literature, arresting them, I will not trouble you. The purpose of these lawless raids, though, was to find something—books, pamphlets, anything— on which to base sedition charges against laborers, and with these in hand to seek long sentences or deportations for them—

the Tzar and his exile system having migrated to America, as
you see!

Throughout all this, consider the worker and his state. He
faces a world in which inordinate profits for a few are set over
against his minute share for what he does to help or create those
great, and so often foolishly used, profits, and then if he com-
plains he is met not only with drastic opposition but open and
illegal as well as unjustifiable assault, and often death. You
doubt? Well, let us take one Porto, of Tide, Indiana County,
Pennsylvania, whom the State Police arrested for murder during the period of economic distress of a few years ago. In order
to torture him into confession, these "up to the minute" American Cossacks, practicing the third degree, tied him to a steam
pipe, beat and kicked him, and then put into his mouth a funnel
through which he was forced to drink water until his stomach
was filled. That not extorting what they desired, they stripped
him, jumped on him, and then put lighted cigarette butts on
his flesh, until reviving from a faint he begged to be killed. The
modern third degree raised to the murder stage! Throughout all
this, though, Porto insisted that he was not guilty. And he was
not killed; that is, he did not die, and finally he was released.
But what of a man's respect for a government that will permit
such a thing, his feeling concerning his personal right to live
unharmed? And can that help to build the security of capitalism
or the government that fosters it? As children, and with horror,
we read in our American histories of the early and cruel custom
of fastening people in stocks or in the pillory or of gagging those
who talked too much! But compare this with our present-hour
capital and labor wars!

But in this connection I also desire to insist that there is no
end to this State police viciousness! It is at its best a criminal
invasion of the rights of the individual under this government,
and the fact that it exists and continues is not only a national
but a world and a race shame and should not be endured. Yet
here is one McHugh, one of the most ruthless of the police in
the Clarence section of Pennsylvania, who, in the corporation

offices and in front of corporation officials, beat one Stabryla, a worker, because he would not confess to dynamiting. He was tortured and told that he would be electrocuted. But on whose order? The State? Not at all! It could only have been the kind of treatment which the corporation's local officials, and none other, think is meet and just for the worker!

Now a strike is obviously not of itself but is brought because of a belief among workers that their condition is degraded, that they themselves are prostituted. Yet the treatment given them during the strike, and on top of the resentment which caused said strike, further corrupts and cankers their minds. First, and in so many places where the corporation owns the entire town in which the workers reside, and because the corporation owning the town so easily secures an injunction against the workers picketing on the corporation property and that means all the property in the vicinity of the scabs—which injunction is invariably stringently enforced by the State police—no effective picketing by the workers is possible. And this is not only unjust but cruel. It is their right to ask others not to take their places. But what intangible nothings the workers may have in the way of rights brings them no more than brutal beatings. Thus, during our always brutally opposed coal and iron strikes, these town-owning companies get injunctions against permitting labor unions to pay the rent of strikers for their company-owned shanty homes or to interfere in any way with eviction— which is contra to State property laws.

These abuses take some such illegal and uncivilized form as this: At Windber, Pennsylvania, for instance, only two of forty-eight workers' families evicted received a sheriff's notice, a requirement by statute. Yet in the face of that, the police dumped all of their furniture in the road, where much of it was broken. More, those strikers, driven to forming tent colonies, are as often illegally harassed there. A tent colony unlawful? No! (Rather uncivilized in the winter when many of them have existed.) Do the corporations or the State troopers have any right to interfere? No! Yet rights or no rights, humanity or no humanity, on June

2, 1922, at Lick Creek, West Virginia, the State troopers raided such a tent colony, cut the canvas, destroyed the stored food, poured kerosene in a churn of milk, and broke dishes and chairs. Then, in Pennsylvania, drunken and reveling police shot into a sleeping tent colony and wounded several members of miners' families.

That such treatment as this unbalances and destroys the workers' minds I can prove. In August, 1927, in Cheswick, Pennsylvania, State troopers, hurling tear gas bombs and swinging their clubs, rode into a meeting of strikers and their families. (Remember, strikes and assemblies are lawful!) Over two hundred persons were injured. One worker became so enraged that he shot and killed a trooper. Besides him, there were two hundred injured who must have been angry at the police and the corporation. But who cares? What matter, apparently?

Then there was the case of John Kashtock, aged 57, a peaceful miner of Pennsylvania, a father and grandfather, who was taken by the State troopers to a hotel. There, for sixteen hours, he was beaten so brutally that he was almost paralyzed. When he failed to arrive at his daughter's home, a short distance away, other miners, incensed by what had befallen him, set out in the rain to search the hillsides for him. At daylight they found him. He had hanged himself to a tree. His wife said that she did not know why he was arrested, and that he told her he didn't know either. He did say to her that a trooper had called him "a big pig" and threatened to kill him if he didn't return to work.

Such tactics as these outrage the sensibilities not only of the workers but also of communities—the town people of these areas who without offense on their part, and despite social guarantees which ought not to be disturbed, must still live under martial law, enforced by corporations which have no least right so to annoy them or harass their feelings. Indeed, in 1922, more than a quarter of a million citizens and business men of the city of Buffalo signed a petition to the Governor to recall the State police, who had been sent there in anticipation of violence during a street car strike. The petition alleged that without justification of any kind the State troopers had committed "unmanly and brutal actions," that they "maliciously attacked law-abiding citizens," and that "irrationally" they "rode on sidewalks, dispersing shoppers and innocent pedestrians, not even heeding the small children and women." Also that they "rode their horses furiously and brutally into stores, scattering merchandise." The Governor, in that instance at least, had to withdraw the State police. But why the State police in the first instance? And why a long series of outrages tolerated before this one brought action? And why the "coal and iron" police? Answer: corporations who control States and cities and fields of industrial activity and feel that by reason of their private property and the defense of the same they are entitled not only to create laws, but police of their own to enforce them!

But the above is no solitary instance. I have reports in connection with other communities, no essential part of the population of which were the strikers, and where, as in a number of important instances, the women and children were ridden down on the sidewalks. Of the extent of permanent injuries, insults, cursing and threats heaped upon citizens not taking part in any strike, I have not space here to speak. These infamous State troopers in one place and another, and at the behest always of corporations conducting their labor wars, have unnecessarily fired revolvers into crowds, terrifying women and children, and arrested and jailed citizens for using the public highways without a company permit! They have even taken a man, as in the case of one Tony Mari, in no way connected with the company or the strike, but who chose to rent a plot of ground to strikers for a peaceful meeting, and beaten him up. And one State trooper of Pennsylvania, after telling Paul Tallo, president of a Lutheran church group there who was talking on the street with a friend, to move on, and being respectfully told in reply by Tallo, although he obeyed and started to go away, that he had a right to speak with his friend on the street, seized said Tallo, pushed him into an alley and struck him on the jaw so brutally as to knock out several teeth! Later when Mrs. Tallo, who heard that the police were holding her husband, attempted to go to him, she was met on the highway by a policeman with a drawn revolver and sent home. Yet for acts like this are the State police of America denounced by our American press? Rather silence, or excuses or applause while their victims burn with an intense hatred of a government so indifferent and so unjust as to permit such happenings!

But this is a mere fraction. State troopers in various States (these cases are too numerous to cite here but can be furnished) have been sent into towns and regions against the will of the sheriffs, mayors, councilmen and duly elected officials, who were powerless in the face of the troopers' rowdyism, obscenity, and total disregard of law. Thus, in July, 1921, State troopers were sent into Corinth, New York, and this over the protests of the Burgess, the Board and the Justice of the Peace, who declared that they themselves could maintain order unaided by the State police, and there, in connection with a strike, abused citizens, terrorizing and driving them about as one would cattle. And not only this, but without authority, they made rules or laws which they enforced by false documents or processes prepared by themselves—a proceeding which was protested by the duly elected officials of the district.

In some places, they have driven citizens to make fake confessions which later the police passed as honest evidence, and even to commit suicide. In most instances everywhere, unless severely restrained, they enjoy starting fights. Thus, McAndrew, a Pennsylvania State trooper, invaded a certain Bittner's restaurant and tried to provoke a row with him. He was only persuaded to depart without committing a crime by others who felt that he was not justified. And though, in 1921, five State troopers in Washington, West Virginia, watched C. E. Lively, a labor spy, shoot Sid Hatfield and Ed Chambers, friends of the mine workers, on the steps of the courthouse there, not a trooper moved to arrest the murderer, who walked calmly away.

Worse, State troopers are all too often a drinking and generally carousing crew. Thus, George Metzger, a Pennsylvania

State trooper, and in his uniform at the time, twice stopped one
Hunsaker, a bus driver, the trooper being too drunk to know
why he held Hunsaker up. More, citizens of various States have
not infrequently testified to finding State policemen drunk. And
it has not been so very long since that I read of a State trooper
in Pennsylvania who, raiding a house without a warrant, burst
into the bedroom where a young mother was nursing her baby
and raped her. Ignorant and mainly lawless, most troopers have
nothing more than the lowest grade school education, and minus
the super-direction of trained army men, they are still sent into
situations which should require courtesy and tact—qualities which
are exactly those our brutal, money-mad corporations do not
want them to have. For they are not sent merely to protect
property but to terrorize and injure those who feel that these
lawless corporations should not be permitted to enslave them.

But does this stir American society to demand sufficient understanding in them to meet their duties? It does not! Nor does the
American corporation heed the feelings, let alone the wishes, of
the public at large. Rather, it desires, buccaneer fashion, to
overawe the public. So, though a State trooper may lock up a
labor organizer in a company building for being a "Red," I
would guarantee that he could not enumerate one important item
of the creed of a "Red" or make plain what relationship, if any,
that creed had to the company or the worker. At best he might
say that the "Red" wants to destroy, but as to the "Red's" ideas
as to what should be established in place of what is, he knows
nothing. And as for any question relative to his powers or duties
or reasons, he would laugh that off with a "Ha, ha! Jesus Christ!
All I have to do is foller orders! What the boss says, goes!"

But are these louts, as I have made them out to be (and as,
according to facts, they actually are) ever punished for their
crimes? Very rarely, indeed! For their victims, ignorant and
poor, are usually some time recovering from beatings, and even
so, can only complain helplessly, having neither the time nor the
money nor the knowledge to prosecute a policeman, or any one,
at law. And should they seek to do so, their reward would most

certainly be more persecution, possibly even death. For by so
doing, and as the American mood now is, they would become
super-radicals, outlaws, and I know not what else!

Yet sometimes there are cases like this. Barkowski, a poor
miner in western Pennsylvania, was taken from a friend's home
by three armed troopers, and at the State police barracks of the
Pittsburgh Coal Company was so nearly beaten to a pulp that he
died the next morning, a crushed chest being his most outstanding injury. And for once, the company physician, a certain Dr.
Patterson, testified that he saw the policemen, Messieurs Lyster
and Watts, kick and wallop the dying man, both before and
after he had received medical aid. According to this doctor's
testimony, he was beaten with a poker until it was bent nearly
double, also with blackjacks and bridle straps. Yet in February,
1930, Messieurs Lyster and Watts were convicted of manslaughter only, not murder which would have carried with it the
death penalty. But that is but one conviction as against scores
of murderers, to say nothing of brutalities of a related nature,
all unpunished.

Now I know that corporations are the first to realize that such
blood and thunder régimes as they sanction and encourage breed
animosity and even revolt, or at least unpopularity. So these same
corporations have men all over the country on salaries of ten
and fifteen thousand dollars a year, who do nothing but think
up ways to make the public like the very systems with which they
are breaking their noses. These clever corporation propaganda
men know that citizens sympathetic to strikers frequently will
not give troopers room and board when so requested. There is
the case also of Charles C. Webber, a clergyman of Pennsylvania in 1922 (I believe my memory is correct but if not, I
can verify), who tried to get the bosses to arbitrate with the
workers, the latter being willing but the bosses unwilling. And
when this clergyman sought to further his efforts by distributing
a pamphlet containing apt religious phrases, he was arrested
for "distributing advertising literature." Yet learning later that
a Commission of the Inter-church World Movement was investi-

gating these State police brutalities, and fearing that the preachers might prove influential with the people and so inimical to
the company, it was decided that something must be done to
bring them to the company's side. In connection with that it
has actually come out through bona fide correspondence that
corporations began to talk of plans to pay teachers and preachers
more salary; in other words, to seek to suborn them by thoughts
of money; to corrupt, if possible, with cash, their natural human
reaction to crime. But to what a wretched end! In order to
safeguard the character-destroying profits of these money fools
at the top!

And already in this connection a sly, if not so amazing, psychological device has been brought into action, and by whom?
For throughout the East for years now, State troopers, or those
who guide them, have been staging "popular" exhibitions of
State trooper skill, such as chariot races at Cobbleskill, New
York, or the crack riders of "G" group galloping through fire
at the Fonda Fair, or other such troopers, at every fair in the
country, indeed, wrestling on horseback or riding in pyramids
or under their horses' bellies. But to what end? In order to
undo, in their hours of peace, the evil reputation they build
for themselves in times of strike and repression! Again, pictures of these handsome gentlemen at their leisure and play
(not work) are shown in hundreds of movie houses, in order,
movies shown in their earlier years. To them the troopers were
all right! They even wanted to become State troopers! But
this, as you see, clarifies the whole subtlety of this State police
system. It shows what a deep and sinister psychology is back
of it all. What a smooth scheme to earn popularity for these
Cossacks in the estimation of the thousands who find other
information in regard to the State police unavailable.

In fact, the trooper system has had for years and still has what
is brazenly called a Publicity Bureau for State Police, located at
432 Fourth Avenue, New York City. And this bureau has not
only established a monthly magazine, with pictures of the hand-
somest troopers mooning over little children or tenderly helping

old ladies cross streets, but has secured endorsements for the State police from hundreds of Rotary, Kiwanis and Lions Clubs, Chambers of Commerce, Grangers and welfare organizations all over the country. In other words, it is really selling State police to the public! But who pays for all this, I would like to know? The State, with taxpayers' money? If so, why? Or the corporations? And if so, why? Also, I would like to know by what need is a branch of the Government entitled to a publicity bureau? And if one for this, why not for State hospitals, prisons, asylums, the Department of Justice and the legislatures?

But remember, these State troopers draw their salary and are lodged and boarded and have their horses bought and are trained at the expense of the taxpayers! Not only that, but as far as I can make out, the financial statement covering their activities gives only obscure information. If you doubt this, look at one: the report, for example, of the State of New Jersey for 1926: "The State Police made $150,000 for the State." I wondered as to that. Upon examination I found that on the asset side were fines collected, and also in this column (to pay for troopers' salaries and expenses, as the balance sheet read), they had added hundreds of thousands of imaginary dollars for each of the following items: value of stolen automobiles recovered, value of stolen goods found, and value of property saved from fire! As though those functions were not already, and properly, assigned to the local police and fire departments everywhere! Also as though "goods found" and "property saved from fire" could be reasonably, let alone accurately, computed! The upshot was, as I found, that the State police of New Jersey cost the taxpayers more than a quarter of a million dollars! It was not an asset but a State liability, assumed (but at whose behest?) by the State and for the express purpose of protecting private property—really corporate property—in its supposed rights, yet really and all too often, its unjust and malign attacks on the individual where he justly seeks to lighten the economic burden so heavily weighing upon him.

But how extensive is this system which I am rebuking? Well, by now, twenty of our American States—nearly half of the total—have complete trooper constabularies, and all established since 1905. And at this writing, an additional one is being sought in Montana, where corporations want to keep the many miners there in subjection. Yet the true reason for it all is always camouflaged by talk of wandering criminals infesting the mountains and with whom the local sheriffs and city and town police cannot cope. Yes? But any one who knows the State of Montana, or the State of Pennsylvania, or the State of New York, knows that that is the boloney, sliced very thick! Criminals are few, as the States' own records show, and mining employees many. Actually, the State police in America originated because industrial leaders, hating the slowness of due process of law and wanting to quell the hatred against the militia (until then used for strike purposes) introduced into Pennsylania and West Virginia the "coal and iron police," a private local force hired by the corporations and commissioned by the State. Though these States later, and motivated by public opinion against private police, set up a supposedly controlled trooper force to contradict these private evils, still in both Pennsylvania and West Virginia, the number of "coal and iron police" has not since diminished. And what I also see is that the twenty States with this outrageous State trooper service are exactly those States with the biggest industrial centers: Connecticut, Massachusetts, Michigan, South Carolina, Tennessee, Alabama, Pennsylvania, New Jersey, New York, etc.

But now I want to set over against the ideas of those who advocate State police my own ideas. They run about as follows. Firstly, they say that the troopers protect rural communities. Well, I have known personally, in Pennsylvania, New York and elsewhere, and ever since this system developed, or for twenty-five years, farmers and other residents, but principally farmers, who have never even seen a State trooper. You see, ordinarily in the great open farming areas, there are no factories or mines, with their attendant oppressions and wars, and so ... well, you know ... the ordinary criminals in those regions—automobile thieves, etc.—are taken care of by the ordinary police. More, the only rural residents who are ever protected by troopers are the rich owners of estates.

Again, these advocates argue that State police make for more efficient detection of crime. But because local police should and really do know the ins and outs of local character and its possibilities, I claim that the town and country police are far more adequately equipped to deal with local ills than these police. Lastly, those who want the State police system say that constabularies are called out only in case of riots or drastic emergencies. But what I protest against is that corporations have these police brought in to prevent riots in connection with their own interests, and their own interests only. You never hear of them being called in to protect workers anywhere, and their history is that of a cruel and brutal attack on all striking workers everywhere. Workers who are peaceful before the troopers arrive are by them excited, and riots are started. They, the workers who obviously have been working honestly and decently for years suddenly become criminals or scoundrels or what you will—of the blackest character—and to be beaten or shot on the slightest pretext. Except for the one instance that follows I insist that these State police work for the corporations, and for them alone!

Additionally, though, as I now wish to point out, it is most jesuitically argued that these State troopers control traffic. Well, I personally believe that a separate force, and a separate force only, should do that—patrol our highways for speeders or fleeing criminals—and that this force should never be called upon in any way to neglect its job for corporation duty. And most assuredly such men should not be turned into Cossacks, trained and authorized to bully and enslave labor. Other arguments to the effect that State troopers do rescue work during catastrophes, and also seize liquor, are merely ridiculous.

In short, everything which troopers do, including strike duty, could more adequately be handled by local forces, representative of the people. If uncontrollable violence is actually occurring, then, and only after the proper checks have been satisfied, should the aid of the State or National Guards be invoked.

And once upon a time our States and their general government actually functioned with only a militia—not State police. And before the arrival of the automobile, with its traffic problems, that process was adequate. But since the automobile, and more especially since now this is used as the chief excuse for the State police, the troopers should be limited to that and the pursuit of criminals on the road.

But the main factor in bringing about the development of the State police system, and that before the automobile was even thought of, was the tremendous growth of our corporations and their power and greed. I saw it in force in Pennsylvania in 1894. But we Americans are, on the whole, I fear, a dull and drudging people. Because of long years of stump-speeches and Fourth of July orations—the usual coruscating bathos of the politician and the hireling and the fool—we have come to think of ourselves as wise, watchful, secure, liberal, and what not else. But under our very eyes, and by reason of the brains and cunning of those who really are shy, watchful, self-seeking, and so secure, our individual privileges, as I have in this particular instance attempted to show, are slowly but surely being pilfered and removed. Consider only the data set forth in the chapters: "Trusts and Banks Functioning as Government"; "The Position of Labor"; "The Constitution as a Scrap of Paper," to name only three! Are we not really sound asleep? On every hand, money, money, money, and always in the control of smaller and smaller groups! And everywhere it is building for itself an autocratic security comparable only to that of the imperialism of Rome, the barons of the Middle Ages, and the royal families of latter-day Europe. We think of ourselves as free, but are we not threatened with a great war, and devastation and death? And at whose command? That of the marching masses? The very thought of it as matters stand to-day is obviously ridiculous. The masses do not plot evil against any group without immense provocation. That is history. It is the individuals of great cunning, and therefore at the top, who order and compel. And these are here shown in their true colors, or I have written lies only.

CHAPTER XIII

THE ABUSE OF THE INDIVIDUAL

CORPORATIONS, the deviously won reward of skyscraper-crowned dignitaries, having catapulted their way (honestly or dishonestly) through meshes of law, public opinion, morals, theories—obviously by reason of some constructive intent on Nature's part as manifested through man—have finally reached that state of centralized power and security in America in which any attempt at opposition, correction, or even criticism, on the part of the small fry is likely to be met with drastic counter-attacks intended in quite every instance to terrify or punish, and so forestall any attempt at the same thing in the future. To realize the truth of this, one need only contemplate the fierce executive, judicial, financial, as well as social, attacks on this or that opponent of the present centralization of all powers in the hands of a few. To-day in America the individual is practically helpless; that is, any individual lower in rank than the top level.

In short, the individual in America suffers from cruelty and abuse, as well as senseless regulation: the kind of abuse and cruelty that is not only ruthless but brainless, and that, except for abnormal money greed on the part of a few, need not exist. Thus, corporation greed in connection with railroads, street cars, busses—in fact, any form of transportation or exchange—has worked untold hardship on the little person, causing him to be pushed and kicked about, browbeaten by officials and their hirelings, ignored and even laughed at by petty officials in every field. One need only consider the street car, bus, or subway—the conscienceless overcrowding; the cars with too few seats, insufficient light and air, dirty seats, floors and windows; and

222

all because by ignoring and failing to supply even the com-
monest decencies of public transport, a few extra dollars can be
made by an inner ring of owners already stuffed to repletion
with money!

Yet no help from any official source to which the public
might turn! Instead, should any complaint be made, insults
from officials, petty magistrates, the police, and the hirelings,
and even thugs, of money-mad corporations, until ten-, fifteen-,
and even thirty-five- and forty-dollar-a-week clerk or worker
in any field is ready to admit that he is a mere nothing, a beggar
or dog or less, in the eyes of those who, by bribery and chicane
and direct robbery in every conceivable form, have been able
to take from him his right to decent service or consideration.
His corporations have not only seized his privileges as a citizen,
but have taxed him to death into the bargain.

One illustration of this was the abolition, not so many years
ago in many cities, of the transfer system from any direct to
any cross-town car line, and vice versa. This meant double
and treble fares for the traveling world which originally had
been assured that in return for a free franchise to the corporation, it would be protected. But no! More millions for more
money-mad dubs, and to be extracted from the many, regardless of their poverty or downright inability to pay! And in
addition, in many other fields, a steady and dishonest increase
in rates for light, heat, water, telephone and other public service,
the while the number of those compelled to use these utilities
grew and grew. And yet, and withal, the corporations, fattening
by this numerical increase, still bawling about confiscatory
taxes and rates not high enough to permit them (the poor
corporations!) to earn seven per cent on their invariably falsely-
represented investments. And so, according to them, no money
for replacement of the wear and tear on their supposedly very
much injured property. And the same therefore, and on this
pretext, left in all too many cases in the shabbiest condition;
no decent service to the public. Go into the men's room or the

ladies' room of a New York City elevated station to-day even, and see for yourself!

And what American has not only suffered from, but commented on, the really infuriating imposition of the American Pullman car, with its stuffy, narrow, and quite public berth, for the use of which he has persistently been charged not only exorbitant but preposterous prices: much more to ride, say, from New York to Pittsburgh than he would have to pay for a room in any of the best hotels of his great cities? And in addition to his regular and already exorbitant fare. And, since our corporations tax as they please, on the "take it or leave it" basis.

And similarly, the control by corporations of prices regardless of merit or (in so far as foodstuffs are concerned) seasonal supply. In New York or Chicago or other big cities, lemons, for instance, remaining at three for ten cents, whether they be plentiful or whether the extra ones have to be allowed to rot in cars or dumped in any harbor or slough in order that this price may be maintained. And this applying to other fruits and vegetables as well. At this writing there are vast piles of farm produce rotting along the railroad tracks which stretch out into the meadows between Jersey City and Newark— carload after carload dumped because otherwise the exorbitant asking price could not be obtained from the wholesaler in New York. And this destruction of food, and in the face of millions of unemployed and thousands of bread lines, not only done openly, but widely publicized. Witness the items in all the newspapers some months ago, announcing a sham battle in California with "surplus" eggs as missiles. Thousands of crates of eggs so destroyed, and in order to keep up prices, the while children all over America were suffering from malnutrition and their parents not only unable to buy eggs for them but themselves suffering from hunger or actually dying of starvation! Is life really mad? Are all men scoundrels or fools?

It is the same with bread. Ten cents a loaf the while hundreds of millions of bushels of wheat lie stored and unsalable!

small office, and behold a tyrant who sees nothing but effrontery in the least desire or pleasure of any one not possessed of authority or property or power. Is it the driver of an automobile? Then it is the pleasure as well as the purpose of the largest as well as the smallest officials connected in any least way with the regulation of traffic (its assumed furtherance, not hindrance) to irritate, browbeat, delay, threaten, and all too often arrest (and for purposes of graft, fine or tax) individuals who are seeking no more than a reasonable and just use of the public roads. And since our American railroads have been seeking to drive the individual bus-owners off the roads in order to gobble up the right to operate buses for themselves, it is no common occurrence to have the petty individual operator annoyed, delayed, and most inordinately fined, until at last, through downright weariness as well as robbery, he is compelled to dispose of his right and allow the corporation to function in his stead. And this by the aid of the local police, the county sheriff, the town marshal, and who not else, in quite every part of America. It is a commonplace, just as the driving out of the individual oil operator by the Standard Oil Company, or the individual coal operator by the combined mining and railway trust, was a commonplace of half a century ago.

In fact, I am now convinced that this is one country that, ever since it was conceived of as a possibility, has been steadily and deceitfully, as well as fraudulently, shunted along the path of individual and later corporate control, as opposed to its written and widely-promulgated determination to make of itself a liberal and helpful democracy in which the individual was to fare more pleasantly and comfortably than ever he had before in all the world! For here more than anywhere else in the world, I do believe, the petty individual has seen himself more thoroughly coerced, robbed and frustrated, and that always in favor of the cunning individual of capitalistic leanings and with a will to power. For where other than here has been developed those superorganisms: the trust and holding company (even the *Holding Company of Holding Companies*) which,

because of its ramifications and strength, is now so completely
in a position to obfuscate law, equity and the rules of government as to have become government, *de facto* if not *de jure*. And
since these organizations have chosen to work evil as well as
good, to abrogate individual as well as government rights, and
to cause to be robbed, restrained, defamed, and even slain, any
and all of those who have ventured to disagree with or oppose
them, they have made of the original plan of our government
a complete failure.

The record is too great and savage to be even more than
hinted at here, but one thing is sure: the illegal, bandit actions
of American financial men in general, and from the beginning—their corporations, trusts and holding companies, their
suborned or threatened courts, lawyers, police, politicians and
officials generally—have so weakened the faith of the little
American in his government that now one of his outstanding
dreams is to obtain, by some hook or crook, an office or uniform
or robe for himself, and thus vested in authority, proceed to
tax or graft upon or otherwise ill-use as thoroughly as the
corporations all those not sufficiently clever to obtain a like
office.

In other words, the American scene in this sense is actually
fantastic. Judges obtain their seats by bribery or corporation
favor (for services rendered, of course) and then proceed to
pass upon the bribery of others. Representatives of the people,
supposedly beholden to the voters for their positions, once
they are elected do the bidding only of the corporations or
bosses and in turn lecture the people on their duties to the
Government and, if you please, its most favored corporations:
the railroads, steel trust, power trust, and what not. And the
little individual, helpless and in the main fearsome because of
what may be done to him as an individual, makes the best of it,
since, as he well knows, neither the courts, the police, nor any
other officials, are for him unless he chances to have the means
wherewith to buy aid. Thus, the little person when arrested
for any offense, however small, all too often finds himself

unnecessarily detained in jail while the judge is busy dining or calling or protracting his absence by any other sort of foolishness. And though the worker may lose several hours or days from his job, does that make any difference? A workingman, a single individual, carries little weight in this régime where wealth and office rule.

Likewise, in some States (Florida, Alabama, Georgia, Texas) men arrested to-day on the pettiest of charges—vagrancy, for one, and because they cannot find work—are at once victims of a virtual Government press gang system. That age-old shippers' custom of employing a press gang, getting a stupid but affable stranger drunk and then hauling him aboard ship and forcing him to slave without pay, was no more iniquitous than the present-day American system of seizing an unemployed man for vagrancy or any other charge and then jailing him and hiring him out as part of a prison gang to work for a private contractor who makes money by paying the officials something and the seized laborer nothing, or nearly nothing—his alleged food and lodging! In fact, until July 1, 1928, when it was prohibited by a State law, Alabama convicts were leased to private contractors and coal mine owners. And under this pagan system, a certain Warden Davis of the State was prosecuted by the State for ordering Convict Robert Knox, who refused to work in the mines, dipped in boiling water, which burned him to death. But how rich the favorites at the State Capitol because of this slavery! Yet despite prohibitive measures in Alabama to-day against contracting out prison labor, flogging the individual with a snakeskin-whip remains as lawful as ever!

Not only that, but the attitude of the Southern white to the Negro as well as that of the Southern landowner to his tenant, the "cropper" with whom presently I will deal, and also that of the average American corporation toward its employees, is of a similar pattern and all equally cruel and evil. In our South, for instance, petty offenders are picked up among the whites and colored to keep the county chain gangs full. In North Carolina, which permits a convict, guilty of only a minor offense, to labor for years, in a chain gang, fixes no limit to other cruelties that may be inflicted on him. Indeed, persons fighting this practice in some counties have found evidence that when the gang is short of men, a much greater number are not only arrested but convicted. And although Alabama, after a bloody career, no longer leases prisoners to private contractors, Idaho, Delaware and South Carolina do. And again, in many States, although convicts in the State prison may not be leased, those in the county jail, mostly guilty of only minor offenses, are so leased, and unrestrainedly, to private contractors who enslave and abuse them as they will. And this is also true of Nebraska, Arkansas and other States—the new American slavery, it might be called, for in thirteen States prisoners are contracted for by private citizens or companies having any kind of grimy work to do: mining, coke-burning, etc., and used to the limit of their strength, and as for pay, for almost nothing, or nothing.

In Virginia, North and South Carolina, the number of men in the chain gangs is frequently twice the number confined in the State prisons. And although experts have declared that this system of manual labor is actually a money-loser (much less efficient than machinery), these counties would apparently rather knock people around, humiliate them publicly in chains, and so totally demoralize them, than appropriate funds for a prison or devise some system whereby economically they might be made self-sustaining and so be considered worthy of at least human treatment. And in at least one case, a city, not a county—and that the notoriously anti-labor city of Greensboro, North Carolina —maintains its own chain gang.

The actual treatment which these poor fellows receive in the chain gangs is an outrage. A cage on wheels, like those for wild animals in a circus, not only transports them along the country roads but furnishes them with their only home. At night, after working from daylight until dark, eighteen of these men, still chained together, are forced to sleep in bunks measuring only eight by eighteen feet. If a man is more than a foot wide, he has to lie on his side, apparently. Drinking water and slop pails are crowded in with them, and men suffering from venereal diseases are in no way segregated. In only one county that I have heard of are diseased convicts placed in separate gangs. Some States, however, have laws enforcing isolation. In winter, the shanties erected for these chain gangs are dirty and poorly ventilated. They are set in the midst of their own sewerage, which, according to the North Carolina Board of Health, contaminates the water. Other reports show these camps alive with vermin. A convict's life here is spent constantly chained, with either single or double shackles riveted on the ankle by a blacksmith and occasionally with spikes a foot long. And these must be worn even while sleeping. But for what great offense, if any? Owing some one five or even three dollars or stealing from some one as little as a chicken!

And more, according to North Carolina laws, a second violation of such petty rules as "no smoking during working hours" calls for a flogging. Yet how inhuman to inflict such cruelty for so petty an offense! But according to the code of North Carolina, this is quite right, for it permits all the flogging which the county physician and the superintendent of a chain gang may agree that a convict can stand! In short, so little significance is placed upon the cruelty of a chain gang superintendent that mainly he is his own guide and law, and more, time after time one such, discharged for inhumane conduct in one county, has immediately been employed by another and for the same work! And though escape itself is only a misdemeanor, a man imprisoned for only a misdemeanor can be shot dead by his superintendent for attempting escape!

Although in my chapter on "Crime and Why" I cover prison conditions in America generally, here I would like to remark that the report of the Tennessee Penal Institutions Committee of March 17, 1931, has just come to my attention, and I feel it necessary to circularize the data contained therein. Although all prisons are not like this, the very fact that such exist at all is shocking. Brushy Mountain Prison was built as a temporary structure thirty-five years ago for 300 or 400 prisoners. To-day, unremodeled, it houses in a four-story building, constructed entirely of wood, 976 prisoners. Wood, as well as the old wiring, makes for a serious fire hazard. Worse, however, is the matter of health. Over 400 men sleep on the fourth floor on beds standing as close together as possible. During the recent investigation, 138 suffering with flu and pneumonia, both highly contagious, slept among the other men. The death rate is sixteen times as high as at Nashville Prison. Sodomy is practiced promiscuously, mostly by inveterate criminals upon the young. (Seventy per cent are from 18 to 30 years old.) More dreadful, if possible, is the fact that the sixty per cent having venereal disease are not only not segregated but also indulge promiscuously in sodomy.

But now let us turn to another phase, that of peonage. For although these cases have been kept secret by the Government over periods, it is known that in 1903, a Federal Grand Jury sitting at Montgomery, Alabama, made 100 indictments for forced labor or peonage as it is called. And in 1907, according to a report of the Department of Justice, 83 complaints against this forced labor were pending. Again, on April 22, 1921, Governor Hugh M. Dorsey of Georgia stated that in February, 1921, a Negro, who had run away after being arrested and brought back twice for indebtedness, was offered for sale by the planter who had illegally enslaved him, and for $55! This same Governor Dorsey told of another case: a Negro who had run away because his peonage-practicing planter employer had threatened him and then hit him in the face. This Negro had been working for this planter for $12 or $15 a month and board. Just before he ran away, the planter gave him $3 for a pair of shoes. On the strength of this $3 debt, the Negro was arrested, charged with swindling, and threatened with the chain gang if he did not return to the planter.

Again, Governor Dorsey revealed that a Negro who had made a contract with a planter to work for $25 a month and board during 1920, but had been paid nothing for months, finally asked the planter for an accounting. The employer admitted that he owed the Negro $65, but paid him only $10, whereupon the Negro ran away. He was arrested and brought back by force.

In the pamphlet from which all this is taken, the Governor cites the case of a Fulton County, Georgia, planter who having taken ten Negroes out of the county chain gang worked them all day at the point of a gun and then at night locked them in. And when two of them ran away, they were forcibly brought back and then whipped, but in such a brutal manner that one, begging to be killed, was shot by the planter and his body sunk in a pond on the plantation. According to this same Governor, one Negro claims to have seen a runaway Negro shot by a Negro supervisor at the command of a white.

The last case I will cite from Governor Dorsey's résumé concerns a Georgia planter indicted for killing eleven Negroes. On April 8, 1921, he was convicted in a single case and sent to prison for life. Yet in spite of this conviction and considerable publicity in connection with all of this data, the system still survives, for the present somewhat secretly. And to this day in the South many Negroes truly believe that their planter may and will shoot them if they tell or complain. Yet in times of crisis, and due to newspaper reporters, in the section, the status of at least some of these tenants, workers or slaves occasionally becomes clear to the outside world. Thus, in connection with the Red Cross flood relief in the South in 1927, it became known that it, our Red Cross of blessed station, contracted with planters to deliver Negroes from the relief station to the plantation again by force, if necessary, when the charity work was over. So much for our Red Cross, its noble services!

But because neither the Negroes nor the poor whites dare talk much, most of these really dreadful cases never get publicity. Yet while some of the States permit men to be brought back for debt, others do prohibit planters from crossing the State lines to force men back, a fact which should be written down to their credit. On the whole, though, this Southern force and violence has its roots, I am sure, in the pre-Civil-War slavery tradition of the South; in other words, the assumed fitness of the Negro and the criminal for slavery, and for slavery only. Yet why? The Negro who works is law-abiding, and if not thrifty is at least economically independent and cheerful, a good and useful citizen. Can it be that due to his somewhat erotic nature, he is offensive to the Northern Puritan (in law, not fact), or is it merely that he is black? In part, its roots may lie in the world-old notion that freedom for the individual is something bestowed by the strong upon the weak, that might makes right, and that the strong may (not necessarily "must") direct the weak and helpless everywhere, and to the advantage of the strong. For the strong, being strong, are right, and the weak, being weak, are wrong or worthless—a doctrine to which all of the money powers of our modern world will most readily subscribe and, in reality, practice. If this and other chapters do not show this, then most certainly my statements are without meaning and of no authority.

Of the practice of peonage in the South, however, Professor S. H. Hobbs, of the Department of Rural Social Economics of the University of North Carolina, on June, 1930, told the Southern Economic Conference in Atlanta that "more than half of all the farms in the South are to-day operated by tenants ... the lowest type of tenure existing in the civilized world to-day, the cropper system, which is just one step removed from serfdom ... and nearly two-thirds of the tenants in the South are whites!"

The laws in some States (Florida and Alabama) state that a worker owing money to an employer may not leave his employ until that money is paid. Yet the payment of it, however small, is no easy matter. For the planters or bosses sell the crop and divide the proceeds, equitably or not, over the heads of the ignorant tenants. Also they, and they only, keep all books and charge such exaggerated prices for rent, food, supplies, etc., that the share cropper or employee of whatsoever walk never succeeds in geting out of debt from one year to the next. In

Georgia also, the code of law which makes running away from an employer when money is owed *prima facie* evidence of intent to defraud, practically secures the worker as a slave, and over very considerable periods of time. For the ignorant tenant or worker, in contracting with his planter employer, is usually made to sign away all sorts of privileges, because not being able to read or write much, he does not understand.

A typical contract is the following cited by the "American Statistical Quarterly Publications XIII," pp. 82-3:

"Said tenant further agrees that if he violates the contract or neglects or abandons or fails (or in the owner's judgment violates this contract or fails) to properly cultivate the land... or if he should become physically incapacitated... or die, or fails to gather . . . crops . . . or fails to pay rents or advances made by the owner, when due, then in that event this contract may become void and canceled at the owner's option, and all indebtedness of the tenant for advances or rent shall at once become due and payable to the owner... in which case the owner is hereby authorized to transfer, sell or dispose of all property thereon... the tenant has any interest in. It shall not be necessary to give any notice of any failure or violation of this contract... the execution of this lease being sufficient notice of defalcation on the part of the tenant, and shall be so construed between the parties hereto, any law, usage, or custom to the contrary notwithstanding."

In other words, this contract puts simply and completely the law into the hands of the planter—such law as he chooses to make and exercise. For it is not binding! There are property laws in the South which have grown up and protect people's interests, but these, of course, are thrown overboard. No delay or any inconvenience of legal resort, as you see! And besides, the tenants never have any money wherewith to investigate or contest such contracts. They are too wholly benighted and enslaved, and by the State! The local politicians and petty executives of all levels in this region will usually be found to be friends of either the planter employer or the system, and at best or worst, extremely unused to taking care of the legal problems of either Negroes or poor whites, and prejudiced against them into the bargain. But why? One must look to the world-old reverence for wealth as opposed to the world-old contempt for poverty. It is something which an entirely different concept of social equity, if such is humanly possible, will have to replace, or there is no hope for social decency in man's relationship to man anywhere in society, any more than there is in wild nature outside society.

To go on with this particular situation in the South, however, a tremendous and extortionate rate of interest is also forced upon these simple and powerless individuals by opulent planters and their merchants. The North Carolina College of Agriculture, in connection with twenty-seven farms in Pitt County in that State in 1928, said that charges for credit by merchants there ranged to nineteen per cent for cash advances and to seventy-two per cent for supplies in advance! And Secretary of Agriculture A. M. Hyde, in his 1930 report, stated that over the entire South, charges by merchants for credit averaged twenty-five per cent, and for fertilizer thirty-five per cent.

But to further substantiate these charges that peonage as well as such abuses as the above exist in the South to-day, I offer the following. These are recent cases—so recent in fact that most of them have not come to trial, at the time when this book goes to press. Fred Burk, a share-cropper of Etowah, Arkansas, was, on March 21, 1931, shot by Pat Cook, a planter. Reason: some complaint in regard to inequity on the part of the cropper. Burk's condition was critical. I mention this case because such quarrels as these are reported by scores in the Southern newspapers of to-day. They exist in such numbers as to be proof, it seems to me, of undue domination by planters.

Again, on January 31, 1931, Ordis Waller, of Bossier Parish, Louisiana, was under bail on a charge of violating the Federal Peonage Act by holding by force four Negro tenants. One Henry McLemore, a well-known planter of Conshatta, Louisiana, was charged, in January, 1931, with unlawfully holding five Negro laborers and share-croppers for alleged indebtedness. Mc-

Lemore, who asserted their indebtedness to range between $125 and $700, went about constantly armed and it is alleged that he would threaten Negroes if they dared leave him.

Still again, James Piggott, of Bogalusa, Louisiana, sentenced to eighteen months in the Federal Prison at Atlanta for peonage, said that he had merely treated his Negroes as everybody else in the South did. Yet on December 28, 1929, Piggott was charged with holding three Negro families totaling thirteen persons on his plantation for a year and a half without pay! It was also charged that they were beaten by him with trace chains and forced to eat inferior food. Not only was every attempt at escape repulsed, but Piggott admitted going into Mississippi and by force, not process of law, bringing his workers back!

But the proof varies. Thus, Russell Owen's New York *Times* report of January 31, 1931, states that no Arkansas sharecropper may move from one plantation to another unless the second planter employing him assumes his debts (if any) to the first planter—a system indicating peonage over a wide area.

Next, on January 28, 1931, the National Association for the Advancement of Colored People wrote to United States District Attorney Mitchell, saying: "Reliable reports reaching us from the drought areas of Arkansas and Louisiana indicate that conditions of peonage are widespread there." And investigation shows that forced labor of this nature is most prevalent in the Red River basin, the inland region of Arkansas and Louisiana and the Delta region. And yet again, Mr. Walter Wilson,* social research worker, sent 118 letters to Southern ministers, professors, Government officials, etc., inquiring as to this matter. I am permitted to quote typical replies.

A well-known lawyer of Houston, Texas, writing in February, 1931, said that peonage was illegal in Texas but because of force illegally applied, was still practiced. He said: "It has a firm hold and terrorizes the tenant."

* *Forced Labor in the United States*, by Walter Wilson. (International Publishers.)

Mr. Covington Hall, of the *Industrial Democrat* of Lees-
ville, Louisiana, on February 23, 1931, wrote: "The 'share-
cropper' and tenant serfdom is confined mainly to the cotton
plantations. In the sugar district, the condition of labor is that
of out-and-out peonage, and it is the same in the lumber industry."

A professor in an Alabama college wrote, on March 17,
1931: "The peonage system of tenantry does exist to a certain
extent."

And Deputy Commissioner of Labor Robert B. Grogg, at
Austin, Texas, wrote, on February 27, 1931: "Peonage, or the
system of tenantry through a credit system that actually binds
tenant-croppers to the land, actually exists in this State, but
the system is so plausibly organized that neither the State nor
Federal authorities have ever been able to isolate a case of
peonage and institute prosecution. The system is not, of course,
recognized by law."

Yet leaving for the time being this depressing illustration
of the wholly inhuman and unsocial and, of course, illegal attitude of the small American employer toward the individual be-
neath him in the economic if not the social scale, we can turn
again to our major corporations and their viewpoint, which is
by no means dissimilar to that of these lesser fry. A corporation like the New York Telephone Company can become so
partial, as well as so indifferent, in their business transactions
as between patron and patron as to cause one—the little man
without influence—to suffer heavily the while another—less
weak—is better taken care of. Thus, in so far as any speedy
installations are concerned, the red flag or check meaning "rush"
is required. But who is to supply or command that? Some one
with influence? Certainly! Otherwise, no courteous, let alone
rapid, installation! One individual or thousands waiting while
a few obtain immediate service. Again, on most railroads in
America to-day, how frequently the local, if not the through,
train is without portable ground steps! And yet heavy people
who cannot possibly step up two feet without help, and so in

danger of a fall! And how many conductors, without a proper sense of their responsibility (due, of course, to the inefficiency of their employers), neglect their work and the public!

But when these same corporations started out, nearly a hundred years ago, how different! Then their securities could scarcely be sold, for financing then was difficult. And hence during their brief period of struggle, and even later when profits were rolling up, all kinds of inducements were offered to the people to persuade them to ride. Round trip and excursion rate concessions! And inducements, because of fare privileges held out, for people to move to the suburbs of all cities along their lines. But now that hundreds of thousands have settled in these suburban towns, acquired property and become interested in the social communities in which they reside, the railroads, instead of dealing with them if not gratefully at least equitably, have long since pushed up the commutation rates until at this time they constitute not only a huge but conscienceless and cruel tax, many of our ogre roads asking and getting three and four times the original rates. Yet yelling "confiscation" when any tax is leveled on them! And indifferent to the question of schools for the children or a job for the head of the family, so often dependent, because of our modern suburban life, upon reasonable fares! Indeed, how great and kind our corporations now that they are so strong!

For always higher and higher rates are desired, and when these higher rate pleas are entered the railroad attorneys present the facts in so misleading a manner. Being shrewd and wise in the ways to power, these railways and their attorneys find it easy to scheme and cheat. Thus, the New York Central recently demanding a forty per cent increase in suburban fares out of New York City, stepped forward with the argument that although their commuters comprised sixty-five per cent of their passenger traffic, they paid only eight per cent of the total fares. But how sly and faked! Do you not really sense injustice to the New York commuter, who from the beginning has not only seen his public property stolen by bribery by the New York

Central—literally billions in property and privileges—and all fair tax rates into the bargain fought to a standstill—but himself in the matter of fares taxed to the point of exhaustion? For of what value is a record of the number of passengers without giving the distance traveled? And how could a commuter riding 18 miles honestly be contrasted as to fare with a passenger traveling 1,800 miles? Yet what about the thousands of miles of track along and through other enormous cities? For considering the enormity of the New York Central's mileage, the length of its various lines, and the great distance traveled by its through passengers, eight per cent of the total fares of the whole system and as the contribution of the passengers who use only about 50 miles of trackage seems O.K. to me.

In this matter of robbing the people, though, our American corporations seem always to me to be trying the one to outdo the other—never in the honest old game of competition, where each one sought to get business by cuting prices on the other, but rather by always raising prices to meet those charged by supposed competitors, who happen to be charging more, not less. And with little Government interference at any time! It evidently does not want to interfere because it does not do so. Thus, right now the New York Central is pointing out that while the New York, New Haven & Hartford Railroad's commutation rate to Mt. Vernon is $10.01 monthly, theirs is only $7.15. Therefore, theirs should be $10.01! Not the New Haven's to $7.15! For that would be lowering rates, and that is practically unheard of in America! Next, all our corporations must sell tickets, or what you will, at prices forced by the strongest or shrewdest company, and these prices always the highest. In other words, never lower a fare; raise it, or at worst, keep it where it is! Otherwise, *confiscation,* the undermining of business, the lowering of the American flag, Communism, and what not else!

In my own city, New York, the New York Edison (an electric company), and as I recall, no better and no worse than any of the corporations the land over, has only this spring of 1931 forced most abusive rates upon its powerless patrons. Forgetful of the social value of a rational balance, even to a corporation, it is perpetrating extortion. It asserts, however, that its plan lowers charges. But what really is meant is that by a curtain of shuffling and rearrangement, it hopes to hoodwink the public the while it is bringing profits to itself. Lower rates but higher bills! The "now you see it, now you don't" system! For what they really do is to cut the price of electric current from 7 to 5 cents a kilowatt hour, the while they proceed to charge 60 cents a month for meter service, a charge never before made and one that really increases the bills of fifty-seven per cent of their customers and those—the poor people. Thus, while the lady of Park Avenue, whose bill was formerly $36.20 for 517 kilowatt hours, saves, under the new apportionment, $10.15 monthly, another woman living in a tenement house, or hundreds of thousands in one-room apartments, and who previously paid only 65 cents for 9 kilowatt hours, now pays $1.05 monthly. Save money for the rich out of pennies of the poor. The eagle standard.

Yet has there been any public outcry as to this, or any defense of the weak by anybody? That voice of the public, the press, has it said anything? Or our so-called political "representatives of the people," have they spoken? In America, I am sorry to report, they are the rubber stamps only that O.K. every corporation proposition; the individuals who "yes, yes" every individual of power. It is America, and that is how the individual is dealt with here.

But how bold, and even insolent, to assess the individual for meters or anything but the electricity which he actually uses! In the beginning, when they were anxious for people to use their electricity, the corporations were glad enough to supply the meters. But not now! And not only that, but they were willing and glad to sell direct to the consumer, whereas after a little while, finding electricity so popular, they must needs devise or at least take up with a third party—likely a subsidiary concern: the sub-metering electricity broker who, like the ticket speculator of the theater world, proceeds to show them how, by dealing through him, they can make even more money. For behold you, he will contract for some hundreds of thousands of kilowatt hours, flat or by the year, paying in advance for the current so taken, then sub-metering the same to apartment houses, office buildings and the like, and locally servicing their tenants, but at rates which yield him a handsome profit and at the same time save the main company the trouble of meter reading, collecting and the like. And at the same time giving the corporation much free money to juggle with. But as for the customer, well, as for the customer in these better apartments and office buildings, he pays, and pays well, more than he would to the company direct. A mere bagatelle, as you see, but also one more illustration of the gross and still growing greed of the wealth of America. It can never get too much and it can never give too little.

But what an undesirable precedent is this meter charge! So unethical! And opening the door to other robberies of the same nature. For next—and why not?—a fixed rate for the wires leading to the house, or the posts or tubes that carry the wires, or a salary for the meter readers! There is no difference in principle. And although just two other cities, Atlanta and San Francisco, have meter charges so far, the former receives for current only 2 cents a kilowatt hour and the latter 1½ cents. Compare these with 5 cents for every single unit of the New York Edison Company's 40 light hours! Yet Mr. Sloan, an Edison president, states that this is the only way that the New York Edison can give New York City a lower rate.

And this following upon America's hope of thirty years ago that with invention and mechanization supplying most of the necessities would come lower living charges, and so more leisure and time for this and that! Instead the rich throw away what the poor man produces and only to keep the rich still more rich. But the individual of to-day as much as ever harnessed to the task of making a living in order that those who rob him may sport! And that in an age when all cooking should be carried on by cheap electricity! More, the New York Edison is controlled by the Consolidated Gas Company. So not only one, but two, and even a score of companies must fatten on a single need of the individual.

In addition, this same New York Edison proposes to assess commercial patrons a demand charge of $1.00 a month. They are possessed with ideas! Corporation witchcraft! Why, building owners alone would pay the company about ten million dollars for installing these demand charge meters!

But now let me add one more illustration of this corporation abuse of the little fellow, and then I will turn to another matter. Our great American telephone company, which is very rich and very powerful now, taxes the individual all that it can; that is, extortionately, and from coast to coast. For practically, the courts and politicians and officeholders aiding it, it fixes its own assessment of the people through the various utilities commissions which now exist in most States and which, by reason of laws arranged by the corporations, have now the power to examine into and fix rates, for the corporations, not the people, depend on that! And in connection with these, this dear American Tel. & Tel. of ours is always "correcting inconsistencies." But these "corrections," as you learn when you come to examine them, are always in the direction of higher rates for the great bulk of the business, with occasional—and not often even there—lowering of them on some minor portion. The method of doing this is termed, by our Mr. Gifford, present President of the Company, "correction of inconsistencies." This *"correction of inconsistencies"* business has already given rise to such clever money-squeezing devices as "person to person calls" and a three-minute limit for one class of calls before an additional payment is demanded and a five-minute rate for another class. Thus, the New York Telephone Company—the greatest of all the great divisions of this great company—is now seeking to increase the rates for calling between 24 and 40 miles and to decrease those over 72 miles. But consider, if you will, the number of calls in the former group, around

New York City alone, say, and with interchange of business between scores of large and prosperous suburbs and other places, and then the number of calls over the longer distance! Now which would have the larger number of calls? Can you guess? How smart you are! So even a five per cent reduction on a high charge for a call of over 72 miles is scarcely the equivalent or proper counterbalance to an increase of from 5 to 10 cents on each of these millions of necessary short calls. For short wires are so busy as compared with long ones. Just the same, this kind-hearted and very large company proposes a cut after 8.30 P.M., when business hours are over! Low charges on the dearth of business; high charges for the mass of it! But, oh, these efficiency experts! How they do earn their money from the company, and how they must sit up late devising these things! Snares, did I hear you say? Or robberies? Yet the telephone company's "line" is no different from that of the railroads and utilities. They all figure on the "up and up."

Telephone from New York to Jersey City or Forest Hills or South Orange, and note the result! For even brief talks, the operators interrupt and annoy you, always pleading for more and more money for the vulture company. And courtesy! They do not know the meaning of the word! Rather, vulgarity and even raw brutal force is their way where protest occurs. Thus, when I found that a friend whom I was trying to reach on a long distance call was out, the operator furnished me with a long report on his whereabouts, of which same, however, I was previously thoroughly cognizant. After thinking to myself that here at last was detailed and careful service, it suddenly came to me that this might really be no more than another corporation trick to get money out of me. And true enough, in reply to my inquiry as to whether I was to be charged for this report, the operator gave me the rate: a third of the total price!

"But why didn't you ask me if I cared for a report on the call, and what I would like you to inquire about the gentleman?" I asked.

"But it's our regulation," she replied.

"But I didn't want it and didn't ask for it."

"But we always do that," she insisted, trying to smooth matters over. One of the present-day American business robberies or "wrinkles," as we call them!

Concerning rate robbery charges, however, I have evidence of what seems to be a misrepresentation on the part of the New York Company. For although the New York Telephone Company stated that the increase to contract business subscribers would be from ten to fifteen per cent only, one Samuel Zirn, of Brooklyn, says that in his Brooklyn office the contract charge prior to January 1, 1931, was $8.06; that on February 1st the bill read $9.38; on June 1st, $9.70, and on July 1st, $10.70. A thirty-three per cent increase for the same service.

And although a man compelled to leave town for a period of time should most certainly be allowed to save something on his telephone bills, especially since he uses no service, the up-and-coming telephone company to-day will not so permit. What, no money for a month or two! Hence, though I leave my studio for two months, and order the service cut off to save money, upon returning and getting it connected, I find myself charged practically as much for this reconnection as I would have been for two months of service!

Yet has the individual any recourse? You know he has not! But is there not the law, and are there not the courts! Yes, there is and are! Try them—at your expense! So the crook who has boodled his franchise through a complaisant council or legislature drives you as though you were enslaved, as, in fact, you really are.

Indeed, for a long time now, as I have shown, our corporations have been free to combine against the individual. And not only that, but even to-day, now, the heads of our great industries as well as those of lesser factories are themselves advocating repeal of the antitrust laws, because, as they see it, these laws have brought on this major depression of 1928-31. But can you imagine a greater burlesque of the logic of eco-

nomics in toto? No wonder voters—poor, misinformed creatures!
—don't know what our Government is all about! Those who
would repeal these laws argue the usual claptrap that these
Sherman and Clayton Anti-Trust laws are the things which
have principally induced overproduction which has in turn
brought depression. And yet, without these laws, most certain
it is that greater and greater mergers, with their illegal but
still enforced power of taxing the people, would have combined
and so taxed the people, even more.

And yet in addition to all this even, the usual American
corporation "blah" concerning courage and the duty of the
American people to fight through, have patience, etc. Yet at
heart their attitude toward all their patrons and fellow-citizens
in general and throughout all of their monopolistic activities
is that of the first and original Vanderbilt (the Commodore
of blessed trust memory!): "The public be damned!"

CHAPTER XIV

THE CHURCH AND WEALTH IN AMERICA

I DECRY the power of the Church and its use of that power, in America in particular! Throughout the world, as all know, the churches are so organized as to have the wealth, size and formation of a great corporation, a government, or an army. And in America, the wealthy individuals who rule in corporate affairs appear to be attracted to the Church by reason of its hold not only on the mind but the actions of its adherents. Politically, socially and otherwise, they count on its power and influence as of use to them. And not without reason, since especially among the ignorant and poor, its revealed wisdom counsels resignation and orders faith in a totally inscrutable hereafter. In short, it makes for ignorance and submission in the working class. And what more could a corporation-minded government or financial group, looking toward complete control of everything for a few, desire?

And besides, the wealth of the Church elevates it to an unsurpassed prestige. The contributions of the congregations of twenty-five denominations in the United States for 1928 was $402,682,961.82. Can the Standard Oil of New Jersey show anything like that? Not even the greatest of our financial corporations can boast either the financial or social or political prestige of either the Catholic, Methodist or Episcopal churches here. Thus, the gifts from the living as well as income on permanent funds and legacies controlled by these twenty-five church denominations in America totaled in 1928 $532,368,714.80. The Methodist Episcopals alone, one little subsidiary of this great group, received in 1928, $98,758,030. The Presbyterians had $75,054,538 to spend. The Methodist Episcopals in the South, a

247

separate group, collected $42,837,679; the Protestant Episcopals $46,088,274, and the Baptists, in the South only, $40,038,259. Obviously this is why the Church (speaking of all denominations collectively) is able to organize tremendous lobbies, and, as I will show, does; also to exercise a preponderance of influence affecting education. And not only that, but to enter upon—and for purposes of social and mental control always—a score of activities which include asylums, hospitals, orphanages, protectories, graveyards, and what not else, all truly functions of government and functions which should never in any way be dominated by either the leaders or adherents of these ignorant and dogmatic religious institutions.

Yet the Church, realizing the power of wealth as well as mentally-controlled numbers, seeks to gather to itself all it can. Each year in America we see its influence grow, the political and "educational" activities of the Catholic Church in particular being everywhere apparent. Thus, the phenomenon of a religious adherent such as Al Smith, seeking from a people whose political as well as mental independence is not acknowledged by his Church, the official (in the sense that an American President has that) control of the same. And not only that, but the spectacle of many of the most grasping commercial magnates in America being elevated to leadership in the Church. The late Haley Fiske, life insurance president, who told his policyholders to denounce Government ownership because their life insurance funds were invested in private utility companies, was prominent in the Catholic movement of the Angelican Church. S. S. Kresge, of 5 and 10 cent store fame, and a Methodist, joined with his denomination in its assiduous fight for prohibition and religious control of public morality. Thomas F. Ryan was not only an adherent but a helpful donor to the Catholic Church, The list is much too long to append here. Yet men of this mental bent not only command the policies of corporate power in America but are evidently, from what I can disclose, an important factor in shaping church pursuits.

That the Church has the money to make itself felt is shown by the table given below:

Church Valuations in 1926

Baptist	$469,835,000
Congregational	164,212,000
Jewish	100,890,000
Methodist	654,736,000
Presbyterian	443,572,000
Protestant Episcopal	314,596,000

But the Roman Catholic Church property alone in America is valued at $837,271,000! The biggest and the worst. But what makes these organizations all the more dominating and far-reaching is that actually, in the large, they offer one and the same interpretation of life. It is the creation of a Ruler, whose intentions, purposes and rules have been revealed to them. More, as I have said, the guiding wish or mood of that Creator is resignation. Hence they are obviously advocates of things as they are. To pry or seek to know or change, as in science, sociology, government, is wrong. The God of each particular denomination knows all, directs all. Resignation to His will, as interpreted by them, is all. Hence they do not, as a rule, advocate the necessity, let alone the value, of change. And since heaven is for all, and the chief business of all is to achieve the hereafter or "sweet bye and bye," why the urge for anything difficult, let alone revolutionary, here? And that is why wealth and government always look upon religion as, if not their handmaiden, at least their "side kick" in these, their earthly adventurings.

Worse, the growing commercialism of America has made it all the more possible for the churches to increase their wealth. Between 1916 and 1926, the value of church buildings rose $2,160,-000,000; that is, an increase of one hundred and twenty-nine per cent. The most striking example in America, probably, of this rise in land values is Trinity Church (Episcopal) at the head of Wall Street. It owns about $15,000,000 in real estate, with an income from that alone of $1,460,000, and it has a surplus of $14,000,000. And all from property practically given to it, and more, in so far as concerns portions of it which can be listed as of service to religion, tax exempt.

That the laws of this or any country should permit any such sums to fall into organizational hands, and especially such organizational hands as set up such claims and commands as those of our religionists, is obviously wrong. More, it is economically unsound, since most of it is untaxed, and permits the rise and support of a privileged class which does little, if anything, more than befog the human mind. For as any one can see for himself, religious doctrines are based on so-called revelation, not reality. And worse, with such wealth to direct, what political, and worse, mental, harm cannot be done! The unlimited use of propaganda! The millions spent on foolish campaigns designed to shape or change public opinion in regard to this or that: divorce, birth control, the falseness of the Darwinian theory, or almost anything in connection with science and history! The blather about saints and cures and bringing all to Jesus, the while taxes are evaded and the scummy politicians whom they endorse, or even nominate and elect to office, proceed to rob the public in favor of the corporations and churches whom they serve! No wonder ignorance, no wonder illusion, when those with power in the religious field knowingly delude and mislead the masses! The things told them! That it is important to vote for this or that crook; uphold religion; it is good for the people to go to war, to put religion in the schools, to give into the hands of these mental bandits the care and education of all children, so that they may be properly enslaved by religion! (A slave, in my opinion, is the man who does not think for himself. A man with knowledge is not powerless.) But always with suave and polished words. For it is not men who are talking, as they assert, but God through them! and so through the mouths of tricksters and social prestidigitators, and no more and no less, comes all this hooey in regard to the hereafter! No wonder then that Russia swept religion away! And it should so be done here! Men should be educated concerning the data of this world and the value to men of a properly organized social life, and the how of that organization, so that they may really live better and be better mentally and physically. But, no! Whisper! God has told me, and I will tell you, and you shall follow and sustain me as my servant who am the servant of God!

But with these enormous Church holdings, as I have said, goes not one cent of taxes on noncommercial property. But there are tricks by which certain denominations, by laying the foundation of a church or school and then resting, can and do hold property for years until, its value having greatly increased, it becomes advisable to sell for an enormously enhanced price, and then, of course, it is so sold. One would think from that that the Churches were a branch of the Government, a public institution, whereas they are only semipublic, being under the control of a special group of patrons, and as such should be taxed and made to pay the same as any other self-aggrandizing corporation.

More, I believe that all of the pursuits in which the Church engages in this country (except æsthetics, which they portray so meagerly, awkwardly, grossly, and unbeautifully) are actually functions of government. And if so, they should be a part of government and not of the functionings of a special and separate, if not private, group of theorists, or worse, political men of affairs seeking, via theory, and worse, revelation, to function as government. I refer to such things as hospitals, protectories, orphan asylums, schools, colleges, homes for the aged and infirm, graveyards, and industries of whatsoever nature.

To show some of the dangers, let me point out how the Church takes advantage of its property holdings, and how practically it profits by the same. Thus, when the Madison Avenue Methodist Church in New York City sold its site for an apartment building and moved to another plot of land nearby, it made a profit of $650,000. But I ask, why should religion be a profiteer? If the State permits them to go tax free, it should at least, should it not? enjoy and participate in any money-making of this nature, which is certainly no legitimate function of religion. Next, in

1926, the Temple Emanu-El likewise made more than $6,000,000 in this same manner. Its property on Fifth Avenue at Forty-third Street, New York, increased in value five hundred per cent between 1900 and 1929. All it had to do in order to garner this increment was to move up Fifth Avenue to Sixty-fifth Street, where it could buy cheaper. A like action in connection with St. Patrick's Cathedral would yield the Catholic Church about $10,000,000. And considering how practical that Church is, it is a wonder it is not so moved. In Brooklyn and the Bronx, the Catholic Church owns several plots of land on which are erected only one-story buildings. What will these be, and what eventually will they be sold for?

But what is worse in connection with this untaxed architecture and the land on which it stands is this. By the overwhelming power of it as mass, if not art, in the eyes of the persuaded followers of any faith, both at once assume spiritual and even mystic significance, thus magnetizing to the organizations controlling them the faith as well as the money of those so mentally led. For it is not only doctrine but doctrine-joined-up-with-material-appearance that so intrigues and deceives the average mind. And in America, as well as Europe, how often the elegance of the town takes its inspiration from its principal religious edifice: in Europe, the Roman Catholic Church; in America, the Methodist, Episcopal and Catholic Churches. The new Methodist Church in Worcester, Massachusetts, is valued at $1,000,000, entailing, in these days of strikes and unemployment, quite an obligation to society, I would say.

Well now, church buildings alone in America, without parsonages, investments, securities, schools, orphanages, hospitals and monasteries, are valued at $3,800,000,000; the parsonages alone, and apart from the above, are reported to be worth $500,-000,000. Furthermore, an estimate in the *Literary Digest* concludes that $7,000,000,000, at least, constitutes the total securities and property of the churches in America. A more definite figure is the actual expenditure of the churches in 1926. This totaled $817,000,000. Well, this is the equivalent of six per cent on more than a $13,500,000,000 investment, is it not? And all for the purposes of the most inane, unprogressive, and often scheming as well as ignorant, social parasites, their crack-brained theories and certainly mentally destructive aims! That they may lead and lord it over fools, or to put it more truthfully, that fools may lead fools!

But mere billions do not in any way indicate the scope of the church—its influence. Much more important is the total member-ship. In all, fifty-five per cent of America's entire population are claimed as church members. Over one-half! And of these the Roman Catholic Church claims thirty per cent. In 1926, 54,576,-000 persons belonged to the various denominations, or claimed to. If this is really true, such an organization can and should mold the mind of the whole populace. But does it? Whether the answer is yes or no, the Catholics, the most reactionary and mind-stultifying of all, seem to be the most efficient. At least they are the most forward in their efforts to direct, politically, educa-tionally, legally and in every way. And as for concentration of effort, well, in 1926, there were 183,505 white Protestant churches for 23,515,000 members—an average of 128 to a church—and 16,615 Roman Catholic churches for 18,104,800 adherents—an average of 1,089 per church.

So this is what the system has to work with. Yet despite this, the country to-day is suffering from a lack of faith, recognized everywhere, but the depths of which may not yet be ascertained. Personally I believe it to be due not only to ignorance but to the dominance in churchly undertakings of economics and its related activities over spiritual development. The Church itself, as much as anything, has made the spiritual life unfashionable, and hence has degraded it. Against the sole hope and inspiration of Christ, it has given way to commercial standards of corporations and just when people need a simple æsthetic and mental haven to escape from corporate speed and complexity. All in all, it has sought to become a moving factor in national life, and by so doing has defeated its purpose of spiritual nourishment. And certainly, the seeking human hearts, so lost from the Church, are something to be reckoned with. Thousands who have followed it from childhood have wakened to find it an intellectual (which includes æsthetics, of course) loss.

But let us see how the Church seeks to influence sociologically, economically and politically, and, of course, seize power via numbers and the control of the same through faith. Orphanages, for one thing; schools, for another; Sunday schools for still another; and then hospitals, protectories, and the like. I want to speak particularly, however, of Sunday schools, schools, and homes for the aged run by churches. For first, the doctrine-flavored educational factor of the Sunday school is shockingly wide in its appeal. In 1926, 212 denominations here had 185,000 Sunday schools, with 21,000,000 pupils—only 3,700,000 less than the total enrollment of all the public schools in the United States! But what is taught in them? An æsthetic appreciation of beauty? Yes? A suggestion of the complicated nature of the organized society in which we find ourselves and the proper understanding of its functions and their value—one's benefits from as well as duties to it as one of its beneficiaries? Never! That would be putting life above death, reality above mysticism, the here and now through which we really live and suffer over and above a mythical and unsubstantiated hereafter in which we are to be rewarded for what we suffer here. Rather a deadly indifference to the correction of those same ills here and now, all reality denounced, feared, buried, the while prayer, the only thing taught in the church which might be turned to æsthetic value, is dominated by a silly, narrow code of sins, confessions and selfish yearnings or needs, pathetically doomed to unfulfillment. In short, every worth-while phase of a proper knowledge of life evaded, the while the antithesis, dogmas relative to a mystical hierarchy which Christ never contemplated, is insisted upon. Indeed, his worded peace, order and unselfishness is almost totally ignored. Or if not, then united with dogma and rules never contemplated by him, and calculated by the Church, particularly the Catholic Church, to give it such power as to chain its adherents to slavish ignorance and obedience throughout their life here. Yet obviously, such power cannot be for the good of the individual here on earth or his government. It is against his mind. And when that is suborned or darkened, by whatever process, what else of value can remain?

From 1906 to 1926, while the percentage of pupils in our American public schools increased only fifty per cent, the total number of pupils in Roman Catholic parochial schools rose one hundred per cent—schools that belie science, deny the powers and plans of any earthly government not profoundly submissive to the mythical heavenly government which they proclaim and administer, and which boldly, and in the main successfully, seek to block all forms of education not wholly harmonious with their antiquated, false and mentally subversive data as to how life is organized and what its proper rewards as well as functions should be. And yet America propagandized abroad as progressive; the people of this country touted as being better equipped educationally as well as in every other way than those of any other part of the world! Only I believe that America is actually becoming weaker mentally, not stronger. And yet, all the rest of the world called upon to bow to the actions as well as the wisdom of this country as of the best, the ideals of the United States Government as mentally, morally and in every other way the highest! Yet Catholics and Jews alike demanding control of the education of their children, for this, for that and the other silly reason: morality, the salvation of their souls, etc., but in the latter sense, most certainly detrimental, since it can only be mis-shaping the wondering, formative mind of the child. And so, instead of joining with the American school system to make it truly constructive mentally, insisting on snatching their children from it either entirely or on any and every day or days they so desire, and for the purpose of having them celebrate this or that dogmatic event, observe this or that holy day, or the life of some fantastic saint whose worship or honor could only be destructive to any worth-while prosecution of education anywhere!

And all this without the least protest as yet on the part of our American educators or our citizens generally. Rather—

whisper!—the Catholics, the Jews, the this, the that, have power and can cast you from office or cause you trouble! And since all is for office or job or money in America, the idea of doing anything for a worth-while ideal, educationally or in any other way, is beyond anybody. Whisper! In a corporation and priest-ridden world it isn't a good thing for the rank and file to know too much, anyhow! It may make them restless! Hence—whisper!—don't say anything! Let it go! It may not be good for business! And so, an ever-increasing number of children in Catholic and other sectarian schools, and all actually being drilled in mental as well as social misvalues. Yet it is known, and can be proved, of course, that these religionists, with their nostrums and their demands, constitute open rebellion against the fundamental principle of nonsectarian education in America. But does that matter? Will it before the education orientation of the nation is totally disarranged?

The following was given out in the fall of 1930 by the National Catholic Welfare Conference:

Pupils in 7,811 Catholic elementary schools 2,283,000
  "   " 2,235   "   high schools 228,000
  "   "   171   "   colleges 102,000
  "   "   77   "   normal schools 9,000
  "   "   187   "   seminaries 18,000

And relatively the same proportions holding for other denominations in America.

But more, the leaders of these sectarian schools, like Dr. Edmund P. Soper, President of Ohio Wesleyan College, arise to say that it is the right and duty of the sectarian educational representatives of America to control what the schools and their professors and teachers teach. And this gentleman gives as his reason that learning should follow Christian principles. But this, according to the present standards of these sectarians, means the acceptance and following of not only dogma as laid down by the religionists, and hence the ignoring of all science, but, and also, the inculcation of the present unrestrained individualism of

Americans as represented now by the money-mad leaders who are dictating not only the economics but the philosophy of the country and using the religionists to help them. And if that is not so, count the ministers and churches now contemplating the state of the tramping masses in America who have one word (as opposed to the word of Capitalism and its present money-madness) to say in their favor. Count them and let us see who and where they are and what the nature of their economic and sociologic programs are!

Dr. Soper also states that his standards would and should be effected by choosing *reactionary* men and that these same should then be allowed to teach with freedom, yet as Christians—which means restraint. More, states Dr. Soper: in case they learn more and change their ideas, the professors must leave! In other words, when they are no longer ignorant enough for the ideals of the sectarian school, they must depart!

Well, in the United States there are 624 four-year colleges and universities, and of these 376 are religious colleges: 75 Methodist, 55 Presbyterian, 46 Baptist, etc. And assuming Dr. Soper's rule to apply, one can see not only what is happening but what is going to happen to true learning in these institutions. Science? History? Learning? Out! Let us have ignorant slave following ignorant master, as in so many of the past periods of recorded history. For what else can come?

But let us return to another of these energies of religion in America which border on and really are functions of government. Homes for the aged, obviously one phase of the business of government, now bring, instead, power to the churches, via the carefully cultivated goodwill and hence, in the main, adherence of thousands of inmates and their relatives—and this regardless of the false educational principles in complete control of such places—false in the sense that they present the sectarian church and its dogmas in the light of truth, its efforts and labors in every field as noble, charitable, etc.—whereas in reality the truth is that these so-called labors and charities are quite always on a paying basis and should not be permitted to usurp the mantle of charity, let alone a proper function of government. They open to sectarian illusion and dogma too wide a door, and that door should be closed.

To make clear what I mean: the median rates per month for residents in quite any of these homes is $30, and the median per capita cost of operation is just about the same. More, in 182 of these homes for the aged, Catholic and others, the old folks work. Thus, one home, at the time of this writing, has 1,100 acres of corn, 25,500 strawberry plants, two acres of raspberries, etc. Last year the old people picked 5,000 quarts of strawberries, 1,000 quarts of raspberries, etc., which the organization marketed. Yet this same is pictured as a Christian charity, the while it makes for Christian adherents of the sect which operates it.

Not only that, but many of these homes have extensive properties which enjoy a natural increment which can but redound to the financial prosperity of the religion or sect operating them. Thus, one I have in mind is located on a 704-acre farm, with numerous timber lots, one of which is 84 acres in extent. Again, a Methodist home of which I know has 125 acres, another 358 acres, and one Episcopal home, 500 acres. These homes also frequently have extensive buildings. Several are valued at $1,000,000 each, and one at $2,000,000.

But to generalize a bit in connection with these homes, let me add that forty-four Methodist homes in America are now valued at $6,639,132 and more, exalt themselves under endowments totaling $3,863,761. Yet for all these investments and gifts, the people in them in many cases live like trusted prisoners. Also, according to the rules in some instances, residents may not leave the grounds, wash clothes, etc., without permission. Furthermore, obedience to these rules is insured, since on entering these old people are compelled to assign to the institution such possessions as they may have—money, land, what you will—which naturally makes them from then on utterly dependent upon said institution until death. In each such institution, a house committee dictates what each inmate may have in his or her room and how the furniture is to be arranged. In addition to that, and regardless of whether they desire it or not, religion is forced on these residents. For pay or no pay, it is good for their souls! And should you doubt the strength of my word "forced," explain, if you can, the existence of the following rule: "... reverent attention during worship is obligatory." And religion, to that extent at least, and in that manner, is administered to the inmates of the following homes:

Homes for the Aged in the United States

Roman Catholic 156
Baptist 20
Lutheran 47
Methodist 45
Presbyterian 20
Episcopal 39
Miscellaneous denominations 148

Quite an influence, don't you think: 475 homes with 27,298 residents?

More than that, our churches have already caught the corporate merger idea and are following their mentors in that field. Thus, in 1906 there was 1 church for 270 population, in 1916 there was 1 church for 300 population, in 1926 there was 1 church for 344 population. But although the number of churches, according to population, is decreasing, the membership rate remains the same.

In addition to this, though, numerous inclusive organizations for specific purposes are bringing about a united effort on the part of the Church as strong as that of any holding company: the A. T. & T., for instance. Thus, already the United Church of Canada has been formed, combining the Methodists, Presbyterians and Congregationalists. And there have been proposals of extensive mergers among others.

That the leaders of this assumed Christianity are themselves bringing to the Church the psychology of our commercial enterprise and order is not only already plain but daily becoming more so. And presumably to strengthen their several positions. Thus, Dr. Harry Emerson Fosdick, for one, at the opening of the Riverside Cathedral, said: "If we were to put an electric sign in front of this church, I know where we would get it. I would steal it from one of the great electric utility companies: 'Public Service, Light and Power' the sign would read." More, the constant use which ministers make of the term "profit," "power house" and other industrial terms, shows that they are accepting as ideals the commercial standards of the day. But contrast, if you will, quite all of Christ's comments on "profits" and "prosperity" and accumulations of wealth in general!

Now one of the movements resulting from Church wealth and prestige in the past everywhere was missionary work. And let us grant that this truly had a Christ-like beginning. For it is a fact, of course, that in the early days of the Church, men did go out and risk their lives and sacrifice comforts for a "spiritual" good which they imagined they contemplated and that decidedly they wished to share with others. And in the early days of the United States, that was true of the missionaries here. Yet listen to an American missionary writing to-day of his work: "Although the sacrificial life of the mission field has been lauded to our paying church members . . . all of these are based on more or less false assumptions." And the reason for this comment could only be that at the present time the Church has drawn such wealth to itself that the day of any form of sacrifice for the missionary is over. He is usually reported as more or less of a lord as well as leader in his various fields of operation. At any rate, certain it is that 15 denominations now contribute $26,000,000 annually to mission work. (Yet for 1900, the figure was only $5,250,000.) And now our missionaries are frequently housed in splendor. Naturally, this has accentuated, and quite reasonably, some prejudice in some of the foreign lands to which these missionaries proceed. For instead of fulfilling the lowly rôle of helpful worker coöperating with those not able to do much for themselves, we find our plethoric missionaries of to-day, and particularly those from America, living richly and acting like lords among the foreign peoples upon whom they choose to bestow their service and whom they stigmatize as benighted. The Chinese, for instance, or the Hindoos! More, an American missionary to India has written that he could testify that "to-day the life of the foreigner there, be he missionary or government official, is the most lordly life on earth."

But what are the aims and methods of procedure of these missionaries who proceed from America into China, India, Siam, and elsewhere? These are interesting, for, as you will see, they have their roots in something very peculiar here. In China, for instance, our missionaries—those of the Protestant persuasion, at least—work with the government there just as closely as do the corporations that have their origin in this land. And with the corporations there also. And are frequently as much the emissaries of American trade as of religion, and even more so. For whereas formerly the missionaries used to go to convey a spiritual message, to-day at least one very important phase of their purpose is to effect as well as share material or economic "blessings" for the natives, such blessings, for instance, as our very material corporations manufacture and seek to distribute as widely as possible; bathtubs, sewing machines, electric lights, or, refrigerators, or in other words, anything and everything that our modern corporations make. In other words again, "Make 'em modern!" That means more business for home corporations, doesn't it? And I am not talking wildly, for only read, as I have done, the writings of our very up-to-date missionaries of this hour. And furthermore, most missionaries now believe that they should be protected with gunboats—they who supposedly represent that Jesus who taught peace! And to show the growth of our missions, the American Baptist Missionary Union, which was organized in 1846 and had nothing to go on, in 1893 had an income of $485,000. And now...!

Well, before I go on as to this, though, I want to speak about John D. Rockefeller and his interest in the matter. Rockefeller, as you know, has always shown an extraordinary interest in the Church. He has been the most conspicuous, I am sure, of all our American capitalists who have exalted the Church with material dignity. In fact, in the early eighties it was that Rockefeller became a vice-president of the Baptist Theological Union of Chicago. And his first interest in the University of Chicago, to which he subsequently gave $35,000,000, related to its then proposed Baptist Union Theological Seminary, to which in 1889 he pledged $600,000. This school was to train men for missionary work abroad as well as the ministry here and soon occupied a social, economic and political position which I will discuss.

As I have related in my chapter titled "Is America Dominant?" to which you will come a little later, Rockefeller in the early part of this century had a big kerosene business in China. He was so powerful (wealthy and protected by American tariffs which aided him in his high prices here) that he was able to undersell the Royal Dutch Shell, thus causing it to lose many millions in China, the field which it was invading. But now in connection with this money given to this Chicago Seminary for the training of missionaries, it is significant to note (and I believe I am treating the matter fairly) that probably it was given with a view to material or financial return for Standard Oil. For as He himself wrote: "According as you put something in, the greater will be your dividends of salvation."

At any rate, as his various public statements show, he well knew the value of religion not only as a sedative in connection with troublesome economic conditions everywhere, but also the great value of missionaries in connection with foreign trade. In fact, I myself have read articles in such papers as the *Review of Reviews,* the *Literary Digest,* and others indicating how the oil-can followed the missionary. At any rate, Rockefeller started his missionary support by an early gift of $400,-000 to this Baptist Missionary Union. Now this organization pivots from ten fields, one in each of the following sections: East China, West China, South China, Japan, Philippines, Burma, Assam, South India, and the Belgian Congo. And in these fields missionaries work from 127 stations and 3,237 outstations. Conceive what that means to American business and then cogitate Rockefeller's cleverness and his charity which has won him so many laurels. They operate 6 colleges, 35 theological seminaries, and 2,608 schools. And their equipment includes 3 printing presses. In this connection it may also be stated that the Park Avenue Baptist Church in New York, which Rockefeller supported and finally established as the Riverside Cathedral, is in the Northern Baptist Convention, which has 3,000 missionaries in China, Japan, Philippines, Burma and the Belgian Congo. And certainly in those fields the Standard Oil Company has flourished. But disregarding the import of this seemingly direct connection, whatever the material results, they could not mentally be less harmful than Baptist or other dogma, and is it not plain that what has been said here certainly illustrates the tendency towards the commercialization of church effort previously referred to?

World-wide mission service has so grown in modern times as to possess organized schools, churches and publications. Along with its own thousands of missionaries, tens of thousands of natives are employed in a staff capacity. And an army of Catholic missionaries numbering 163,615 strong prey on foreign peoples from their 95 jurisdictions in China, 44 in India and Burma, 14 in Siam and Indo-China, 30 in South Africa, and 33 in South America. In fact, the Catholics claim 6,000,000 members in Asia and 3,500,000 in Africa. Management of these Roman Catholic mission branches is under the Catholic Sacred Congregation for the Propagation of the Faith. The personnel for this project is trained in 5 universities, 309 seminaries, 1,117 superior schools, and 836 professional schools. Also, the Catholic Sacred Congregation for the Propagation of the Faith uses 164 printing shops. Is it any wonder then that the world is being overrun with this Catholic inanity? Or that America, so interested in trade from whatever source, should aid in the great work?

Now in this connection, it may be explained that universality has always been the goal of the Roman Catholic Church, whose missionaries have always begun where imperialistic armies left off. And while it is true that there are millions of non-Christians in many countries unexploited by capitalism, still where money is invested, it is always noticeable that the missionaries turn. And there are 500 American corporations in China. Yet when the missionaries come, Catholic or other, it is supposedly to claim a land for Christ. But in the light of the Rockefeller view of it, the capitalistic patronizing of the Chinese movement as a whole is quite explicable. And so, no wonder that China has been found such a stirring field for a new kind of missionary enthusiasm! In America, however, owing to the number of missionaries that issue therefrom, it might reasonably be considered to be Christianized and hence a pleasant place.

But now for a change consider the attitude of the Church toward the economic and social ills of the individual at this time. His unemployment, his abuse when he is employed, the immense class and individual injustices, which go unscathed save for wild words here and there, by the immense organizations which set themselves up as not only the teachers but the practicers of the teachings of Christ! You have seen (since I have shown where and how) the Negro disfranchised and burned in the South and rarely wanted in any white church. Also the capital and labor wars in which the minor individual has during decades past, and more so now than ever, been denounced, underpaid, starved and beaten, the while the Church in all its phases and under whatsoever sectarian banners it marches has stood by and done nothing, studied neither the economics, the sociology nor the government of the all too real world in which these laborers are compelled to live, nor how and why they are so compelled to live. Not the Church! For it is not the poor who build the magnificent church edifices of this day or pay the largest salaries, though as usual the Church, whenever it approaches the little man, and regardless of his inability to pay much, does so with a tin cup. More, when he comes to the church for anything, if he comes at all, he pays, and plenty! So much for a marriage—so many dollars; so much for a baptism; so much for a funeral service; so much for a mass or special prayers; so much for a plot in a carefully conducted—financially speaking—religious graveyard; so much for a bed in a charity hospital; so much for a bed in a home for the aged, or *no bed;* so much for the poor-box; so much for the "shrine of the little flower"; so much for his children's education in a sectarian school; so much for membership in the "Catholic Boy Scouts"; so much for the favor of any saint in the immense and entire roster of saints, although disguised as an offering! And tickets, tickets, tickets, for this, that and the other, and which the faithful must invariably buy! But as for help for the faithful in their great struggles, well, that is, in the main, the business of the general public, non-Catholic as well as Catholic, is it not? Or the State? Or the Government? Yet all of whom in their turn do as little as possible, or, in other words, pass the buck!

Yet when it comes to rounding up the faithful or "selling" the idea of religion to the masses regardless of its benefits, note the new and quite up-to-date, also corporate, methods of handling this great problem. It is none other than our old and effective friend *propaganda,* vitalized by the use of money for publicity and directed by the best of our American publicity agents who cook up the same "hot dope" on the churches as do the professionals laboring for the great railroad and manufacturing systems in this country. These publicity agents, as things go now, take any sermon anywhere and, regardless of its dullness and inanity, proceed to give it a snappy head and lead, whereupon it is sent to the local or metropolitan newspapers. Thus, Edward L. Wertheim, one of New York's well-known religious publicity agents (the Church must have them as well as the circus!) rewrites news for the Greater New York Federation of Churches, the Fifth Avenue Presbyterian Church, Calvary Church, Grace Episcopal Church, Manhattan Congregational Church, etc. The H. S. Howland Advertising Agency publicizes for the Church of the Intercession; Walter Irving Clark, of Philadelphia, manages publicity for the Presbyterian Church of the United States of America; Herbert D. Rugg is editorial secretary of the National Council of Congregational Churches; Dr. Steele reports and propagandizes for the Federal Council of Churches of Christ in America, etc.

These publicity experts write feature stories which must bring wide popularity and acclaim to the ministers represented, or there will be no publicity agent or at least no pay for his work. For as in other practical fields, his labors must bring results. Yet contemplate this in connection with the mental refinement and method of Jesus, who said: "Whosoever shall exalt himself shall be abased; and he that shall humble himself shall be exalted." Many churches or groups of churches now employ such "go getter" publicity agents. Some of them, unfortunately, are trained according to the standards of New York's second-rate newspapers, so that to-day editors are not infrequently in receipt of word that the sermon the following Sunday in this or that big church is to be so striking (and it is given a shocking but meaningless title to arrest popular interest) that a special reporter is sought by the church to cover it.

But the church brings its moral significance to bear just how? I do not see how any one can do otherwise than indict the various organizations carrying on the following petty and foolish regulation campaigns when the world is so full of such severe psychologic as well as economic ills as have here in this volume been shown. Contemplate, for instance, the platform of the Lord's Day Alliance Movement in America, drawn as it has been and fought for by Methodists, Presbyterians, Congregationalists, Baptists, Episcopalians, etc. By disseminating endless syndicated stories and sponsoring bills to the end that a thoroughly "blue Sunday" may be universal, it seeks to prohibit the following on Sunday: concerts, plays, movies, debates, skating, dancing, rail and water excursions, baseball (even amateur), garage repairing, and all entertainment, as well as the sale of candy, delicatessen merchandise, etc. But considering the real ills of the world, and those of America in particular—the state of the little man here—what an annoying and profitless interference with private life! You are to be good or religious whether you want to be or not! But such petty ways of being good—sitting idle and folding your hands!

And this backed up by the Lord's Day Alliance speakers all over the country! Indeed, the business of bawling "Sin!" in connection with nearly every amiable interest, recreation, or weakness of the living men and women of the world is typical of almost every phase of our present-day American religions. And the result has been to make it all so shallow and hollow as to suggest—and that presently and without external interference or opposition of any kind—a complete and final internal collapse.

But to consider further for a moment this business of this Lord's Day Alliance in making America better, religiously at least. For one thing, merchants doing business on Sunday were recently arrested in New Jersey. South Carolina arrests Sunday golfers, etc. You cannot buy gasoline on a Sunday morning in Georgia, nor go anywhere in your shirtsleeves. So it is with this minute dictation of personal life by all church factions. Rules are handed out to be followed to the letter, whether they are for the betterment of the individual or not, and frequently backed up by the argument that they are divine law—an argument carrying no more weight than any other idea or interpretation of life by any earthly being. Thus, the Roman Catholic Church widely denounces birth control as against divine law. Well, in one sense one can understand this when one remembers its great need of the child from whatsoever source in order to turn it, before six or at least by twelve years of age, into a Catholic. But why the rest of America or any other government should decry something so temperamentally and economically valuable as this to human beings at this time is more than I can understand. Certainly those held closest to this anti-birth-control position are among the most degraded representatives of society to-day, the poorest and most unfit.

True, some Protestant denominations state that they favor birth control, but they beleaguer its use with so many reservations as to make it taboo to all save the diseased and poverty-stricken.

And yet consider, if you will, some of the problems to which the American Church, if it would (had the heart, brains, initiative) could turn. There is child labor. And humanly the Church might battle against that! But does it? Or there are the thousands of men and women who are compelled by the New York subways and elevated roads, the bus lines, railroads, etc., to work eight, ten and twelve hours on Sundays. And to work in addition seven days a week. Couldn't the churches and the Lord's Day Alliance do something about that, especially since by so doing they would give work to so many of the present-day unemployed and prevent them from desecrating the Sabbath by so working? And will it? Well, wait and see! More, there is unemployment insurance. And what does the Church do about that? Or old age pensions? Or our inhuman prison conditions? Or peonage in the South? Or forced and inhuman labor anywhere? Pah!

But the churches do not—and more, cannot—so wisely or tenderly act, because it is against the interests of the capitalists, and the capitalists, being the opulent subscribers to the Church, cannot be repelled by having the Church go against them. Who does not know that? Thus, our capitalists, or our corporations or both, and all such so minded, control the Church in America to-day. Yet in order to keep the minds of churchgoers off the essential truth of this, the priests and ministers and all of their sinister, if silly, organizations and societies are busy over "issues" and "doing good," all of which are not good at all. In short, the congregations of the various sects, as well as the under dog of any or no sect, are to be kept ignorant in order that they may be dominated.

More, I decry the ignorance of American ministers who so viciously direct millions of lives and whose seminary-filtered knowledge has absolutely nothing to do with the reality of to-day. And in this connection, consider, if you will, the silly, unspiritual emanations of our great pulpits, and at this time. The sawdust or confetti sprinkled upon our assembled American dunces! "Getting over the Blues"; "Being a Good Sport"; "Seeing it Through"; "You Can!"—fitting themes for individuals hired to make bad times seem good times, or the unbearable ills of mankind bearable, but hardly laudable from a pulpit voicing the communism of Christ! And these from some of our best pulpits the land over! The trouble is that neither science, politics, economics, sociology, history, taxation, government are truly, if at all, taught these creatures who are later to lead the masses to Christ. They would prove too disarming. Nor does it help that three out of every eight ministers in eighteen white denominations and more than three out of every four ministers in the three largest Negro religious organizations; that is, forty-one per cent of the Protestant ministers and 6.6 per cent of Catholic priests, and one minister out of five in the cities and one out of two in the country, are not graduated from any college or seminary. For even so, before they enter upon any sectarian church, must they not be adherents of that faith and talk whatever "revealed" nonsense is ordained by said faith? And should they talk otherwise, is not the corporation-financed American world certain to blacklist, denounce and pursue them? The absence of any minister or priest of any standing uttering a single worthwhile economic thought in connection with the present immense social crisis should tell the story, should it not? Either they have not the brains or they have no conscience!

But to return to Church mentality, to say nothing of liberality in any sense. Thus, so great a conference as that of Lambeth in the Anglican Communion in 1930, and one lauded at the time as being liberal and even radical and thus marking a turning point in church history, busied itself with such folderol as denouncing divorce and proclaiming that "Sex is holy, and therefore the relations of man and wife are holy," and added that "Trial marriage destroys the reverence and discipline for both body and mind on which the happiness of married life so signally depends." Also, birth control was given quite a setback by a statement that desire for children should govern sexual intercourse. And such little rules and narrow dicta as: the Protestant Episcopal minister can marry divorcées only by civil ceremony; the Catholics cannot marry them at all; and more, a civil marriage, to that organization, is neither legal nor binding. In other words, it is not that Church that owes allegiance to any State but rather every State owes allegiance to that faith, and is looked upon in that light by that faith; i.e., as a subject state, to be led and guided by that wholly political organization which has now dominated the minds of the masses to their confusion and ill for nearly two thousand years!

Yet with all this quite fantastic lack of mental understanding, and with all its irritating and at times devastating potency of numbers, the Church plunges headlong into politics and economics. For instance, the National Catholic Welfare Conference in America, endorsed by the Pope, functions exactly as any other lobby, although the Catholics will not admit that it is a lobby. This lobby seeks to and does influence education, immigration, marriage, divorce, eugenics, censorship, what should or should not go through the United States mails, control and sterilization of the incompetent, etc. More, it has several methods of leverage. Firstly, in so far as it can without treading on the ground of stronger powers, it sees that laws governing these restrictions are not violated. Next, it furnishes all manner of aid to the Roman Catholic broadcasting stations, which work night and day in its noble behalf. Lastly, the "Catholic Conference" also has a news organization which sends "canned" editorials to the Catholic papers all over America, and likewise news items under the supervision of a former Hearst newspaperman.

And the quite terrorized awe with which Americans of all walks of life and belief or nonbelief touch upon anything relating to the Catholic Church! Its rumored power and machinations, and the definite reality of the same! While other countries —Spain, Mexico, Italy, France—retain the courage to denounce and even regulate the Roman Catholic Church (in 1925 a separation agreement was drawn up between the Roman Catholic Church and the Government of Chile; Mussolini in Rome is closing Catholic clubs and playgrounds and dissolving the Catholic Action, etc., etc.), America stands in either ridiculous fear or reverence. Whisper...no one must say anything about it here! That is the attitude. No one dare even justly attack its policies or their meaning, or its mental and social effrontery. Is it overawing in politics? Silence! Is it working secretly in the American labor unions to control labor? Silence! Is it doing its best to undermine the mental freedom of the American school? Silence! Beware! No one dare say a word, for if one does, the Church will pursue that person and do him up! Imagine! Consider only the whispering campaign against Al Smith, nominee of Tammany Hall and the Catholic Church for the Presidency of the United States in 1928! Did any one dare say openly he was just that, or that once in office he might favor those wretchedly practical and wholly power-seeking organizations? Hush, hush! Attack Catholicism? Silence! Vote but don't talk! It's too powerful! It'll do you harm! And so, Al Smith defeated, but by an enormous *silent* vote. And to this hour, whisper, whisper, or silence! But just why, in this connection, have the American people lost their courage to say out loud what they think? Are we so weak, so characterless, or socially meaningless, that we dare not discuss with this Church what its policies, and more, its political and social intentions, are? And since when?

The Lord's Day Alliance, which, as I have said, is an interdenominational organization, keeps lobbyists in legislatures all over the country, trying to get this, that and the other inane law passed. Numerically, if not mentally, weighty, and the ballot being a weapon which it can use, a group like this is able to and does at times bear down on the helpless individual quite as does a trust. As an example of the bills sponsored by it, I offer the New York State Jenks Bill, outlawing Sunday baseball (including even playing "catch") before 2 P.M. More, this Lord's Day Alliance lobby defeats on an average of forty State bills per year. Recently their lobbyists in New Jersey defeated thirty-nine commercial bills which they believed would interfere with Sunday reverence. Yet it is this form of visionless and trivial pettiness which makes of America the asinine, nonintellectual specimen that it is to-day.

But now for the Methodist Board of Temperance, Prohibition and Morals. The wealth of this particular institution may indicate something of the means at its command to carry out its propaganda. To begin with, it is housed in a luxurious building of marble and limestone very near the Government buildings in Washington. More, here fine apartments are rented to senators and representatives—perhaps of the right persuasion. Next, this Board was created and is now dominated by one Dr. Wilson, formerly a soap-box and platform orator on local option in the Northwest. Wilson got himself into the good graces of the Methodists, and later headed their simple little society out in Topeka, Kansas. Within a short time thereafter, though, he had reached the above described proportions. And to his organization and its buildings now come subscriptions from all over the country and from all sources, financial as well as religious. It has even been charged that its subscribers include not only our corporations anxious to take the minds of voters off the trust movement and government ownership issues, but also bootleggers who, finding that this war against liquor serves them in their trade and its profits, are ready also to contribute. I include the idea for what it is worth. Certain it is, though, and as any one with half an eye can see, that if those who are of influence in America to-day really wanted Prohibition as a benefit to the people, it would be enforced. But is it? Our futile churches talk and collect money, but in New York City alone are thousands of speakeasies, and the number for the United States must be colossal. Yet to what *political* dimensions has the above organization reached! It functions, and there is liquor for everybody!

Yet the following other church organizations have also fought for Prohibition, and collected money so to do; the Southern Methodists, under Bishop Cannon; the Presbyterians, the Disciples, and semiofficially, the Catholic Father Matthew Society and the Association of Catholics. The Methodist Board

of Temperance, Prohibition and Morals sends out about 2,000,-
000 columns of news annually. Its platform includes compulsory
teaching of the Bible in public schools, uniform marriage and
divorce laws (I suppose all to be as stiff as New York State's);
no cartoons, jokes or songs that are immodest, and in this category, according to their avowed principles, goes European art;
no professional or collegiate boxing, no tobacco, etc.

In sum, in America as elsewhere, the Church—speaking of
all sects and creeds as one—has consistently expounded views
calculated to make the underdog content with his wretched lot,
and in all crises which have meant hunger, abuse, and even death,
as in our great labor wars, has left him to do as best he may.
More, the Church, and particularly the Roman Catholic Church,
is more concerned with a system of sins, confessions, judgment,
punishment and rewards relating to the hereafter than it is with
the world of to-day, its economics, politics, sociology and government; that is, in any honest or helpful way. More, it leaves,
as it always has, the underdog to suffer as he may here, the while
it seeks to turn his eye on supposed grace hereafter. So true is
this that from an American Federation of Labor symposium on
religion, influenced, of course, by the current religious attitude
of Americans and their churches in general, I gather that its
chief philosophy is that the poor should help the poor, since
the rich will not, neither their trusts, banks nor government,
and that in doing so they will bring about a Christlike contentment, if not better wages. And more than that, questioning
a religionist voicing such views on a street corner a few years
ago, I found from his own confession that he was then and
there being paid by a certain religious organization to preach
such views. But who was financing the religious organization?
I have often since wondered!

But to further illustrate what I mean, let me add that when
four strikers were shot down by sheriffs and their deputies
(maybe private police) during the recent great textile strike
in North Carolina, James Myers, industrial secretary of the
Federal Council of Churches, down there to help the workers,

was invited to make the funeral address. As usual with our present-hour religionists, who if not consciously are still subconsciously corporation-minded, he made this his opportunity to advise strikers, who were out against indecent conditions, to fight no longer and choose the way of love! Not only that, but I personally can name scores of cases where ministers have refused to do anything for strikers, or where ministers who have aided strikers have been attacked by capitalistic representatives.

Yet the Church goes in for politics in a big way in legislative elections for Congress and State assemblies. Religious participation in economic issues pervades all political life. Many of the great denominations have economic research bureaus which outline reforms. The following sweeping issues have been made their business: support of the World Court, the League of Nations, lower tariffs, reduction of armaments, regulation of school curricula, subversion of the Monroe Doctrine, etc. Our churches have also meddled in Government investigations, sought to have Japanese admitted to this country, and have asked pardon for convicts, etc. And in 1926, under the leadership of ex-Ambassador Gerard, Bishop Manning had ten Episcopal bishops protest the United States proposed Treaty of Lausanne with Turkey, because Turkey was non-Christian. Yet the beneficiaries of this action, if you please, were British oil interests!

And more, economic as well as spiritual pronouncements are alike heightened by a supposedly divine authority. The claim of the Roman Catholic Church is that the Pope is the Vicar of Christ and the Vice-Regent of God over men under divine authority. And accordingly, everything possible is done, even to this day, to make this seem true. Will some one kindly page Mr. Einstein or Charles Darwin? Indeed, Pope Leo XIII, in his Encyclicals published in New York in 1903, stated: ". . . over this mighty multitude God has placed rulers" (the Roman Catholic bishops) "with power to govern, and He has willed that one of them should be the head of all." The Catholics, likewise, are great on show and mystery, honoring men by making them "Knights of the Equestrian Order of the Holy Sepulchre in the United States," "Officers of the Militia of Christ," and this and that!

But all too often, this religious interference in economic issues takes the form of being in no true sense leadership but merely the making of excuses for capitalistic actions. Thus, the Committee on the War and Religious Outlook merely excused the war, because obviously denunciation of the same as unchristian would have been opposed to the sentiments of their great material patrons. In amelioration of their peculiar attitude, they added that one set of standards existed for the State and another for the individual. This was the verdict of a committee of professors and ministers, which under the chairmanship of the Very Reverend Harry Emerson Fosdick sat to pronounce on this matter in 1914.

And of course, and long since (always, in fact, I judge), politicians enlisted the spell and domination of the Church as a means of finding favor with the people. By this method, and under the leadership of President Harding and Secretary Hughes, the Washington Treaties relating to the Great War became very popular. And S. Parkes Cadman, a very popular if not any too well-informed, and maybe (I do not know) too sincere, Englishman functioning as a minister in the United States, has expressed the highly ideal economic view (an epitome of that of hundreds of ministers in America and elsewhere to-day, I think) that the Golden Rule is at this hour in practice because millionaires give to charity! Well, that makes this dear United States of ours a Utopia, doesn't it? And this book a joke! Just the same, though, if at another time this same Cadman had called the Communistic theory of Marx a very powerful economic analysis—which he did—how would he reconcile our present corporate economic state with that or with the Golden Rule? And if he could not, should not that cost him his present American religious prestige? I hope so!

P.S. I have tried here, by facts, to show the subtle relation of money and economic policy to religion and capital, also that capital has changed religion into a far different thing from the teachings of Jesus Christ. In conclusion now I offer the conviction that in due time this particular alliance of Church and Capital is quite certain to result in the downfall of religion in its present secretarian and dogmatic form. And, may I add, good riddance!

CHAPTER XV

FIRST, I want to show the financial racket behind charity. A major portion of the private funds raised for charity shoot from the professional skill of firms that make a business of drives on a percentage basis. Another large slice of the total gifts of about $50,000,000 a year, given by the people for educational, philanthropic and religious purposes, comes from legacies and other voluntary donations. Only a very small portion of the drives are managed by amateurs.

These money-raising corporations in New York City in 1928 numbered at least twenty. Typical firms are the John Price Jones Corporation and Tamblyn and Brown. In re this latter firm, Tamblyn as director of membership extension in the Atlantic division of the American Red Cross, managed over 60 drives for Community Chest funds and the Red Cross. It didn't take him four years to raise $30,000,000. In addition, $40,000,000 more were raised in 80 drives for better housing projects, the prevention of crime, a medical center, a cathedral, four memorials for deceased Presidents of the United States, for colleges, State universities, preparatory schools, theological seminaries, hospitals and missionary groups. For this, that little firm received six per cent commission—a figure in the millions—of the many millions given by the people supposedly to charity. Then I know it to be a fact that other firms charge even a higher commission —ten per cent or more.

There are so many of these private groups that are making devastating percentages that such cities as Minneapolis and Grand Rapids have already decreed that campaign managers must first be investigated in order to try to weed out the worst grafters and fakers.

One means which these charity racketeers employ to raise funds is lies and improper use of government officials and groups. Recently in New York City such cases have been discovered among city employee associations. The racket centers around getting advertising by the above dark means. Here are two cases. Of advertising sold for the Municipal Court Attendants' Association, about $23,800 went to the racketeers and only about $3,000 to the Association. Then again, promoters for the annual benefits of the Veteran Firemen's Association and the Veteran Officers' Association sold from 60,000 to 100,000 tickets to dances in a hall with capacity for only 2,000 people.

This ceases to be smart-aleck stuff when it concerns the unemployed, suffering in millions. It rather becomes a monument of the tragic failure of the whole American system in force to-day. Especially when such a big portion of unemployment relief is so managed to-day. It gives cause to pause and consider the waste, the futility, and impossibility of these methods. An example of this is the following great scandal (one discovered and exposed out of probably numerous similar cases) in Philadelphia.

In May, 1931, an investigation of MAYOR MACKEY's COMMITTEE FOR RELIEF OF THE POOR AND UNEMPLOYED, with Charles B. Helms as director, was started by City Councils of Philadelphia and the District Attorney. It was brought out that "high pressure" telephone solicitors of the Mayor's Committee used the name of a Philadelphia Hospital to secure funds, also the name of the American Legion. They even used blind men as solicitors. These promoters managing charity shows contracted with a hospital and nurses' alumni to put on a benefit performance and give the hospital the "gross receipts" less ten per cent commission to the promoter. Each year, as a result of the performance, this promoter has given the hospital sums ranging from $350 to $450, with his alleged ten per cent deducted. He has actually collected $5,000 to $10,000 on each performance. It was revealed that during his four years of so-called charitable service, he has netted about $30,000 while the hospital received less than $1,500. Joseph E. Rose, a promoter, was used also in arranging charity shows. He was grilled on the stand, and testified that of $86,807.11 in receipts from two shows they put on at the Metropolitan Opera House, only $44,093 was disbursed for relief. In one entertainment at the Opera House, $52,000 was received, of which $22,500 went for expenses and $7,000 to the promoters. The ticket selling was all handled by these "high pressure" solicitors. They even called up a man in Pittsburgh and said that they were speaking for the Mayor and asked him to send $500. People were likewise telephoned in the name of the Mayor, and asked to contribute huge sums for Philadelphia's Shelter for the Homeless and to buy "milk for starving babies," and many of those so solicited did contribute. Yet Charles B. Helms, the director, said that he had permission from the Mayor only to sell tickets for benefit shows and secure advertising in programs and nothing else.

Yet, according to the true American standard as it operates to-day, Helms' agreement with the Philadelphia Mayor was a twenty per cent commission to the promoter. But, in practice, they took even more. An audit of the books showed that 64 cents of every dollar solicited went to the promoters.

New Jersey's latest exposure is a parallel to that of Philadelphia. There seems to be no limit to abuse of the people. The capitalistic pirate philosophy impregnating America makes nothing sacred, not even obligation to society. State Senator Roy T. Yates spent New Jersey funds for the aged and jobless on his mistress. Department of the Treasury checks for hundreds of dollars were made out to this woman, supposedly for her research work on pensions, etc. How vast the sum is which was so blackly spent in this way from the meager relief funds is not made public.

Then here in New York City only recently, Irving Weisser, Morris Holland, Harry Siegel and Edward Cornez were caught selling tickets at $5 to $20 each for a concert. The proceeds from it were to be given to the unemployed, so they said. Yet it is alleged that they took for themselves sixty per cent of the money.

Always in America it is the organizer who unjustly gets the lion's share of the money—even though the money is for the unemployed, with their drastic needs. For in America with its purely materialistic and individualistic outlook—the devil take the hindmost—the idea of doing anything for any one else without a large personal return is taken as a joke. To begin with, any one who asks for charity in so purely materialistic a land is looked upon as a failure, a down and out, some one without brains and skill, and so fit only for the poor house, the jail or the Potter's field. The damned fools never stop to consider the immense inequity of a system that grinds the face and breaks the back of the worker in order to enrich some schemer or trickster who can think faster and more slyly and cruelly, but who, in so far as the general welfare of the nation is concerned is no more valuable than any thief or housebreaker. He is worse, for he steals more and wastes more.

Hence, what is one to say except "of course" of the raisin racket (the sale of raisins as well as of apples by the unemployed) whereby as a recent examination of this practice in San Francisco showed, a ton of raisins costing $100 sold at $1,000 in five cent boxes. The 300 unemployed selling them averaged about $1.50 a day profit, while the promoters took a forty-five per cent profit. And that would be and, no doubt, was, advertised by our kept press as a great and successful drive for the jobless. Also as a complete cure.

To point other phases of the financial racket in charity, though, I want to discuss the proportion of charity funds that really reach the needy, if ever. This question I know to be one of great concern among the hundreds of thousands of citizens called on every year to give more than they can afford to charity. And justly is it their concern, and the concern of every one with any sense of economy whatsoever.

Let us take the New York Charity Organization Society which has an elaborate mail connection with donors in whom they try to instill a proprietorship over the poor by sending them elaborate reports of dramatic cases they (specific donors, themselves) are supposed to relieve through the organization's efforts. (All wrong as a system, since equity in government itself would make needless all private charity.) One means by which this organization does this is through the *Bulletin,* a weekly publication for donors, costing $4,000 in 1930, and bringing in $10,000 in spontaneous giving. But here, as you see, out of $10,000 in all given to charity, only $6,000 remains for genuine charity use. And yet only a small part of that goes to the poor. So judge for yourself as to the value of organized charity in such a world crisis as that of this hour.

But now look at this astonishing budget of funds set aside by the Rescue Mission in New York for the year ending in November, 1930:

        $15,000 for office expense
        $15,000 for advertising
        $25,000 for salaries
        $44,000 for radio broadcasting for funds

and only $5,000 to feed the unemployed! And all in the name of God and charity, both of which, of course, should be overthrown.

Yet charities all over the country are really no better, and all pay fat salaries to their racketeers or promoters, or shall we call them honorable sponsors, those sleek and haughty sponsors of the poor. In Syracuse, New York, the manager of the Community Chest Funds receives a salary of $10,000 a year (wait till you see who contributes to such funds and how poor these contributors are!). In Auburn, New York, the Community Chest Manager is paid $5,000 annually. Out in St. Louis, the overhead reaches $160,000 a year. The social worker at the head of charities in Pittsburgh makes $9,000 a year.

Also, twelve executives of the American Red Cross each receives about $5,500 annually, twelve more about $7,000, one $10,000 and another $12,000 and formerly $15,000.

In the matter of charities, the example of the corporations as regards salaries is being followed. An executive of charity gets as much money as a similar corporate executive. This is the domination of Big Business philosophy throughout all economics. But it is all wrong for executives of either group to take so much away from the poor. If you do not find this fundamentally unwholesome, consider the following case:

It was published lately in the Lowry District Herald of Minneapolis that the Community Fund was a racket and that while $1,250,416 was raised last year in the drive, nearly a million dollars went for the payment of salaries alone. The Executive Secretary, Otto Bradley, it is stated, received $14,500.

To sum up the proportion of charitable gifts that ever reach the needy, Louis Hacker in the *New Freeman* last year stated that a typical chest fund turning over $5,000,000 a year, distributes but ten per cent of it in cash to needy persons. In fact, an amazingly small proportion of the poor ever get anything but advice. The money goes for salaries and expenses of this kind of charity.

And now we come to Walter S. Gifford, President of the American Telephone and Telegraph, and my personal financial pet, who says that people who ask how much of charity money actually reaches the poor, do not understand modern charity, which is to arrange matters so that relief doled out in the form of money will seldom be needed. I, on the contrary, claim to understand modern charity. After I show how charity functions, I am prepared to answer my dear, darling Gifford, by showing whether or not modern charity is managed to lower the standard of the poor, while the rich, not even contributing money, take the profits from these poor. And Mr. Gifford's own A. T. & T. is a fair illustration of what I mean. His charity is charging the people burdensome rates which are being protested against in Illinois through the courts; in Amarillo, Texas, by boycott and, at various times, in other places, by the score. Yet this is of no avail to the people. And his charity to his employees—he pays them impossibly low wages and then gets large contributions for charity out of them. And with the installation of dial telephones, lays off hundreds of employees. But do you suppose that rates are lowered to compensate to the public for doing its own work with the dial apparatus? Not to be thought of! Mr. Gifford's "charity"!

But now, consider the legal aid charities in America, whose cases have increased from 20,896 in 1900 to 150,234 in 1923. There were 72 private or government legal aid societies in 1924 in America. These societies operating in some of the biggest cities are private charitable corporations, i.e., those in New York City, Boston, Buffalo, Cleveland, Cincinnati, Milwaukee, Providence, Newark, etc. Anyhow, these private corporations do about one-half of the entire work in that field in the United States. And charitable as it may seem, most of these corporations charge clients a fee—registration charges up to $1 and ten per cent for winning a money claim. And about twenty-five per cent of the cases are claims for wages to the client which the employer has refused to pay so that ten per cent to the society has considerable meaning, when you think of it. Another large group of cases are on domestic relations and another on debts, etc. Other services are miscellaneous. These legal aid societies work very closely with labor unions, which may or may not be open to suspicion. The government ones, especially, are open to racket. For politicians have already ruined the one in Dallas and injured two more. But since the standards of our present-day politicians and government officials are largely those of capitalism and to hell with the underdog—the process and result is not without logic. But does a legal society like this ever protect the rights of the "Red" anywhere? Show me a single instance!

More of this legal aid "charity" is practiced by regular corporations, unusual as it may seem. Of course, the matter of papers for foreign laborers in their factories is very important to them. Such corporations furnishing legal aid are the great Ford Motor Company, Yellow Cab Company of Chicago, the Youngstown Sheet and Tube Company, etc. R. H. Smith, of the Boston Bar, says corporation legal aid is a failure because the men do not feel free to tell their affairs to the company. This means that they cannot. The company would object, and at best refuse the case. And, too, as Smith says, if claims relate to the employing company, what can a worker get by going to that company to collect the money?

I have shown enough, though, I think, of how charities steal from the people for gluttonous personal benefit; now I want to point out some of the crazy projects and causes they sponsor when they do spend money for "charitable purposes." The Community Fund in Minneapolis, for instance, and among other things, aided the Woman's Occupational Bureau by $3,700 a year, yet this bureau finds positions for salaried women (mostly college women) at a fee of thirty-six per cent for the first month's salary, and no less. Also, this Community fund gave $8,000 to the Women's Community Council, which largely instructs fashionable women on home-making, i.e., care of oriental rugs, interior decorating, etc. Of course, Minneapolis with her thousands of unemployed and starving had no better use for her money. I can understand that. And Mr. Gifford—what would be the opinion of that suave gentleman?

Another antiquated and asinine use of the charitable gifts to the Community Trust Fund is for the "survey." Mark that, and you can judge for yourself how charitable "surveys" are. They start out to find what the real social and economic needs of a community are in order that later they can do the right thing and never waste any time on the undeserving. So it is when the whole social system is wrong. Cleveland's first survey from such a fund was of the school system, and cost $48,000. Then, in 1917, this same organization spent $35,000 to survey recreation and again in 1920, $50,000 for research on vice and crime. Chicago's similar fund, likewise, has indulged deeply. Just one survey of jails set them back 7,000 "bucks." But the world's craziest, most inane bunch of hypocrites, loafers and fools is sponsored by this kind of a fund in New York City. Read them. Agree?

St. Stephens College,
University of Jerusalem,
Girl Scouts,
Westchester County Girls' Association,
Jeanne d'Arc Foundation, and
The Author's League.

Such is the racket of charity. But these rackets are encouraged by a system which not only indirectly forces poor people to give, but are now evolving systems of genuine force. Solicitation by friends embarrasses people. It is an unfair and, after a fashion, dishonest thing to do, since it involves unescapable personal criticism, often unjust and decidedly sly and unfair. Yet it is widely practiced. One way is to have workers "give" while the company foreman, on whom their jobs depend, looks on. By such subtle force, company officials coerced and still coerce employees. Thus during December, 1930, workers in Youngstown and Warren, Ohio, laid off or working full time at part time pay, were browbeaten into a "voluntary" charity drive. In the steel industry, mills have assessed and do now still assess, one to two days' wages a month for the community chest. Voluntary, as you see. But the worst is this. It is called the Civic Fund Plan, conceived in Canton in 1925, by officials of the United Alloy Steel Corporation, so you know it's charitable. By it, 40 cents out of every $100 wages is constantly deducted from the workers' pay for the Community Fund. No aye or nay by the robbed worker. Of course, they proclaim that a worker may give or not as he chooses. But the coercion is there. Or what else can the following mean? In 1928, the average pledge from civic fund companies was $5.39, and from non-civic fund companies, where a man was still not free by any means, but freer than in the above groups, $2.96. But certainly not the poor man's desire brought about the following: over 16,000 employees in 82 Canton companies are subscribing by the outrageous "Civic Fund" system. And lest you believe that the worker does not give too much to these fake funds, let me quote from a report of the Association of Community Chests and Councils on November 18, 1930, concerning the oversubscription in the Community Chest campaigns:

"In every city a large part of the increase has come directly from job-holders—persons who may at any time have to turn to the chest for aid." The devil is almost up to the hindmost. Likewise, it seems to me that depriving people of their independence, as they are deprived when forced to accept charity, tends by the very acceptance of that charity, to make people more complacent, as they should not be.

Yet I stop to think, what good does it do, to coerce men to skimp? And when they have so extremely little? It doesn't seem to me that thus forcing a man is going to make him more social—rather, much less social, of course, as any one who understood the situation would conclude. And what is Mr. Gifford's answer to that economic thesis?

To offset the worker struggling against an overpowering, entrenched system of racket, set the rich man's "charity." He scatters his money to the European and Oriental winds with a ruthless, but typically American hard-shell disregard of those suffering here. Thus there is John D. Rockefeller, Junior's, gift of $2,000,000 to the City University of Paris, and another of $2,000,000 for a museum in Jerusalem. For the year 1929, New York contributed $15,000,000 for the Near East Colleges. Then Morris Schinasi gave $1,000,000 for a hospital in Magnesia, Asia Minor, and so it goes, with America's little babies undernourished and starving.

The gross mistake in our ways of doing things in America is so evident from the needs of the people and the inadequacy of present relief, that these things should be signals to the most conservative that this economic arrangement in America is a failure. Thus, the cost of caring for families in need in 1930, was about or over $40,000,000, an increase of eighty-nine per cent over 1929.

In February, 1930, the daily average number of men who stayed under the roof of the Municipal Lodging House on 25th Street in New York City, was 1,100. Of its first 14,000 men admitted in 1930, 6,000 were there for the first time. This contradicts somewhat the brutal view of capitalists and their spokesmen, government officials, trade unions, etc., that many men won't work and are habitually unemployed. People were and are really suffering. A ten per cent increase for the first eight months of 1930 in demand for free or partly free service was reported by 36 hospitals of the United Hospital Fund of New York. The people's load kept piling up. Charity organizations in New York had 58,666 cases during November, 1930, as opposed to 17,061 in November, 1929, an increase of more than two hundred per cent.

Unemployment gnawed more and more into American society. People have been and are frantic. At one time in New York there were 82 breadlines with 50 of them on Manhattan alone. And still unemployment and its need for relief waxes. In New York City, $3,175,000 was spent in February, 1931, by 11 agencies for 30,000 families, an eighty per cent rise over the preceding year. By January, 1931, 9.4 per cent of the total population of 19 cities in America were out of work, able to work, and looking for jobs, and 1.8 per cent were laid off without pay, were able to work and wanted to. And, of course, only one person in about every five works.

And in relief, how often is the worker treated like a dog! What a welcome is given the jobless wanderer. You know how agencies boot him around. Or what graft some one receives from selling vile food to soup kitchens. In April, 1931, in Oklahoma City, an edict was issued against the camping of the unemployed on the banks of the North Canadian River, and this while a soup kitchen on the spot was giving out 7,500 meals daily. Always the unemployed individual may roam or drift where he pleases, to find work, if he is lucky, or just a way to get along temporarily, or even, after a little time, death.

Relief to the unemployed makes the racket of charity all the more revolting, because that relief is so thoroughly inadequate. For example, how is the following for justice? In February, 1931, in New York City, 750,000 jobless men were losing $80,000,000 monthly in wages. What this sum had previously brought was then taken care of by giving them $2,100,000 monthly, dispersed by 1,200 charities. Besides, while New York's private agencies reach only 12,000 unemployed, the Director of City Employment service estimates that there are 800,000 jobless. Think of the financial drain that this is on the middle class, for most people, oppressed by the stigma that accepting charity is degrading and not realizing that their bad condition is due to false economic principles and direction, borrow from their friends, relatives, etc.

Thus we see a wishy-washy charity racket (still so, despite Gifford, etc.) working inadequately.

But what are some of the inner meanings of that racket? Although it is not obvious on the face, the brunt of charity comes upon the burdened taxpayer. First, to dismiss such an outrage as the Salvation Army, let me state that the National Information Bureau report in 1924 showed that the Salvation Army handled only a very slight amount of the relief work in any place. Thus while private charity amounts to little, the demands of public charity increase. Consider this in regard to municipal agencies. In 17 years, according to a report of the Welfare Council, New York City, in October, 1930, the sum which municipal societies have spent for aid to people as distinguished from institutions, has increased from $229,000 to $6,000,000, or 2,500 per cent. This shows a whole trend in America. People can no longer live under the régime of monopoly with its artificial prices and ruthless attitude toward the worker, so the people must and do seek direct aid.

Who bears this added burden tightening with the growth of monopoly? Does private charity? Do Community Chests?—private in the sense that they appeal by drives. A report in 1931 by the National Association of Community Chests and Councils shows that more than seventy-five per cent of the local relief has come from public treasuries—mostly municipal. The taxpayers' money. And do the wealthy give much to that other twenty-five per cent, constituting all charity, except by government appropriation?

Abraham Epstein, asserting that the rich contribute only a little to present-day relief, estimates that although 357,825 persons in New York fill out income tax returns, only about 45,000 of them have contributed voluntarily to charity. Thus it is that while public relief work has increased one hundred and fifty per-cent, private aid has grown by only fifty per cent. And in Chi-cago the private agencies don't pay out half as much in relief as does the city. Again, in a large industrial town like Detroit, with its great corporations, ninety-eight per cent of the relief in 1928 came from public funds. This doesn't look commendable for Mr. Gifford's colleagues. Thus, the local treasuries taking care of this are so burdening themselves by great debts with their weight of interest to more of Mr. Gifford's colleagues, as to harness the people down to big taxation, and, by this same token, depriving them of education, health, improvements, protection, etc. But can our people be made to see their situation? Can they be made to think? I wonder.

Another meaning of the charity racket is that these organiza-tions, the biggest things on earth, so overawe with their grandeur and "success" that they obtain a following and then use it to benefit business interests. Thus, in 1929, the Salvation Army put up a 12-story administration building and auditorium on 14th Street, New York City, from whence they proceed to drug the worker with the religious trust and faith dope that makes him a mental slave. For as a man knows, so is he free, and since this dope is not knowledge, he is not free. And yet this very ignorant and destructive "Army" spreads its black wings to 79 countries and colonies, and administers many millions of dollars worth of property. It is exceedingly strong in England, Canada and Australia.

The American Red Cross is a little higher-class aid to busi-ness. It, too, has great wealth, about $19,722,003.52 book value of just its securities held as of June 30, 1930, let alone tens of millions in other funds. Also the American Red Cross makes friends all over the world for the American merchant. But by what right? Money, that's all. Money is the only right, according to capitalism, as I have shown. Thus, the American Red Cross offered help in the Japanese earthquake relief, gave $2,500,000 in 1922 to mitigate distress in Greece and Smyrna, etc. On November 26, 1924, it was written that during 1923 the American Red Cross appropriated money and organized relief in 43 disasters in many parts of the world.

But I can do even better than that. I can show a direct help to business, and this assistance is not usually thought of as a function of the Red Cross. Yet it is their policy and practice. In case of disaster, i.e., flood, earthquake, etc., the Red Cross aids every kind of business; boiler works, hotels, grocery stores, restaurants, garages, etc. Their aid usually consists of taking inventories and paying for repairs. Naturally, few businesses fail after this Red Cross procedure.

Yet out of all this wealth and wide relief, what does the worker get? Here's an example of Negroes in the World War. After a battle in the Argonne Forest, the 92nd Negro Division with its wounded was sent to the rear. The wounded were sent to the base hospital near Treves, France. Red Cross nurses there, organized from Texas and Georgia, refused to aid Negroes. For that reason, the wounded were laid on the ground and warned that they would have to take care of their own wounded. After lying on the ground half a day, these men, many of them gassed, were taken to a French hospital at the solicitation of a French general. It is unintelligence that makes people follow any and all of these prejudices instead of humane viewpoints; most prejudices are created by the capitalists so that they can "justifiably" make a cheap laboring class.

The worker, likewise, gets his standard of living lowered by the Red Cross which ruins his wage scale. At the last conference recently of the Tennessee Federation of Labor at Nashville, a resolution was passed calling the Red Cross a scab organization. The Community Fund of Cleveland, another charity, also, for which bosses had forced workers to contribute and organized labor was besieged, advised scabbing. More, the 1930 drought in the Central States brought but six cents a day of Red Cross relief in Arkansas, the while in some sections all relief was refused unless applicants would dig ditches, clear brush or clean cemeteries for 15 cents an hour, Elsewhere, the Red Cross in this relief gave workers three days' work a week, but with pay in merchandise from private merchants instead of money.

Thus, the standards of labor are voluntarily lowered by our private and also public charities, and apparently intentionally so. Thus, in New York on February 23, 1931, the Emergency Relief Committee, according to complaint, put some men to work at less than the union scale for charitable institutions. And prior, November, 1930, thousands were employed through charitable groups for a full day's work at $3 a day when the union rate was much higher.

But the Red Cross is perfectly willing for the small communities to be saddled as the rich want them to be and are causing them to be. The Red Cross is a thoroughly capitalistic institution. Therefore, the Red Cross opposed national unemployment relief through themselves, but financed by the government. And last year when this question was in the air, John Barton Payne, Chairman of the Red Cross, made statements as to the Red Cross financial condition to the Appropriations Committee of the Senate. The People's Legislative Service said that he greatly underestimated the Red Cross resources. In fact, the former said that the Red Cross entered the fiscal year, July 1, 1930, with $44,000,000 in hand or substantially assured. Although the Red Cross said that this was too much by $20,000,000, later, when the vice-chairman in charge of finance for the Red Cross checked the figure arrived at by the People's Legislative Service, he admitted that the latter was right. And when the Senate voted $25,000,000 for the Red Cross to relieve the unemployed, the Red Cross stood up, defying Senatorial authority, and refused the money.

And when labor tries to fight these lower standards, the Red Cross practically forces them to quit. For instance, this spring, the miners of Gallagher were refused aid by the Red Cross because a labor dispute was going on. This policy of the Red Cross practiced over and over again, establishes them as a strike-breaking and hence anti-labor institution.

In Danville, Va., laborers struck against inhuman conditions. The sister of the late Manager Fitzgerald of the Dan River and Riverside Mills was head of the local Red Cross. She flatly denied relief to strikers. That kind of situation has existed time and again in America. It is an issue to-day.

Yet American standards of living were too low already. In 1928, the Conference of Social Work reported that of 2,354 wage-earners of the skilled and semi-skilled class, two-thirds of the families had incomes insufficient for the minimum standard of living budget set by the Chicago Council of Social Agencies. In 355 families there were other sources of income, i.e., boarders or wives' and children's work, borrowed money, gifts, etc. In 108 families, the wives worked so hard outside as to make home-activities impossible.

But that was in the days of prosperity, when the people were supposed to be well off, as Mr. Gifford is constantly reiterating. And now during depression, the standard is so much lower. Thus, Grace Abbott, chief of the U. S. Children's Bureau, told the American Red Cross Convention in April, 1931, that at least 6,000,000 children of the 45,000,000 in the United States were subnormal because of insufficient food.

On October 25, 1931, James Fieser, acting Chairman of the American Red Cross, said: "Reports reaching the Red Cross indicate that a serious health problem may face the nation for several years to come as a result of curtailed diets, inability to pay for medical and hospital expenses, and withdrawal of the funds for local health work." But as to relief in this crisis? The Red Cross? No. Chairman Payne of that organization says that the Red Cross "does not extend national relief in unemployment." There you are.

Another alarming trend in America which shows the effect of charity and the economic system upon the workers is child placement. These charity organizations, including the Red Cross, encourage the brutal separation of children from their jobless parents. Child placing in homes is becoming more and more prevalent. Yet many placements are with foster mothers, unadapted to children, and hence produce unsocial children as members of society. This is occasionally so because many children who cry or are mischievous—nothing unusual in children—are given up as a bad job by impatient foster mothers, who have no understanding of children, and all this makes them feel that they are not wanted anywhere. The number of children taken from homes where they are wanted and put elsewhere with no love, and the growing movement in America toward this as a necessity, is cause for Americans to stop and wonder again as to the worth of the present economic system. The following gives some idea of the extent of this. During the year ending June 30, 1931, Jewish charities in New York report that by 18 child-caring institutions they helped 10,496 children, 5,205 of whom were admitted to institutions and boarding houses, and 5,291 were supervised before placement. Then, in a report of May 30, 1928, the State Charities Aid Association in New York City made public that it had placed its 41,130th child in a family home. There's a sample in only one state. This family disintegration shows in part at least the economic failure of America.

But this charity racket with the economic implications, indicate as I have just brought out that capitalism is aided by these charity efforts, not injured. The corporations do not want to be assessed very much for unemployment, and they are not. They let local governments and these charity aid people do it for them. Otherwise, that is, if there were Federal aid by Congress, the national income taxes would go to the unemployed and have to be increased, and this is a situation which the rich do not want. To show the difference it makes, while New York individuals and corporations pay about thirty-three per cent of the total Federal income tax, the amount of the nation's unemployment there is only thirteen per cent. So whether the rich give in charity, or pay local taxes, which is so much better, still they will contribute only one-third as much according to their income in order to provide the same degree of relief in their state as will the people generally.

To show that corporations don't want to be assessed much for the depression and resulting unemployment, look at this estimate on, say the A. T. & T. companies:

If a group of five telephone companies contributes to charity	$ 385,000
of this, employees contribute	285,000
the corporations' share being	100,000
Then there is a corporation saving by omitting the usual salary increases, because of depression ...	1,000,000
Less the corporation gift to charity	100,000
Leaving a net saving to corporations of	$ 900,000

In fact, the corporations are so determined to flatten out the people and to have their charity system, which merely makes the poor man poorer, work, that corporations are themselves beginning to subscribe to charity. Besides, these little gifts are supposed to make the corporation seem more benevolent. But are they even legal? The corporation directors cannot lawfully give away the stockholders' money. If they charge it back on the people by high rates, as inwardly, of course, they must, it is hypocritical, and very much so.

Yet our corporations have consciously adopted the brassy policy of contributing to community chest funds. Thus, in 1929, our corporations gave twenty-two per cent of a total of only $59,000,000 raised. And the major corporate support came from a small group of companies. This evidences all the more that this "modern charity" racket is the policy of the Rockefeller-Morgan interests. Because their men are directing. Walter S. Gifford, President of the American Telephone and Telegraph, whose companies are making gifts to chests, and who is managing President Hoover's unemployment relief, is certainly the head and front of this system of getting all out of the people by making them live off each other. And Owen D. Young, President of the General Electric Company, fairly comes next. In short, our capitalists are bound together in this charity policy. These very facts of corporation giving were compiled under the sponsorship of such men as Walter S. Gifford, William C. Procter, Gerard Swope, Felix Warburg, etc.

All charity is dominated as much as industry by Wall Street. The board of directors of the Red Cross includes a copper magnate, a steel capitalist, a banker's widow, several society women, and generals representing the United States Army and, of course, favoring war which the capitalists want also.

In fact, charity in general is controlled by the trust crowd who use charity to keep up monopolistic prices, to lower wages, all of which improves the rule of monopoly for themselves, but at the same time forces such conditions on the masses as the following: In May, 1931, in New York City, four of the biggest charity organizations began advising the poor to borrow on their insurance policies, even though they lost all protection. This stranglehold on the people is what makes capitalism a failure. Nor would any reform be any good. Look at the reforms in Europe—the unemployment insurance in France, etc. They are mere pittances to the poor, and harness them to nothing at all from birth to death. This constitutes the greatest tragedy of mankind.

But out of a very few more facts I add to the above, I have one idea that, in a nut-shell, shows the absurdity of present-day charity dominated by wealth.

Another method of giving relief in unemployment is by loans of companies to their laid-off men. These are to be repaid when business improves. The capitalistic scheme is just one to keep the means of livelihood from the people unless the people can enrich the already rich by paying high prices in capitalistic stores, for instance;—stores where monopoly keeps the prices high and all stores are that way. Of these loans, the International Harvester Loan to employees is weekly and merely for living expenses—no installment payments or old debts can be met with it. Then the General Electric limits loans to $200. The Southern Pacific and United States Steel also loan. Some companies require interest.

Then another form of relief. Railroad companies like the Rock Island, the Northwestern, etc., have their independent relief.

Still, here is a vastly different method of mitigating distress. In the winter of 1930-31, Chicago counted her unemployed through data from the schools. Since she found 30,933 families claiming immediate distress and inability to pay rent so pressing, the State Commission on Unemployment undertook to guarantee the rent of tenants recommended by accredited welfare agencies.

One more form is the State gift to private charity; the States have thus spent the taxpayers' money in the hundred millions.

And recall the other methods of financing charity—the wild promotions schemes, in fact, the scores of ways—and the whole through a score of conflicting, wasteful processes.

What does this chapter mean to you? It is worthless, if it doesn't make you sense the haphazard anarchy of the whole régime of Capitalism. How false its price values and its profit dicta! How true it is that America needs a uniform, scientifically planned system which will divide work and the means of life's enjoyment and improvement among the people. I dream of no imaginary Utopia, but rather I call for an examination of Russia's methods which show much less waste and more equity.

But under the Rockefeller-Morgan banner of "modern charity," with Walter S. Gifford, President of the American Telephone and Telegraph, as its exponent, the rich are really accepting charity from the poor.

CHAPTER XVI

CRIME AND WHY

THE Government's system of capture and punishment is assumed to protect people from crimes of violence. But what are these crimes? Facts show that ninety-four per cent of them are crimes against property. In the United States at the present hour, twenty per cent of the total number of crimes are burglary and entering; nine and four-tenths per cent larceny of $40 or more; thirty-four per cent, pathetically enough, larceny of less than $50; four and eight-tenths per cent robbery; and the enormous figure of twenty-five and eight-tenths per cent of America's total crimes stands for automobile thefts. Add them up and get the illuminating surprise I got. Ninety-four per cent of America's crimes are against property! But the robber, for all of his robbing, gets but a pitiful $1.30 for each year he serves in prison at Sing Sing; he who commits larceny, $38; and the burglar only $2.

Yet crime—or the price of keeping people safe from these small money peculations—cost America $13,000,000,000 a year (N. Y. State Baumes Commission estimate, 1928). The very recent Wickersham National Commission puts the figure at over a billion dollars but says that the amount is so staggering as to be impossible to estimate. The Philadelphia *Ledger* calls $1,000,-000,000 "but a fragmentary figure for the annual cost of crime to the American people." But is this not something which should be hushed? Should Americans know how their taxes are wasted? The root is in the system of private property, of course. It is not due to traditional American independence and revolt, nor is it due to Southern European immigrants, etc., as many sociologists would have one believe. Rather must one conclude that the social

and economic basis which can afford to and does pay $13,000,-
000,000 annually to protect itself from these petty thieveries is
also responsible for them. And I think I can show why. It does
not cure or even modify the cost of opposing the petty thieveries.
They grow, instead of lessening, and their cost grows with them.

But private property rights really signify license of the
individual or his corporation to make and keep for him or
itself the major portion of any created or controlled wealth, in
the creation, if not the control, of which others, and many
others—laborers, principally—always share, and this in the
face of the millions who must be satisfied with $30 a week or
less and as against the multimillionaires' $30,000 every seven
days or less. And as usual, the little individual does not get
$30 or $20 or $10, or even $5. He pindles through it all on
almost nothing. And yet thousands of people, as everybody
knows, need much more than the current allotment of $30 a
week or less to the skilled worker permits. Their natural im-
pulses and ambitions have no financial outlet.

More, both phases of the present-day trend of capitalistic
economics—depression and prosperity—only aggravate property crime. Look at unemployment! I sense something penetrating in the reasoning of a formerly jobless convict, who said:
"When a fellow is out of work, his mind gets dopy, and when
he sees something he wants, he's going to get the money somehow!" Dr. Weisz, Dr. Tugan-Baranowsky, Tarnowski and other
noted statisticians have tried to prove, and with some success,
that crime increases with unemployment and other phases of
economic depression. And right now, during this most severe of
unemployment years, I read of bombing threats against the
Harlan plant and the Pennsylvania Railroad shops if they do
not give employment. (Of course maybe the threats were faked,
but I assume not.) And in New York State, the total criminal
convictions increased from 1928 to 1929 sixfold. My most recent report is from the Tombs in New York City where 905
prisoners are being housed in 280 cells as of September 20,
1931. They are hissing and shouting against the kind of food

given them. And what about the crime increase in New York City
during 1930, the first year of severe unemployment? In that one
year, the felony arrests increased three and three-tenths per cent
and murder and manslaughter eighteen per cent over 1929. And
while in 1929, automobile thefts numbered only 8,760, in 1930
there were 12,731 in New York City alone.

Yet even prosperity itself, the prosperity that takes too much
for the few and gives too little to the many, foments outlawry.
The madness of material things (most of which are hideously in-
artistic, and yet in America encouraged by every sort of price
reduction and installment payment plan) makes people run
amuck, hooting and snorting to heap up more and more possessions, mostly worthless, and lawfully or otherwise. This highly-
charged and, as things go to-day, mainly forced prosperity gives
people the idea that they not only must have everything but that
actually they *can* have everything. "It's yours!" "Take it!" "You
can!" Do you recall these go-getter slogans? They are typical of
individualism and go-getter prosperity—the proper slogans for
the same though as exemplars of a social philosophy, they are not
so much. They leave too many behind. And these many, infested with these ideas, and not making enough money to keep
up with this prosperity blah do resort to taking property illegally.

More, many people cannot possibly live under the pauper
standards set for the masses by those who are strong and so
acquire control. Without, mayhap, the necessary constructive
skill to win anything much, they are still too vital to endure
grinding poverty. So in New York City alone, one person in
every two hundred is arrested each year for a felony; that is,
a major crime. Indeed, it would look almost as though religion
and patriotism notwithstanding, men simply will not be chained
to a system which to-day refuses them even a modest share of
the world's earned wealth, the creation of which, in part at
least, is theirs. Convict Floyd Peters, in a reformatory, said:
"What do I want to study civics for when I can get fifty or
sixty dollars a night sticking people up?" (I happen to know

the civics teacher and I don't wonder at this remark from an alert fellow.)

On the contrary, if money, as in Russia, were so distributed —or rather, equitably awarded—that the people could live decently for a respectable amount of labor, they and their children could certainly achieve an environment more adequate, in the sociological sense, for their development and comfort. As it is now, in America at least, the few have the conditions which (supposedly, at least) make for real betterment; the many, few or none of them. Let me illustrate. One individual whose case I studied had a drunken, quarrelsome father who kicked him about, a mother subject to insane spells, an epileptic aunt, and, for want of anything better, of course, he slept on roofs, wherefrom, and by reason of haphazard companionship, he was intrigued into becoming a "pigeon thief." Finally, for stealing some little thing, he was convicted. It was not a government oil field he stole, or he would not have been convicted! But here, as any one can see, economics, with its accompanying wretched environment, and possibly (not necessarily) poor blood, were against him, and may have weakened him. And if so, most certainly his was not a case for a jail or even the present-day reformatory or "protectory," with its antiquated psychiatric and medical methods. Any one can, or at least should, see—as I view it, at least—that a more equitable distribution of wealth, and hence decent living conditions, would probably do more than any protectory or reformatory or other forms of economic restraint or correction for such an individual as this. In short, the thing to reform—and first of all—is the social system surrounding the individual. Proper social economics would, of course, effect proper social surroundings, and if these are truly molding, as in many instances they seem to be, such economics should reduce crime to a marked extent. At any rate, in cases of severe insanity or epilepsy, propagation of the species should be prohibited. As for this particular boy, he as well as others with his related background, might become, under different economic conditions, independent and a benefit rather than a burden to society.

But our present economic system, with its domination and so guidance by the super-individualist, his trust, his bank, and his government, makes for the average man a grinding mechanical existence which brings about crime, or at least error. For to men of the caliber of the average criminal in our American penal institutions, this life of ours, with its rush through subway tubes to work, this hustling efficiently and steadily at business every day, and then whirring the night away at roadside pleasure resorts, movies and other entertainment, is something which they are not fitted, either by intelligence or physique, to meet. More, a majority of delinquents (so called) have never passed the sixth grade educationally, and never could. Wretched social conditions from which they derive, as well as lack of mind and means, bar them; in short, they never really share in the life just described. Even where they attempt it, they not only fail dismally, but land in jail.

But the answer is not jail, and should not be! These simple-minded individuals, forced, as they are now, to bump around like shuttles in the grim machine of life, might be settled at something they really could do: some form of routine and, where necessary, very simple tasks, but with pay in some form— sufficient, at least, to make possible diversion. Or, as in Russia, the State should provide that divertissement. At any rate, they are, in the main, in so far as crime is concerned, not accomplices in the real sense of the word, but rather children, who, like children, always, and nearly always unsuccessfully, follow the lead and the orders of some shrewder person who can seldom, if ever, be caught. He is too shrewd and uses them. So while they do his bidding, it does not follow that they should do the paying entirely. But can society be made to see that? And will it ever trouble to do anything about it? It would certainly be less expensive than the present system.

There is much talk to-day of sex liberty and the crimes attributable to it. And there are many crimes attributable to it:

murder, theft, and what not. But are the thousands of men from all walks of life now in jail there because of sex? What nonsense! A very small percentage of the total crimes of to-day spring directly from sex offenses: rape and sodomy. On the other hand, it is only fair to say that many property crimes are leveraged by sex. Thus, Convict Mark Snell (quite typical in this respect, I think) said to his captors and subsequent legal mentors: "I was living in a furnished room with a girl, and after the robbery I gave her the money, and three days later she married another fellow and squealed on me."

In another case, a seventeen-year-old boy tried to swing a hold-up to buy clothes for his sweetheart, even younger than he, because her mother told him he needn't come around unless he could bring her dresses. But this, and the case above cited, are, as any one can see, motivated by economic injustice rather than by downright evil in the heart. In fact, while sexual impetus is in part behind such crimes as that of Convict William Case, a man of good industrial capacity, who raised a check from $18 to $1,800 in order to take his married girl friend, who was trying to get a divorce—which alone would have righted the case—out of town because his parents objected to her, still the chief cause was poverty—the inability to achieve a relatively adequate economic freedom.

But who bothers to sort out the conflicting economic, social and other motives here, and to mitigate accordingly? Or to study the economics of the social arrangement by which they are so sharply checked? Or cares whether such young fellows become embittered? Show me the American who would even recall such emotional tragedies, let alone brood over them with any feeling of understanding! Who is stirred enough because of such things (that terrible crime in Amarillo, Texas, for instance) to agitate for lenient divorce laws? No one!

I, for one, believe that divorce laws more in accord with nature and science than our present religious theories could do more to reduce crime than many another propounded palliative. But at that, they would have to be associated with a fair economic distribution of the material means of living. For sex and economics walk hand in hand. Note the old saw which reads to the effect that when poverty enters the door, love flies out the window. Even so. Yet at that, I fear that in no economic scheme can sex be altogether eliminated as a cause of crime. It is too wholly the very core of life. At the same time, though, a loosening of such idiotic religious dogmas as that which cause either a woman or a man to feel that she or he, for whatever alleged reason, owns one the other for an entire lifetime, might induce a penetrating and helpful psychology.

Indeed, many criminals, whether of low or high origin, are not to blame. What about a Marquis de Sade, he with an inborn desire to torture women? Or the mystic and weird Landru, with his twenty-one murdered wives? Should not both of these have been dealt with medically rather than criminally? And just so with our unreasoning chronic criminals, in most cases simpleminded and mental morons. Surely they are not to blame. For these recidivists at times actually disintegrate mentally, become technically demented, until having finally lost their minds altogether, they are exactly like mechanical toys, not thinking or talking and not knowing whether they are eating bread or prunes. But these, I believe, should not be allowed to live. They are too much of a burden on the treasury of any society and should be eliminated. On the other hand, with ten per cent of our population affected by epilepsy—which, as has been discovered aside from causing fits also causes complete forgetfulness (amnesia)—censure and blame for crimes might well give way to a more humane understanding. These people should be committed to laboratories, not prisons. Their endocrine glands should be studied.

The interesting thought in all this to me is that supposedly seventy-five per cent of all criminals are recidivists of one degree or another. They have previous criminal records, and if released would, supposedly at least, go back to crime. Yet does that really mean that if there was any other way in which they could make a few thousand dollars, they would still return to crime? I doubt it! My personal feeling is that with economic equity, as here indicated, only those most hopelessly unfit mentally and physically to cope with the present-day drive or grind, would fall back. The others should not. Hence, the necessity of a reconsideration of our economic life in its entirety—a modification of our survival of the fittest scramble—or the admission of an Emperor or Cæsar, and at once.

But to look at another phase of our crime cure. For one thing, such prisons as do exist (and how many there are!) present such a distressingly bad social influence as to make for crime, not its cure. For have we not seen—and how often, recently!—hunger strikes against vile food, the great prison riots against their savage control by henchmen and plain grafters and crooks, the evils and weaknesses of our laws and penalties which should never condemn so many of such people to such ill-considered and wholly neglected social hells? Indeed, present prison conditions in America, as the recent Wickersham report shows, induce more crime, not less. For instance, in many cases these prisoners live like animals, in some cases the sexes not even segregated. Also, the kids of to-day, arrested for the slightest misdemeanor —maybe spitting in subway trains or walking on the grass in Central Park—are shut in the same cell betimes with a lot of hard-boiled criminals who electrify them with gangster lingo and gangster trend of thought—"Centuries" ($100 bills); "Four grand" ($4,000), etc., etc. In New York State alone, hundreds of prisoners beyond the capacity which can be accommodated decently are herded into Sing Sing, Great Meadow, and Clinton. County jails, such as those built at Jamesville in 1901, at Rome in 1882; at Ontario and Queens in 1895; at Schuyler in 1866, and Ovid in 1846 (eighty-five years ago) have never been remodeled, enlarged or even slightly improved. And you have read about Auburn, Columbus, Jefferson City. Indeed, anything may and does happen in these places: mutiny, suicide, attempted escape, murder, or at best there is induced an attitude of revolt and lawlessness. But what an environment for social thought or training! No wonder so many come out angry at our so-called

organized life and rail at its shams and its brutalities and then
return to crime!

More, crime is increased because the incorrigible defectives
and insane prisoners mixed with the young and more intelligent
ones retard any chances for improvement. Again, the dark cell
or starvation method to keep prison order makes convicts rebel.
A fine way to encourage people to a better life! Men in prisons
should work and be paid for their labor, so that upon dismissal
they would not only have money for a fresh start but a bit of
technical skill in some field wherewith to pay their way through
life. They should be trained to do something. Yet are they? The
1,300 prisoners discharged from Welfare Island in New York in
1930, and not permitted to do any constructive work while there,
received a mere twenty-five cents, not enough to keep them from
stealing unless a job were forthwith provided. But what job for
one who has no training, and usually the very one who should have
a lot of it or be dismissed from the world! And yet for these, what
insults, dismissals, hunger, and where crime is again indulged in,
more punishment! By the way, these authorities who gave only
twenty-five cents to each departing prisoner had the quite
large sum of $40,000 which was supposed to be used for this
purpose. But was it? And yet we sniff at Russia, which at this
hour fits the convict into its social and economic life in and out
of prison. And its real motto is not "Go!" but "*Come* and sin
no more!"

Indeed, not only is crime actually induced, as I see it, by the
economic inequities of our present social order but also it most
certainly could be lessened. But not by the slack business or
political methods with which everything in connection with our
prisons and their industries to-day is managed; the grafting and
abuse so constantly charged and so constantly rebelled against
by the criminals themselves; the numskull guards, with their
low intelligence and lower conceptions of their duties and
powers; our total social indifference to everything that happens
to any one who once charged with a crime and later sentenced
and punished is looked upon as a pariah. Yet at Clinton, a New

York State prison, where a foreman was supposed to be on the
job in the shirt and clothing industry, there was not any on
duty for months. And the result? Well, what would be the
result? Disorder, indifference, contempt for the prison régime as
a whole. Again, at Sing Sing, its brush and mattress department,
such manufacturing standards as would have caused the workers
to respect their work and skill were never insisted upon. The
product never did meet market requirements, or so it was testified. The goods turned out were not saleable. In the same prison
also, the shoe business as well as the knitting and hosiery industry also were allowed to dwindle, thus conveying to the
workers thoughts as to their own futility. Again, at Auburn,
New York, instead of making only license plates, as is now the
case, the men might be kept busy by also being allowed to make
all street and highway signs and so possibly arrive at that
feeling of efficiency which comes with activity. But no, this is
not permitted! Yet I think that all prison industries should be
put on a paying basis. Their products should be allowed to enter
the open market and the State should be forced to pay the union
wage, or nearly so.

But of all disintegrative and degrading things in connection
with our American prison life, graft is the worst, and it is on the
increase. The data is too voluminous to permit of recitation here.
Yet certainly to a very great extent it is due to our poorly conceived and wholly inequitable economic system which gives too
much to one and too little to another. For through a fairer economic distribution of all the wealth nationally created, much, if
not all, of this graft could be obviated. It would not be needed,
and certainly the guards as well as the prisoners in our peniten-
tiaries could be made to feel that they are not being savagely but
helpfully dealt with by society and so could be made to feel less
savage and unjust to others. That is rather obvious, is it not? If
not, then most certainly graft should be punished with death!

As it is now, though, our prisons are inspired, inside and outside, by gangsters like Barnet Bertsche, Bugs Moran, Legs Diamond, and the famous Alphonse Capone (as ceremoniously

treated and respected, apparently, as if actually he were a constructive leader of import). More, these racketeers, conscious, I am sure, of so much that is inequitable in our social system, set out to seize such power and means as they may for themselves. And hence our great and illegal bootlegging system which now no longer confines itself to the mere granting of liquor concessions but has organized (by buying off the Government) a tremendous lawless syndicate to which must subscribe all gambling houses and resorts of vice or their owners, and even such rum runners as the Government pays to annihilate said syndicate. But to what end? And is there any one who will insist that there is no possible change? And that, when openly the police and party leaders, our mayors, and who not else, quite openly receive money to permit these resorts to remain open? Instead, though, and inspired by the tremendous profits from this form of robbery, and for every one concerned, we have now developed the racketeer in other realms—the bandits who, unless they are secretly bought off, now cause strikes, threaten to and do carry away property, as in Chicago (great truckloads of property), and by employing professional gunmen, kidnapers, and so on, so impress our acquisitive, if not exactly respectable, corporations as well as legitimate business men so much so that by now fifteen per cent of the price of almost any office building goes to the gangster just to keep labor on the job.

But what is the remedy? As I see it, by equitably reorganizing society, paying labor justly, and reëducating the grafter or, failing that, imprisoning him permanently. But instead of that, behold competition stifled, the Government mocked, the prisons filled with small-fry lackeys, and the world filled with capitalists exacting not only exorbitant prices for everything but themselves perpetrating atrocious crimes against society. Gunmen and gangsters, as I understand it, and right now, control ninety necessary economic activities. Their enormous profits? Hushed! In vain do I search the law reports for Government prosecutions of these men. Where is the United States District Attorney who will pierce the mystery and stand forth with the "straight dope"?

America, effete politically, needs a national bracing-up, a complete change of heart.

In the wider aspect, as I have shown, property plus graft makes criminal punishment into a thing which it should not be: a process plus a result that is not the aim of punishment. Punishment's just mission is care as well as where possible reformation for the physically, and hence socially, unfit; i.e., recidivists and those sexually weak, and murderers. And I insist, and re-insist, that if profits of labor everywhere were more equitably allotted to all who work, and if graft were punishable by imprisonment, or in extreme cases by death, these economic brutalities would cease.

For I insist that our present property distribution, while characteristic of wild nature, is not the way of organized society which, and that quite plainly, has risen in the face of these wilder ways—an attempt, apparently, at a peaceful and so more pleasurable existence, and as such, worthy of the serious contemplation of man. And that is why I say that inequitable distribution is so serious and really predominates over all other crimes. And worse, incorrect wealth apportionment engenders a tremendous and disgusting, and even infuriating, disproportion which is useless in the search for happiness, and more, breeds so much ill as always to spell in the long run the seizure or ruin of so-called vested interests. In sum, the profiteers at the top eventually die of the ills they engender at the bottom. Nor can these ills under unjust distribution be halted. Only the system itself may be reformed, not the ills without changing the system.

And if that is not true, why have not years upon years of social training, reformatories and the like done something toward the dissipation of crime, not only in America but anywhere and everywhere? For only look at crime here and elsewhere! Dr. Christian, head of the New York State Reformatory at Elmira, probably one of the best heads of these institutions in America, and with one of the best institutions of its kind under his care, and with only youth under his direction, states that seventy-five per cent of the young men there have committed other crimes before the one for which they are now suffering; also that they are, in the main, too young or too poor or too defective to have accumulated any means for themselves. And that is why I say that it is because of the inequitable profit distribution of to-day that they cannot and will not live under the social strain they are compelled to endure, without crime. They are not meek enough, and for that reason cannot be ground down to the pauper life that in the main confronts them. Pride, ambition, love, envy, greed, etc., all talk in them as in others, but without in their case sufficient social understanding or a decent economic background or "break" to content them. But is that the fault of the men at the top or the men at the bottom? And who does not know which? It is said by people who don't count that these men would not work if they could. My studies of the psychological influences of many lead me to believe that with the proper reward for such work as they can do, they would work.

But when one speaks of "proper reward," of a more equitable distribution of the profits resulting from labor of the hand as well as the brain, one is striking at the very roots of the ghastly inequity of this hour in which we live, and which, as all can see, gives into the hands of a few private manipulators of money billions upon billions the while the immense majority trudge gloomily in the shadow of want and the fear of disaster. And after so many of them so ably and willingly labor at the task of creating not only the supply but the demand of organized society! And not only that, but there will come to organized society its proper level and trend only through the tramping mass at the bottom, the individuals at plow, loom, counter, switchboard, station, who still make possible the thing we call organized life. Will they ever be made conscious of their duty —the mass out of humble homes, from which many strong and beautiful events have taken their rise?

Yet, as we see to-day, not only is money hoarding and money domination wholly inequitable, but its treatment of crime is a complete nonsuccess, and its reforms of less than small help to the whole body of present-day organized society, but crime itself is increasing. For, firstly, the real criminals of our present time are not those who can be detected, or if so detected, seized. I refer to our principal overlords of to-day and of a hundred and a thousand years past. They are too strong, too shrewd, too sly, and below them, and how pathetically and ridiculously (consider only the opening facts of this chapter), run our principal minor criminals, the racketeer and gunman, who shrewd though they be are still not as shrewd as and certainly no more ruthless than our corporation tyrants who to-day enslave and starve them, and then in strikes or attempted reprisals of any kind murder "by law" or by the gun direct those who seek to release themselves from such slavery. But all so unnecessarily! Economically calculated and distributed, there is certainly enough of worth-while things in the world for all to enjoy a reasonable share. (But this panacea won't appear in all of its glory by dreaming about it. Rather it would take fiery spirit and action.) And surely there is room for all. The functioning of the cells in that immense social system, the human body, prove as much. Because each of the cells in the immense system which is *us* gets enough to eat and do, they are healthy and that is why we live. Cannot the exterior states created by these same cells—our governments—which through us *they* make —be made to function as well? I believe so. Yet as an offset to what might be said, let me add that the American Bar Association Crime Commission says that at this writing there are at large in New York 30,000 criminals and in Chicago 10,000. Also that the annual murder rate in America has increased in the last twenty-nine years exactly three hundred and fifty per cent; also that in 1904 there were in the United States only 57,000 prisoners, and in January, 1927, there were 96,125—an increase of over sixty-eight per cent.

Yet it is said that America leads the world. Undoubtedly it does, but in what? Crime! Even Italy, supposedly the most intemperate and vicious in crime and actually, in fact, the only country whose crime record comes anywhere near ours, doesn't have half the crime that there is right in our own back yards. Not long ago, in the whole of England and Wales, with their oppressive industrial conditions and strong class distinctions, there were only 151 murders in a single year, but during this same period, Chicago had 389 and New York City 262! All in all, America had fifty times as many as Great Britain. And so it is with all kinds of crimes.

But does our Government, or the people who make our Government, sense either the economic import or the sociological drift of this? Yes? Furthermore, the Government itself, national and local, will not always admit that there is crime. It is not good for business! It does not look good to do so! So in one month, in Chicago, the captain of a certain district recorded only 37 crimes of violence and camouflaged all the others—a total of 141!

And yet the Wickersham Commission which just reported on crime would and did designate no causes. Yet America has to face the cause of crime which is inequitable participation in resources, produce and manufactured goods.

CHAPTER XVII

WHY THE BALLOT?

THE most meaningless thing which the trudging American of to-day possesses is his right to vote. The ballot! The value he sets on it—the numskull of the country store, the village corner, the farmers' grange! *His* senator! *His* governor! *His* President! Bah! And that in the face of the ills they have not only permitted but aided to descend upon him! Of all the farces in the world to-day, and especially in connection with the marching mobs who endure anything without a murmur, the vote is the greatest! And yet the millions of Americans who firmly believe in and trust the candidate elected as the choice of the majority of the people! Oh, the glories of theoretical justice! Would that I might stir even a few with the actualities!

Elections, of course *should* bring to issue a series of important questions which would justify respect for the ballot. But do they? Consider only the trivial issues concerning which thousands of politicians rant and ballyhoo on street corners, in halls, in the press or over the radio, at $1,000 a night! The Republican Party is better than the Democratic Party! The ass or scoundrel Robinson is no greater than or not as great an ass and scoundrel as that ass and scoundrel Jones! Tweedledee and Tweedledum! Yet always visible in the background the local, state or national boss! And over the shoulders of the boss, whoever he may be, the leering, acquisitive, ironic and sardonic corporation, its owners, banks, lawyers, courts, and its Government! Tara! Let us have bands and flags and processions and words, for they serve to fool the fools, as the tricksters and sharpers well know.

Yet the actual affairs of this, our nation or country, can be put so that almost anybody can understand them, even the politicians, if they but would. Actually, people would not need to do very much studying before they would become wise enough to sift this raw corporation hocus-pocus and dispose of it. But will they? And really, how can they? The corporations would put the fear of corporation-God into any politician who tried to bring this about, and the press would wash it over nicely. If you doubt this consider the countless small town papers owned by the likes of Gannett and what and how news is printed! Also the sly and wholly dishonest editing or incomplete reporting of America's supposedly best and more "upright" newspapers, corporation minded and bent as they are!

Yet the ballot of to-day theoretically would effect and conduct a government as favorable to the majority (instead of to the minority, as it is now). For according to these impossible ideals whatever the mass desired in fairness, it could most certainly and by right of numbers have. But will it ever have it? Will general and unchanging misery ever cause people to do anything for themselves: strongly protest, let us say? Well, maybe! The French did. And the Russians. But we Americans? As things stand to-day, is it not quite obvious that we prefer—actually prefer—to vote for a troop of reprobates and ruffians rather than for any decent or intelligent men? Consider only our local bosses, their nominees and their victories! Consider the men whom Vanderbilt, Gould and Sage bought!

Of course, not all politicians allow gangsters to sock people in the jaw or bump them off nor does every officeholder permit power to be held by gangsters. Yet those now serving permit people to be "soaked" five cents on every quart of milk as well as to pay exorbitant and even robber charges to all of our entrenched corporations and their monopolies the while wages lag far behind and unemployment sinks more and more into the limbo of the defeated and the dead.

And yet the ballot is supposed to render protection. But how can it, under the present system, with neither public interest nor vigilance behind it? The voters are asleep or at the ball game. Neither their minds nor their hearts appear to be where their welfare truly lies. "Eyes and they see not; ears and they hear not." But do I really need to repeat that the ballot is meant to be the means of managing responsibly all Government affairs? Neither the City, State nor Federal Government needs to pay five or ten times what everything is worth. They merely do so because of lack of grit in the men who have the ballot, and hence in the men whom the ballots elect. The graft scandals of our cities and towns, and the crooks and fakes, all duly elected and applauded, what put them over? Individual indifference! I think so. New York, Chicago, Philadelphia, Pittsburgh—well, all of our cities and towns. Look at them. The crime! The waste! The graft! Yet what does the voter care about waste? Where is his lost sense of economy? I suppose the reader will laugh when I suggest that of every fifty or sixty million dollars wasted by the Government, from five to fifty dollars is probably his money. Still, millions of voters march annually to the polls to cast ballots for men who only half-do their work; and office-seekers and, worse, officeholders now multiply so rapidly that from three to ten men are hired for every job, and hence must loaf and graft and sell out their government or their electors in order to keep themselves there.

But believe it or not, the ballot is not actually designed to favor either the corporation or the crook—his lawyer, his governor, his judge, his elected thief. Voters might and should secure the things they need: bridges, roads (and I don't mean with enormous interest and profit to bankers and contractors, either, but for proper and reasonably-priced public service); a fair day's pay for a fair day's work; also decent homes; decent factories without child or human slavery. For the vote is not supposed to place in control of government men who see only the opportunity to add millions to their already ridiculous fortunes but no money for the improvement of the State or its people. Consider only Mr. Rockefeller, of whom I have written, and then consider the thousands who walk the streets hungry! Actually the ballot is designed to command fair investigation, legislation and enforcement. But does it? And where does the error lie?

Every workingman can use the ballot. He is told that by its use he can better his lot, obtain higher wages, the five-day week and the six-hour day. He is told that by the ballot child labor can be reformed. (And I have shown where and by whom it can be absolutely stopped.) Even now you can hear this or that candidate saying what he can and will do about unemployment. But by and large, what does the ballot bring labor? At this moment very likely the President is appointing another committee on unemployment. And committees, committees, committees in every field. But what will be done with the statistics gathered by the last year's committee? They will be filed and forgotten. For statistics of themselves are helpless. It is the men behind the statistics who count, and where are they? In office? At work for those who need aid? If so, how is it that any unemployment insurance, when it does originate in any State, is designed to be paid for by the laborer rather than the boss? Can it be because the laborer is making a big fuss to have it, but not thinking as to whom he elects to aid him in the matter? And will he eventually be forced to pay for his own indifference or dullness? The chances are he will, because he knows nothing and seemingly does not care to know anything concerning the forces working against him. But the forces working against him know that, and count on his indifference or ignorance, or both.

Government issues get close to the clash between labor and capital. They make corporation rates which the people pay. They regulate wages. But do they ever do anything for the masses? Do they ever actually make reform a success?

The ballot is calculated to place people in position to express their thoughts freely. Yet here in America they do not appear to know, or maybe do not even want to know, that the Democratic Party or the Republican Party is not even an avenue to accomplishment unless they are prepared to force that accomplishment from the men they elect or appoint. And there may

come a time when they will do this. Who knows? Anything is
possible. Yet so far indifference, an immense and most painfully
expensive inertia, due, I believe, to the American single-track
concentration on money—but curiously, money made in business,
not politics (which is for crooks) or the responsible management
of his own government and for himself, really the best-paying
business for the little fellow that there is. I doubt whether he
has ever thought of that. A complete reorganization of our
present capitalistic system, or better yet, its disestablishment,
is what America needs. Reform has been a failure because
all independent political parties have been put down and now
there are the two old parties by now so wholly controlled by
the one real party: the money-bag holders or Big Business.
Yet does the American Federation of Labor, that staunch be-
liever in insipid reform, ever run independent tickets! No, their
reform isn't even that good.

For instance, the ballot, in dual or multiple form (more
likely in multiple than any other party form) should let the
American voter in on foreign affairs. It should determine where
and how American imperialism is to be felt. But does it? The
ballot should say whether American cannons, in the guise of
"intervention to protect the American citizen," are going to
blow up thousands of foreign natives. But does it? Now you
tell me! Yet since this is a democracy as things go, the ballot
should dictate concerning who is to fight, die, spend millions
on a war caused by such a bewildering maze of tripe and propaganda that nobody ever knows what caused it. But does it? The
common people should have the privilege of saying at the bal-
lot-box whether they want to sacrifice their lives in a war which
merely makes big business for corporations. Yet do they?

In the foregoing I have partially listed what the ballot is
intended to signify. Now I would like to present something of
what really does occur. In almost any election, the publicity
chairman gets, say, $25,000 a year. And our campaigns cost
millions and millions of dollars. And we vote and vote until the
sight of another ballot or the announcement of another campaign

is sufficient to either bore or infuriate one. Votes on quite every conceivable pretext, either asinine or positively evil. And at every election and for whatsoever purpose, up steps the "one hundred per center," the lover of liberty, the flag-waver, the moralist, the religionist, the this, the that, and votes and votes and votes! And now it is to elevate a common fool like Harding to the presidency, or now it is to take his party heirs and assigns, Coolidge and Hoover, both of them parts of his cabinet, and do the same. Again, as in the State of California, where a single railroad, the Southern Pacific, helps decide who shall be nominated, who shall say what about the elevation to the positions of senators and assemblymen of scores of nobodies (and each one blah-blahing louder than the other as to his honesty, loyalty, faithfulness to the interests of the voters), the voter is still told that he is doing it all, and made to believe it. Yet once elected, these corporation servants, as every one knows, at once kowtow to their real masters, the money lords of their State or of America, and do their bidding, and their bidding only. And should one of these voters step forward with a complaint or a request, well, he is lucky if he escapes subsequent pursuit and injury. Yet is anything more in the way of performances expected by the voters? Is not what every one really knows beforehand expected: that those elected will serve the corporation, and none other? And if you don't beleve it, look at the unchanged and unchanging power of the Southern Pacific in California and every other State that it serves!

Yet Americans seem to like to vote, just to be voting. It makes a holiday. There are bonfires, speakers, wars in the newspapers, insults and charges and counter-charges. What matter if those they vote for have received their nominations because they have flirted with and made promises to corporations? Is it not still delightful to vote for them? Flags, bands, orations, newspaper and radio palaver, the already hundred-year-old ballyhoo concerning patriotism, the greatness of America, its future, the evil character of the opposing party, the excellence of the one to which you belong! And although ad interim (between elec-

tions, that is) you will be ignored, betrayed, spat upon, your
labor and property pilfered, is it not still delightful to vote?
Our great national holiday—the first Tuesday after the first Mon-
day in November! Our banks and stores closed. No work to do
until to-morrow! Liquor in private places! Street fights! Joyous
and yet betimes bitter and lunatic arguments, with fisticuffs
added for good measure! And on the morrow the winners announced. And the losers also! And the nation's corporations
smirking over the working of the well-oiled system of electing
whom they please, under either party or none: some particular
label of their own gotten up for the occasion, mayhap.

I think of the nomination and election of one William Sulzer,
once a governor of New York. And then of his speedy de-
thronement by the reigning boss of the day, Charles F. Murphy
of Tammany Hall. And this regardless of the hundreds of thousands of votes cast for him. Said Murphy, himself a corporation tool, was angered because of some slight disobedience on
the part of said Sulzer. And here are the details, very much
condensed.

William Sulzer was a Democrat. Charles F. Murphy was the
big chief of Tammany Hall. The New York State Legislature
was controlled by Tammany. Sulzer went into office as Governor
of New York on January 1, 1913. He had not been in office
more than a few months when his administration was myste-
riously harassed and insulted. The fury reigned until he was
impeached for not spending all of his campaign funds, which
witnesses testified they gave him to do with as he wished. The
impeachment was, of course, ridiculous. Impeachment is a Constitutional resort to be used only in case of serious malfeasance in
office. However, Sulzer, in his short term (January 1, 1913, to
October 17, 1913) had tried to instigate new and better ways
of doing things and to eliminate crooks—some of them members
of that same Tammany Hall. And for that he was booted out,
all of the New York newspapers frantically arguing not only
as to the necessity but the honorable honesty of it. Murphy,
of course, had enough control of the Tammany legislature to do

it. But why did he want to? Sulzer, in an interview to the press, said that the impeachment resulted when he refused to appoint the men demanded by Murphy. He said these were usually selected for the Governor by Murphy who sent to him a certain Judge McCall, who told him what the "big chief" (meaning Murphy) wanted.

Poor Sulzer! Merely an example of the futility of balloting in America. There have been scores like him in New York and elsewhere. Just let an elected official disobey his corporation or the boss who represents the corporation which pays for this or that! If you doubt this, take a look at the State of New York. Quite anything can be done to the voters there, and without let or hindrance. Judgeships can be bought and sold, and are. A political, semi-religious organization in New York City that has functioned fairly uninterruptedly for seventy or eighty years can say who and who not is to be nominated; what powers, emoluments, etc., they are to bestow upon banks, corporations, the police, and for how much in hand paid. And yet hundreds of thousands of voters in New York will march earnestly to the polls year in and year out and vote and vote and vote for the same swine who have but one object in view, and that is to fleece them as thoroughly as possible. Need I do more than call to your attention the latest New York City political scandal at this writing still being aired: its public servants impeached or questioned—and what for? What they did and how they did it: rewarding the voter with robbery, perjury and what not! Or let me sing a little song of names: Connolly, Vitale, Mancuso, Vause, Colly, Walsh, Ewald, Tommaney, Healy! And all within a year or so.

In this same New York investigation by the Hofstadter Committee now in action, James A. McQuade, Brooklyn Democratic leader and Register of Kings County, deposited $547,-254.03 in the last six years and three-quarters during which period his salary was between $9,000 and $12,000 a year. Sheriff Thomas M. Farley here deposited $360,660.34 in six years and three-quarters on a salary of from $6,500 to $15,000 annually. Then at the present date, the Grand Jury investigating Allegheny County recommended an indictment against the Mayor of Pittsburgh, Pennsylvania, for countless contracts for expensive city supplies, not given to the lowest responsible bidder in accordance with the law. But America is full of this political corruption as every one knows and it would serve no purpose to go on with endless examples of it. It exists, however, from these small positions to the highest ones.

Sometimes Government officials and banks or corporations work together in the most corrupt manner. In New York just a little while ago the banker Ferrari, with an unstable network of trust companies, etc., under him, put his man Warder in as superintendent of banks in New York. And because Ferrari arranged with one of his wild-cat realty corporations to let Warder have a Riverside Drive apartment, furnished with Oriental rugs and period furniture, the official let his sponsor's bank mergers pass unregulated. And not only that, but every time a bank inspection was due, Ferrari took Warder's family to Atlantic City or paid their fares to Europe or gave the wife jewelry, or had his unsound Lancia Motor Company arrange to give Warder a couple of $3,000 or $4,000 motor cars. And yet Warder and Ferrari are but two instances.

Corporation alliance with Government officials is one of those subtle abuses which has honeycombed American politics and American life, really. For example, during the great miners' strike of 1927, a certain Judge Langham signed an injunction against labor union meetings near a coal mine at Rossiter, Pennsylvania. This judge had several thousand dollars invested in coal companies of the vicinity. No wonder he was interested in stockholders' profits rather than decent wages for labor! Always there has been too much interest of government officeholders in bank and corporate projects. Years ago Thomas Jefferson denounced this state of affairs. By no fairness should a public official own stock in a company concerning which his government vote or action will enrich himself. By this means, many officeholders in the government have become well to do. Not only that, but vastly more important is the fact that these men directed the whole political policy of America toward the rise and domination of the trusts. How much their private enrichment through these corporations influenced political policy cannot readily be ascertained.

Well, as it looks now, it would appear that people like corruption. A powerful gangster is bowed to and served and photographed and interviewed. An Al Capone or a Dion O'Bannion or a "Legs" Diamond is patronized by senators, journalists, judges, and society. And people who think gangsters are only to be found in gambling dens and houses of prostitution are old-timers. The Manhattan & Bronx Fish Dealers kept off all outsiders by strong-arm force and took one hundred per cent profit, according to Court testimony. And independent flour truckmen, outside a graft ring that had set up to graft upon and regulate said trucking, were beaten up or had their business taken away, or both. Then add the same type of racketeering in connection with chickens, eggs, every food. Millions of dollars go to New York racketeers. And in this connection, let me add, undertakers must pay gangsters or see their hearses demolished. Laundries pay $1,000,000 annually, according to evidence, and truckmen $5,000,000. Yet this is only a tithe of what the American voter is getting out of the pleasure and privilege of voting! But do the people ever turn a hand? Bootleggers use city-owned barges in New York harbor. At least one case was made public last year. Hundreds of people walk by the open saloon at the corner of Fourth and Charles Streets, with its large new American flag suspended over the bar, and laugh! But when all is said and done, the joke is on whom: the corrupt government or the people who permit it?

In fact, nowadays people cannot elect non-partisan officials. For always before being nominated or even considered for nomination, they are seen as to their views and leanings. And later in office they certainly obey their backers, usually our banks and corporations who must see to it that the Government is properly managed. And the only men put up by either of the two great parties are not only devoted to capitalism but are also opposed to drastic reform or any reform, which in itself is a confession of our social and political failure. For, according to them, all is well; no change is needed. To prove my assertion I quote the National City Bank on the Presidential campaign of 1928: "There is no issue between the candidates that is likely to make a disturbance in business circles." No, indeed! There was none, and yet an immensely numerous people fired to a spasm in connection with Prohibition, while life and death matters, such as a living for themselves, were in the hands of a corporation-minded group. And for further proof that both parties are controlled by money, look only at the Hoover-Smith campaign. That in that campaign the Republican Party, for which tremendous sums were raised by manufacturers to elect Coolidge, stood pledged to a high protective tariff is shown by the testimony of J. R. Grundy, President of the Pennsylvania Manufacturers' Association, who so stated. Also, the higher tariff was passed. And in everything—Muscle Shoals, soldiers' bonus, the matter of Government aid to the unemployed—did Hoover obey those who put him in office?

Yet this not subtle but quite open relationship is obviously a baneful thing. It arranges all for the strong as against the weak. Candidates of all degrees of importance have corporate connections and help. It makes no difference whether he is a future President or County Judge, this lineup with the big interests usually holds. There is no limit apparently to what their backers will and do spend to put them in office. The corporations and their interests have the money and they know how to spend it. Yet no matter what the cost of their men may be, the corporations never fail to place them in office. The Republicans spent $3,000,000 to elect Calvin Coolidge. He came high, apparently. Only in extenuation of the same it was given out that to circularize 1,000,000 voters cost $100,000. Well, Pennsylvania had 2,000,000 registered voters and Illinois 3,000,000. Not only that, but there were daily radio speeches costing not less than several thousand dollars a week, over the radio trust system in which Rockefeller is interested. And posters, pictures, stories, meetings. The capitalists know full well how to make the people like a candidate—how he should appear, what characteristics should be played up to appeal to the sympathies of the credulous voter. Besides a campaign in Pennsylvania looking to the reëlection of a certain Senator Pepper cost more than $1,000,000, while another, that for William S. Vare, successful candidate, cost $600,000. So judge for yourself.

Despite my saying that labor, by the ballot, is said to be able to do much for itself, here are a few actualities concerning the matter. America has no national child labor law. The Constitution doesn't say enough about liberty, the pursuit of happiness and such in dealing with a question like this. So the Supreme Court, always sensitive to corporate desires, can knock out a law on a technicality or two, and in this matter of child labor, did, as elsewhere I have shown. But does the child actually labor in such a "progressive" country as the United States? Of course, since this "progress" is only for a few, anyhow! So, in spite of the ballot, which might be used to drive out child labor, in Rhode Island, forty-one per cent of all youngsters working. And in Connecticut, labor pay in general is so low that sixty-four per cent of the children start working at the age of fourteen. More, in Alabama, the payrolls of 16 iron and steel plants show that only about twenty-eight per cent of all employees are on an 8-hour day, nearly forty-two per cent on a 10-hour day, twenty-seven per cent on a 12-hour day, and of these some work alternately six and seven days a week and twenty-two per cent work on a straight 12-hour 7-day week. And on the basis of its commercial salubrity, that interesting and constantly voting State invites other corporations to come as quickly as possible and enjoy the going while it is good. In fact, the businessmen of Birmingham, Alabama, advertise in northern magazines for capitalists to come down and start factories. One advertisement read that in that city 106,000 women and children over ten years of age were unemployed and that they would be glad to work for $10 a week, and in many cases for less. That means that children will be recompensed, as they are already in the Carolinas, New Jersey and Pennsylvania, by partial starvation, tuberculosis, ignorance and the like.

What the laborer needs, of course, is, in good times, legislation against the easy borrowing that starts all kinds of hokum business. Banks could be regulated if there were enough individual spirit in the land to study and regulate them. When people see loans mounting, they should protest, not in words only but by their votes. The laborer needs regulation against any sort of overtime work. The output of factories might and could be effectively limited and made more uniform. Yet can any one of these reforms—without a complete change in the form of government here—a government of workers of whatsoever walk or type—be put through without the other? It cannot! Even the dream of regulating American wealth by the ballot appears to have vanished. Such is the total failure of the ballot. As much and as often as the American people vote, it is obvious that they do not expect their votes to do anything. It has actually come to be believed in America that although "Big Business" and prosperity offer no financial relief to the rank and file, still nothing can be done about that by voting. For by now, as the little man sees it, the "big man," meaning the corporate master of wealth in America to-day, has him down. He has, because he has the money, the lawyers, the police, the courts, the church, the newspapers, the publicity and propaganda bureaus, the army, the navy, the Government in all of its legislative and executive forms, and the moment he begins writing or talking or indicating in any way that he is in favor of any change or method of lightening the load on his back, he is at once suspect: a radical, a Bolshevist, a socialist, a Red, a disturber, and as such and so, subject to all the terrorism which has now become a feature of our everyday American life. So his faith in his voting, or its value, might be supposed to be absolutely nil. But is it? Does he not vote? He does! To me one of the real wonders of the world! For why? Why not rather stay away from the polls, or if not that, at least organize some form of party protest that would mean at least

"We protest!" But no, that does not seem possible either, because the average voter has so little time and so little money, and worse, apparently so little brain, to devote to such a thing. He must, at present at least, be stirred and worked for and directed by those who wish him well. Yet what local as well as national opprobrium attaches to one who would do so! The scoundrel! The Red! The radical! The undesirable citizen! One can hear the newspapers, the radio, the pulpits, our glorious apostles for things as they are! And yet, six million or more men out of work, prices about as high as ever, a winter at hand, and Mr. Hoover holding a conference with a Mr. Doak or a Mr. Gifford concerning unemployment relief!

And yet, let us reconsider the actual position of the little man under our Big Business system. As it works now, the ordinary laborer, union or non-union, works his head off for a time, under the national speed-up system, and then has to hang around the house for a year or two out of a job, and with no money to live on. Yet do Americans really want this lunatic "prosperity" which the corporations are for ever trying to pump up? And the resulting depression. Yet what happens to one who even mildly opposes the corporate will? As Rob Roy McGregor, campaigning for Samuel Insull of Chicago against senators favoring public ownership, said: "Capitalists easily kill these fellows by making them out to be Bolsheviks and radicals." And I am myself astounded at the power of those words: "Red," "radical," "Bolshevik." How can it come about that people in such great numbers will shrink from or be repelled by anything, however beneficial, because it is thus slyly and dishonestly called something which they do not quite understand?

More, even the slightest reform is battered to pieces by lobbies of the great trusts, shouting this and that or privately buying right and left, or "legally" interposing this or that. Look at Muscle Shoals, and injunctions, and child labor. All have been smashed by the lobby resources of the trusts. All have been fought by the utilities lobby, disbursing $1,000,000 annually on this for the last three years.

Consider also the career of a man like Henry T. Oxnard at Washington. For years the Sugar Trust employed him at a fat salary to spread its propaganda. Even eighteen or twenty years ago, a campaign costing the Sugar Trust $1,000,000 was the order. This lobbying and actual killing of people's issues and substituting for them those of the banks and trusts takes place not only in Congress but in every State legislature and on down the line. Right now, the Irving Trust Company of New York has a crack New York lawyer working with the legislature in the State capital at Raleigh, North Carolina, at a salary of $6,000 monthly. "What's wrong with that?" inquires every good American? Well, let's look at it. The Irving Trust Company, through its own mistakes, has placed poor loans and loaned so much money on notes that the taxes aren't enough to pay the interest let alone even the notes. Hence the banks, after burdening the people thus unjustly, seek through this lawyer to get laws through the legislature, making the people pay for it all anyhow. In short, harness them right down by a taxation sufficient to pay interest on the notes, interest on the loans, the notes themselves, the loans, and even this salary of their crack lawyer, through whose work they can so drive the people. And this same condition exists at West Palm Beach, in North Bergen, New Jersey, and elsewhere. And add to this, if you wish, the thought of the many other financial houses working on the common people with this same type of lobbying. Loans to Government, a rich source of income for the banks, have become a general American menace. For all you have to do is to obligate the Government, and then you are set. For are not the people the Government, and vice versa? And when you have the Government, haven't you the people in the hollow of your hand? And can you not squeeze as you will?

As I stated, though, in my Chapter, "Our Banks and Corporations as Government," the lobbyists have their source of direction within the great offices and halls of metropolitan financiers.

These offer a force as calculating and selfish as it is diversified and omnipresent. Yet you can actually hear the American blockhead voter, stuffed as he is with corporation propaganda in a hundred forms, arguing that these corporation lobbyists are opposed by non-trust lobbies like the American Federation of Labor lobby, the anti-saloon lobby, etc., and that these, with the honest, watchful newspapers, are sufficient to keep America from being run by corporations! And this in the face of the fact that while the common people (more than ninety-nine per cent of the population) never have prosperity, the corporations and their banks have it constantly!

But can the American voter be brought to exercise any real thought in connection with this? Or indeed in connection with anything relating to economics, politics, or the science of government? Are our people going to be forever brain-bound by the Democratic and Republican parties? Certainly it is a little difficult to resign oneself to this thought entirely. Yet, an executive of the American Federation of Labor in New York City told me with pride at their achievement that it was the A. F. of L. which kept Socialism out of America! And he added that they were working to do the same to Communism. Yet imagine the mental state of a people who cannot rise above these meaningless (except for purposes of graft and betrayal) Republicans and Democrats and their obsequious American Federation of Labor! And to-day because of this mental state, the fascinating social development offered by the Communists being fought in so far as possible, silenced all along the line! Their leaders are termed seditionists and made to serve ten- and twelve-year sentences. So it is across this whole United States. Yet might not some phases of their political theories be tested? They might apply to American problems. I certainly think they do, just as certainly as I see that the brainless lockstepping of our voters behind these two old parties gets nowhere! Yet must it be that we Americans will continue to let these undemocratic corporations fill us with sly propaganda to the effect that anything other than a Democrat or a Republican is "Red"? But supposing one is "Red" in that sense, what of it? Judge Runyon, in dismissing a case, told Henry Gold, a Communist, that he "hoped now that Gold would still be able to look with kindness on government in general." But in the main, our judges, courts, lawyers, newspapers, police, all try to make everything other than capitalism seem no better than anarchy. And all Americans are supposed to believe that and want capitalism. But do they? And if not is it any wonder then that all dignity and force has been stripped from the ballot as a means of change or reform?

The government of the United States was organized in the beginning, and that purposely, so that the will of the people was to be interpreted and followed. Despite that, however, we have ruling to-day only the voice and the will of money, and none other. And so, why the ballot? For if it cannot be made to mean anything, why vote and spend all the time and money it takes to do so, when a few powerful corporations will tell us what to do, and be glad to do it? More, they will *make* us do it, just as they do now.

A year ago I said: "Move Wall Street to Washington!" But I was kidding or trying to be ironic. For as dumb as I am, do not think that I do not know that it is there now and not so much secretly as openly ruling. As to that, and as they see it, we Americans are not even worth deceiving any more!

CHAPTER XVIII

GOVERNMENT ownership, a principle socialistic but in no way communistic and not to be confused with the nationalization of all wealth as well as all industry as advocated by Communism, is thoroughly established in this country as Constitutional, and this despite the free competition and free business phases implied by the Constitution itself. I state this so carefully because as argument and propaganda go now, it may be assumed by many that it is not. But let us see.

The first case of this kind which early reached the Supreme Court was that of the city of Portland, Maine. Because of high prices due to monopoly and because of delays on the part of private dealers, this municipality set up a coal and wood yard as a permanent business. Speaking for the Supreme Court, which declared this action of the city of Portland to be Constitutional Chief Justice Taft, usually a stout prop for "big business," stated that the Government could engage in any business to help the general public.

The next case to be tried by the Supreme Court was against the Non-Partisan League of North Dakota, a far more daring phase of socialism and certainly directly against the current American practice of corporation control. Yet this scheme, as I stated in the chapter on "Our Banks and Corporations as Government," openly launched to counteract the abuse of monopoly in North Dakota, was an inclusive, State-wide socialization to further agriculture, grain elevators, factories to manufacture farm implements, banks, housing accommodations and other things of that order, all to be established with the aid of State funds; also the sale of grain and manufactured mer-

329

chandise was to be carried on by the State. Yet this program, so contradictory to established methods here, was also declared Constitutional.

Again, in November, 1924, the voters of Lincoln, Nebraska, started a wholesale and retail gasoline and oil business. The Standard Oil Company, viewing this as socialism and hence as an invasion of its private or corporate domain, took this case to the Supreme Court. Its brief for this trial read: "If a city may confer on itself by charter provision power to engage in such business, then the power exists whereby such city can socialize all industry and business within its limits ... and thus transform itself into a purely socialistic community.... Can these be under Constitutional government as it now exists?" When the Standard Oil attorneys finished their argument, Chief Justice Taft told the city lawyers that they need not reply to the case further. The city of Lincoln's participation in business was deemed Constitutional. Although in the former cases the city and State pleaded private monopoly as a defense, it was not argued in this case. Here, despite the fact that the city oil business actually competed with and affected prices of Standard Oil, this argument was not used and the decision was based on whether the public business was for the general good.

Again, the Farm Board, to which the Federal Government appropriated $200,000,000 for the coördination of the whole farming industry, but which was a failure, its action under capitalism worsening instead of improving the condition of the masses was still an attempt at Government control of one phase of capitalism which attracted world-wide attention. In fact, from examining the various opinions of the various local Chambers of Commerce concerning the Farm Board, one gathered that they most definitely looked upon it as competing with individuals in their private struggles for profit. Hence anathema. Said one such opinion: "There has been imposed unbearable hardship upon business enterprises unable to maintain their position" (i.e., making millions by causing market fluctuations, I would say) "against discriminatory competition from the

Government. We condemn as a permanent policy the employment of public funds for the purpose of participation in business in competition with established agencies." In other words, Government direction as well as ownership and control of various commercial and economic functions, in America, was here condemned.

Yet the foundation of the issue I am going to discuss rests on actualities. Already our capitalistic form of Government has engaged in business and has not only so engaged but competed in these pursuits: housing projects, gas and electric companies, fuel yards, ice plants, abattoirs, milk supply stations, laundries, insurance, banks, grain elevators, and mills. At this moment the United States Government owns capital stock in the United States Housing Corporation, the United States Spruce Production Corporation, the Panama Railroad, the Inland Waterways, also banks, steamship and river boat lines.

I acclaim present-day government ownership as a fact which in practice shows up the waste due to the high profits exacted by our American corporations, their financial and other agencies; in sum, all of the present abuses of the corporate system: social, political, economic and legislative.

In this connection let me examine, and for your benefit, if you please, the insurance business. The New York State government, through its Workers' Compensation Department, not only writes policies fifteen per cent lower than do the standard insurance companies, but it likewise pays a fifteen per cent dividend, which makes each $100 premium $2.75 below the rates charged by the regular insurance companies. And more, this government fund not only pays its pro rata share of taxes, but grows constantly, and is the present largest carrier of workers' compensation. Yet in Ohio, which also has a State fund, the fund there is even cheaper than it is in New York State. These compensation groups were formed because eighty-seven per cent of the workmen's policies in private companies lapsed, inability to keep up with the payments being the reason. Also, in 1928, 1,759,000 policies in the private companies were surrendered and 5,800,000 lapsed, so that for every person realizing any profit on his investment, eight lost all or most of their money.

Is it any wonder then, my dear reader (and I hope you are a corporation-minded reader at that, for this happens to be a good point!) that a State system grew up to help stop these abuses? Also, I would like to add, should it seem singular to you that a government can (and where it undertakes so to do, does) undersell any private company? And could that possibly mean anything to the public at large; indicate, for instance, that corporation abuses might be ended by nationalization of quite everything after the communist fashion? Or perhaps the fact that in 1928, eighty high officials in private insurance companies drew salaries of $3,480,000 will throw some light on this thought. The fact is that 30 cents of every $1.10 paid into private insurance companies was and still is, for that matter, used for salaries and dividends to stockholders.

To further develop this phase of the issue, I am going to prove that even the United States Government as it is now capitalistically organized not only can be successful in business, but that it can and does show up the excessive and even cruel and brutal profits of present Wall Street management in private business. If you are not prepared to believe that, witness what is now going on in our corporate world. We will begin with the Federal Government, which has just spent hundreds of millions on waterways which it knew would go to the dogs unless something was done to revive river traffic. Neither the railroads nor anybody else was interested in developing such traffic, however. If they had been, the Government never would have interfered, you may be sure. Yet in 1924, Congress formed a regular corporation called the Inland Waterways Corporation. It had six advisory directors and the Secretary of War was ordered to delegate all powers to a chairman whose authority was to be absolute. In connection with this, Congress voted $5,000,000 for capital stock which the Government was to hold. This corporation then organized the business of operating freight boats up and down the Mississippi and

Warrior Rivers mainly, at a rate not a great deal less than the railroads charged. For this purpose they maintained their own wireless and insurance. Yet soon the Inland Waterways, prospering greatly under Government control, took over a bankrupt railroad which they bought from the Southern Railway and in two years made a six-per-cent profit on that. More, this very conservative business, reckoned a dead one by financiers, made such excess profits that in 1929 the Inland Waterways had increased its book value to $19,756,350—nearly four times the amount Congress put into it five years before. For that reason the capital stock was increased to $15,000,000 in November, 1929. Now the United States Government still owns the stock of this flourishing corporation. It is a part of the assets of the United States Treasury.

Of course, the financiers do not want the public to know the truth concerning these Government ventures in business. And possibly it was for that reason—who knows?—that *Business Week,* a publication, not only failed to consider the facts but apparently sought to delude the people by saying that a Farm Board shipment of wheat with this Inland Waterways Company "may mean more grief for the taxpayers who support this barge line." In fact, capitalist propaganda is always full of just such insults and insinuations, and always intended, and most unjustly, to disparge these Government-owned ventures.

But despite this success, the capitalists continue to roar out the doctrine of government inefficiency in business, also to belittle (in some instances rightly, in others unjustly) officeholders' business ability and to make fun of the crooked politicians as if under no circumstances could a public officeholder have integrity. As a matter of fact, though, some officeholders do have integrity. Concerning the Government operation of the railroads in wartime, and of which I have already written, the railroad owners said: "Look at our railroads! What a failure wartime operation by the Government is!" Yet in connection with that, I want to drive home one fact, and that is that not even the private owners of our railroads, with their self-proclaimed genius for business, could carry on transportation on the rates charged during the War under McAdoo. Furthermore, my proof is that immediately the railroads were returned to their private owners, these rates were increased. And that our private and corporate railroad financiers had the malicious and unmitigated "crust" to cite as proving that the Government had no capacity for business! It did not raise its rates as high as it might have. It did not pocket as much money as they would have.

Another of their arguments was that since the Government had taken over the operation of the railroads, there had been a general increase in taxes which they were now compelled to pay. And that was true. But these increases were due to the War, and everybody paid pro rata, the railroads no more than any other, if as much. But had the Government been so inefficient and wasteful in business, would the money owners have found it necessary to yell about it so much? Wouldn't it have been obvious, rather than so suspicious, that almost the entire American world doubted their sincerity? Besides, would not the public itself have complained? Yet it did not. No, the truth is that the Government in business, in that instance at least, apparently managed so well as to indicate clearly the avariciously unfair profits which our private concerns were taking, and this was, of course, the dreadful and infuriating thing. Also, it could threaten Government competition in many fields other than railroading—a possibility of which our lordly and at present domineering corporations are most horribly afraid.

But to display even more the undue profits of private corporations, let us set over against our private utilities those of Canada: their publicly-owned ones. In Ottawa, the average cost of electricity for homes at this time is less than one cent per kilowatt hour (the amount of electricity necessary to burn a 40-watt electric light bulb for 25 hours), whereas here in America our small-town residents pay 15 cents per kilowatt hour. And throughout the whole of Ontario, the electricity is less than 2 cents, the while we Americans in our homes burn electricity costing an average of 8 cents per kilowatt hour. Yet with only a three-cent reduction on the American side, over $200,000,000 of the people's income every year would be saved. But that's why our American power trust won't reduce the rate!

But do not assume that a large number of towns and cities have not already realized the exorbitant financial drain on the masses which comes with private corporation control of such matters. Corporations have no interest in what is equitable; merely in what the traffic will yield. On that account, not so very long ago the city of Cleveland, Ohio, went into the electric light business and cut the rates in two. The city of Seattle, Washington, where private companies charged the people 12½ cents per kilowatt hour, finally introduced a city-owned plant which now furnishes electricity to the people for 5½ cents per kilowatt hour. And these cities are not losing money; they have a surplus. In Henton, Texas, for instance, the publicly owned electric light and gas works pay two-thirds of the town's taxes. In Jacksonville, Florida, with a population of 167,000, the electric light department under government ownership returns over $1,000,000 a year in taxes. Then, too, the Hydro-Electric Commission, which runs the system in Ontario, has a surplus of $80,000,000 and by the end of thirty or forty years will have paid back all of the capital which it has used.

But supposing honest Government operation in this field to reach the stage of real competition with these private concerns, what happens? In 1906, when the Province of Ontario, Canada, went into partnership with 380 municipalities under the direction of the Hydro-Electric Power Commission to carry on a utility business, they aimed at complete control. They bought companies and now own plants and transmit electricity. Due to their business, the private utility rates in Canada have since been forced down from nineteen to sixty per cent lower.

Yet while the Canadian Government proceeded to help its people in this way, Americans here were left by their Government to their corporations, and more recently, or since this last great depression, to charity. For where their electric light bills have become so large that they cannot afford electricity they have been resorting to the nearest alms agencies and receiving from them, if anything, kerosene lamps. But who is to blame for this: the masses, their Government, their trusts and banks, or all?

To show further how severe competition by the Government in business can affect a private concern, look at Lincoln, Nebraska. In 1913, the Hon. William Schroeder of that city's government commission put through an ordinance establishing a municipal electric plant. The first rate charged was 9 cents a kilowatt hour as opposed to 13 cents by the private companies, who then dropped theirs to 9 cents. Shortly thereafter, though, Schroeder again cut his rate, which was met, and so on, until finally with the people of all the surrounding cities still paying from 10 cents to 15 cents, those of Lincoln were and now are receiving electricity for from 3 to 5 cents per kilowatt hour.

And finally Chanute, Kansas, the taxless city. We are informed that Chanute's $122,610 budget for 1931 will be met chiefly out of earnings from the town's municipal gas and electric plants. Their rates are the lowest in Kansas, and from them the electric plant will contribute $42,100 and the gas works $60,460. The balance comes from court fees, interest on deposits, state road tax and other sources. In fact, ever since Chanute went in for publicly-owned utilities five years ago, taxes have steadily declined. Last year's earnings met the entire budget. The earnings are building a $350,000 memorial building and a $75,000 airport.

But whether all this is worth anything to you as data or political or economic theory depends on whether you believe in Capitalism as you now have it, or in a nationalization of industry and credit under the people, not under or to the private profit of banks and corporations.

But I cannot go into all of the municipal utility plants now functioning profitably in America. As a final fair example, I will, however, take the one in Colby, Kansas. There a government-owned plant pays all of the city's bills out of its surplus income. Not only that, but during the last two years, Colby has built

$200,000 worth of pavement. After paying this bill and salaries, $45,000 still remains in the treasury, a move in the direction of social equity which however weak should hearten those who understand and desire true nationalization.

Since, as you can see, Government ownership is well established as a method to which the people can resort if they wish, a sweeping movement to hold back the inordinate greed of private corporations has so developed as not only to make possible many a public municipal utility but also to launch voters across the whole country on a national drive against private ownership of big projects. One of these, Muscle Shoals, its fate still hanging in the balance, has enough immediate resources and latent power to supply several cities. As a matter of fact, ten States could and should be supplied with electricity by Muscle Shoals. Developments in the Tennessee River above it should add seventy-five per cent to the present power. In addition, the chemical plant which the Government built there during the War could furnish enormous amounts of fertilizer to the farmers. But what will happen? Already Presidents Coolidge and Hoover have vetoed three government ownership bills. The Power Trust wants it; that's the explanation.

And yet again, there is the Colorado River project—or Boulder Dam, as it is called—the third largest water power project in the country and one which, when completed, should supply Arizona, Utah and California with electricity at about one-half cent per kilowatt hour to companies which in turn should transmit and sell it to the people in their homes at not very much more than that. But will they?

This dam as high as a sixty-story building will hold the water back for 100 miles. Not only that, but a number of tracts of wasteland in that western area can be made rich and fruitful by this water. Imperial Valley, Palos Verdes Valley, and Yuma in Arizona, which now have to be constantly protected by higher levees each year, would stand unharmed by flood. But now, theoretically, as America stands to-day, should this be a private or a governmental monopoly? And under which system would it do best by all? But do not write me as to this.

The proposed water power plant for the St. Lawrence River would create, it is calculated, twice as much power as the Boulder and eight times as much as Muscle Shoals. And New York State, which, second to California, has the greatest amount of already developed power, wants to develop the St. Lawrence as a Government project. And what a boon to all forms of industry in the Mohawk Valley that should be! From the St. Lawrence, electricity could likewise be sent to New England and maybe to New York City. Or New York State, like the Hydro-Electric Commission of Ontario, could go into the transmission and distribution business.

But in connection with all of these things arises the question as to whether government operation of these projects should be achieved. And while I believe that the principle of government ownership and operation should be greatly extended, especially in the electrical field, still I know that government ownership, no matter how advantageous and economical for the people, is at present so powerfully thwarted by corporations as to be certain to fail unless a great social change takes place. But are the American people as yet, and for all their ills, ready for that —sufficiently interested to make it?

For thus far certainly our private trusts are making such financial strides—won, of course, by their abusive and dictatorial practices—as to give them the power to block most effectively this entire government ownership movement, desired or not, or if not that then themselves to seize and operate the Government through these nationalizing methods but of course for their own private enrichment and entrenchment in power. Imperial Russia owned its railroads as did Imperial Germany, but to what end in so far as the masses are concerned? We all know. But that is not the import or direction of this book. Its arrow, if any, flies to nationalization by the masses and equity for all workers, not drones, in every field.

But as things stand now, these corporations of ours have the spirit, as well as the means, to conquer the world, financially, and with their desire pointed toward national as well as international control our present public ownership program may as readily prove an arrow in their quiver as in that of the worker in his mass form and extent. That this is no exaggeration is attested not only by the known ambitions of our industrial giants, but is inherent in the very philosophy of economics, sociology and government which animates and directs them. Thus, they do not believe in the power (if not in the right) of the people to govern themselves, or in a government to greatly help the masses. They think of the masses as fools and numskulls, always to be outwitted and betrayed by those who are shrewder and stronger. And as for equity—what is equity? The protection if not the propagation of the many by the strong? What nonsense! God helps those who help themselves! The devil takes the hindmost! Up then, we who are strong but few, and seize the reins of power! They are ours by right of brain! The mass, as ever, shall march to our music! And thus far at least, certainly the American mass stands agape and afraid. It does not know what to do about the armed Goliaths who now so sinisterly tower above it. And now, as I have pointed out, these have the means, as the strong and the few in any past age or day have always had. They have the guns and to-morrow may roll the drums and call "March!", and march we will, I presume, since so few appear ready to fight! And our new Cæsar will be a financier, you may depend upon that! None but one who is a master of economics, if a Cæsar it is to be, will rule the world as it is now organized!

For only see how the events of our day are shaping up to that one end! American money owners are in scores of foreign countries to the extent of many billions of dollars, and in every known industry, so much so that even in this difficult year for America's working people, her gilt-edge lords have billions wherewith to *increase* their foreign investments. And right now, as during years past, their profits mount excessively. Every one knows the commonplace of American business: put in $50,000 and in twenty years a $3,000,000 concern blossoms on unfair accumulation of profits. And hundreds of minor businesses yet still of good size bob up around us, only to be united in but a little while into one of our hundred or five-hundred-million dollar corporations. And then the stock and bond issues of this same, touted and sold to an ignorant and confiding public as gilt-edge, the result, as usual, enormous profits for the primary owners of the corporations but for no others.

Indeed, this power of our corporations to rob the people and in addition dictate to the Government is also strong enough unless they themselves turn to it as a means of control, to crush the present agitation for Government ownership. Yet even that cannot be understood without further examination of their profits and therefore their rates, their power to accumulate money with which all else is done: politics financed, lawyers hired; judges, senators and what not elected; the whole political aspect of America colored by their ideas. Thus, when I passed through Wisconsin last summer I found the farmers there paying from 9 to 11 cents a kilowatt hour for electricity. The Northern State Power Company charged its subsidiary, which supplied the farmers, only one cent per kilowatt hour. The profits—$2,000,000 yearly—mostly enriched the Byllesbys in Chicago rather than helped the thousands of citizens who needed and deserved a betterment of their financial status.

Yet our money owners always justify, and morally, of course, their right to rob the people by arguing that their prices and profits permit of increase to the workers in general in the forms of lowered rates or higher wages or both. But do they? And to how many? Facts show that in so far as the electrical world is concerned, and a very large world that is to-day, labor cost per kilowatt hour between 1912 and 1922 dropped. Next, in the same period, utility operating expenses also declined from sixty-seven per cent to sixty-two per cent the while income increased $250,000,000. Yet the rate for consumers—which is the real test of the social value of any public utility—and during these greatest years of these holding company developments in the utility field, and with their acknowledged efficiency measures —shows a decrease of only $.004 per kilowatt hour!

Likewise in the shipping world, labor stands as but a fraction—and a slight one at that—of the total operating expense. Yet instead of the general well-being which money-owners have always avowed would seep down to the masses, more and more of the people are leveled to a mediocre and even difficult standard of living. I am not speaking now of the abnormalities of "hard times," but rather of such general conditions as are now prevalent in the automobile and other industries, where by reducing by machinery millions of skilled laborers to really the unskilled class, and then speeding those up, we have an illustration of the system which can only weaken and reduce the mass to a very low level and make the owner and controller of the machine of production and its government all the stronger and all the more dictatorial.

Still, as yet the American people do not appear to see that their faith in their corporations is lunatic. For the utilities as well as all other forms of corporation control answer complaints as to hard times, unemployment, wretched living conditions for the many, with generalizations as to taxes, foreign trade, the depressing results of the people investing in the stocks and bonds of the companies which they themselves so woefully mismanage. Thus, right now, the utilities answer the charges of high rates and unemployment by pleading, first, of course, the high wages paid (and you have seen what these amount to), and next, by asserting that while they themselves are taxed to death by the Government, State and county municipalities operating electric plants as well as the Hydro-Electric Commission of Ontario, pay no taxes.

Well, I am able to reply to that. In Nebraska, Government-owned plants undersell the private concerns on electric light power from 4 to 7 cents per kilowatt hour. And as against that, and while charging higher rates, the corporations pay a tax of but two mills per kilowatt hour. More, while the utilities here argue that the Ontario project is supported by the Govern-

ment, the Hydro-Electric Commission of Ontario is also taxed
two mills per kilowatt hour, although it is true that the rural
lines there are partially subsidized. But contrast with this, if you
will, the fact that in 1930, with almost every factory suffering
from a depressed market and with many closed down because
of the abundant previous production which could not be distributed, or working on part time, or undergoing strikes and
other labor disputes, or unable to sell much to the millions of
jobless, still the corporation, who had in no way insured the
laborers against these calamities, possessed a rich surplus of
profits.

In fact, according to figures from a New York statistical
organization, the gross revenues of ten of the nation's leading
public utility corporations, in the decade from 1921 to 1930,
increased over 177 per cent. During the same period, this authority states, the ratio of operating expenses to income dropped
from 63.55 in 1921 to 55.10 in 1930, while earnings to fixed
charges increased from 2.06 to 3.63, a gain of about seventy-
five per cent. The total revenue taken by these ten big utility
corporations in the ten-year period is given as about
$627,684,000.

Figures from another source indicate the prosperity of big
utilities even in times of depression. Profits of electric utilities
increased by nearly $44,000,000 last year while the rest of the
country was struggling to keep its head above water. This was
the greatest gain ever made in the industry. It would be unfair
to ignore the fact that the prosperity of these huge units of the
national power trust is in a certain sense a source of economic
stability. Had profits fallen to a minimum or been converted
into losses, it would have been necessary for them to make re-
trenchments. On the other hand, it is being recognized that
undue concentration of the nation's wealth is responsible to a
large extent for the depression. The utilities, with their control
in the hands of a privileged few who reap the real profits, are
leading contributors to this concentration. The big earnings that
accrue from utility prosperity for the most part do not get into

the regular channels of business and industry for the benefit of all—they go direct into the hands of the very rich to be hoarded or used as reinvestments to act further to concentrate wealth and income.

In fact, as in the power trust, so in all other phases of our commercial life this money-madness dominates. It has even resulted, as any one can see to-day, in intensive installment-selling of quite anything here in America—the business of forcing by high power salesmanship, the individual to buy or undertake far more than he can carry—a mushroom form of profiteering which constitutes no petty issue and has pushed many an individual into a wretched corner. To illustrate, ninety per cent of all pianos, sewing machines, and washing machines are purchased on installment contracts. And, of course, this type of financing runs between fifteen per cent and twenty-five per cent higher than cash payment—or, in other words, we see usury resorted to for the purpose of aggrandizement.

And of these profits, a great part, as I will show, is being used to seize industrial control abroad, and another $1,000,000 a year is still reserved and used by the utilities here to quiet, by propaganda, any agitation in favor of Government ownership. Think back on my chapter "Our Banks and Corporations as Government"!

In regard to this matter of foreign control, I propose to recite—for the present, at least—but two or three things. When the recent revolution in Cuba broke out, who were the chief advisers and friends of the dictator Machado, despised and resented by ninety per cent of the nevertheless helpless people— since there, as elsewhere, the money, guns, airplanes, army, ships and all the remaining paraphernalia of war wherewith to overawe had been carefully garnered into the hands of Mr. Machado. Plainly the chief American investors, the security of whose property depended on his administration and the really great investors are concerns and corporations represented by the Chase National Bank and the National City Bank. And with a quick

slaughter of the innocents, that particular attempt to force the
money-sucking corporations off their backs was quickly put down.

Next, consider the revolution in Chile, where under the dictator Ibañez (nicknamed by some "the bloody"), quite all of
Chile's raw materials had swiftly passed—say in the last twenty
years—under the control of our United States bankers, under
the leadership of the Guggenheim interests. United States investments at the time of this revolution amounted to $600,000,000.
And previous to this (1927), the reorganization of the copper
and nitrate mines there, through the "rationalization" process
known to the Guggenheims, had cost 30,000 workers their jobs.
In consequence, the national revenue of the government had
suffered a deep slash. And this made for hard times. Dictator
Ibañez then sought to obtain new loans from Wall Street in
order to avert a financial debacle. But Wall Street at that time
was facing the dangerous maneuvers of British imperialists in
Chile who were trying to recapture their former political control
over this national middle-class. And having no binding contract with Ibañez, it was able to desert him. He then installed a
Fascist dictatorship, the purpose of which was, via the landlords, small merchants and the imperialists, to throw the burden
of retrenchment and suffering upon the workers and peasants.
This is what eventually produced the disastrous uprising last
September. But note the present of our American millions taken
out of America and used to enslave a foreign people!

Next, in so far as this particular point is concerned, note
the distressing failure of the leaders of the labor government of
Great Britain to maintain the principles of their party in the
face of a national crisis, since that indicates one thing very
clearly; i.e., that the international bankers really run the world
and that governments, when it comes to a showdown, are merely
puppets in their hands. World developments of the middle
months of 1931 and all of epoch-making importance, in England,
Germany, Chile, Cuba, China, and where not else, bear out the
present contention that for years now power has been gravitat-
ing from the hands of government into the hands of those who

own and control a huge portion of the world's wealth. The international bankers, with their huge financial power and ability to smash or bolster currencies, exchange and credit, stepped in at the English crisis, made their demands and got them. The result was the resignation of the loyal members of the MacDonald Government, the forming of a coalition government that later balanced the British budget but at labor's expense.

Or again, look at the present international situation concerning the war debts of Germany to the United States. This debt to the Federal Treasury is secured by a first lien on German industry and taxes. Yet knowing that, New York bankers subsequently loaned fabulous sums to the German cities, states and corporations. These great sums were the moneys of clients and depositors of the New York banks. But now the National City Bank and the Chase National Bank, both of New York City, and both as stated by Senator Shipstead of Minnesota the interested parties, are trying to lessen the debt to the United States Government, thus making safe their German debt. And this when a first lien is always prior to a second. Also when the bankers consciously loaned money to Germany although the bankers knew of the prior lien—that German reparation debts to the United States had better security than the more recent debts for money loaned by these bankers. The experienced bankers probably knew beforehand that they could lower the reparations debt by political maneuvering (which should never be tolerated) and thus make their own loose financial actions good.

But the greatest mal-force, as I see it, among these our rapidly increasing money-machines called corporations, is the old "holding company" idea of John D. Rockefeller, most likely, which originated about 1890, and for the purpose of keeping under single control his grasping oil industry. But one of its greatest exemplars to-day is, I think, the above power industry of which I have been talking and which, in so far as salable (and sold) electricity in America is concerned, expended some tens of billions of kilowatt hours in 1927. In regard to it—this holding company idea, I mean—our corporations, through their law departments, advance the argument that a very central organization such as this, with banking connections, can all the more rapidly furnish capital to modernly equipped operating plants, since it can accept in return stock in such concerns as it fosters. In other words, an easy step to world monopoly. And, by way of illustration, we have Electric Bond & Share, a stock-holding and selling corporation which represents other corporations only and, as you may be sure, only such corporations as are in good financial condition. Yet see how this centralizes control. And in one sense legitimately, since holding companies grow up because of the difficulty of carrying on a great national or international business under a score of conflicting State or national and even international laws. And if one were talking of government control and operation such as one sees in Russia, say, that would be well enough—a natural national method as opposed to a score or more of private methods. But in private hands! And in but a few private hands, at that! For by the piling up of holding companies, one company that buys but a fractional share in one—yet the same carrying with it complete control in that company,—a slight fraction of an immense total investment—can and does eventually direct the whole of it, however divided.

And so it comes about that by now five holding companies direct half the utilities in America. And as an example of this pyramiding, I will cite this: the Texas Power & Light, which operates a number of individual plants, is yet held by the Southern Power & Light, a holding company whose stock is owned by the American Power & Light, another holding company which in turn is managed by the Electric Bond & Share, whose capital stock is owned entirely by the Electric Bond & Share Securities Corporation. But is that not a stair leading to the chamber of a Cæsar somewhere? Either that or the whole thing is a hoax and there is nothing to be afraid of. But isn't there?

For while some of the holding utility companies appear to have grown up in a natural way, others appear to be the results of but one purpose: the desire on the part of one or a few magnates somewhere in America or abroad (or both) to control a lot of money with a very little money. And though utility men still argue that the holding company, performing, as it does, technical services for various operating concerns, grew up naturally enough and will so continue to grow, still many companies, like the Middle West Utilities in 21 States, were not merged for efficiency but rather in a grab-as-grab-can scramble for private or group control of any possible operating company. And not only that, but many such were purchased under such competitive and hence high prices that for many years the people using the service provided by them will certainly have to pay rates on this overcapitalization rather than on the small or real value that underlies the whole business. Thus, to illustrate, the Mohawk Hudson paid $347 a share for the Syracuse Lighting Company, when the book value of that same was only $116. None the less, the Mohawk Hudson Company will certainly want, and get, six per cent, or as near that or as much more as possible, on that $347, and out of the consumer, who will have to pay the rates which will provide it. Next, the Narragansett Electric has an overcapitalization of nearly $17,000,000. And who pays the interest on that, do you suppose? The holders of the $17,000,000? Now, really! Then as against the law, millions of dollars on utility books on which the people pay rates are unaccounted for—in New York State, alone, $163,000,000 with $32,000,000 unaccounted for on the Niagara Falls Power Company books for 10 years.

But now as to and what if anything is being done concerning this strange and almost mystic growth and how, if at all, it is ever to be regulated. For already various courts have decreed that a Public Service Commission may not regulate the stock issues of a holding company. And again, our National Federal Trade Commission, more or less giving up in despair before these dreadful complexities of finance, has already said that the control of a majority of the voting stock of the 23 reported holding companies is in the hands of fewer than 25 stockholders, and that this group, with an investment of about $600,000,000, controls operating companies with an investment of $2,000,000,000. (Please pause sixty seconds on that, and turn east or west or any other old way, and pray or meditate silently, for as I see it, there are few matters more serious at the moment!) For what group is this that holds all this? (Or maybe—who knows—just one or two men! Rockefeller, say!) At any rate, as yet the public isn't allowed to know anything. And again, the State of Massachusetts has long since decried the holding company as a device "too confused in itself for any effective regulation." Thus, this new holding company, or its sponsors or Cæsars, may do as it pleases or they please, may it or they not? Charge or tax the public, say anything, since the Massachusetts Court holds that this, their device, is "too confused in itself for any effective regulation." And as if in confirmation of that, we find, in connection with these holding companies, items such as reserves for replacement and depreciation treated as the holding companies say, not as the Government or any one State may wish. In short, no State any longer has any effective authority over these tremendous national enterprises. They are their own law and fix their own profits. Reform is futile. Change and change only in a radical way can bring order out of this chaos. These financial spiders do not really know the complexities and ramifications of their own cobwebs.

But now once more as to these profits taken from these immense *misuses* of capital: these corporations which have slowly but surely developed a political and managerial strategy too subtle as well as too strong to be either understood or regulated by government, as it is now capitalistically constructed. As we are seeing to-day, they maneuver developments of all power sites and almost everything else for their own financial increment, and theirs alone. But cannot any one with half an eye see how this increment is to be used? Is it not already manifesting itself as a form of imperialism, and an American imperialism at that, which now seeks to take financial and so all other forms of control throughout the world? Have I not spoken of England,

Germany, Chile, Cuba and somewhere in a previous chapter have I not listed the amount of our foreign investments? The one point I wish to make here is that obviously this immense sum of money is or has been taken from America by its corporations. And that money is not now controlled by the United States as such, or its people, but by a few banks and their associated corporations. And it is the financiers of these same— mostly our financiers, as you may well guess—who are the ones who are so busy functioning not alone as businessmen but as government, not only here but everywhere, abroad and at home. And have I not shown how our State Department, as well as our Army and Navy, can and is being used for furthering of their purposes, and none other—Nicaragua, Mexico, Chile, Argentina, Brazil? And will this adventuring be stopped or regulated unless some consciousness of the same and its meaning to the rank and file of this country dawns on the individuals who make up that rank and file? For now it is to be either a financial Cæsar or a nationalization by the workers of all walks and hence for the benefit of all since under any sane readjustment all should and will be made to work. Which is it to be?

For in opposition to Cæsarism, what is to be placed, if anything? The ballot of the American voter? And just after I have shown that he is not interested in his ballot and cannot or will not be made to think, and so cannot or will not vote intelligently! Yet dismissing him as a nonentity, as one well may, then what? The desires and powers of such elements as mentally and materially still remain uninfluenced, or better and best, remain uncontrolled by these immense pools of money and their directors, and who still desire something less than Cæsarism (the material Cæsarism of a Morgan or a Rockefeller, say) and who still look to or at least wish for an enlightened middle mass which may yet save the world from this crass and purely material dictatorship now so near at hand? And if so, what is their weapon to be? Socialism or an American form of Communism? Most certainly one or the other. And hence, as I see it at least, nationalization by the masses themselves, the only contra weapon which such an idealistic group could offer or employ. National or public ownership and control of everything, all public utilities and, in addition to those, all private adventures and enterprises of any kind. For if you are to destroy an evil (and if capitalistic control of everything is not an evil, what is it?), then most certainly you must do more than control the largest of the great utilities. But, say you, that is Communism, and given into the hands of wild-eyed theorists... whereas, in the case of capitalism... well, in the case of capitalism, what? Have we not just seen?

At any rate, any sane mind must by now have halted. For already in America and everywhere else, but more particularly in America, Capitalism has already shown its true aims: world domination by a group which concerns itself not so much ("by no means," I should say) with the welfare of the mass as with the welfare of its sons, daughters, its group. And that, well, certainly that is Cæsarism! And now which will you? For what has become of democracy for which the whole world was made to suffer by that last immense and purely materialistic war? Does it actually speak in America as it should, or anywhere else to-day, unless it be in Russia? You know that it does not! The day of the little man, his significance, his care, has gone in America and elsewhere, and forever, apparently, unless... unless... well?

morals, social intercourse and economic life, boys and girls should
be instructed concerning the existence and meaning of organized
society—matters now so ignored by the State which should insist
on them, and fought by the Church which is determined to insist
on their duty to God and itself as the representative of God on
earth. In fact, the first word a child hears is "God" and instead
of being made to see, as soon as he is old enough to think, that
the important thing is not what God dictates, but what effects
his actions, good, bad or indifferent, are likely to have on others,
as well as himself in this integrated plexus which is organized
society, he is told only that they are offensive to God—a creature
whom he cannot visualize, let alone directly obey. But I repeat
that the child's acts should be interpreted to himself in the light
of their meaning to the world about him. Boys and girls should be
made to understand organized society—its various and beneficial
functions and their part in and to it.

As it is to-day, though, the Church dictates rules concerning
the family as well as the State. The first of these is the duty
of the State, as well as the individual, to God, and next, man's
duty to reproduce himself in order to maintain the State and
presumably please God. Also, the Church teaches that marriage
is instituted by God for the purpose of propagating the race.

And people are still supposed to have children because it is
their solemn obligation to God. But, as I see it, is it not better
to so contribute to, understand, and appreciate society as to
bring about the wish to continue it, its achievements, in short,
what we have and see around us, rather than to feel or believe
that we do this because God so orders? If so, then most certainly
children should be taught the useful and lovely things of life, so
that they will be able to and wish to extend them to their children. With this broader view, child-bearing and training would
come from an intelligent sense of society and one's duty to it—
the wish, if such a wish were involved by it, to continue it rather
than destroy it. And this from a satisfaction with life as it is or
can be organized, rather than from any vague duty to a decidedly

remote and rather dubious Creator—that is, a directly creating Creator.

Now care of the child is the first function of the family. As it is now, though, the cheap religionists throughout the world declare this a responsibility imposed by the will of God. But I would have children taught the basic principles of society: i.e., that the young should not be deserted by their parents because doing so would thrust too big a burden upon organized society as a whole. Children should be taught the meaning of society so that they themselves in their turn may desire to care for their children, and also so that they would know how to care for them, and so that they would have the means to bring them up.

As it is now, though, all too much of the child's social education is based upon religious training in the home. And this precisely follows the methods of the Church. Thus, the first thing a Catholic child is taught is to make the cross, to signify that Jesus died on the cross to redeem mankind. Next, the child must perform other acts equally mysterious to him; i.e., the Hail Mary of the Catholic Church, or the "Now I lay me" of the Protestant home. This builds up a series of mystic symbols, having no bearing upon anything around the child. Hence, these religious acts besides being meaningless, crowd out almost any contemplation of the presence, significance and meaning of organized society as such. Worse, when the child, possibly an intelligent little creature, seeks to know the why of some garbled religious version of his social and economic and scientific place in life and nature, he is told that God knows best and that what he is seeking to understand is not anything for him to worry about—that it is his duty to accept and obey. Or that God wants little boys to be kind to other little boys. Then the youngster, wondering how people know that God is right, is told because He *is*, He is always right. Yes?

But as I see it, the training of children in their social relations —national and international—should be the main function of our public schools. Boys and girls should be made to see themselves as a part of a great mass of people with whom they are connected and to whom they are socially, economically and, in other ways, responsible as co-sharers not so much of this immense and mysterious nature—all well enough for later and more contemplative years, as of all the benefits of that immense mass-coördination known as organized society of which obviously they are such intimate co-sharers. Early and clearly as it seems to me they should be apprised of its immense ramifications and duties of which they must be a part, however humbly so, connected with it all by the fact that they live in a house built for them by others, ride in automobiles manufactured for them by men like their fathers; eat food grown by farmers, shipped by railroad clerks, cooked by their mothers; and in return for all this, that it is their as well as their father's duty to help to build houses for other people, or build roads, or sell gasoline. In sum, children must be made to see that they are only a few members of a wide race with other little boys and girls all over the world. They must be taught that neither the necessities nor the more interesting and pleasurable phases of their lives can be had without the contributions of all of the individuals of the world working to supply them. In fact, everything that comes up in the classroom or in connection with education in general, should be explained to the children in its relation to this social organization of which they are a part. Should a little boy or girl bring the teacher flowers, it should be asked: "Do people like flowers; why do people like flowers?" etc. Thus should the school training concerning society replace the old, meaningless, because unthoughtful, religious training of the home.

The next dogmatic command of the Church in relation to the family is the duty imposed by God upon the individual to be clean for the sake of the family. But children should be taught that not so much God as society in its organized form demands this, and that not only sanitation and the prevention of disease, but æsthetics as well, exact this of all. To be sure, that mother is pleased to see their little hands clean because they look nice, and cleanliness keeps them from getting sick, need not be wholly ignored. The personal relation always remains, in some form. But if mother knows anything of organized society, she is likely to add that, if boys and girls are dirty, they finally get sick, and cause others in society to become sick also. Indeed, children should be made to realize that they owe it to their mothers to keep from getting sick because mothers worry, and in turn might become sick themselves. Daddy worries and cannot do his work so well, which may inconvenience or even injure some other member of society who deserves better. He has to pay a big doctor bill, so that maybe mother cannot have a new warm coat she needs. The children owe it to the other children to keep clean and well, because diseases are catching and other children would thus miss out on their school work.

According to the Church again, which is the main teacher in this respect, all so-called moral acts form the bases from which the soul takes its flight to heaven. Thus if little children do not want to smolder and sizzle in the flames of hell, it is their duty to be moral. Such are God's orders. Hence, supposedly, God threatens little children with punishment which is not true, unless for God be substituted organized nature of which society is an outgrowth. But organized nature does not voice any direct command. It is organized society that does that or should. But that brings the immediate duty of correct information as to all this back to society, where it belongs. For such an order on the part of God suggests nothing to the child of the immense and valuable organized life about it, or its real, because equitable, obligations to that life. Instead of "Thou shalt not kill—it is against the will of God" (that mysterious, befuddling will of God!) the child should be told: "Man should not be killed because you yourself wish to live, not be killed; and don't you want your little playmates to live? You would hate some one to take your life away from you or away from your daddy. Then your mother would feel terrible and she'd have such a hard time. You want to live, don't you? Daddy and all the other daddies and children all over the world want to live, and if you want to be permitted to live unharmed, then you must wish for and see to it that all others are not harmed. Well, then, for that reason, you must not kill any one. If you kill any one, then the other people think it is so terrible that they put you to death, so that you won't kill more people. They put you to death by having the government do it. The government is really organized society, and does things to help the whole of organized society."

According to religion, God gave the command not to steal. People tell children not to steal because it is wicked or it is not right. This method of treating the subject springs from religious and not equitable sources, and shows no intelligence in the teacher. Neither does it arouse or satisfy thought in the child. Yet children should be made to understand that what they steal from some one else that some one else has worked to obtain; more, that it is of use or a source of comfort to the owner. If goods are stolen, the owner is deprived, and as the thief himself would not wish to be deprived by another person. One of the children would not want another to steal his new red pencil bought from money earned by washing the dishes or sweeping snow from the sidewalk, or by his father's work. Worse, if the stolen goods were sold, the buyer would consider it his. Look at all the persons involved. When stolen goods are sold, the money received is taken unjustly because no work has been done to earn that money. The stolen goods were taken unjustly because they were not gained from work for the good of society in general. An individual must work for society in general; that is, for all the other people in the world, because all these other people are working for that individual.

Again, religion teaches us not to bear false witness. That is not totally the same as lying, which is something which should be explained. As to lying proper, that is not explained. The child does not know what it is all about, or what relation it has to society in its organized form. He is merely told to tell the truth, because, according to God, one must tell the truth. But intelligent children can never grow up mentally on that type of argument. To render children intelligent to the people and life surrounding them, an explanation of the misery caused by falsehood should be made. If a child, because he wanted to play Indian at his house longer, told his playmate's mother that he was not there, think of the worry it would cause the mother. If a boy refused to tell whether boards around an uncovered manhole were dragged off by him because he wished to play with them and later was afraid of being punished for endangering the lives of others, he might be shown that safety and telling the truth is an obligation to society which adds to the comfort of all. Certainly, a child would feel badly if another took his dog and then lied about where the dog was.

The same with burglary. If one person has a right to break into a house, so has every other person. The child should be taught that burglary is a dreadful violation not only by the breaking of locks, thus exposing to the world property which has been worked for, and even stealing that property, but also to the privacy of the people which all the world alike demands. The same goes for robbery, which is by force. The child should be made by the State, through its public schools, to comprehend how dreadful this would be for itself or those closest to it, its parents or relatives. And from there, the argument could and should be extended to society at large, and that for the reasons thus shown, Government (which should also be explained for what it is—mutual aid and protection) makes laws against such robbery. In short, children should be made to understand that these laws are for the good of everybody. And equitable personal gain is the first and best argument. If you do not rob anybody, they may not rob you. For instance, supposing mother was straightening a closet upstairs when a burglar came in and stole daddy's watch. Mother might faint; she might be so nervous for months that she could not do her work. She might instill fear into her children which could darken their whole lives. Daddy's watch might be a gift which could never be replaced. Or Daddy might not have the money to buy himself a good watch again.

The Church also considers revenge a sin. But again, its admonitions are lunatic, for it dismisses organized society and replaces it with God and his personal commands. But the child never sees God, or hears him personally commanding anything. But the units composing organized society it can and does see. So that, by not giving children reasons or explanations based on the necessity for organized coöperation on the part of all members of society, the Church of to-day in any of its forms or sects is working a great harm. It is delaying, not aiding, the growth of organized society, with all its possibilities for good. For any true explanation of sin must show that it is not against God in person, as the Church insists, but against organized society, which may or may not represent a God. The Church itself does not know. But anyhow, in regard to revenge, the child would have a much fuller view if he were shown that every one would be in constant fear, or in a warlike state, if all persons wanted to get revenge. Life, of which he is a part, would be a jungle and not a state, in which all should find themselves reasonably at peace. Rather, if they felt some one was going to do something to them for revenge, neither the children nor their families would dare go out on the street or into the garden. Hence, children, and for these reasons relating to organized society, should be directed that there are other ways of settling disputes than those which seem unjust. They should talk nicely with the person and try to explain their point of view, and, if possible, bring about what seemed to them a just settlement. If a just settlement cannot be reached, they should consult the teacher, if the matter is important, as grown-ups go to law, or, if it is unimportant, it should be forgotten.

Again, the Church makes it a sin before God to be an accessory to another's sin. Well, so does the law make it an offense to aid in another's crime either before or after the crime is committed. But to the Church, advising, commanding or provoking another to sin, or consenting to or partaking of the results of another's sin, or concealing or defending it, is also a sin against God. But to introduce God is to belittle the force and sufficiency of organized society in these matters which is not for the good of either organized society or the attitude of the child, and it should be stopped. It is not only enough, but best that the child should be made to look to organized society for all its rewards and punishments, and not elsewhere—for so, and only so, will organized society be made into the helpful and effective thing that it should be. Thus, if a little boy advises a girl to mark in a book owned by the school, the girl may do it, and have to stay in for recess, as penalty, because those books are to be kept in condition for all children to enjoy. Hence, the little boy should be shown that he has encouraged the girl in something depriving her of pleasure and necessities—her recess. Or supposing some one led him on to a point where he had to suffer for it. Dramatic representation of examples should be forced upon the children, so that they themselves might meditate as to the same, but, of course, in the light of their experiences so far.

Still again, the Church, in the name of God, tells the child to be kind. But I consider that the little ones, even very little ones, should be made as much as possible to understand the equity of balance on which all society is necessarily based. People are kind because they want others to be kind to them. They do not steal because they do not want others to steal from them. They do not lie because they do not want to be lied to. And while that may be of God, his voice has not as yet been directly heard. It is men who, by bitter experience, have found these things out for themselves and organized themselves accordingly. As to teaching the child all this, well, one might say to it: Perhaps in some cases, as in illness, one person cannot make the effort to be kind. Then the other should be just the same. But on the whole, kindness should be returned. If one little girl ties another's sash, the other should be willing to please her friend likewise. If each child is kind and considerate of the other, they will be much happier, and that is the object of organized society, which desires to improve and, more, make pleasant the relations of all. In other words, kindness is everybody's obligation to everybody, to make people happier. Therefore, it is an obligation to society, not to God, hence why bring God into it?

The next group of orders from the Almighty concern social bearing. Jesus died to redeem our sins, one of which is pride. Of course, a child should not have so much pride as to prevent it from walking with a poorer or duller companion, or help an unfortunate whom it might not really fancy with his arithmetic. But is that something the child owes to God? Rather, is it not a debt to the downcast boy, a member of society, and hence a debt to society?

But I might run through many such things—covetousness, anger, despair, fear—and all to the same end, dismissing the direct will of God and setting in its place the individual's duty to organized society of which he is a part and a beneficiary, or should be. (And can be.)

The reason for making despair anti-social, let us say, is that almost always despair lacks a sound basis. A person despondent about one thing is forgetting all the other phases of life. Besides, the despair of one person makes it difficult for others to help. Again, fear should not be given up because it is a sin against God, but because in a world where society is understood and maintained in the manner here proposed, fear would not be necessary. Yet the Church plays up to the great fear—the fear of death— by offering people the supposed opportunity to live forever elsewhere by communion, by unction and the forgiveness of sins here. But contemplation of death is a sorrow at the loss of all the loveliness here, and should not be overemphasized since our stay here may yet be made reasonably sufficient. More, courage and the desire to make life here worth while should be man's contribution to the society of which he is a part and whose functions he desires to improve if not perfect. And for that, more than anything else, as he might be taught, he may well be remembered. At least, helping to the perfection of the social organization of which he is a part here, is his one best bet,—not by contemplating a possibly satisfactory hereafter.

Also, as we know, economic matters are likewise regulated, and to the letter, by religious doctrine. For the Church not only teaches that orphans and the aged should be cared for, but the Church itself proceeds to build and operate homes for the aged, orphan asylums and its partisan schools by the thousands. But this, as I have already shown, has enormous economic as well as social

importance, and all detrimental. For these either are now (as in
Russia) or should be, functions of government. It should never
be permitted that they be seized upon for religious propaganda.
Rather, they should be operated by the State not only for the
immediate need they serve and good that they do, but as a
means of promulgating the principles of Society. For by entering
upon these functions not as a matter of equity but rather in the
name of religion, God, divine charity, etc., the Church gnaws at
the State and does its best to render effete its economic program.
But it is the State and not the Church which should enter upon
and strengthen that program. As it is now, industry, patience,
obedience and temperance are forced on the people by the
Church, not in the name of equity and with a proper emphasis
on the just rewards of the same, but in the name of God which results in their betrayal by the individualist who believes in no
equity, but only strength and power and privilege for himself.
Worse, such doctrines and admonitions as, "Cast your burdens
upon the Lord, and he will sustain thee" or "God is my unfail-
ing supply," only misdirect the people, thwarting their natural
social sense. That "God will take care of you" must give way to
self-knowledge and vigilance. Yet as in the present world crisis
what do we find, i.e., the Church bawling about relying on God
and looking to God and praying when really if it were worth its
salt it would be helping actively in the work of organizing society, so as to prevent the economic misery we now see. But no.
Except for rendering the labors as well as the meaning of organized society weak and all but useless, the Church is useless.
To illustrate, I will state that to-day, (September 21, 1931) I see
in the news page of Sunday sermons of one newspaper, where
the Rev. Dr. Donald Bradshaw Aldrich, of the Protestant Episcopal Church of the Ascension in New York, says: "I believe
the world is sick. But I do not believe that its industry and commerce, or even its politics are unsound!" No.

But such statements can be no more than an echo of the pious
capitalistic wish to quiet the people. The people are thus made
fools of. And the middle class, cocky and ignorant, is little bet-

ter than the lower class, and fully as much the goat of the capitalists who gouge them at every turn. This marching middle class, this marching regiment of saps! Here's what this same minister said to them on that same day. (He knows them for what they are!) "You will be asked this winter to contribute to all sorts of agencies of social welfare . . . and you can be counted on. Why? It is the reason that you are in church this morning." And here is still another economic study from St. Patrick's Cathedral and of the same date, the Rev. Francis A. Fadden speaking: "Hard times may get people away from the love of God" (capitalism) "but people must continue to stave off any distress by believing in God with all their soul and heart. God brings security of mind, and life is too big for any one man to do without the consolation and faith he would get in this way." Yet our trusts and holding companies, their lords and masters, appear to do so and with the greatest ease, the while their contempt for organized society as such is shown at every turn.

In fact, the worst phase of religion and dogma as opposed to the necessities and hence the rules of organized society is the same business of teaching reliance on God as opposed to equity in society itself, from which and from which alone can come that security of mind which springs from earnest personal effort, backed as it should be by equitable and hence fair government. Yet at least (admit the religionists) the mind should be secure. But as to that, and as you see, I propose something deeper and more sound. I acclaim an economic security which, if people cease these unintelligent obligations to God, and understand and take seriously their obligations to society, will result. Yet reliance on God is still to this hour a very strong urge, drummed upon as it is by the comfortable and meaningless religionists who live—and only live, mark you—by the benighted minds and stulted labors of those whom they lead.

But instead of being taught this submission and weak servitude to God as a philosophy of life, children, as I see it, should be taught their rights. One would think in going through school that the individual American citizen had no rights. No mention is ever made of them. I would, however, instruct pupils concerning their property rights. They should know certain things: that notice should be given before eviction; that when a place is rented by the week, there must be a week's notice to leave before any one can be put out, and with a rental by the month, a month's notice in advance is necessary. This would save a lot of corporate abuse to the worker and his family. Of whatever the system of government the people should know their rights.

Next, I would inform children in the public schools of their business rights. A child should know that the law will not uphold a contract without consideration. This could be explained by saying that when two men made a business deal, i.e., when one sells property to another; money is paid for it or some important right given up, such as agreeing not to engage in business in the vicinity for ten years. More, people should be made to understand fraud. These matters would lessen the number of oil, gas, etc., leases all over the country by uninformed farmers to great corporations. The corporations are now leasing gas lands from the Pennsylvania farmers at 25 cents an acre per year, and drilling gas wells thereon, paying $10,000 and $15,000 a day.

In fact, all should know about life, not death, their social and all other rights, be their forms or their character what they may. Thus, all Americans should know and as opposed to knowing the hour of mass or services on Sunday, their police and other social rights and privileges. Thus, and before going to Church even, they should understand that a man cannot be arrested without a warrant except for a felony; that is, a major crime like burglary, murder, etc. Also, they should know that the police cannot legally break in doors in order to enter a house except in case of felony. More, they should be fully informed of their State laws on weights and measures, on unions, strikes, and picketing, plus their Constitutional right to assemble without hindrance and to speak as they think.

More, all children to-day should bristle with knowledge of these rights as well as the following, which is the most important of all. It is the real basis of organized society. A man is supposed to receive from society for his work the necessities and comforts of society made by other members of society. If the people only understood this and were alive, the poor and the middle classes would not be so submissive to their oppression by our present-day corporations or their predecessors, the divine-right masters of the past. Yet although the Church has long made oppression of the poor a sin, it has done nothing that I can see to lessen it. And what is it doing now, it, or its voice of God thundering (supposedly) through it. Anything? Rather, as I have just pointed out the Church has made the first duty of the individual his responsibility to God. But society, as we see it to-day, does not bear out the notion of God's duty to the individual. For we see how he fares. More, any examination of the life about us would show the obligation of the individual to be to his fellow and to none other. Also that it is the business of government of which he is one to so conduct its affairs as to insure that every man, woman and child will come by those necessities and comforts which this aforementioned obligation implies.

And hereby do I proclaim that every man and woman who is loyal to God as opposed to organized society, its necessities and benefits, is either mentally incompetent or a faker! Loyalty is not owed to some mythical spirit, but to one's fellow-men, and by this, understand, would living be enriched and beauty for its own sake be born. And how vastly sweeter that than the present life of misery for so many here. And mostly because of that mythical and impossible future life promised by religion. For putting the obligations of life where they actually belong, that is, one to another, and representing those obligations at their best, does not do away with any personal God, if there is but best represented on earth all of those attributes which he is supposed to represent and of which it is written that he has spoken and commanded.

CHAPTER XX

FIRSTLY, in connection with this I would like to characterize, if possible, at least some of the magnates whose personalities cannot somehow be separated from facts so far stated in this book.

To begin with, let us take the old Commodore, the elder Vanderbilt who trusted nobody, In burly style, he lorded it over all, and sneered at silly luxury. Even in his old age he could not write. Not even his son, William H. Vanderbilt, cared much about learning, although he possessed a private art gallery of fabulous value—but because it was the mode. And like the elder Vanderbilt, Sage was also a miser. More, he was no hypocrite in the matter of either morals or charity. He had neither. J. P. Morgan, by the force of his personality and mind, crashed through mountains, legal or commercial. He proclaimed his wild individualism as fiercely as does a lion. And all of these idolized financiers of ours "go-getting" to its ultimate in respect to money!

Along with their relentlessness, these men only sometimes joined construction with destruction. Sage and also Gould actually ravaged much they touched, and then left it, in order that they might plunder elsewhere. Gould plundered the Erie and then the Union Pacific. In the case of the Erie, there was, to put it mildly, a minimum of constructive effort. For many of these magnates understood nothing of railroad management or development.

On the other hand, Rockefeller, no matter how destructive of his competitors, at least managed the Standard Oil constructively and with vision. One of the first things he did was to construct a vast number of tanks to store overproduced oil. And so early as 1874, he was constructing barrel factories and obtaining tank cars and terminals. Soon also he had fleets and depots on three continents for his foreign trade. Although at first there was a waste of ten per cent of the crude oil in manufacturing its by-products, Rockefeller not only worked on this problem until by 1903 there was almost no waste, but he also manufactured all kinds of by-products. This organization of his—a marvel of efficiency—was really possible because Rockefeller secured for executives, as he himself said, "only the big ones, those who have already proved they can do a big business." Even big inde-pendents who warred against him at first were converted by him to monopoly, were given lots of profits, and were to the end faithfully and belligerently for him.

Yet almost all of our American magnates have deluded the public as to their true motives. Thus, when Colonel Stewart, Chairman of the Board of the Standard Oil of Indiana, was at-tacked during the Teapot Dome scandal for having accepted in bonds $759,000 from the Continental Trading Company of Canada, he first denied and then admitted having done so, and after Rockefeller, Jr., mild offshoot of his more drastic sire, tried to have him removed because of this connection with the Teapot Dome scandal, or so he said. As a matter of fact, though, Rockefeller, Sr., held more stock in the Standard Oil of New Jersey than the Standard Oil of Indiana. The latter company, opening out commercially like a parachute, had for a long time been infringing on the New Jersey company's ground. Rocke-feller, Jr., disapproved Stewart's methods and probably took advantage of his opportunity to finish him. Yet the Washington *Star* said later: "The leading figure in oil has voluntarily and whole-heartedly joined the Senate in its attempt to clean up the Teapot Dome mess." So you see how magnates are. Nothing is beyond them—stealing, bearing false witness, bribing or taking bribes, and then turning, as in this case, to save their own hides, by aiding the pursuing enemy!

But let us study them some more—these American financial

geniuses of ours. Thus in 1862, when Vanderbilt chartered boats
for the Government to ship soldiers to New Orleans, he charged
the Government extortionately, as the following shows:

Name of Ship	Price under Vanderbilt charter	Price for which the same boats had previously been chartered by the U. S. Government
Eastern Queen	$900 daily	$500 daily
Quinebang	250 "	130 "
Shetucket	250 "	150 "
Charles Osgood	250 "	150 "
James S. Green	250 "	200 "
Salvor	450 "	300 "
Albany	250 "	150 "
Jersey Blue	250 "	150 "

Despite the price, these boats were so dreadful that the
people investigated the matter. Also, although Vanderbilt was
supposed to furnish water-worthy boats, many of those chartered
were hopelessly decayed, out of date, and in some instances,
mere small lake craft unfit for the sea. Just the same, Vanderbilt was never tried, let alone punished, for this.

More, our magnates, early and late, have not only maliciously
refused to answer official investigating committees on questions of public concern, but when it has suited their interests,
have given perjured testimony. Thus, although for years Russell Sage perjured himself with the statement that his taxable
personal property did not exceed $2,000,000, after his death it
was found to be worth $40,000,000. And August Stein, an ex-
pert accountant, testified to the Hepburn Committee of 1879
that an examination of the books of the Erie Railroad showed
that Gould himself must have taken $12,000,000 from funds re-
corded for construction and equipment, but never so used, and
still more from stock manipulation. Yet on such loot the Gould
heirs later became social leaders. Let me add that in 1888 Rockefeller testified before the New York Investigating Committee

that he had not been interested in the Southern Improvement Company. It had developed, however, in 1872, in testimony before a Congressional Committee, that he was owner of 120 shares in that company. Other Standard Oil men owned enough more shares to give Standard the largest interest in the Southern Improvement Company. Rockefeller testified that the Standard Oil did nothing to lower competitors' profits—which needs no comment here—also that he did not receive railroad rebates— which he did, and had from all the great systems for the previous sixteen years.

Yet *en passant* I would like to ask here (and answer) what did Rockefeller think of labor, any or all of the questions relating to it? Well, this! He considered that he was doing a great thing for the laboring man by giving him a job! And you know at what wages. Also, J. P. Morgan, testifying before the Industrial Relations Commission in 1915 and dealing with this same subject, stated quite blithely that he had never thought about when children should go to work, or how long or for what wages human beings should work. Yet think of a man in his position—one of the chief beneficiaries of organized society as he had found it at his birth, being so wholly individualistic— selfish and unsocial as to say this—or perhaps—except from the point of view of profit—never giving these all-important human issues a thought! Yet he owned the Mercantile Marine Company, which paid wages of $10 a week, and when the Commission asked him if he considered this enough to support a family, he answered: "If that is all he can get and he takes it, I suppose it is enough." But coldly and untruthfully argued, as I see it, for he left out the paramount fact that under our present industrial system, and sometimes with blacklists and lockouts, for good measure, a man must take a job because it is the *only* one he can get, which might suggest that it is NOT pay enough. Also what man so dumb or so wholly selfish as to believe that organized society was made for him alone—or any little group that might rise to power through the opportunities and profits made possible by the very existence of organized society. For assume that it was a very little society or tribe of which he was a part—a tribe, the dangerous surroundings of which compelled every man to share in the labors and the resultant profits almost equally, as is all too often the case. And he set himself selfishly apart to do as he pleased. (The tribe be damned, as it were.) How long would his presence be tolerated and how soon he would die, or be driven out to die, a reward exactly equal to his selfishness! Would he say then that he knew nothing about labor—or what was enough or good enough for one as opposed to what was enough or good enough for another? Or all? Imagine! Why, had he ever troubled in his life to contemplate his own or any other's body—that of a fly, a worm, a dog or a man, he would have known or he could have learned that there was no least chance of its functioning as a living organism unless every single cell or atom in it was economically and socially provided for—with food, work, rest, elimination, and all cared for by the *body-state* as a whole— every cell and every atom coöperating and healthily—otherwise, no body-state, and no life for body or cell or atom. And surely he was not so dumb that he could not have known that. Yet debonairly there he sat on that occasion and contemptuously added that he didn't even know what collective bargaining was. Not that some militant but unsuccessful labor unions hadn't tried to make him aware! More, he added that directors never paid any attention to labor problems! They were not sufficiently important to men of large financial vision! No? Well, a worker-ruled world as in Russia thinks differently.

The rule by force and anarchy, as exemplified by the activities of these magnates, though, brought about in America the ultimate triumph of and rule by family. And what I mean by family follows. Thus, when Commodore Cornelius Vanderbilt, the first magnate of his family, died in 1877, he left a fortune of $105,-000,000. The public froze with astonishment and fear as if a miracle had taken place, and so it was for those days. But by 1893, the Vanderbilt family wealth controlled 12,000 miles of railroads on which the gross earnings were about $60,000,000 annually. In addition, and to show the nature of the expansion of an active family fortune in our swelling American financial world of the past hundred years, let me state that in 1908, only about thirty years later, the Vanderbilt fortune had grown to $700,000,000. In other words, one branch after another plunged in to win and then to keep for itself. And at an age as young as forty-five, Jay Gould the first, possessed a fortune of $100,000,000.

Now where, as in this land of ours, profits are as great as they are and where holds this rule by force, it does not take long to buy up an appreciable part of the wealth of the country. For after all, American wealth is not limitless, as I will show by comparisons at the end of this chapter. And so early as thirty years ago, 55,000 miles of railroads were under the Morgan influence. More, while in 1904 (according to the Legislative Investigating Committee of 1906) the New York Life Insurance Company was spending $204,019 and the Equitable Life Assurance Society $172,698 to corrupt Albany, Morgan was controlling the stupendous funds of these companies. In fact, by then he had taken over so many of the great banks of America that all in all he managed about $10,000,000,000 of the nation's wealth.

But I want you to see to just what extent family supremacy exists in America to-day. So please trace quickly with me the Rockefeller ascension:

Standard Oil Dividends

1870-1882	$ 11,000,000
1882-1895	118,000,000
1895-1903	275,000,000
1903-1911	314,000,000

Total dividends, $718,000,000 in 40 years. Only dividends!

Of course, this sounds like quite a lot of money. But the true meaning of it cannot be obtained without comparison and investigation of its uses. This money then was so used as to make Rockefeller an actual banker, for it was loaned; millions of foreign exchange were sold by Rockefeller and his were experts in collateral. Your natural impression from this might be (I do not know): "Oh, yes, a little banking on the side." But that is not true. *Rockefeller's money far exceeded the resources of any bank in America, no matter how great.* The great National City Bank of that day had capital of only $25,000,000. And now again in the year 1911, as you may recall, the Standard Oil Company was dissolved, Well, that dissolution furnished some facts, since in the process they could not very well be hidden. And so I am able to make another little table: Here it is:

Increases in Stock Value as Shown at That Time:

Standard Oil of Nebraska .....from $115 to $ 350 a share
Standard Oil of California .... " 140 to 200 a share
Standard Oil of Kentucky ..... " 150 to 1,000 a share

And at that time the Standard Oil of Indiana paid 850 per cent in dividends in one year. So that when a stock dividend in this company was, on February 6, 1912, declared, a gift of 29 shares was made to every shareholder who was the owner of one old share. And each share of Standard Oil of Indiana before that dividend sold for $7,000 each. So multiply!

Yet Rockefeller's wealth continued to pile up, as from a rushing avalanche. For by 1922, the American voters with their votes sound asleep all this while (liberty, equality, fraternity, you know), we have the following stock dividends—veritable bolts of power!

Standard Oil of California 100%
Standard Oil of New Jersey 400%

Or in other words, between 1911 and 1922, Standard Oil stock increased in market value over $3,000,000,000, and in stock dividends $1,000,000,000. As for cash dividends, they also totaled $1,000,000,000. So add.

But to visualize the repeater speed multiplication of Rockefeller's fortune and hence power, and all purely individualistic, as you may well guess, and so wholly indifferent to the well-being of all the massed atoms in this or any other body, just imagine yourself to be the owner of an original share of Standard Oil of Indiana, worth, say $100. After twenty-three years, the book value of this share was $2,520. From the dissolution of the Standard Oil in 1912 on to the year 1923, cash dividends on this investment brought $8,220 and stock dividends $36,500—a total of, say, $47,000!

As I said before, though, the Standard Oil, because it was an illegal trust, was, presumably, in 1911, broken into 34 parts. Only the trust wasn't really dissolved at all, because the same owners controlled all the identical companies, and the management remained fundamentally unchanged. Yet by 1924, just one little part of that illegal trust, the present Standard Oil of New Jersey, had more wealth than even the whole illegal trust had in 1911! And this is only one of all the many great companies that now function as parts of the really now great organization or *international* power dominated or controlled by the Rockefeller interests.

In fact to-day, I now believe that all of the great money interests or organizations of America, or both, are managed by allied persons, and these not so numerous. I believe, for instance, that the great Rockefeller and Morgan influences are thus handled now. And I base it on the following facts. The J. P. Morgan banking interests, with which others such as the First National Bank coöperate, are very closely aligned with such trusts as the United States Steel and the American Telephone & Telegraph Company, which in turn is aligned with the Rockefeller interests.

But, my dear reader, this pile of trusts is put together very intricately, and it cannot as a whole be understood without knowing its parts. So take a fresh breath! And watch closely, for now comes a little discussion of the American Telephone and Telegraph Company, a subsidiary of the above Rockefeller group—Mr. Rockefeller, our first and true American Cæsar.

For one of the major companies owned by the A. T. and T. is the New York Telephone Company. And court decision after

court decision (and all, oh so nicely arranged!) has sent it along
the golden road of profits. Yet to me the facts in regard to it
mean nothing if not that this New York Telephone is an ex-
tortioner of the worst type. Yet even before the various court
decisions which have so helped this ambitious company, it was in
good financial condition, paying over eight per cent dividends,
and since 1896! In March, 1922, though, it petitioned to be allowed to base its rates on the following valuations:

> Cost of property $247,000,000
> Cost of reproduction 373,000,000
> Fair and reasonable value 323,000,000

And on April 18, 1923, the United States Supreme Court, being
called upon for a decision, let these figures stand.

But one chief engineer of the New York Telephone Company,
testifying before the New York Public Service Commission on
November 8, 1920, stated that a fair rate-making value of the
New York Telephone Company's property was, for 1919,
$107,000,000, and as of August 31, 1920, $117,000,000. Only the
same engineer a little later signed an affidavit to the effect that
the fair rate-making value of the same property in 1919 was
$181,000,000. Hence he must have made a little mistake some-
where. Or...

But then comes the annual depreciation, for which the people,
by the rates fixed for them, must pay. And this is:

> For 1921............$13,000,000 depreciation
> 1922............ 15,000,000 depreciation
> 1923............ 17,000,000 depreciation
> 1924............ 20,000,000 depreciation

And how much of this faked depreciation?

A certain Mr. M. H. Winkler, lawyer and authority on this
New York Telephone Company, says that "charges to expenses
under the guise of depreciation are $9,000,000 a year in excess
of all amounts necessary to meet actual requirements." Mr.
Winkler also added that "$164,000,000 in excess of original cost

less actual depreciation costs New York Telephone subscribers $13,000,000 a year beyond what would be a reasonable return to the company on its investment." Yet the courts let that sort of thing pass. And the telephone user pays.

But for sure-fire information, let me also refer to the Chicago Telephone Company. Back in 1923, the Chicago branch of the A. T. & T. demanded an increase in rates on the service there on the ground that the existing rates were inadequate. And after due examination, the Illinois State Commerce Commission, a body to which such matters were referred there, fixed upon a lesser rate than that which this corporation demanded or might charge—not what it wanted! But did that feaze the Chicago Telephone Company? On December 21, 1923, it was, on a Federal court plea, of course, given an injunction saying that the lesser rates ordered did not have to be charged until the restraining suit brought by the company had been decided by the courts, and then, if the telephone company lost, and then only, the additional rates must be returned to the patrons. Only personally, I do not understand how any injunction in this case could have been given in good faith, since the change of rates ordered by the State Commerce Commission also applied to coin box phones. And how could any money possibly be eventually returned to the users of coin boxes? And were not they then to be robbed? And by a Court order? Ask Mr. Gifford who is now doing charity work for the unemployed. Maybe he owes some of them nickels.

But among other things charged by the Government at that time and in that suit was that the Chicago Telephone Company paid the Western Electric Company, a subsidiary of the A. T. & T., the most outrageous prices for equipment. Also that this was done because Western Electric, A. T. & T., and so, of course, the Chicago Telephone Company, were all owned by the same men. And the public to pay for it! Yet in this case, a citation of law previously referred to which reads (and backed up by law decisions upon law decisions) that a controlling ownership of the stock of one company by another does not by any means raise a presumption of control by the first company over the second whose stock is thus owned smoothed all that out. In other words, you may own a company, but you don't control it. You don't bother, maybe? But don't you? Or doesn't the A. T. & T. and other such monopolies do such things? No?

But the most ridiculous thing in this whole case was that it didn't come to trial in the United States Supreme Court until April, 1929, by which time $11,000,000 of extra rates had been collected and invested or at least something done with them, you may be sure! And then the Supreme Court, on December 1, 1930, remanded—that is, sent back—to the Federal Court for Illinois, this by now very old and, of course, highly involved case—the money of the telephone users still tied up, you see! —because of incomplete and ill-arranged data. Only, wasn't seven years long enough time in which to get this matter of the mixed-up data straight? And then, to send it back to the court which had previously decided for the Telephone Company!! And can such movements really be in good faith? Can any one but a telephone beneficiary truly think so?

But now for a glance at the various companies owned by this same American Telephone & Telegraph Company, a subsidiary, as I told you, of the great Rockefeller group. Here they are:

Bell Telephone Company of Canada
Bell Telephone Company of Pennsylvania
Lehigh Bell Telephone Company
Chesapeake & Potomac Telephone Company
Chesapeake —& Potomac Telephone Company of
    Baltimore City
Chesapeake & Potomac Telephone Company of Virginia
Chesapeake & Potomac Telephone Company of West Virginia
Cincinnati & Suburban Bell Telephone Company
Diamond State Telephone Company
Illinois Bell Telephone Company
Central Union Telephone Company
Indiana Bell Telephone Company
Michigan Bell Telephone Company
Mountain States Telephone & Telegraph Company
New England Telephone & Telegraph Company
Central New Hampshire Telephone Company

Coos Telephone Company
Eastern Telephone & Telegraph Company
Westerly Automatic Telephone Company
White Mountains Telephone & Telegraph Company
New Jersey Bell Telephone Company
Commercial Union Telephone Company
Cattaraugus Union Telephone Company
Southern Bell Telephone & Telegraph Company
Wisconsin Telephone Company
Southwestern Bell Telephone Company

and so many more that I won't stop to copy them down.

Yet with all this wealth gained in methods heretofore described, what does Walter S. Gifford, President of the American Telephone & Telegraph Company, and in August, 1931, chosen to aid unemployment relief for the coming winter, plan? To give any of his very large company's money? No! Mr. Gifford, having publicly stated his plans for next winter, is not going to get money from the corporation's fat treasuries, but rather intends to organize nation-wide drives to beg money from common people all over the country for unemployment relief. (Last winter they took up exorbitant collections from meagerly-paid workers!) Well, the New York *Times* has already said editorially that Gifford is just the man because he has the means of communication. And Mr. Hoover, in other words, has said the same. Yet Gifford is aiding unemployment as rampantly as he can by, at this very time, dismissing hundreds of girl operators in New York City because of the new mechanical dial system of telephoning. It's not so much a work saver as a work dodger since it puts the work which should be done by the telephone company or its poorly paid employees over on the public who pay the same old rates or more. But as for money or work—well, you know how dumb are the common people in America! And besides, are they not sufficiently well sustained by slogans?

But now where does the A. T. & T. come in as regards the workings of these other big trusts? Well, together with West-

ern Electric, the Radio Corporation of America, General
Electric, Westinghouse, etc., it controls the entire radio business.
This is accomplished by its control of 4,000 patents. And it
grants the use of these to the public or to such corporations and
organizations as are not competitors in any of these fields. But
let a competitor step up and ask to use a patent, and he is
charged anything the radio trust cares to ask! Thus, no competitor can become strong; he is affected by signal disadvan-
tages. For these companies manufacture ninety-five per cent of
radio apparatus. So, Constitution or no Constitution, this particular corporation markedly interferes with the rights of the individual here and will continue to do so.

To be sure, on May 14, 1930, the Government instigated an
anti-trust case against these companies, yet all radio decisions
up to the present writing point to the conclusion that the Government will do nothing about the radio trust. For on June 24,
1931, the Radio Commission held, by a 3-2 decision, that 1,403
licenses held by subsidiaries of the Radio Corporation of America
could be renewed. Yet by 1909, according to Gustavus Myers,
who wrote that memorable book, "The History of American
Fortunes," the Standard Oil Company already owned the General Electric Company and previous to that or during the great
panic of 1907, that great oil concern had already forced the
Westinghouse Company under its oil ownership. And more,
while, in 1919, still under Standard Oil, the General Electric
organized the Radio Corporation of America. But a subsidiary
of it, the Radio Corporation of America Photophone with Western Electric had a monopoly on all the apparatus of the enormous "talkie" motion picture business. And in the trust also
are the Radio Corporation of America, Radiotron, Radio Corporation of America, Victor, etc., etc. Be calm and read slowly.

Besides this trust, though, which it so obviously controls—
or dominates, take your choice—the Standard Oil interests have
also wide ownership in railroads, utilities, coal, coke ovens,
ships, banks and insurance companies. (Would that the Govern-

ment or the corporations were compelled to publish all the inside facts!)

I cannot, however, really estimate Rockefeller, Jr.'s income. Yet since he has most of his father's stocks, the reward annually must be enormous. More, the conservative New York *Commercial* stated that about 1905 Rockefeller's annual income was not less than $72,000,000. Over these sixty years of violent profits, all invested and themselves making violent profits, the scope of Rockefeller money must be much greater than is realized. Realty trust is built upon trust and the income, where? Consider, for one thing, the old ramshackle four-story houses in the very heart of Manhattan Island—three immense blocks of them from Fifth to Sixth Avenue—bought up at low prices by the Rockefeller interests and finally now being torn down for Radio City, or what might better be called Rockefeller City. This city of skyscrapers, costing heaven only knows how much—is to be equipped and devoted to the development of world-wide radio entertainment, but all controlled by Mr. Rockefeller's radio trust. Well?

But let us look upon our America in general, where the banks and insurance companies hold mortgages on over one-third of the business and residence real estate and on one-fifth of the real estate of the farmers, among whom tenantry is increasing, and where above all, Rockefeller, Jr., looms as the trust giant. And here I propose to ask what portion of America Rockefeller really owns! According to the Federal Trade Commission Report of 1926 on national wealth and income, the estimated total value of the

Metal industry was	$10,000,000,000
Food industry	5,000,000,000
Textile industry	4,000,000,000
Steam railroads	17,000,000,000
Telephone, telegraph and radio	1,000,000,000
Gas and electric	2,000,000,000
Oil	3,000,000,000

But now examine that, and you will see whole industries worth only a few billion dollars. But Rockefeller is more than a billionaire! He has probably several billions personally and more indirectly under his control. In sum, I proclaim the fact that ROCKEFELLER IS RELATIVELY THE PRESENT OWNER OF AMERICAN INDUSTRY. Yet this same man wrote a book called "Labor and Capital—Partners." Yes? Of course, the conventional capitalist philosophy intended, I believe, to appease labor (coöperation, labor's ownership of stock, etc.) and put forth by all of the high-powered public relations counsels for corporations.

As a matter of truth, though, what does the Rockefeller ownership and control mean? I believe that it makes Rockefeller, Jr., more than any other, the ruler of America, and by the laws of this country, his son, Rockefeller, the third, a prince after the old tradition—as much born to rule as if born of a king and under the law or faith of the divine rule by kings!

In closing, though, I want to say that I have here sought to show the gradual exploitation of America's natural resources and the accompanying anarchy. Yet the process is still going strong to-day, in the utilities and elsewhere. And under the control of a few persons, our trusts wax and exploitation grows by leaps and bounds. In fact, just now not one but all our corporations are closing in on the people. They want money and ever more money. The right to expand and tax and most of all the right to say what type of thought about all this is to be thought by the small American who finds himself thus controlled and ordered and taught to think. But will he always think as ordered? The class differences here, with wealth as the standard, are far wider and deeper than the intellectual differences of human beings.

My argument though is really not so much against Rockefeller or Gould or Sage (because there were countless other commercial figures just as bad) but AGAINST THE SYSTEM! America, as I see it, should be reorganized on a non-competitive basis commercially. The waste of the business methods described in this book should be eliminated. They are savage and unsuited to a highly organized, civilized society. They are not suited to the welfare of society at large at all! The cry of our people should now be:

WE WANT A GOVERNMENT FOR ALL THE PEOPLE!

NO ENORMOUS WEALTH IN PRIVATE HANDS!

WE WANT EFFICIENT MANAGERS FOR THE BENEFIT OF ALL AMERICANS!

CHAPTER XXI

IS AMERICA DOMINANT?

A YOUNG democracy shows within itself healthy trading activities among more or less evenly successful contestants. In the course of time, however, via inheritance and opportunism, these same sift and shift until finally a few, vying for the cream of the possibilities, attain their goal by any means whatsoever, lawful or not. Then the giants, joining forces, become tyrants: a sign of decay. Dominance over foreign countries goes with this decay of capitalism.

American dollars are the source of the imperialism of the United States. Where are they? Two billions invested in Canada, a billion each in Mexico and Cuba, six hundred million in Chile, half a billion in Great Britain, and about a hundred million each in France, Venezuela, Peru, Bolivia and the Philippines. Apart from native resources seized upon by the individual for his own private aggrandizement, almost all of this money was made through the American worker: the excess profits created by his work—clerk, office man, salesman, laborer—so that to-day, and with the aid of money pooled at home (but by no means equitably distributed there), American wealth is running the railroads and utilities of nine other important countries. It does the manufacturing of six first-rate nations and exploits oil in twenty countries. In fact, commercially America has been and is turning the world upside down. In one year, money from this country may be found installing thousands of telephone exchanges —not private phones but exchanges—in Spain, Mexico and South America. The United Fruit Company, one of our great corporations, owns $24,000,000 worth of banana plantations in Honduras, $4,000,000 in Guatemala, $8,000,000 in Costa Rica and elsewhere, and for that reason is forcing an economic change which improves the workers of those lands inconsiderably, if at all, the while it makes for greater fortunes for its already inordinately wealthy owners. Yet that again means that more laborers are to be exploited in still other lands and climes.

Fox Films, for instance, has subsidiaries in 49 countries, and Henry Ford is all over the map. No part of the world seems so remote that the shine of the American dollar is not meaningful. Apparently even China provides a familiar hearth for American financial gatherings, for there we find Bethlehem Steel, Lee Higginson, Standard Oil, and J. P. Morgan and all thoroughly at home. Ditto the omnipresent, omnipotent Guggenheims, du Ponts, Dohertys and Dohenys. American guns and regiments and missionaries keep these "nationals" in countenance.

Yet does this money so freely sent abroad and invested work for generally better working or living conditions in America or in the country to which it is sent? Do you really think so? When Standard Oil had everything in Mexico it refined oil there at a profit of six hundred per cent, but sold it elsewhere (in the United States, for instance) at the market price. And not only that, but some of these American companies abroad have quadrupled their activities in the last three or four years. Thirty or forty per cent dividends, even four hundred or four thousand per cent, set the pace. And in this connection, I want you to stop and pay homage to the facts for a moment. I want you to sense their import, because on them depends your judgment of America's present and future position.

These foreign investments have amassed great wealth in America. They have helped to bring in so much capital for all kinds of domestic enterprises that Americans send (or did send until recently) twice as much manufactures, raw materials, food to Europe as European ships brought to America. In fact, the upshot of the whole commercial situation is that several times more gold is coming into this country than is going out, and it has been so ever since the World War. America's position is one of distinct advantage. For example, the following are the debts of leading German banks as of March 31, 1931: of 5,636,000,000 Reichsmarks, 37.1 per cent is due to the United States, 20.4 per cent to England, 13.9 per cent to Switzerland, 9.7 per cent to Holland, and 6.5 per cent to France. A committee of bankers under the leadership of Albert H. Wiggin, Chairman of the Governing Board of the Chase National Bank, said, in late August, 1931, that Germany's short term credit of $1,200,000,000 must be extended six months. Governments were to legislate to render this legal. Yet Wiggin had no official or semi-official connection with the United States Government. Isn't that an indication of world-dictation by American banks?

With a sufficient surplus of things to be sent out, of course world prices could be controlled. Herbert Hoover has listed American copper, cotton and oil as possibilities. But at this point I want to show that there is a great distinction between the effect of commercial exchange of goods and the investing of capital in foreign lands. A trader is aided by having his foreign customer prosperous, but to the banker investing, very often the client's bankruptcy is a most profitable opportunity.

The key to this vast entanglement of profit-making is that these foreign enterprises of ours are all maneuvered and directed by four or five important New York banking houses; among them, Kuhn, Loeb & Company, Lee Higginson & Company; J. P. Morgan, John D. Rockefeller's National City Bank. This latter bank alone, by the way, operating under the name of the International Banking Corporation, has banks all over the world. More, the J. P. Morgan interests have the Foreign Finance Corporation, the business of which is financing foreign enterprises. So consider, if you will, the activities and possibilities of coercion and influence of such firms! And all this, remember, in a time in which the philosophy of external affairs is being emphasized, disarmament harped on, and "aid and development of uncivilized countries" spurred. To me, this is the sign manual of a most conservative and imperialistic government; also of a government directed for a few and according to the group theory of that few. For was it not so under Disraeli, Palmerston and Salisbury in England? And certainly America's position now seems to be shown, strikingly enough, by the fact that the greatest part of her foreign investments is in petroleum, fruit, oil, meat, sugar and minerals, rather than in the far less productive public construction and manufacture which comprise the foreign investments of many other countries. This hold of America's on basic industries often puts her in a position dominant enough to control a country's entire finances. A fact imperialistic enough in its significance, surely!

To understand America and get some perspective on her in this sense, I want to show her in relation to other countries. Without this, there can be no vision. And looking abroad, we find among the money lords (and the only equivalent of our own) the Cortlandts (European du Ponts) and the Rothschilds (Continental Morgans). And these, as well as several other bankers abroad, have already, American style, swung Europe in upon some quite arresting imperialistic quests. So much so that even here in the United States, where financial domination by Europe is least expected, the silk and oil industries at least show an appreciable influx of foreign investment if not control. So that, taken together, American plus European money, in this highly individualistic form, dominates the income of the whole world. For side by side in all mineral, railroad, fruit, meat and oil projects everywhere, England marches with America. And in spite of the fact that Germany's great corporations were broken up after the War, German investments to-day rank third in Argentina, Chile and Brazil. In fact, Berlin and London—their fortune families, I mean—live on trusts. And from them spring such networks and alliances as would be illegal under American laws. I question, however, that their trusts are any stronger than the Wall Street interconnected holding companies.

But the boldest, most aggressive, most imperialistic of these foreigners is the Royal Dutch Shell. Unlike the Standard Oil, which for years confined itself mostly to one country (America) for its supply and limited its activities to the refining and shipping of the oil of that country, the Royal Dutch Shell, a Dutch and English company, not only prospected for oil all over the world but as it did so closed, as far as possible, every source to outside companies. Oil in Asia, Europe, South America, Mexico, on islands everywhere, and even to a large extent in the United States, was speedily and boldly preëmpted, and this under the very nose of our Standard Oil. In other words, Shell beat the Standard on its own ground, so that to-day Deterding, its wizard, has every strategic place nailed. Both ends of the Suez Canal, a Shell station on the Cape Verde Islands, halfway between Africa and America, one station at the Panama Canal and another at the entrance to the Gulf of Mexico! Shell owns 80 companies and surpasses everything with its fleet of tankers. Even at that, this no more than counterbalances the Standard's activities in European markets.

But does this success of the Dutch-British Shell satisfy the British or perfect a stable alliance? On the contrary! For antipathetic to British imperialism and its desire for world control, the Royal Dutch Shell not only has an alliance with the French, but it invests in many places, even floating a portion of its stock in Wall Street so as to make a good impression on Americans. Naturally, these acts make Shell appear a little too independent for the British. They do not control it entirely. In consequence, England, always the cautious gray spider of the North, and with her state-directed Anglo-Persian Company, safeguards an oil supply of her own for her navy. She does not trust Shell or any other international company to that extent, the while America does. Usually, governments hide their imperialism behind trusts. Only in a few cases—Turkey, Poland, Roumania—have governments tried open seizure.

But these exploited countries dealing with imperialistic empires such as ours, or their international trusts, are fools, or else they are corrupted or coerced by corporations or governments working for corporations. For they do not appear to understand as yet how powerful trusts, once in and in control of certain enterprises in their country, can kick them around and finally enslave them. At any rate, the Standard Oil in Bolivia is not only overlord of the oil of that land, but by agreement can and does operate railways, trams, harbors, telephones, telegraph and public utilities. More, some South American countries which have been insane enough to grant sole concessions to either British or American firms (only to regret the domination of a monopoly later) have had a devilish time afterward trying to let in investors from other countries. Still, they keep granting concessions to these foreign giants, most likely because of the faithlessness of their own local "representatives," the assumed patriotism of their leaders or "statesmen." Thus, right now, the whole nitrate industry of Chile has been formed into a monopoly under the joint control of American and European bankers and their investors. And for this, the Chilean government, giving 150,000,000 tons of recoverable nitrate to Cosach, the monopoly, and lifting the export duty of $12.32 a ton on this industry valued at $750,000,000, receives only a mere half interest and $21,000,000 in cash and $36,000,000 in bonds for the next three years!

More, our own International "Tel. & Tel.," the world extension of the great American monopoly, has a concession from Chile to run the telephone and wireless service there for fifty years. And unless the government of Chile buys it out at the end of that time, then this concession becomes self-perpetuating! And what a petty chance Chile will have should the International Tel. & Tel. not wish to sell, as it probably will not! At any rate, and whatever settlement is made, it will be at the corporation's price.

And what a price! Those who pay the present American telephone rates can well guess.

Of course, mind you, this sort of thing always begins most pleasingly. Diplomacy is like that. So are its lawyers. So much so that when about three hundred thousand telephones in Argentina, Chile and Uruguay were linked with twenty million in the United States and Canada, President Hoover and President

Ibañez of Chile exchanged the most amiable greetings. But what will these smaller countries do in ten, fifteen or twenty years from now, when they are paying American prices for everything and being paid, as in Cuba and elsewhere, the starvation wages of their own land, and, into the bargain, being threatened by our American regiments come to protect our "nationals" and their holdings? Well, wait and see! But is it not likely that then these simple governments will have to eat the dust of their own mistakes? It is! For the smiling corporations with whom they have but now agreed so amicably will be bleeding them with high rates. One needs only to recall the policy of these very great corporations at home. And will they change their spots abroad? What, these embryo governments! *They* presuming to quarrel with an American corporation when that American corporation can call upon its own private government to shake its fist!

But turn for a moment to China, and what do we see there? Not only monopolies but contracts giving American corporations a preponderance of profits and privileges. Not so long ago, the New York *Herald Tribune* stated that while 136 American firms existed in China in 1914, 400 flourished there in 1920. And during the frantic American prosperity era and foreign commercial expansion from 1924 to 1929, the number again increased. In fact, Chinese business is being more and more avidly solicited; for instance, in 1914 American exports to China amounted to about $24,000,000, and by 1924 they had risen to $124,000,000, more than four hundred per cent increase.

To illustrate, Aviation Exploration, Inc., a Delaware corporate subsidiary of Curtiss, now carries air mail for the Chinese government. Its contract is with the Chinese National Aviation Corporation, a government corporation capitalized at $10,000,-000. By the terms of the agreement the American company uses its own equipment and operates the air mail line. But the American company is guaranteed 3,000 flying miles per day and receives $1.50 in gold per mile for carrying mails on a plane of less than 800 pounds capacity; $3.75 for planes 2,000-

2,800 pounds; and $4.50 each mile for planes 2,800-4,000 pounds. That's $4,500 per 1,000 miles—less than the distance from New York to Chicago. How much does one of those planes cost? This mail charge seems terrific. A more important fact is that this company is given a monopoly and exclusive right to extensions—an eternal monopoly in China for air mail. Its present air lines are between Shanghai-Nanking-Hankow, Nanking-Tsinan, Tientsin-Peiping, Hankow-Changsha-Canton.

Another important contract is that of the R. C. A. of November, 1928, which calls for the construction by the National Reconstruction Council of China (the Chinese Government) of a radio station at Shanghai for R. C. A. use. Also, the Automatic Electric Company, of Chicago, in November, 1928, contracted to install an automatic phone system in Nanking, the Chicago concern to be paid a huge initial sum and to own the system unless paid for. I'd like to know the outcome!

And here's a deal that must be profitable to the Robert Dollar Company. It is between the Dollar Company and that same National Reconstruction Commission of the Chinese Government. By this contract the Commission is to build and run a radio station and handle all messages from ship to shore and from shore to ship, *free*. To insure this, the Dollar Company deposited ninety-five per cent of the cost with the Commission, and this is to be returned to the Company. After that, the Dollar Company is to pay rent, salaries, part of the interest on cost and of depreciation, and a monthly royalty of $6,500 Shanghai currency (much different from gold, which the Chinese Government must pay the corporations on most contracts requiring Government payment).

But what international business struggles have not ensued in this foreign investment field! And may not! In 1911, for instance, Bethlehem Steel signed a contract with China to build her a navy yard, a coal station, and to supply all materials to construct ships. But do you suppose Japan would let America have a powerful Oriental station? She would not! The contract, though valid, blew up. Nothing was done about it. One govern-

ment, with its trusts, forcing another government with its trusts!
And then, of course, the United States Government ordered that
all this remain a secret. But later up bobs that other grand im-
perialist, Great Britain, with a contract to build China a navy,
and this despite the American contract. And England and Japan
having an international understanding of some kind—no particular quarrel between England and Japan—the thing appeared to stand. Yet China, as all outside imperialistic governments know, having no use for any navy other than to let the
same be used by said outside imperialistic governments for
their benefit, the needlessness of such a navy at last appeared
to become very apparent there. At any rate, China suddenly
ceased its "demand" for one, thus ending that quarrel.

But aside from that, there was a previous business war of
a major concern in China which resulted in the first recognition
of Royal Dutch by the Standard Oil Company. It went this way.
The Standard Oil, in China several years before the Royal
Dutch, was fighting competition by selling oil in foreign countries far below even the cost of production and making up the
deficit by high American prices, protected by high American
tariff (please note that!) established for its benefit. For months
after the Royal Dutch appeared on the scene, the Standard was
therefore able to slash prices thus giving Sir Henri Deterding,
the head of Royal Dutch (and who lost nearly four million dollars through this fight, and on just kerosene alone), quite a large
ache. Yet he would not give way, and finally losses on all sides
being very great, our Standard agreed to split the Chinese
trade fifty-fifty with the Royal Dutch.

Yet a little later, see the same two tearing at each other in
Mexico. The mighty Standard, in first again, is now being fought
by Royal Dutch Shell, joined in this instance by several independent American groups, all opposed to Standard Oil or Mr.
Rockefeller and all, of course, supported financially, under those
circumstances, by Morgan. And in consequence, international
tangle! American trusts against British. Also, and in the same
fight, American money against Americans. Also, American money,

but under British laws, against American money. And all in Mexico, a country foreign to both. No wonder France, observing all this and without oil herself, wanted the combination of allies to stick together in order to guarantee her a supply of oil after the War. But when the Standard (a corporation, please notice, not a government!) refused to do this, France (and hardly to be blamed for it, either!) entered into an alliance with Great Britain for her naval and domestic oil. But then, Johnny-on-the-spot, up pops the United States Ambassador to France, Mr. Hugh Wallace, with demands from the United States Government for France to open to the Standard Oil the same opportunities and privileges in France as were being granted to British companies. (See my chapter on the Government functioning as clerk for the trusts.)

But these have not been and are not now the gravest clashes. I am thinking of the enormous differences in price levels between the United States and every country which she is exploiting. For it is ridiculous to expect that economic conditions here can be maintained, if all the rest of the world is poor and depressed. And this foreign labor and these foreign raw materials cost, comparatively, scarcely anything. So it comes about that America, in connection with her shipping, is now having difficulty over just such a question. Because in America raw materials and wages make ship-building here twice as expensive as in Britain and other countries, Americans, rather than build their own ships, pay billions in freight for foreign steamers to carry their cargoes. To alleviate this, the United States Shipping Board sought to and did build a number of ships which later it sold to private companies for a song. For in spite of all of this uneconomical and even unethical use of taxpayers' money to help our American trusts abroad, about thirty per cent of our American goods is now transported by native ships.

But with this trouble over price levels goes the tariff, which is too high and eliminates the possibility of foreign countries paying with goods instead of money. And since most foreign countries have no money, exports have slumped. So now the surplus of agricultural products to be shipped out of this country is diminishing while industrial exports mount. Hence our American farmers suffering. But is any campaign, as in Russia, organized to mitigate their distress? There is not! Rather, capitalists would have us believe that the farmer's status is inevitable—which it is not! And worse, these foreign sovereignties, bucked by this stout American tariff of ours, have retaliated and now threaten England and the United States in their imperialistic business quests. In fact, hourly this business war becomes worse and more violent. Look at Cuba to-day. The Sugar Trust here got an import duty on sugar as high as the cost of production in Cuba. This was to keep the sugar trust's price up but outwardly the tariff was supposed to protect the beet sugar industry here. In this way the American people have paid extra for sugar, a sum larger than the investment of the whole beet sugar industry. And as for the Cubans, they are poverty-stricken, distressed, insecure, dying and rebelling.

But now to go back to this business of our great trusts and their holding companies, with all of the wealth they have accumulated in this country (and without, in the main, a decent return to labor in its larger aspects here), invading these foreign lands, seizing upon their principal industries or resources and then calling upon the American Government to protect them, and at its expense. Do they obey the laws of the lands that they invade? Do they help the people of the country really to better themselves and so make for their advancement? If you think so, study Cuba—with a Guggenheim (Harry F.) as the American Ambassador Extraordinary and Plenipotentiary since 1929 and hated as the associate adviser and approver of Machado, the thoroughly hated Cuban dictator! (At a banquet in Santa Clara, Cuba, the dictator is said to have stated to his hearers: "My government is an honest and just one, and here is the American Ambassador at my side to prove it.") Or Chile, where the Guggenheim control of the nitrate industry eventually resulted in the overthrow and flight of the dictator Ibañez. Or Nicaragua, where our troops and ships are regularly called in to protect an American-directed dictatorship. Or Haiti, or Venezuela, or Santa Domingo, or even far China, where our boats or troops or this or that are always being called in to protect American property and the interests of our "nationals."

In fact, in so far as the United States is concerned, its State Department as well as its every diplomat in the whole gamut of its legations, acts upon the sacred principle that it is the right and duty (bugaboo) of America to protect the person and property of her citizens abroad. And apparently even when American demands are against foreign law. For although the revised Mexican Constitution made no provision for assessment of property lost by revolution, Mr. Fall, under President Harding, demanded such assessment for American citizens. Yet the latter not only seek, in such foreign countries as they invade, privileges contrary to the law of that country, but they ignore or evade what laws they find there. Only consider the *meaning* of the following principle of *extra-territoriality*, as it is called. America, and along with other imperialists, and by a decidedly unequal and imperialistic treaty, has her own courts in China, and these courts are in no way bound to Chinese law. Yet China, actually believing that the League of Nations meant what it said when it declared its intention of making peace, asked the League Council in 1919 to annul the Chino-Japanese agreements of 1915 on the ground that they were made under duress. Japan defended herself by impudently saying that all China's treaties of late years were made under duress. Since which, China is absolutely at the mercy of imperialism. So much so that when Chao-Hein-Chu, delegate from China to the League of Nations, sought on September 11, 1925, to have it change the unequal Chinese treaties under the League clause: "to advise reconsideration ... of treaties ... which might endanger the peace of the world," nothing was done. And most of China's grievances were not even mentioned at the Washington Conference.

But now consider, please, how Americans also ignore or evade foreign laws elsewhere. The whole principle behind intervention by the United States is that when one of her citizens buys property in a foreign land, that property is no longer subject to the law of that foreign land. Firstly, the United States government does not treat Latin American states as sovereign but instead abrogates their property laws. American landowners, for instance, and to this hour, are not touched by the Mexican agrarian law. (We are too strong to let that country run its own business—too strong and too kind to ourselves.) Another of our Government's principles, and quite like that of England of the old days, is to make treaties at the point of a cannon, even though coercion yields no enduring contract at law. Yet that is the way these imperialists of ours force concessions for petroleum and some other things, and the way in which some of these exploited countries have been brought under our influence, or, as in the case of the Philippines, complete control. For, one is compelled to ask, what honorable principle was there in getting the Philippines to fight with the Americans under Aguinaldo against the Spanish with the promise of independence, and then stamping out with blood this same Aguinaldo's independence movement? Then, too, in 1898, the Congress declared Cuba "free and independent." But in 1919, the United States explained that "independent" meant a protected state and that "free" did not signify full freedom of action but just enough so that Cuba might, in international diplomacy, hold as a theoretical legal entity and retain her personality. Yet not her real freedom, which to this hour is dominated by American capital—American trusts and banks. If you don't believe it, go to Cuba and see ninety-five per cent of the people objecting to the American-financed Machado régime but unable to get out from under without revolution, which is again being attempted and fought against by American money, which has had immense and profitable concessions there as well as the cheapest of labor. Not only that, but it was our governing Americans of the day who told Cuba how to write its Constitution and forced it to say that the United States could go down there at any time to maintain the existing Cuban régime. Is Mr. Machado, approved by the Guggenheims, the Morgans, the Havemeyer heirs, etc., staying in or getting out? And if he goes, will not the powers install his like? Inevitable!

Also, the United States, in loaning to France and England $8,000,000,000 and sums to every other country in Europe except Scandinavia, Holland, Spain and the war enemies, not only knows that she can use these same loans for political persuasion but also has no qualms against such action, although as yet she has not offended in any great measure. Just the same, when Roumania sought to nationalize its oil, and so did, and our American oil corporation objected, the United States so indicated, at the same time reminding Roumania of her loan.

And just at this point, if you don't mind, I would like to touch on our loans to China. China, as you may or may not know, was first preyed upon by England in 1842, that country having built up a thriving opium trade between India and China, opium being actually smuggled into China by England, and against China's will. When China tried to stop England's profitable activities, England forced her will on her by war. Another cause of clash become more pointed at this time. During the 18th century, the East India Company had lots of trouble with the tariff in China; it would not pay what China asked. Finally, the British Empire sent Canton the tariff rates which China would be allowed to charge British companies, and for reply China charged twice as much. Then England immediately declared war, and in 1842, the Treaty of Nanking, resulting from England's victory, limited China's tariff to five per cent, at which per cent it still stands, controlled by the quite visible forces at England's command—her armies and navy.

On November 8, 1858, a similar treaty, limiting any tariff on British goods to five per cent, was drawn up for Shanghai. Later, the number of commodities entirely exempt from duty was enlarged by the Treaty of Tientsin in 1900. According to this, no duty whatsoever was to be charged on products to be consumed by foreigners—a tariff yoke which has been straining the whole Chinese population for nearly a hundred years! And how this has weakened the resources of China and made possible fabulous incomes for foreign traders—a terrific on-slaught of graft by force!

After the Chinese-Japanese War, China was in a precarious financial state. Between 1896 and 1898, a Franco-Russian gov-ernment loan and two joint Anglo-German government loans of £54,455,000 were made to China, with the customs as security, the customs to be administered by the International Maritime Customs Service. Foreign powers stepping in and doing as they wished because of China's weakness! But we will see about the result to the Chinese people.

Also, Europe early began eating up China in still another manner. Because England triumphed over China in the opium war, she demanded that Hongkong be ceded to her! And Hong-kong was so ceded in 1841, and remains a concession of Eng-land's to this day. Again, Kowloon, opposite Hongkong, was ceded in 1860, and the Kowloon Peninsula, by a lease in 1898, became "Her Majesty's Colony of Hongkong." Previously, how-ever, France had stepped in and got a few concessions. This stirred England's great sense of rivalry, and determined not to let France get ahead of her, she, in 1886, got the Chinese to let her rule Burma *with full authority*. Again, in 1890, Sikkim passed to England in the very same way. And still later, in 1899, when Russia, also in for plunder, seized Port Arthur, Eng-land leased the harbor of Weihaiwei, and still later the foreland, Shantung. Yet of 150,000 people here, only 200 are whites. And certainly, England's reasons were not to protect her great popu-lation migrated for trade purposes to Shantung. Rather, she made it clear that she was to be permitted to erect fortifications there over 1,650 square miles of this strategic point. Hence for Shantung exists the status of a colony under a government sub-ject to the Crown. Revenues are from land tax, road tax, wine, and an opium monopoly (a common thing in the Orient, which is one of several continuous opium monopolies).

These concessions, plus the foreign loans concerning which the great international clique was to step in and collect customs, caused so much hatred that by 1900 the Boxer Rebellion arose.

Yet China was again beaten, and this time she was given something to put her in her place. The Boxer indemnity, which China had to pay for wanting to be free, was £67,500,000—all China could stand, as we will see—and £7,425,000 of this went to Britain.

At this time the United States took her share by insisting upon Chinese students coming to American universities at the expense of the Chinese Government. And all told, this Boxer indemnity proved to be such a terrific load (China was so poor that she couldn't pay) that the balance of the Imperial Customs (England had many commodities let in duty free) was raised to five per cent, likewise to be collected by the English customs officers. During this period, after the Boxer Rebellion, the English Foreign Office shaped its policy on the advice of big companies (British) in China and the China Association. But these great foreign drains on the Chinese taxes not only kept the people down but also reduced the Chinese National Government almost to bankruptcy. The Chinese annual deficit in 1911, when the revolution broke out there, was between 20,000 and 70,000 taels. When this clash was over, Yuan Shik-Kai united China under his own banner. A loan to China was then arranged by a group of American, British, French and German bankers. But their terms were so high that China instead sought to make a contract for a loan with some Belgian bankers, and at a much lower rate, whereupon all previous smaller loans arranged for with China and in process of being supplied from time to time by these same four powers, immediately ceased, and China was forced to cancel her loan from the Belgian bankers. And the United States Government of that day well understood Wall Street's participation in this insidious deal, and the like of which is being repeated in China to-day.

But more as to this loan. Russia and Japan were included with the four power bankers. And arrangements for this enormous loan were secured by a national salt tax, this tax to be managed and collected by these foreigners. This China denounced, even to the extent of the whole loan. But when China would not accept their terms, the powers shut off all finance. Therefore, China, without a place to turn for money, was bankrupt. It was Shylocked, and by American bankers along with the rest. Indeed, about this time, these activities of our American bankers were denounced here in the United States, so much so that the Wilson administration was compelled to keep Wall Street from participating in this loan, which was finally concluded between China and the other five powers. (This was before the World War; after the War, United States bankers participated.) And that salt tax was administered by Chinese and international representatives, and unless they could make it pay, by the International Maritime Customs. The Chinese people were outraged. To comfort them, the Chinese Government asserted that unless it could be paid, national bankruptcy was at hand, and pathetically added that it had reached the stage where if this loan was not accepted it could not meet the terms of its prior loans, which would themselves begin to be collected (taxes) by foreign agents. (Foreign agents must be accepted in any plan.) In other words, China was dying, and America, after the World War, was helping as to that.

To show the enormous grasp of foreign bankers on China's finance I will list the items China owed in 1913:

Liabilities due by Chinese Government (this includes arrears of Boxer Indemnity, repayment of advances, treasury bills, interest and sinking fund of previous loans)	£4,317,778
Liabilities soon maturing	3,592,263
Provincial loans	2,870,000
Disbanding of troops	3,000,000
Current administration	5,500,000
Reorganization of salt tax	2,000,000

Yet in 1920, the American Government was all for a consortium to loan China money. And this was formed, and with the United States in the ring for the first time. Wall Street wouldn't be held out any longer. Although this consortium was outwardly an international affair, actually it was dominated by four powers:

United States, Japan, England and France. It keeps China from borrowing money from any other source. China must pay their high rates. An example of this drain is the present Nationalist Government bond issue: seven issues of $175,000,000 in all from May, 1927, to October, 1928. These are secured on what used to be considered poor and merciless security: customs and taxes on tobacco, stamps, kerosene (used extensively in China for illumination) and gasoline.

Hence now China is practically bankrupt. In 1925, her total revenue was only $345,000,000. To show how China skimps along financially, let me state that forty-five per cent of her funds consisted of loans and bond issues secured on the necessities of life: salt, flour, wheat and petroleum; and only a bare fifty-five per cent of her income was from revenues during the period from June to November, 1928. The bankers (our Americans with them) have China in a position where they extract every pittance the populace can bear. So ever since 1920, the United States has demanded and received a share of this commercial and financial loot.

But now to some of the other abuses involved in this business of foreign loans. Thus, for years the United States used, and is still using, her influence to keep foreign nations from making loans to Central America and the West Indies. They must deal with us or not deal at all. Nor may foreign investors trample these lands unrepelled. Concessions for their development to any but Americans are immediately vetoed. If by some ruse they are not vetoed, ultimatums stating American demands are enforced by marines, bayonets and machine guns. Thus, during July 1924, eleven Latin-American countries were officially directed in finance by Americans. Yet the misery of these foreign peoples! Their protest at our interventions! More, during recent times, the United States has, on thirty occasions, sent troops or battleships to seven sovereignties to enforce her will. And you don't call that imperialism? She has made virtual protectorates of Cuba, Panama, Haiti and Nicaragua. And look at the period of time in which the United States has maintained a government in

Nicaragua although opposed by eighty per cent of its people.
American marines have functioned in Nicaragua for twenty-two
years. The result of this policy? The most backward of all
nations there. And in Hawaii, after three thousand natives were
put to death, Americans took over the customs and rewrote the
Constitution. Also, when a rebellion was stirred up in Colombia
some time ago, our American President took that country under
our protection.

To show the instability of this policy—American corporation
attacks on these countries, seven of the twenty Latin-American
constitutional governments were overthrown by revolution
during the year ending February, 1931. In Argentina, Brazil
and Peru no national elections have been held to obtain the
will of the people of the new government and Dominican
Republic elections were declared fraudulent by the courts.
Now our King Hoover visits our possessions (Porto Rico) in
order to emphasize that subtle allegiance. And by way of
so doing, he reminds them that they are by us "endowed with
liberty, freedom, self-government and individual opportunity
through incorporation under the American flag." In other words,
their individual opportunity to slave for an American corporation on wages too meager for a decent living! Yet the policy of
Secretary of State Stimson is to recognize Latin American
governments whether their people approve or not. Duly
elected governments there have been overthrown and the latter
government recognized by the United States without people there
approving said overthrown government. All the United States
needs for recognition is failure of a foreign people to dis-
approve which means that they had no opportunity to vote
and were unable to revolt. Yet recognition by this country
means foreign loans to the overthrown government and hence
its maintenance. Since the United States adopted this policy,
there have been more revolutions than ever before in their
history. So answer for yourself my question: "Is America dominant?"

More, in our *Congressional Record* it is written that Wall

Street financiers can offer opposition to any exposure of the American situation. But the real truth is that our Government recognizes that it is only an errand-boy for the corporations; in other words, for the select few. For it is only the trust in America that has not only the wants but the initiative and power to acquire results in connection with them. Thus, when the Mexican Government under Diaz tried to break up the Standard Oil's monopoly by granting concessions to the Englishman, Pearson, an insurrection "of the people" broke out. (Strange cause for an insurrection!) And, of course, the United States was for the insurrectionist, Madero, who was for the Standard Oil. (A peculiar policy when viewed in the light that our Government is now inclined to intervene against the revolutionists in Cuba!) At that time a Mexican minister told the United States Senate that the *Standard Oil Company* (leaving the American Government out of the picture entirely, as you see) had made a treaty with Madero to the effect that if he (Madero) was made President of Mexico, he was to grant oil concessions to the Standard Oil and take all of Pearson's away. Then too, according, to an American ambassador to Mexico, documents in the State department at Washington prove that the Madero revolution was financed by Standard Oil. Still later, some interested Americans, out for all they could get, supported some half dozen Mexican insurrectionists in another revolution, the purpose being the maintenance of peace and order. Again, in the fight against Pearson and British capital, the Standard Oil, with a promise of a hundred million dollar loan to the Mexican Government, told it that if certain concessions were granted to Standard, the revolution would die on the spot. During this period thousands of dollars were paid to bandits for their services. However, and just the same (as much if not more money being on that side, I suppose), Pearson remained in Mexico and his Mexican Eagle Company was finally bought out by Standard's great rival, the Royal Dutch Shell. The underlying principle is the clash of nationals which makes domination of a single trust or country impossible. In this deal, the British Government gave such aid to the Royal Dutch Shell as to cause the allegation that it was controlled by the British Government. Doubtless there is influence, although England depends on her Persian Oil Company for her navy supply.

But see how secondary is the United States Government throughout all this. For obviously it is not this Government that does all the intriguing and troublemaking. It is the trusts and corporations, and then afterward they get the Government to do the threatening and fighting. And as for the people whom this Government is supposed to represent and in whose general interests, and theirs alone, it is supposed to act, do they count in all this? You know they do not! Yet throughout this entire Mexican-Standard Oil shindig, our dear Government did its best to help the Standard Oil by such devices as it could, such as not recognizing the Mexican Government's Constitutional provision to prohibit foreigners from holding mineral lands unless United States citizens were exempt from this ruling. Of course, a few Americans—those who were the originators of those hundreds of American Chambers of Commerce all over the country which preach our good will to the world, also the investors in our forty Standard Oil companies and our owners of seventy per cent of the American capital invested in Mexico—were interested. And these few, after a time, plunged wholeheartedly into the work of exposing (on this occasion, at least) these Mexican scandals. Whereupon, thus exposed or "razzed," our State Department turned to hushing up everything, going so far as to keep the exposed material not only from our American but also the European press. But all this for the benefit of the imperialists and their investors, not for the American public at large. Not at all!

So now I come to the place where I can answer the question: "Is America dominant?" And the answer is: "It is!" But should one repeat the old tush that great countries everywhere fear the United States? What difference does it make that another important individual, a German Supreme Court Justice, fears American imperialization? Every one knows that wars start through some such entanglements as those mentioned here. And that only such strong and imperialistic-minded governments as ours and England, and for that matter Japan, can start them is obvious. The reasons are always the same: the desire to rule and show off and be the big fish in the little puddle. What else? More, it is history that within the past four hundred years the world has fought against Spain, France, Germany and England because of their desires in this direction. And possibly the world will fight the United States or a group of which dominantly it will make one. And now, as ever, the danger-fields for war are numerous. Communists abound in Central America, China and elsewhere, and their united stand against these increasingly imperialistic adventures of our foreign-going corporations should and do bother them in the care of their billion-dollar investments. Hence, war.

More, these American trusts of ours are now being barred from oil activities in Palestine, Mesopotamia, Burma, India, Persia, and the United Kingdom. And what may that not lead to? Indeed, a policy of favoritism exists in fifteen other countries which cannot, of course, but infuriate our world-adventuring money-kings. And are they going to endure this foreign discrimination, and especially when they have such a numerous and docile people as Americans ready to do their bidding? Only look at our regiments in China now! And those that were in Russia in 1919, 1920 and 1921, without the knowledge, let alone the consent, of the people who were really paying for them—the rank and file of Americans!

But where is the next Marne to be? Who is to lead the next attack? Where is our next world-leader to sit, and what will his throne be like? By wars thus far have capitalism and imperialism grown, and war it is that creates the first flair for big business and its tremendous undertakings. Under its pressure thousands of listless persons proceed to work and increase incomes. And of course, if America wants to fight, the only economical thing to do is (following the German theory) to be prepared and clean up the enemy before the enemy cleans you up! But apart from

Big Business and its predatory aims everywhere—its desire to elevate the few and suppress the many—are there so many who desire war, or so many real enemies? I think not. Rather, they have to be made, always, and by abuse abroad as well as propaganda at home. Any school child should know that by now.

But more important still is this: Are there war preparations? And if so, are the American people being told about them? For I do not believe that the people of the United States at this time want war. They are not, I think, imperialistic, and could easily, apart from direct abuse on the part of an outside power, be friendly with all. Then why this infernal interference on the part of our corporations with other people's business—their desire to dominate everybody? And why should they not be checked and put in their proper places? For actually, for all they think and seek to do for themselves alone, they are of the people, by the people, for the people, and should be taught who their real masters are: the people themselves! And if that does not satisfy them—the satisfaction of working with honor and distinction for all—then let them get out—these mighty leaders who can only blunder a great nation into war and misery—and let the reins be taken by people big enough to know that organized society cannot go on without the work as well as the sustenance and the care of all!

As it stands now, though, with America—the financial leaders, I mean—daily and hourly they appear to wish to be more like England was before the War (and still is, apparently): always ready for conquest, and so war. For in England its leaders alone can declare war. And here, our leaders are beginning stiffly to hold to the same idea: that of themselves as the ruling class. They want to elect our presidents and governors and legislatures and judges and what not else. And now do so. And not only that, but by the power of money to rule the whole world. But, do we want to imitate England and Japan and the old Russia? For although England has commanded a powerful position because her financiers have "laid" for "backward" peoples, I still do not see in the British Empire any model to imitate. The idea that underlies it is *passé*. It will no longer work. For as we see to-day, the English people, millions of them, and for all their imperial sweep, take only a meager living from life while a select array of royalty and title controls and enjoys its wealth. And such royalty and title! But these so-called supermen never really care for the rank and file. They do not even understand them. It is their business, as they see it, to keep the rank and file below and themselves on top. But does it follow that the somewhat enlarged vision of the mass anywhere to-day is likely to accept that? I doubt it. See Spain, Cuba, Mexico, Russia. Isn't there a change at hand, and for the better, not the worse? I think so.

Anyhow, I know of two things that should help break up American imperialism. The first pertains to war. Nations never fight without an issue. And always the few make the issue. As it is now, though, our American people merely follow orders, and they know it. Yet likewise they know also that this is supposed to be a free country and that men at least pretend to vote for what they want. Now declaring war is the world's greatest act of sovereignty. And whether that should be decided by the people or by "the few" (meaning the corporations who are merely after "big business") is something concerning which many otherwise not so socially well-informed are beginning to ponder. And if ever they conclude that the many, and not the few, should decide this, the dreams of the individualist will have to give way to something besides thoughts of personal profit and personal or family dominance or he will be too small for the job in hand.

And when I think of America in this connection, I wish to say: "You claim to be a democracy, yet do you realize that not one phase of your various international problems comes to a vote?" And because of this I propose an amendment to the Constitution which shall declare that war can be declared only by a vote of the people: a two-thirds majority.

In the second place, there is a way to stop not only some but all of the brutal phases of American imperialism which I have recounted in this chapter, and that is an absolute change of the economic system, so that wealth is more equitably distributed.

But to achieve that, only "the many," not "the few," may declare war. After that, the many, and not the few, must proceed to enforce that equity in wealth—that is, participation in produce and such for effort expended—which is now debarred by this present control of it by the few. And when that is done, they (the many) will achieve their desire for a non-imperialistic nation and will presently present a fine native race economically fitted to pursue its personal interests and talents. And an excellent and even inspiring example that should be; something like that which the democratic-minded fathers of this country had in view when they dreamed of the thirteen colonies as a nation.

And now in substantiation of all that I have said, I wish to quote the statement of Colonel Henry W. Anderson, conservative Republican from Virginia, an American corporation lawyer of position and note, who as a member of the Wickersham Committee, a national commission recently appointed by the President to investigate and report on "Lawlessness and Law Enforcement," was finally compelled to conclude as follows:

"Offsetting the many admirable qualities and achievements of American civilization are certain general facts of which the student of present social conditions must take cognizance.

"The American people acquired in the virgin state what is in many respects the most favored and fruitful area of the world's surface. They have existed as an independent people for only the short period of 150 years. Within this time they have destroyed the original occupants of the soil or driven them from their lands with little regard for their rights.

"They have converted substantially all of this great area, with its immense natural resources, from public into private ownership. They have exploited these resources for private gain to an extent which, in some instances at least, already threatens exhaustion. They have created the widest spread between the extremes of wealth and poverty existing in the whole world.

"They have developed degrading slums in the cities and ignorant, under-privileged areas in the rural districts, which stand as menaces to social health and dangers to social order. They have conquered many of the forces of nature and made them servants

of man, but have so organized and developed their industrial
system that it tends to make of man himself a cog in a relentless
machine, without the inspiration of personal achievement or the
contentment which springs from social and economic security.

"They have created the largest body of laws and the most
complex system of government now in existence as restrains and
controls upon individual and social conduct, but every stage in
their development has been characterized by a large and ever-
increasing degree of lawlessness and crime. They have engaged
in at least one war in every generation.

"No candid investigation can ignore these facts, or the con-
clusions which they naturally suggest."

CHAPTER XXII

SUGGESTIONS TOWARDS A NEW STATECRAFT

CAPITALISM is a failure in America to-day. This dénouement
Karl Marx foretold by deductions of economic laws almost a
hundred years ago. To me, his was one of the most amazing and
brilliant contributions to learning. Imagine the mind that could
then accurately predict conditions as they are to-day! And his
was an age before any of the great European cartels or trusts
or before American monopoly under Rockefeller and others.
I would put Karl Marx ahead of such renowned economic phi-
losophers as John Stuart Mill, Voltaire, Rousseau, Fichte and
Hegel. And to-day Marx, with his learned and true study, "Das
Kapital," is dismissed by the American press and capitalist leaders as "radical"; the people have been educated no further than
thus to stigmatize a great philosophy. Just the same, that philosophy was the basis of the old Socialist movement, corrupted
by capitalistic pacifism, and later the Russian Communist
system.

Capitalistic failure here is evidenced by the fact that no longer
is economic balance maintained. I mean by that that equity of
consumption does not exist here. America can produce but is
unable, for want of money, to buy what it makes. In other words,
the people create a wealth which in the field of consumption is
denied them. On the other hand, the rich have the power to erect
wastefully Empire State Buildings, Radio Cities, Chrysler
Buildings, General Motors Buildings, what you will, and to build
enormous mills to supply millions with food and clothing; to
create automobile, radio, furniture, paint, glass, metal, lumber,
coal and oil businesses sufficient for the needs of multitudes; to
organize speedy transportation by steamship, airplane or rail-

way; yet the masses are unable to obtain these commodities and facilities for their own use in any but an extraordinarily limited way. Of course, large profits can be made from selling at high prices to the comparatively small number of persons who can get enough to pay for these various things, but actually this means, and just the same, the deprivation of the worker who makes them but cannot buy: really grinding down the masses to benefit the rich. And because of that, I am led to think of the great Roman Empire.

The way of Rome was to conquer and live off captured plunder. Conquest upon conquest—not the natural manufacture and consumption by the people themselves—was counted upon to replenish the great Roman treasury. And so long as conquest lasted, so long did Rome endure. Yet throughout the period of conquest, were the many, as opposed to the few, looked after? They were not! And after the conquest period ended, the subjection of the masses, as was natural, continued. They had nothing before and they had nothing after. More, throughout its period of conquest and domination, the money barons of Rome taxed all colonies as America is to-day taxed by corporations. And as the rich and powerful of Rome gloried in their colonial profits from trade and agriculture and basked in luxury, giving nothing in return, so do (or do they not?) the Rockefellers, Insulls, Fords, Guggenheims, du Ponts likewise to-day. For Rome had not the economic intelligence to see that political endurance depended on *exchange* of consumption for labor; in other words, on balance. And all that its lords could do was to take, pilfer, and rob. The Roman genius which had the constructive and organizational force to build to itself an empire became effete and was lacking in sufficient economic philosophy and understanding to keep that empire going. And so it is with our capitalistic leaders of to-day.

For has Rockefeller as yet offered one creative idea for the alleviation of any of the economic ills of America to-day? Or J. P. Morgan? Or Samuel Insull? Or General Atterbury or Alfred P. Sloan? Not one capitalist or any of his factotums has as yet made one constructive move! And why? Because it is against his own interest!

What happened to Rome was this: though the average university research worker is sure that the Huns and the Goths or the weak-minded emperors caused the downfall of Rome, an intensive scholarly study has disclosed that many of the colonies, once fruitful, finally failed and disappeared, not because of Goths or Huns or any other invading tribe or body but because of starvation due to grain taxes and money extorted from them by Rome. And America, in the course of time and under the directive forces of to-day, may, and I feel reasonably sure, will (unless a great intellectual light very presently illuminates it) meet with a like decay. Why? Because science and a panoramic look at economics through the centuries show that nature's way is a balance. Conceive for a moment the physical balances of the universe. Atoms, stars, the sun, planets, men, countries—the atoms within the human body and all other bodies from amœba up. In fact, all history of governments shows the same balance between the ruling power and the masses as the sun in nature and the planets. The executives of a nation can, by the law of nature, take no more power to themselves than the people will that they take. In America that has been done rabidly, as this book testifies. In Russia it cannot be done. When the equity or co-extension is lost, a change occurs. Maybe that change is a French Revolution or a Russian Revolution; maybe it is the destruction of a planet.

Personally I am for a reconstruction of our American economic life in order to restore that balance. And by that balance I mean equity of consumption among all the people. And not ten or twenty or fifty years from now, but now, at once! Also I feel that to work *to* such a goal, a strong central authority secured and controlled by the people themselves cannot be escaped. More, I think the people should inform themselves of this, and know always—be absolutely sure, in fact—that this central authority is working for them all and not for any private interest in any shape or form. Also that all facts and transactions should be open to the people. No hypocrisy. Without this, construction and respect for this construction can never be.

For never did a powerful constructive government exist which was not autocratic or oligarchical. Even Soviet Russia is that—autocratic—but with this difference that both its ideals and frailties counter those of the autocracy of other lands and systems. For, whereas in Soviet Russia, the government cannot rise above, step over or abuse the people, every other government has been able to go as far as it liked, or could, in oppressing the masses—America included. If you doubt this, only thumb through your history books and see. Consider Athens and Rome, dominated by the money interests of their day. And next the European kingdoms throughout the succeeding centuries. Visualize, for instance, the world's constructive and yet autocratic figures. Queen Elizabeth, Louis XIV, Frederick the Great, Catherine the Great, Napoleon. And to-day, Mussolini. All—every one of them for the few as against the many. Also, on the other hand, consider Stalin, who with his small oligarchy, the Central Executive Committee of the Communist Party, rules his land for the utmost benefit of the workers. Yet American capitalistic writers state that though Russia is "an oligarchy of the worst, most domineering form," the United States is a free land where every man's will by his vote governs. Yes? Well, that is the bunk, as any honest man with any brains at all, can see for himself. Corporations, corporations, corporations. And all with government at their beck. And all with the power to tax and bleed. Instead of a Stalin or Workers' Central Committee, the corporations and their banks rule here, and rule for their own oligarchical pockets all of the time, not for the masses!

I have shown, I believe, in preceding chapters that America is ruled by a Wall Street oligarchy. And Republicanism, so called, in the form in which it exists in England and France to-day, most certainly narrows down to conservative, if gracile, moves by and for the banks and their corporations and those whose private holdings are represented by these things. Even Germany, recently alleged to be socialistic, is now becoming so reactionary as to attempt to quell Communistic dissension. Even the reparations the Allies were able to get out of Germany by force of war are now being decreased to forfend against Communism seizing upon Germany. But the bankers ground the German people down to the limit.

But what I propose is an executive power for the American working masses not unlike the Communist Central Committee in Moscow, but composed of American men and women (if there are such) who have made a thorough study of the social and economic ills that to-day engulf America. For you cannot escape needing brains in some form anywhere. Only instead of being in office at the instigation of monopolies, trusts and cartels, as is the case with present oligarchies, and therefore serving their personal interests only and saying to hell with the rest of humanity, the whole system must be cleansed from the very bottom, its very heart! The voice and the will of the people must again be heard if ever as yet they have been heard. All private fortunes, as in Russia, must be abolished. The idea of an unearned inheritance by any one must be ended, for it is unfair and cruel. Men must not only not hope to come by great fortunes by inheritance or chance or theft, but they must not hope to make great fortunes by what they do, since so few can do so much as to deserve a great fortune, let alone administer it wisely once they have it. Rather, let us say to them, as did Aristotle over two thousand years ago: "See, we will give you fame, the acclaim of those whom you have served and benefited!" And in addition to this honor and recognition, security and peace, but no more. For it is enough.

Yet even this proposed central authority for America must have as its sole motivation the well-being of all of the people rather than that slight aid that may slip their way after the corporation giants or lords, their wives, concubines, friends and heirs, are gorged. For how obvious it is that under private control so little is equitably distributed. Rather by favor and in willful ignorance or savage and usually erratic domination is anything done, and despite our large trusts and organizations of all kinds, unwisely, most certainly with no general view which in organized society is the very base of equity.

Yet what can alleviate this corporate grip upon America? In this book, I have shown the uselessness of reform under the present methods of production and private property. Therefore, as I see it, nothing but a fundamental change in the whole system can do it. The present foundation is crumbling; the weakness is basic—absolutely at bottom and cannot be patched up or repaired. Hence, I now ask, how is it possible to change the foundation of the American economic structure? I would answer for *the masses to build themselves new institutions.* For under our present methods the working class is being destroyed—it is dying from insufferable conditions. This class must be joined by farmers and the entire middle class whom the financial barons have bled and defrauded. The cultural influences of the middle class with frequently slightly more leisure, must join up with the working class to whom they are far closer than they realize, and bolster it up.

For indeed, the sacredness of private property is an illusion, as shown by change and death. Hence and instead, the proposed new government must have the power to confiscate and turn into state property all of the basic industries: coal, lumber, food, steel, etc., as well as their means of transportation. Some might think that those owning stock in these corporations might be paid for their holdings, but I do not agree. In my judgment, they must take pot luck with the rest of us, fall in with the necessary changes in the spirit of our early pioneers and make a new and better scene here and now. Too long have they been the beneficiaries of inequity, and must learn, however grimly, that that is true. Let them forget the past. It has been a fine dream for the few, but an evil one for the many, and must give way. Besides, what have they to fear? The fate and the life and the living and working conditions of every other man—improved as equity would improve them. And is that so bad? Only a coward or a parasite would say so. Personally, I welcome the change.

Not only that, but this central control which now will be should have authority to confiscate such homes of the rich as well as other institutions, private, civil, religious, as might fit into any purpose of the state: educational, recreational, reformative, medical or charitable; or any other really urgent need of the new state or system. Of course, in suggesting such things, any one to-day is more than likely to be faced, in the capitalistic press and elsewhere, with the assurance, and without in any way consulting the masses, that the American people don't want these things! But don't they? I rather fancy myself that they do, or will!

Next, in the new constitution which I feel should supplant the old, a clause similar to that in the present Russian Soviet Constitution might, and I think would, guarantee official domination by the masses, rather than private interests, of all plans or acts. And that central authority should consistently be held to fight for the people as a whole and in a manner I shall describe.

The source of this government authority constitutes a very difficult problem, because by and large the people appear never to understand. They let whosoever will—priest, political demagogue, corporation executive, arresting and fascinating individuals out of nowhere—as in Mussolini's case—tell them anything or everything: that the country is being run for the good of the people; that this good depends on private ownership; that things are all right as they are; that a plan like this should not be developed hastily without due trial (which trial never comes about); that this plan wouldn't work, etc.—all of which is false. Yet in so far as the present situation is concerned, it would seem as though the basic facts at least must by now be seen by every one; i.e., that corporations charge prices which the public, under wages from these corporations, cannot pay; that the Government leaves the people, not the corporations, to get along as best they may; that the corporations always get value received

and hence must for financing the activities of the two political parties which, as every one by now knows, are mere semi-
annual or quadrennial circuses, intended, via red fire, oratory,
scare headlines, noise and what not, to distract the attention of
the marching masses from the underlying issues, which are never
allowed to appear but which, none the less, have the seeming if
not the real endorsement of the people. For that is the sole
value of our present two-party system. And certainly, compared
with that, my proposed system, working to give the utmost to
every one, is infinitely better.

Of course, any person or group informing the people of these
political views will have powerful enemies: the trusts and their
allies. Subtle all-controlling and tireless enemies of which the
people must beware! Worse, experience in other governments
(Russia, in particular, at present) shows that not even the most
active educational program fostered by the workers' leaders
can train the minds of the masses in these truths and principles
sufficiently to guarantee, by reason of general understanding
and appreciation, their continuance. For have I not shown how
continuously and quite idiotically the American people here
vote—yet to what end one can see. And for that reason I
think the Russian elections are now limited. The franchise
there is denied, and rightly, I think, to such interests as remain inveterate enemies of proletarian welfare: to the clergy,
for instance, which was at first let alone (approximately for
ten years) but later disfranchised because they were shown
to have defended the large private owners, kept property for
private and not public use, and lived off the masses. For this
same reason, bourgeois private dealer classes and the kulaks and
all large individual landowners were swept away. They were not
and could not be made public-spirited. Fear—always inspired by
an individualistic and hence capitalistic world—prevented them
from being so. Lenin saw that, as did Marx. In their absence,
though, the Russian Government holds elections among its
soviets in factories, villages and collective farms, which of necessity leaves out multitudes of the population. Even the elections

for the Central Executive Committee concern a list of candidates made out by the Communist Party and any other list advanced is discredited. Then the Central Executive Committee elects its executive; its Stalin, for instance.

For this reason obviously the Russian Soviet system is an oligarchy, and a strong one. I think, however, that the aims of the same to pool all wealth and distribute its fruits equitably among all fully justify this dictatorship. Yet, as I have said, Russian leaders cannot rise above their masses. The masses are on top and the executives exist only as means to that end. So how much better that than the dictatorship here of the likes of a Rockefeller, whose oily billions can and do build Radio City on one of New York's most costly real estate areas, the while the wages of most of the Standard Oil employees are cut! Since Americans are much better educated and since means of publication are so highly organized, the American population should not offer quite the same difficulty of education as do the Russian. And who knows, we might be the ones to materialize Aristotle's very beautiful dream: a state controlled by and for all and giving equitable honor and recognition, but not wealth, to those most deserving it. His plan is worth rereading weekly —in our schools, for one place.

As I see it now, though, the laws on public opinion would not be a great deal different in America under such a régime from those at present ruling. Treason, as now, would and should be construed as an attempt against the government. Although the present interpretation of "sedition" as meaning advocacy of a violent overthrow of a régime I believe limits the free exercise of public opinion, still I also believe that such a limitation is justifiable under such circumstances as envelop any new government, the people of which have not as yet learned thoroughly to understand. In an older government, well established, complete freedom of public opinion should be granted. Yet you may note here in connection with this that our present declining capitalistic system in the United States, and after scores of years in which to indicate its value to the people, does not feel strong enough to do without the most stringent of sedition laws, certainly in a large majority of the States. And yet, why? Is it not really because it has not rendered any equitable, let alone altruistic, service which might be supposed to secure it in public esteem, and hence must fall back on a National Espionage Act as drastic as any anywhere?

I also believe that a strongly centralized authority such as I propose should, as now, have full law-making capacity so as to be able to legislate, and quickly, as circumstances might warrant to preserve the government for the welfare and purposes of the masses as a whole. Also, as now, it should have an appeal to courts, the same drawing their power from the same electoral sources as now. And the government should not merely have lawyers to prosecute criminals, but, as in present-day Russia, lawyers to examine defendants and prepare their briefs. And as now, persons should be able to defend themselves in court, and without government opposition or malice toward any such defense.

Working out such a change—though—presents the utmost difficulty in this country where influential thousands neither understand nor care about the tribulations, struggles and heartbreaks of the striving, hardworking millions. Yet just as I would be the first to urge a change that would equalize opportunity and welfare, so would I be the last to want the brutality which might accompany such a change. Rather do I advocate, as in Russia, a gradual, though sure, reassembling of the economic life over a period of years. To be sure, capitalists and magnates and the American Federation of Labor, etc., are always defiantly saying that Communism can never be established here—that it by no means synchronizes with the spirit of the American people, their restless and creative individualism. Yet why does it not? I saw no lack of individualism in Russia, creative or otherwise. Arts and invention appeared to be flourishing there as here. At any rate, I would prefer to have the American people say what they want, rather than have the corporations, depending as they do to-day on the police, the press, and the pro-capitalistic officials of the Government, say it for them.

In connection with that proposal, it seems reasonable to me that the new government, for the time being at least, might be thoughtful of the personal welfare of such earnest individualists who under present capitalistic systems have shown constructive if not always equitable intent. They might be looked upon as victims of an older day and given opportunity in the new. But on the other hand, those who should proceed to retaliate in any manner would, as I see it, have to be held guilty of treason or of sedition and restrained or punished accordingly. For some, as has been shown, Russia retains the death sentence, particularly for damage to its present activities by inveterate class enemies. And to me that is right. Besides, does not death go with treason to the United States Government? However aggrieved because of the loss of privileges, they are still traitors and should be dealt with as such. True, the kulaks (wealthy landowners) in Russia are evicted, deprived of all their property and exiled to work in the lumber regions of Siberia. But for those making genuine attempts at impairing the government and therefore the common good, this is well enough. For how is one to deal with one's enemies in any such great issue? Yet once the new systems were installed, I would be the first to relax the laws and to deal as leniently as possible with those who offended or sought so to do.

And in so far as America is concerned, actually I believe that some forms of private trading might remain, for a time anyhow, but just how much and what their fields would be a matter for executive conference and debate. However all of such traders' and dealers' earnings should and would have to be carefully checked, as in Russia, and all beyond a certain income taken and credited to the government as taxes. On the other hand, and as in Russia, I am sure that all basic commodities, such as iron, steel, lumber, coal, electricity, transportation, sugar, flour, oil, cotton goods, etc., should be prohibited to private adventure and handled exclusively by the government. And since experience in Russia has shown that individual dealers, in order to prosper, had to charge four or five times as much as the government which supplied quantities of those things, doubtless private dealers in those products would be in the course of time forced out of business. Besides and at any time, the government should be able to fix its own prices in such a way as to make its own dealings with the masses and in all commodities a business success.

Our Government, as I see it, should also carry on the major phases of manufacture and sale by the present trust method, since that has been proven efficient by capitalists. Only in this case, the immense profits of large scale production and distribution would, and should, enrich the government, and this should naturally tend to lower prices to every one as well as make for the physical as well as mental profit of the individual, he being the first care of the state. In connection with that, each industry should be organized as to section, with a centralized authority over all mills or mines or factories or farming areas growing particular crops.

In short, farming must be carried on in the manner of a corporation or collective, which was the suggestion I made in Russia in 1927-28. For as I understand it, the large corporation farms in Kansas to-day make more money than do the private farmers aggregately possessed of the same area and facilities. And with proper and efficient planning in this realm, production and, in consequence, valuable and nourishing distribution should reach a high stage. The size of such corporations or collectives and their results should depend on the nature of the agriculture, dairy, or activity in question. One farm (a collective) in Russia is 500,000 acres in extent. Others much less. But in order to effect efficiency in industry and farming, the Russian Soviet's experience shows that a highly developed organization is paramount, and for that reason I have the feeling that America would be as effective, if not more so, in this field as in any other. For naturally, apparently, we are an inventive, industrious and resourceful people, and because of that I suggest—for farming purposes in particular—a complete staff organization such as that of the army's, but with an agricultural rather than a predatory objective. And such officers once in command should, by reason of almost military agricultural training and understanding, effect the smooth-running of the world's foremost need: assured agricultural production and distribution.

Under this new arrangement also, as I see it, our American farms and industries should deal with labor in the following fashion. As the majority must labor now in the United States, so would men have to be employed at some phase of these industries. And it should work out better than it does at present. For under this system, and as opposed to what is now, men would have free choice of any work they would like to perform, providing they had the capacity for it. And in that connection, labor should be paid for the amount of work done, and no more. Yet it should be paid well. Only those who could not make a comfortable living in accordance with the high standards necessary to be maintained should then be analyzed as to industrial as well as individual factors, and subsequently put either where they could maintain themselves or, failing that, should be paid, quite as other laborers, according to the amount of work done, whether at plowing, sowing, reaping, or what you will, but for limited hours of work—eight, seven, six, five. But these failing to support him, he should be relegated to some special home or institution.

Since farming is seasonal, in winter this skilled farm labor might well be transferred to factories or work relating to the care or distribution of farm products, which could be as easily arranged for in winter as in summer. This was a suggestion I made in writing to Russia in January, 1928.

To continue, supervisors should go about to see that all work is well done; i.e., the ground not half turned over or plowed shallow; and a wage deduction should be the penalty of haste and carelessness. Without this labor method, one industrious person might well be saddled with an undue proportion of the work, whereas another, less industrious, would be receiving an undue share for his lack of skill or intentional idleness.

Under my proposed plan, also laborers could be protected by long period contracts, as they are in Russia if they care to sign, as well as appropriate insurance in every form. As it is to-day, and as we all see, a laborer can be thrown out with a day's notice. Not only is this properly a duty of the government but also those forms of social welfare work now seized upon by religionists as well as charity workers in general—the Red Cross, the Salvation Army, the Catholic and other churches, with their hospitals, protectories, etc.—are properly functions of government, and as such should be taken over. Thus, all insurance should be handled by it, and not as now by private corporations or trusts. Next, workers of all ranks should be secured against unemployment, illness, injury, permanent disablement and death. Yet as it is in America to-day, our streets are as full of unprotected cripples and hold as many beggars as a medieval cathedral. Yet a very pathetic and unjust thing, for they should be given appropriate work or taken care of and barred from the streets.

For why should an American Red Cross pay enormous salaries to wasters the while spending what seems to me a dishonestly low fraction of its receipts on actual aid? Or again, why should a sociologically and economically as well as politically ignorant Salvation Army debase all that is beautiful and poetic in religion to the bellow of a cornet and the jingle of gay tambourines the while begging? Admirable as any religious theory may be, it should never in any state, as I see it, be bolstered by any form of economic or social authority which would permit it to pose as an avatar of charity or the principle of charity. In the first place this is wholly uneconomic and socially as well as organizationally wrong. For in any well-conducted state, there should be no beggary, let alone religious orders dispensing charity—and for their private glorification as well as emolument. It is not adherents to any religion, but the government of adherents to organized society that should do this. (And how effectively that would dispose of most religious authority or its excuse!) In short, and as in Russia, all material aiding of individuals should be denied the Church. It should be the business of the state, and that of none other.

In fact, as I see it, all education should be arranged and paid for by the government. And in that connection, religion should cease to function in all schools and colleges. For what it asserts is not, as a rule, related to fact—which is the business of education—but rather to mysticism and theory. Therefore, all should go as far intellectually as they can and wish, and free. More, full freedom should be given all professors of any field of knowledge to teach the results of their scholarship, and not, as now, and especially in the sectarian world, be compelled to face a denial of the right to do so. More, all teaching should be denied the Church, either in school or Sunday school. And no religion of any kind should be taught anywhere until children are sixteen years of age. Then if they choose, and since at that age they are better fitted to comprehend any life data than at five or six or ten, they might be allowed to examine the great data of life. And as all informed persons already know, laws of this nature are working out very well in Russia now. Such ethics as tend to forfend crime and induce honesty and the like should be fully taught in the lower grades but as a matter of social training, of course.

The greatest confusion concerning such a government as I propose relates (in the minds of most persons) to what is to happen to the individual under a system of equity of consumption. The fear springs principally, I think, from the thought not that they are not going to be as well off as any other—which is nonsense—but that they are going to be denied what they now have—that is, more than the next fellow. It is the idea of equality of opportunity and privilege that sickens them—for they are so sure, whatever their own asinine thoughts about life, that the other fellow is so much lower mentally or æsthetically and, as for him being improved—pah!—he should not be allowed to improve, for that would most certainly infringe upon their

imagined superiority. And they are absolutely sure that they
need or at least should have and enjoy privileges of one kind
or another not common to all, however sociologically and or-
ganically unfair. But this is, in the main, groundless, or at best
or worst on their part, selfish. For firstly, equality will be
only relative, not absolute. For as all know, the greatest of all
wealth is *mental,* and with sufficient mind one may effect literally marvels with a very little material. It is the true difference between all men and all women, and that difference
cannot be eradicated either by law or education. It can only
be humanized. Yet the essence of the new system should be the
leveling of all material things: no voluminously wealthy and
no destitute. And the pivot of the system would and should be
that all must work in order to eat. Yet to such a forward and
industrious system many do and will object. It is so antagonistic
to all our American theories so far, but not to our true needs.

Thus, Daniel Willard, of the Baltimore & Ohio Railroad,
recently said that he would want his children to live in a fashion
similar to his way of living. Well, Mr. Willard has worked and
established an easy status for himself under capitalism, but
perhaps it was not always so with him, and perhaps he did
not fare so badly even then. At any rate, it could not and should
not be as he wishes. Rather, the state should approach all without prejudice and solely with a view to ascertaining their true
and most valuable capacities. And once the object of the state
were thoroughly made clear—to bring all to a decent living
level—I cannot see what grounds any one would have for com-
plaining. For every one who sincerely worked should, and
under the new system would, have the necessities as well as the
comforts of life. Every one! As for those who could not or
would not work, they would be looked after, for they are the
fruits of whatever social and economic system is or has been
and as such to be cared for. We did not make ourselves. We
are but products and, accordingly, heirs of a system that is or
was. Yet in so far as possible, as I have said, the individual
should be allowed to choose his pursuits as now, and could be

so allowed. But it should be the business of government to fit him into what best he could do, and at times, of course, regardless of exact aptitudes. For one cannot always have everything everywhere, not even under capitalism. So all should work at something and all should have two good vacations a year with pay.

But Robert Scripps, of the Scripps-Howard newspapers, is afraid that he and his fellow capitalists would lose their jobs. But as I see it, all they would lose would be the enormous incomes which they do not really earn and cannot personally use, and which therefore they should be compelled to share with others. For what can any one individual do with millions and billions except to exercise his judgment in connection with his use of the same and to pretend that his judgment or use of the same is better than that of any other? But is it? Has capitalism proved that? And just where and how? In most cases, the same men who lead and construct and direct could, if loyal to this new form of government, manage and compel as now. For most certainly the really capable or superior individual would have about as much chance to advance as now. For are not the wise always needed? And since wisdom is power, the wise are certainly most likely to rise, and once there they would be furnished with the necessary facilities for wisdom's work. The only difference would be that instead of building merely for their own and their wives' and children's pleasure and social superiority, they would plan and project for all. Also, those in the arts would have like opportunity for individual achievement and recognition. It is so in Russia to-day. There is no distinction but that of the mind, anyhow. Every one who has held otherwise has come to naught. Few, in fact, have disputed this doctrine. Even such a sponsor as Voltaire, who believed that property brought a man distinction, is now known *only* for his mentality, while many of his contemporaries, infinitely more wealthy, are totally forgotten.

Americans! Men and women! The forces of change are deep-seated and subtle, yet sure and swift in their approach and final determination. And the situation in America, like the constantly moving and shattering and rejoining energy of the universe, is being changed, and will continue so to change. It is life. And as life there need be no fear of it. More, it is adventure, and who is so mean as to fear adventure? Not forever can our capitalists, land trusts, and banks continue to aggravate the economic struggle by establishing their scores of mills, their trusts and holding companies, among unknowing people, paying them almost nothing! Not forever will eighty-five per cent of the people, as now, live on incomes below the minimum decent wage, while the other fifteen per cent hoard and dominate the rest! As it stands now in their great land, only one per cent of the stocks are owned by workers, including managers and executives. Less than one per cent of the total population of America trades on the stock exchange. And of these, less than one per cent of the people, a very few individuals, controls banks, railroads and industries. In fact, Dr. John H. Gray, head of Department of Economics, Graduate School of the American University, and formerly chief analyst of the Interstate Commerce Commission, writes: "America is to-day not only the richest nation in the world; it has the greatest inequality of wealth and the most centralized ownership and control in the history of the race.... Furthermore, the acceleration of such control is greater here than in other countries ... we are rapidly moving towards a unified, centralized, monopolistic control of all credit and wealth.... But the problem of monopoly here bids fair soon to become as important as it was in England three centuries ago. To check the movement towards monopoly in England cost Sir Francis Bacon, the leading mind of his age, all his property and titles; Charles I his head; and James II his throne. It was the immediate cause of a long and devastating civil war."

And may I add that not even that, of course, stopped monopoly in England. It is not so easy. Men are required for that—*men*. And not trudging dubs or Caspar Milquetoasts, speculating forever as to the dangers and the costs.

Yet many a change has swept the political world which was

previously not taken seriously. And even in my day have I not seen the death of the idea of royalty, with its claim of royal blood; the rise of Communism and its trial? And can nothing more happen? Yet these but a few hours since were considered impregnable—their disestablishment a fool's dream. Yet every era is a reaction to and at the same time an opposition to the past, and this that is now coming is not less so. Private gain may, and I now believe will, give way to gain for the whole, under which many more may rise. Yet how different from Mr. Charles M. Schwab's cruel and relentless law of $30,000,000 in bonuses to officers and $15 and $20 a week to laborers of great strength and industry! But out of this approaching change, what may not come: men and women how wise and strong, and how eager to find a surer and more pleasing way of life!

INDEX

A

Adair vs. U. S., 168-169.

Agriculture, see "Cropper" system, Farm Board, Farmer, Nationalization.

Airplanes vs. railroads, 102-104.

American Bar Assn., 144.

American Federation of Labor, 21, 27, 204; and the ballot, 316, 327; betrayal of labor by, 126-127, 179, 181, 193, 199; and church, 273; favoritism toward capital, 179, 181, 190, 200; inadequate leadership and mismanagement of, 106, 107, 126, 178, 183, 186, 191, 193-197, 199, 417; limitation of membership, 179; and politics, 181; salaries of officers, 183. See also United Mine Workers, Unions, Child Labor.

American Tel. & Tel. Co., 144, 375-377; rates, 74, 243, 282, 294, 377.

American Union Tel Co., 39.

Anglo Persian Oil Co. Ltd., 386.

Archbold, John D., 78-80.

Argentina, 385, 387.

Atterbury, W. W., 67, 99, 107, 108, 110, 409.

B

Baker, Geo. F., Sr., 12, 87, 158; Jr., 87.

Ballot, and foreign affairs, 316; futility of, 312, 313, 317, 318, 319, 321, 322, 326; indifference of American voters, 144, 313, 314, 322, 325, 327; potential power of, 314-316, 323-324; purpose and use of, 314, 315, 328.

Banks, Chase National, 54, 343, 345, 384; First National, 373; Irving Trust, 326; National City, 54, 322, 343, 345, 372, 384; profits and resources of, 53-56; regulation of, by ballot, 324; supremacy over Government in U. S. and abroad, 55, 326, 344, 345, 384.

Bethlehem Shipbuilding Co., 12.

Bethlehem Steel Co., 184, 383, 389.

Bolivia, 382, 387.

Boulder Dam, 59, 337.

Brazil, 385.

Brotherhood of Locomotive Engineers, mismanagement of, 182.

Brotherhood of Railway and SS. Clerks, 126-127.

Buses, ownership of lines, 108; vs. railroads, 95, 102-104, 107, 122, 227.

C

Calvinists, theory of equality, 155.

Cameron, Wm. D., 102.

Canada, American investments in, 382; publicly-owned utilities, rates, 11, 334, 335, 338, 341.

Capitalism, failure of, 1-30, 110, 112, 153, 174, 178, 278, 308, 408, 416, 424.

Carlisle, Floyd L., 11.

Carnegie, Andrew, 135.

Cash Sales Act, 31.

Chain Gangs, see Convicts.

Chain Stores and System, 4, 76, 83.

Charity, abuse of individual by, 278-280, 283, 287; as aid to business, 289, 290; burden on poor and taxpayers, 288, 296, 377; child placement, 292-293; Civic and Community Funds, 284-286; contributions to, by corporations, 199, 294-295; dominated by corporations, 295; foreign, 6, 286; forms of corporation, 295, 296; inadequate private, of rich, 288-289, 393, legal aid, 283; management of drives, 277, 278; mismanagement of funds, 278, 279, 280, 284; profit from, 280;

427